# Patterns of Change
# Change of Patterns

## Linguistic Change and Reconstruction Methodology

*edited by*
Philip Baldi

Mouton de Gruyter
Berlin · New York 1991

Mouton de Gruyter (formerly Mouton, The Hague)
is a Division of Walter de Gruyter & Co., Berlin.

♾ Printed on acid-free paper which falls within the guidelines
of the ANSI to ensure permanence and durability.

This paperback contains selected articles from the original clothbound edition of
*Linguistic Change and Reconstruction Methodology*, edited by Philip Baldi (Trends
in Linguistics. Studies and Monographs 45).

*Library of Congress Cataloging in Publication Data*

Patterns of change, change of patterns : linguistic change and
  reconstruction methodology / edited by Philip Baldi.
       p.      cm.
  Includes bibliographical referenes and indexes.
  ISBN 3-11-013405-5 (acid-free paper)
    1. Linguistics change. 2. Reconstruction (Linguistics) 3.
  Comparative linguistics. I. Baldi, Philip.
  P142.P38     1991
  417′.7 — dc20                                        91-34032
                                                           CIP

*Die Deutsche Bibliothek Cataloging in Publication Data*

**Patterns of change, change of patterns** : linguistic change and
reconstruction methodology / ed. by Philip Baldi. — Berlin ;
New York : Mouton de Gruyter, 1991
  ISBN 3-11-013405-5
NE: Baldi, Philip [Hrsg.

Typesetting: Arthur Collignon GmbH, Berlin — Printing: Gerike GmbH, Berlin
Binding: Dieter Mikolai, Berlin.
Printed in Germany

# Preface

This volume contains fifteen of the original thirty-eight papers presented at the Workshop on Linguistic Change and Reconstruction Methodology held at Stanford University, July 28-August 1, 1987. These fifteen papers, plus the editor's introduction, constitute an unrevised selection of representative articles from an earlier, much larger volume published as *Linguistic Change and Reconstruction Methodology* (Mouton de Gruyter 1990), which contained twenty-eight of the original thirty-eight papers.

The current selection of articles was made on the basis of several interlocking factors: first, it was felt by the editor that these articles represent work that is in the best tradition of historical-comparative linguistic research, and that they deserve the additional visibility that this shorter volume will provide; second, the selected articles address issues which are timely and appropriate in the context of current trends in historical and comparative linguistics, and which should be brought into the open scholarly domain, especially that of advanced students and non-specialists, as soon as possible; third, each one of these papers addresses methodological concerns which are central to ongoing progress in the field of genetic linguistic, and thus form a common theme which merits their regrouping in a more compact presentation. Though the approaches are varied, and the languages which are treated in these selections are as different as they might be, the common thread of methodological rigor and proper representation of data stand as a pivot point in each. For these reasons they have been chosen to form a shorter and more accessible collection from the original group.

The re-publication of this selection of papers from *Linguistic Change and Reconstruction Methodology* provides the editor with another opportunity to reflect on the Stanford Workshop from which the present and earlier volumes have arisen, and to discharge once again the pleasant duty of remembering those individuals who were instrumental in making that meeting such an enduring success. The meeting was a five-day long series of workshops, formal presentations and debates sponsored entirely by the U.S. National Science Foundation (Grant # 86-17435), held during the now biennial Summer Institute of the Linguistic Society of America (LSA). The pleasant setting and intellectually rich atmosphere of the Stanford LSA Institute provided a special attraction to the scholars who were invited to participate in the Workshop on Linguistic Change and Reconstruction Methodology. During that Summer Institute more than four hundred linguists and students of linguistics were in residence at Stanford, providing a stimulating concordance of language study, theory, and description which is unavailable in any other setting.

Bringing together thirty-eight scholars from around the world for a successful conference and two follow-up publications requires a blend of good organization, good planning, and good luck. From the beginning, this project was blessed with all three. The good organization owes much to the staff of the Stanford LSA Institute, who were cooperative and helpful in every detail, important or trivial. Overall thanks are due to Ivan Sag, the Institute Director, who ran what is in retrospect one of the most successful LSA Institutes ever. More specific acknowledgment is due to Kathryn Henniss, Sag's tireless and eternally cheery assistant; Gina Wein, the administrative aide of the Department of Linguistics; and Michelle Collette and Sonya Oliva, the efficient pillars of the Departmental staff. Their helpful cooperation, together with the fine facilities of the Stanford LSA, provided a guarantee that details of housing, space, food, entertainment and a rich atmosphere for all participants would be satisfactorily met. And they were.

The good planning which made the Workshop a success, and helped to bring this and the earlier volume to life, is due in no small part to the efforts of my secretary, Mrs. Connie Moore. She handled the complexities of travel, scheduling, and other arrangements with professionalism and good cheer. Without her efforts, this undertaking could never have gone as smoothly as it did.

The good luck is a bit harder to pin down, but it does have a general outline. There was the good luck to have had such a helpful and cooperative professional as Paul Chapin overseeing the Linguistics Program of the National Science Foundation. There was the good luck to have received such an enthusiastic response to the original Workshop proposal, both from the NSF reviewers and from the invited participants. There was the good luck to have found replacements for some last-minute withdrawals from several of the pre-organized discussion groups. The final bit of good luck was for me personally to have chosen historical-comparative linguistics as my primary area of inquiry, and to have had the opportunity to serve scholarship in this area in some small way.

I would also like to thank several people who were helpful with the manuscript for the volume: Helyn Gareis, who copy-edited the original manuscript with me; Sebastian Uijtdehaage, who helped with the original indices; Margaret Saunders of de Gruyter, who guided the present volume to publication; and Connie Moore, who helped with typing and correspondence. Finally, I should like to acknowledge several scholars who were helpful to me in an advisory capacity throughout the project. They include Eric Hamp, Henry Hoenigswald, Lyle Campbell, Bob Blust, and Bill Schmalstieg.

University Park
August, 1991

# Contents

# Contributors

*Philip Baldi,* University Park, Pennsylvania, USA
*M. Lionel Bender,* Carbondale, Illinois, USA
*Barry Blake,* Bundoora, Victoria, Australia
*Robert Blust,* Honolulu, Hawaii, USA
*Lyle Campbell,* Baton Rouge, Louisiana, USA
*Robert M. W. Dixon,* Canberra, Australia
*Ives Goddard,* Washington, DC, USA
*George W. Grace,* Honolulu, Hawaii, USA
*Henry M. Hoenigswald,* Philadelphia, Pennsylvania, USA
*Steve Johnson,* Armidale, New South Wales, Australia
*Stephen Lieberman,* Philadelphia, Pennsylvania, USA
*Samuel E. Martin,* New Haven, Connecticut, USA
*Marianne Mithun,* Santa Barbara, California, USA
*Calvert Watkins,* Cambridge, Massachusetts, USA

# Introduction: The comparative method

*Philip Baldi*

The matter of methodology in historical reconstruction, and in particular the method of comparative reconstruction, is a point of recurring concern among practicing historical linguists. For more than a century now, the field of historical linguistics has been trying to refine the goals, techniques, and assumptions which guide their efforts to recover the linguistic past.

There are many issues which one must consider in any attempt to capture the central notions involved in the comparative method. Chief among these issues are its universality, its replicability, and its limits. Universality is a central concern, for a method which is effective only with certain languages, or types of languages, is of limited general value. Replicability is also a crucial issue, for a method which yields different results to different investigators can lay no claim to a scientific basis. The limitations of the method are also of pivotal concern, for the time-depth and the uniqueness which can be attained by reconstruction techniques bear enormous implications for the status of proto-languages.

As is commonly known, most research on linguistic change in the twentieth century has been guided by principles, methods, and assumptions which were formulated in the nineteenth century. It was of course during the nineteenth century that the Indo-European and Finno-Ugric languages provided the main empirical foundations for modern theories of language change and, more crucially for our purposes, for the methods used to study such change and to recover the past. Indeed, as has often been pointed out, Finno-Ugric was recognized as a linguistic entity in the eighteenth century, and was scientifically established as such by Gyărmathi in 1799. His work, especially in the comparison of inflectional systems, was very influential in the nineteenth century when such scholars as Rask and Bopp were beginning systematic investigations of the Indo-European language family. Work on the Indo-European languages during the nineteenth century was so successful that it seems to have set the theoretical and practical standard for much comparative research, serving as a kind of methodological focus for carrying out studies of genetic linguistics. This focus has resulted from the long and well-established traditions of the Indo-European languages, and of Indo-European scholarship. There is a wealth of written data from this language family, with salient materials from every stock; it has a wide geographical and cultural spread, stretching from Europe to India at the time of its discovery and now spanning the globe; it has a rich time depth, with recorded data stretching deep into the second millennium B.C.; and it has a relative homogeneity among its eleven well-attested branches which facilitates comparison and reconstruction.

The models of description and the associated theoretical positions which have emerged from the intensive comparative study of the Indo-European and other languages contain at least the following central notions relating to the establishment of genetic units and the reconstruction of proto-languages; from the beginning, these notions have been applied to non-Indo-European languages, and the apparent universality of their usefulness is a basic premise of historical-comparative linguistic analysis.

1) A significant percentage of cognates in core vocabulary areas must be demonstrated in order to establish genetic affinity between languages. This is a crucial step in the comparison of lexical items across languages, which allows the formation of reconstruction hypotheses. It further involves the notion that there are reliable ways to recognize borrowings, onomatopoeia, and accidents of linguistic history which result in chance lexical similarities, none of which can play a part in either the postulation of a genetic unit or in the reconstruction equation itself.

2) Phonological change is regular; that is, all tokens of a particular phonological type will change in the same way across time, under like conditions. Because of the principle of regularity, in which exceptions and irregularities are explained by further subregularities, one expects to find consistent and systematic sound correspondences or matchings between cognate forms in cognate languages. This is the Neogrammarian legacy: sound change has no exceptions that are not governed by some recoverable rule. A claim of genetic relatedness must be substantiated by sets of recurring correspondences in phonological systems, and replicable reconstruction can only proceed if some form of the regularity hypothesis is adopted.

3) The regularity of systematic correspondences between related languages makes possible the application of the comparative method, which is a procedure for postulating reconstructed proto-forms on the basis of the attested evidence of the descendant languages which have already been shown to be related. It is based on the principle that sets of recurring phoneme correspondences between two related languages continue blocks of positional allophones from the parent language (Hoenigswald 1960: 132). The comparative method requires data from at least two languages, though in both principle and fact many more can be placed into the reconstruction equation. The comparative method is supplemented by the ancillary procedure of internal reconstruction, which generates hypotheses concerning the earliest recoverable evidence from within a single language by investigating the internal alternation of linguistic elements.

Reconstructions based on the strict application of the comparative method can be verified by reference to independently established typological principles. These principles, which in part define linguistic universals and establish parameters for structural configurations at every level of linguistic organization, provide an external check on the empirical validity of a reconstruction.

4) Sound changes can be recovered from written data. Because of the long written traditions of many of the Indo-European languages, we are endowed with physical orthographic evidence of changes in individual languages as they are recorded through time. To understand and interpret these orthographic representations, we must have a thorough philological understanding of the texts themselves, and a sensitivity to the writing habits and traditions of a diverse group, from illiterate stone cutters inscribing monuments, to vulgar citizens scribbling graffitti, to semi-educated scribes recording documents, to skilled language users. All of this allows us to plot changes in the physical linguistic record, to interpret them, and to integrate them into our theoretical views of sound change.

5) Analogy of various sorts — phonological, morphological, lexical/semantic — can (re)condition sound changes. The recognition that the forces of analogy can confound the operation of a regular sound change by either causing it not to apply, or by obscuring its results, has played a highly important role in the formulation of the traditional comparative method. The rich array of analogical processes which work sometimes in cooperation, and

sometimes at odds, with phonological processes has resulted in a
strengthening of the notion of regular sound change by providing
a series of mechanisms to explain some types of irregularity. And
while the unpredictable and non-formalizable nature of analogy has
itself been a point of interest and debate among historical linguists,
its dominant role in language change, at least in the Indo-European
family, is denied by no one.

6) The relatability of irregular forms, especially irregular morphological forms, is an index of genetic affinity among languages,
and an important tool in the recovery of proto-stages. Implicit in
this notion is the assumption that language change in general is not
only regular in its operation, but that it leads to greater regularity
in the resulting linguistic system. Such regularity is consistent with
the notion that speakers must be able to preserve communication
across generations, and that the system which results from a change
or series of changes must be general enough to be learnable. Irregular forms (i.e., those not derivable by general rule) are largely
historical residue and are of necessity limited in a language system;
they are not generally introduced in the process of language change.
When such irregularities are found to correspond across languages,
this is a clear index of genetic relatedness.

Of course, one might then legitimately ask why it is that, if sound
change is regular, systems remain full of irregularity? The answer
to this is a paradox: sound change is regular, but often creates
irregularity, especially in paradigms where one form may not fit the
environment of the sound change at work. On the other hand,
analogy, which is irregular and unpredictable in its operation, creates regularity by eliminating allomorphy between forms. Take the
example of Latin rhotacism, whereby $s > r/V$____V, using the word
*honōs* 'honor' for illustration. By the normal application of the
rhotacism rule, the oblique cases of *honōs* are as follows (singular
only):

nom. *honōs*
gen. *honōris*
dat. *honōri*
acc. *honōrem*
abl. *honōre*

This paradigm is irregular in that there is an allomorphic variation
between the nominative stem *honōs* and the oblique stem *honōr-*.

The irregularity is resolved by the analogical restructuring of the nominative form to *honor,* thereby reestablishing a monomorphemic stem *honōr-* and restoring regularity. What is curious here is that the analogical restructuring of the stem to *honōr-* throughout the paradigm is unpredictable, despite the regularity it creates. Other candidates for such a restructuring process like *flōs, flōris* 'flower' or *mōs, mōris* 'custom' never developed nominative forms *\*flor* and *\*mor.*

In general, the six criteria just discussed, as well as the many additional subcriteria and associated methodologies, are based on a conception of language change which is for the most part phonologically based. The techniques of linguistic reconstruction which have proven especially useful in the recovery of ancestral stages in the Indo-European languages are most appropriately characterized in terms of phonological processes. The "ripple effect" of phonological change as it reshapes morphs, and ultimately can result in a reorientation of grammatical categories and processes, is a characteristic feature of change in the Indo-European family. This is not to say, of course, that there is no independent morphological or grammatical change, or that there is no independently established comparative morphology or comparative syntax. But one thing is clear: there is no regularity principle or Neogrammarian hypothesis for either morphology or syntax; the method keeps coming back to phonology.

These notions concerning linguistic change and reconstruction have yielded tremendously fruitful results in the Indo-European family, and have, as I said above, set the methodological standard for research on language change in studying non-Indo-European languages as well. An illustration may be in order.

When we claim that two or more languages are genetically related, we are at the same time claiming that they share common ancestry. And if we make such a claim about common ancestry, then our methods should provide us with a means of recovering the ancestral system, attested or not. The initial demonstration of relatedness is in many ways the easy part; establishing well-motivated intermediate and ancestral forms is quite another matter. Among the difficulties are: Which features in which of the languages being compared are older? Which are innovations? Which are borrowed? How many shared similarities are enough to prove relatedness conclusively, and what sort of similarities must they be? How are these weighted for significance? What assumptions do we make about the relative importance of lexical, morphological, syntactic and phonological characteristics, and about directions of language change?

Though all of these questions come into play in any reconstruction effort, we begin with the following assumption: if two or more languages share a feature which is unlikely to have arisen by accident, borrowing, or as the result of some typological tendency or language universal, then it is assumed to have arisen only once and to have been transmitted to the two or more languages from a common source. The greater the number of features that are discovered and securely identified, the sounder the relationship.

In determining genetic relationship and reconstructing proto-forms using the comparative method, we usually start with vocabulary. A list of possible cognates which is likely to produce a maximum number of common inheritance items, known as the basic vocabulary list, provides many of the words we might investigate, such as basic kinship terms, pronouns, body parts, lower numerals, and others. From these and other data we seek to establish sets of equations known as correspondences, which are statements that in a given environment, phoneme X of one language will correspond to phoneme Y of another language consistently and systematically if the two languages are descended from a common ancestor.

In order to illustrate the comparative method we will briefly and selectively choose a few lexical items from Indo-European sister languages, restricting ourselves to fairly clear cases:

|       | 'mouse' |        | 'mother' |        | 'nine' |
|-------|---------|--------|----------|--------|--------|
| Skt.  | *mū́ṣ-* |        | *mātár-* |        | *náva* |
| Gk.   | *mûs*   | (Dor.) | *mā́tēr* |        | *enné(w)a* |
| Lat.  | *mūs*   |        | *māter*  |        | *novem* |
| Goth. | *mūs*   | OIc.   | *mōðir*  | Goth.  | *niun* |

|       | 'dead' |        | 'dog' |        | 'race, kind' |
|-------|--------|--------|-------|--------|--------------|
| Skt.  | *mr̥tá-* |      | *śván-* |      | *jánas-* |
| Gk.   | *ámbrotos* 'immortal' | | *kúōn* |  | *génos* |
| Lat.  | *mortuus* |     | *canis* |     | *genus* |
| Goth. | *maúrþr* 'murder' | | *hunds* |  | *kuni* |

|  | 'I am' | 'vomit' | 'old' |
|---|---|---|---|
| Skt. | *ásmi* | *vámiti* | *sána-* |
| Gk. | *eimí* | *eméō* | *hénos* 'last year's' |
| Lat. | *sum* | *vomō* | *senex* |
| Goth. | *im* | OIc. *vāma* 'sickness' | Goth. *sineigs* |

We will concentrate on the nasals *m* and *n*. Lined up for the comparative method they look like this:

|  | 'mouse' | 'mother' | 'nine' | 'dead' | 'dog' |
|---|---|---|---|---|---|
| Skt. | *m-* | *m-* | *-n-* | *m-* | *-n* |
| Gk. | *m-* | *m-* | *-nn-* | *-m(b)-* | *-n* |
| Lat. | *m-* | *m-* | *-n-* | *m-* | *-n-* |
| Gmc. | *m-* | *m-* | *-n-* | *m-* | *-n-* |

|  | 'race, kind' | 'I am' | 'vomit' | 'old' |
|---|---|---|---|---|
| Skt. | *-n-* | *-m-* | *-m-* | *-n-* |
| Gk. | *-n-* | *-m-* | *-m-* | *-n-* |
| Lat. | *-n-* | *-m* | *-m-* | *-n-* |
| Gmc. | *-n-* | *-m* | *-m-* | *-n-* |

Before we begin reconstructing, we must be sure that we are comparing the appropriate segments. It is clear that this is the case in 'mouse,' 'mother,' 'dog,' 'race, kind,' 'I am,' 'vomit' and 'old,' but less clear in 'nine' and 'dead.' What of the double *n* in Gk. *enné(w)a*? A closer look reveals that *en-* is a prefix; thus, the first *n* is outside the equation. Similarly with *ámbrotos* 'immortal': the *á-* is a prefix meaning 'not' (= Lat. *in-*, Goth. *un-*, etc.), and the *b* results from a rule of Greek in which the sequence *-mr-* results in *-mbr-*, with epenthetic *b* (cf. the parallel process in Lat. *camera* > Fr. *chambre*). So the *m*'s do indeed align, leaving us with a consistent set of *m* and *n* correspondences:

$m : m : m : m$            $n : n : n : n$
←————————→        ←————————→

These alignments represent the horizontal or comparative dimension. Next we 'triangulate' the segments, adding the vertical, or historical, dimension:

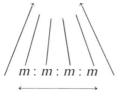

Finally, after checking all the relevant data and investigating their distributional patterns, we make a hypothesis concerning the proto-sound. In these two cases the most immediately evident hypothesis is that the proto-sounds were *\*m* and *\*n*:

At this stage of the analysis we are claiming that *\*m* > (develops into) *m* and *\*n* > *n* in the various daughter languages.

Neat correspondences such as these are more the exception than the rule in historical-comparative linguistics. It is far more common to find sets in which only a few of the members have identical segments. But the method of comparative reconstruction, when supplemented with sufficient information about the internal structure of the languages in question, can still yield replicable results. Consider the following data:

|  | 'stand' | 'old' | 'race, kind' (gen. case) | 'be' |
|---|---|---|---|---|
| Skt. | *sthā-* | *sánaḥ* | *jánasaḥ* | *ástu* 'let him be!' |
| Gk. | *hí-stāmi* | *hénos* 'last years's' | *géneos (génous)* | *éō (ō)* 'I might be' |
| Lat. | *stāre* | *senex* | *generis* | *erō* 'I will be' |
| Goth. | *standan* | *sineigs* | (OCS *slovesa* 'words') | *ist* 'he/she is' |

We are concentrating here on the correspondences which include *s*, *h*, *ḥ*, and *r*. In 'stand' we find the correspondence set *s : s : s : s*, with the initial *h* of Gk. *hístāmi* the result of reduplication of the root initial *s* and its replacement by *h*. This replacement reproduces the pattern we find in the initial sound of the set 'old,' namely *s : h : s : s*. In final position we find *ḥ : s : s : s* in 'old' and 'race, kind.' And in medial position we have *s : Ø : r : s* in 'race, kind' and 'be.' What is or are the proto-sound(s)?

A brief look at the languages in question takes us straight to *\*s* for all four correspondences. For the first set 'stand' we have complete agreement of correspondences, and *\*s* seems a reasonable reconstruction in the absence of evidence to the contrary. For the second set, we can see a pattern by postulating that *\*s* > *h* in Greek initially (*hístāmi, hénos*), a weakening process found in a number of languages. This weakening is further evidenced in the forms *géneos* and *éō*, where medial *\*s* > ∅. The final *ḥ* of Sanskrit *sánaḥ* and *janasaḥ* results from a specific rule of Sanskrit by which final *s* after vowels becomes *ḥ*. And the medial Latin *r* in *generis* and *erō* is the result of rhotacism, whereby Latin consistently converts intervocalic *s* to *r* (cf. *flōs* 'flower', (gen.) *flōris*).

From these few, admittedly simplified, examples we see that the comparative method, when supplemented by adequate information about the internal structure of the languages in question and by a consideration of all the relevant data, seems to produce consistent and reliable reconstructions of ancestral forms. It is with such methods that Proto-Indo-European has been reconstructed.

Research on a wide variety of the world's languages has shown that there are many strict phonological correspondences of the type found in Indo-European languages. For example, some American Indian languages allow for the orthodox application of the comparative method of reconstruction with consistent results. These results have been so impressive that it has even been said that some of the American Indian languages are more Indo-European than some Indo-European ones. Similar results in both grouping and reconstruction have been achieved in the Austronesian, Dravidian, Finno-Ugric, and many other families. The end product has been a continuous vindication of the comparative method in some quarters, and the repeated demonstration that its applicability extends beyond its original domain.

But doubt lingers along several lines. First, it has been asked whether the method is both circular and too powerful, in effect guaranteeing its own success. This is because the practice of historical linguists and the theories and methods they profess to be following may be quite different from each other. Critics would claim that the real-life application of the comparative method goes something like the following: first make an informed guess about the cognacy of the languages to be compared; next decide what forms are cognate on the basis of a kind of loose semantic relatability; next reconstruct forms by applying internal and comparative reconstruction methods *sui generis*; then explain away exceptions and irregularities by appeal to analogy and other well-established notions; and finally build "semantic bridges" which adjust results in order to arrive at a more or less unique form with a consistent sound-meaning correspondence. Points that skeptics of the comparative method consistently raise are the relatively small number of "good cognates" (i.e., those in which appeal to explanatory devices outside the comparative method is unnecessary), and the often wide disagreement among scholars on the reconstructions themselves, especially those involving polymorphemic structures.

There has also been a lively controversy over the matter of lexical diffusion, as developed primarily by Wang (1969). Wang's original claim was that sound changes spread gradually across the lexicon (words change), and that phonemes frequently are not the minimal units of historical phonological change. This contrasts strongly with the original Neogrammarian position that change affects all words that include the sound according to their phonetic environment (sounds change). These apparently opposite positions have been reconciled by Labov (1981), in which the different types of changes are shown to apply to different types of phenomena in the linguistic system ("We have located Neogrammarian regularity in low-level output rules, and lexical diffusion in the redistribution of an abstract word class into other abstract words classes," Labov 1981: 304). What is especially noteworthy in Labov's resolution of the paradox between lexical diffusion and Neogrammarian regularity is the fact that it has been achieved in research on modern English dialects in American cities, thereby demonstrating the applicability of historical methodology to current phenomena. It strengthens the position that historical linguists should carry out their research as if all change were regular.

In addition to the disagreement over the integrity of the method itself, questions have been raised for decades over its applicability to languages of widely divergent typologies, or to languages with social, cultural, and geographical characteristics different from those of the Indo-European languages. Doubt seems to flow along several different lines.

First is the matter of the phonological basis of linguistic change which is so much in evidence in the Indo-European languages. The comparative method relies on sound correspondences; what, then, can it do in language families where sound correspondences are irregular and inconsistent? Boretzky (1984), for example, has argued that change in the Arandic languages of central Australia seems to proceed more by abrupt lexical replacement through borrowing than by gradual phonological change. Moreover, these lexical replacements are frequent, and cut deep into the core vocabulary commonly held to be resistant to borrowing. Furthermore, the conditions according to which these replacements take place are difficult to imagine in large language families with many speakers, considerable geographical spread, and complex stratified societies. These conditions include borrowing/replacement because of death taboos, which proscribe the use of common nouns contained in the names of tribe members who have died. They also include notions such as secret languages, mother-in-law languages, language loyalty and shift according to marriage patterns, and a number of other conditions which promote a certain pattern of change which is not easily adaptable to the traditional notions of regularity, graduality, and the like.

A second area of disagreement over the comparative method concerns its usefulness in the establishment of long-distance linguistic relationships and remote proto-languages. This is an active controversy in historical linguistics today, and it is touched on in several places throughout this volume.

Whether linguists can reliably reconstruct distant genetic relationships and establish phylum-level proto-languages is not only a matter of method, but of philosophy of science. At issue are such questions as the following: What counts as data? What are the requirements on semantic relatability? What are the ultimate determinants of cognacy? How much strict regularity is required in phonological equations? How much internal reconstruction can or should be done? What is an acceptable time-depth? Is it legitimate to use a reconstructed proto-language as an intermediate stage (common language) in the reconstruction of an even more remote proto-language?

A brief discussion is in order. Greenberg (1987) has claimed that the native languages of the Americas can be classified into three main genetic groups, with ninety percent of them in what he calls "Amerind" and the remaining ten percent in the groups he calls "Na-Dene" and "Eskimo-Aleut." This contrasts with the more generally held view, according to which about one hundred fifty families can be established, and according to which deeper relationships are so far poorly demonstrated. Greenberg's classification is based not on the application of the orthodox comparative method, but rather on the technique of "multilateral comparison." The emphasis is strictly lexical. Multilateral comparison looks at a relatively small number of words across a relatively large number of languages, and attempts to expose similarities in form and meaning among the words which Greenberg believes betray genetic relatedness among the languages. The large number of languages used in the comparison typically increases the chance for similarities, and the lack of a phonological correspondence requirement across cognate forms makes the procedure considerably more liberal than the comparative method as described earlier. Of course, it is important to bear in mind that the goal of multilateral comparison is not reconstruction, but rather classification, though it is not clear that the method of multilateral comparison was instrumental in Greenberg's classifications. There are no asterisked forms in Greenberg's lexical comparisons. (For a complete review of the issues, see Campbell 1988.)

There are asterisked forms in other long-distance work, however, and we must not let the shadow of Greenberg's bold but unorthodox classification darken the light on other phylum-level reconstruction efforts. In particular we should mention here the new efforts to reconstruct Proto-Nostratic as a parent language of the Afroasiatic, Kartvelian, Indo-European, Uralic, Dravidian, and Altaic language families. Though no less controversial than Greenberg's classifications, the reconstruction of Proto-Nostratic has proceeded along more traditional lines, and the results have to be reckoned with by traditionalists (who favor family-level limits to reconstruction) and by non-traditionalists (who favor phylum-level reconstructions) alike.

Many of these issues are for the future to decide. The present volume presents research from six different language groups, both genetic and areal, in an effort to address some of the basic methodological issues we have been discussing. Though not all the papers address these matters directly, and some raise points which we have not touched on in this discussion, we can nonetheless uncover a *communis opinio* among contributors: the comparative method works. While it is true that the method has flaws, it nonetheless allows for a general replicability which strongly indicates its internal integrity as a method. Furthermore, the method has a general applicability, not only to Indo-European languages and those that behave like Indo-European languages, but to languages and language families which differ markedly from these. This includes the languages of Australia, in contrast to what Boretzky has claimed. Finally, on the matter of the limits of the method, there is less agreement, but still consensus. The comparative method has limits, both practical and methodological. The people who use this method are constrained by human limitations, and the availability and accessibility of all the data required to make remote speculations are severe. Yet one must not stop trying, for the search into history should never be proscribed by our failure to find ways to do it.

## References

Boretzky, Norbert
  1984        "The Indo-Europeanist model of sound change and genetic affinity and its application to exotic languages", *Diachronica* 1: 1—51.
Campbell, Lyle
  1988        Review of Greenberg 1987, *Language* 64: 591—615.
Greenberg, Joseph
  1987        *Language in the Americas* (Stanford: Stanford University Press).
Hoenigswald, Henry M.
  1960        *Language change and linguistic reconstruction* (Chicago: University of Chicago Press).
Labov, William
  1981        "Resolving the Neogrammarian controversy", *Language* 57: 267—308.
Wang, William S.-Y.
  1969        "Competing changes as a cause of residue", *Language* 45: 9—25.

# Summary report: American Indian languages and principles of language change

*Lyle Campbell* and *Ives Goddard*

In the 1924 edition of *Les langues du monde*, Antoine Meillet wondered "if the American languages ... will ever lend themselves to the establishment of precise and complete comparative grammars" (Meillet 1926—1936, 2: 61). The following year Leonard Bloomfield, citing Meillet's statement, wrote that he hoped that one of the results of his paper "On the sound system of Central Algonquian" would be "to help dispose of the notion that the usual processes of linguistic change are suspended on the American continent" (Bloomfield 1925: 130). The work that has been done on the historical linguistics of the native languages of the Americas, a small part of which was reported on at the Stanford conference and is printed in this volume, demonstrates that language change in the New World is not different in kind from what happens elsewhere in the world, and that correspondingly these languages require no methods of reconstruction based on assumptions that would be invalid for other languages. A consequence that this fact has for the present report is that no uniqueness can be claimed for the general topics here surveyed. Nevertheless, the specific cases presented and discussed will serve to illustrate the state of historical linguistics as it is practiced by Americanists.

It should be mentioned at the outset that the specialized knowledge of the Americanists who participated in the Stanford conference does not encompass all the linguistic families of the New World, and in particular extends only minimally to South America. We feel, however, that we are representative of a general consensus, one that grows out of the cross-fertilization that characterizes linguistic work on the languages of the Western Hemisphere. Three general factors to be considered are: the history of this research and its goals, the nature of the data, and the nature of historical linguistics in general in North America. We consider these in turn, and then take up the specific questions addressed by the participants of the conference concerning the relevance of American Indian studies to historical linguistic concerns in general. A more particular factor is the relationship between the historical study of Indian languages and their descriptive study, and the consequent tendency for historical linguists working in different families to work on different types of problems.

## History of research

Research on American Indian languages has been dominated from the beginning by a desire to determine the origin and relationships of the languages of the New World. This has tended to put an emphasis on distant relationships before the details of the closer relationships were worked out (see below). It has led to the use of data that would produce quick and putatively convincing proofs of relationship rather than data that would require a specialized understanding of the particulars. As a consequence, the use of lists of similar words to demonstrate linguistic relationships has been a fixture of the field from Grotius to Greenberg (Slotkin 1965: 97 – 98; Greenberg 1987 a). And, more generally, there has often been a greater degree of tolerance among Americanists for proposals of distant genetic relationships than among linguists working in the more established language families. This long-standing focus on distant relationships has distracted the attention of those outside the field from the lapidary and often perhaps unspectacular reconstruction of the histories of individual language families that has moved forward with increasing refinement throughout the present century. To cite an illustration of current interest, Greenberg's attempt to set up distant relationships while ignoring the concrete results of the family-level historical work (Chafe 1987; Goddard 1987; Campbell 1988) has been correctly and rather pointedly characterized, by a commentator whom Greenberg (1987 b: 664) himself regards as sympathetic, as work that "cannot be located in the main tradition of comparative linguistics in the Americas" and whose conclusions "are of little interest to serious comparativists" (Golla 1987: 657, 658; cf. Golla 1988).

Out of the limelight, meanwhile, as historical linguistics has developed, its techniques have been applied in the New World as elsewhere. For example, Otto Stoll (1884, 1885) formulated a number of Mayan "sound laws", indicating:

> These changes follow regular phonetic laws and bear a strong affinity to the principle of "Lautverschiebung" (Grimm's law), long ago known as an agent of most extensive application in the morphology of the Indo-European languages. (Stoll 1885: 257)

Similarly, Eduard Seler's (1887) Mayan historical morphology and syntax was squarely in the Indo-Europeanist tradition of the time (Delbrück 1888, 1893). Both Stoll and Seler, working in the 1880s, used the newly minted methods developed by the Neo-Grammarians. While American Indian historical linguistics has benefitted greatly from general developments in historical linguistics, it has also contributed to the development, if only in its own small way. For example, there has been some impact from the work of Bloomfield (1925, 1928) and Sapir (1913, 1914, 1931) in establishing that sound change is regular in unwritten languages, and from the work of Boas which inspired areal linguistics in Europe, from whence it returned to become important in American Indian studies (Jakobson 1931, 1938, 1944; Darnell—Sherzer 1971; Campbell 1985; see below).

A more difficult subject, perhaps, is the effect on American Indian historical linguistics of the state of the art of historical linguistics in general in North America. Historical linguistics has certainly tended to be the step-child of linguistic programs, and many linguists appear to assume that it is simply some sort of algebra that any linguist can manipulate (and no one else can evaluate). When the constraints of accepted historical method have seemed too restrictive, new, less rigorous methodologies have been proposed in order to produce results more easily. A notable example is Carl Voegelin's unfortunate distinction between comparative-method linguistics and phylum linguistics (Voegelin 1965; cf. Voegelin 1942), which at bottom reflected the misconception, widespread in North America, that the comparative method is a method for proving languages to be related by using sound laws (see also, for example, McQuown 1955: 502; Longacre 1967: 119—120). On the contrary, the comparative method is a method used to construct hypotheses about the undocumented history of related languages by systematically comparing their features. It need not involve the use of phonological information of any kind, though this is often useful and, to be sure, the formulation of sound laws is an important part of working out the linguistic history of a language family or a directly documented language. Any shared or similar feature that must be explained as an independent genetic inheritance in each of the related languages can be turned into a piece of linguistic history by the comparative method.

The relationship between the historical study of Indian languages and their descriptive study has been significant. In fact it often seems that the function of historical linguistic study is, for many scholars, to provide a way of gaining a perspective on the synchronic and typological problems that are their first concerns. As a consequence of this factor, and no doubt also because of the typological differences that exist, there seems to be a tendency for linguists working in different American Indian language families to look at different types of problems. Linguists with an interest in syntactic typology concentrate on historical syntax; linguists working on phonologically complex languages focus on historical phonology. It is an open question whether this situation can be turned to crossfertilization and mutual enrichment; if it simply continues to reinforce the parochialism that sometimes seems to characterize the field at present, the insights will soon dry up and the impact of American Indian historical linguistics will be small.

## The data

Data on American Indian languages are for the most part much less abundant than for the Old World languages that provided the basis for the development of historical linguistics. It is a commonplace to observe that historical sequences of documents are generally lacking, although it is sometimes possible to find earlier materials that shed light on historical questions. An example can be cited from Seri, which pluralizes nouns by a number of complex patterns, including vowel ablauting; one pair, which has to be treated as suppletive, is *kʷíkke* 'person, Seri' and its plural *koŋkáak*. Alphonse Pinart's recording of these words in 1879 as ⟨komkak⟩ and ⟨kmike⟩ (presumably *komkáak* and *kmíkke* [or *kʷmíkke*]) resolves the sup-

pletion as an additional ablaut pattern (on the consonantal frame
*k m k k*) and permits the recovery of several pieces of quite recent
linguistic history (Goddard in Bowen 1983: 248; for a number of
examples of this type from Mayan languages, see Campbell in press
a and this volume).

The general thinness of the documentation of American Indian
languages has consequences for historical linguistics beyond a
negative effect on the possibilities for directly documenting
change. The documentation typically does not include the abundance of texts that, for Indo-European languages say, provides
the evidence for the contextual associations of words and elements that form the basis of etymology. There are exceptions,
but these are almost entirely unexploited for this purpose. For
many Indian languages that are considered well documented there
may well be attestation from only a small number of speakers,
often only one, speaking on a limited range of topics. Also, for
these languages, information is typically sparse or lacking on the
natural synchronic variation that reflects the historical changes of
the past and adumbrates those of the future. On the positive side,
the absence of standardization means that American Indian languages are generally documented in a form closer to natural,
spoken language than is often true elsewhere, and where information on variation is available there are research opportunities
that so far are largely unexploited.

## The techniques

The native languages of the New World provide a laboratory for
the utilization and examination of the full range of historical linguistic techniques. There is no reason to believe that linguistic
change differs in the New World in ways that require assumptions
and methodologies that would not be applicable elsewhere. Where
the effects of regular sound change have been interfered with by
special factors, our axiomatic assumption of regularity allows us to
recognize this and gives us a starting point for explaining the
phenomenon. The data reported on by Krauss and Leer (see Leer,
this volume) present challenges of this sort (see below).

The complex morphology of many language families provides the opportunity for using reconstructive techniques on challenging data, but, by the same token, the data are rewarding for sharpening these techniques. Langdon's paper (this volume) is an example of this.


## The role of typology

Mithun (this volume) reports on the wide range of applications that the use of linguistic typology has had in the study of linguistic history in the New World. Descriptive typology has provided a guide to realism in reconstruction, and in turn diachronic typology has been enriched by the increasing knowledge of the patterns of change found in numerous linguistic families of the Americas. As elsewhere in the world, the study of linguistic history has contributed to the understanding of synchronic and typological questions, bearing on universal claims and the like. A strong tradition in New World linguistics cautions that typological similarity cannot be assumed to provide a key to genetic relationship, but typological sophistication in the evaluation of the cooccurrence of features can provide a principled basis for evaluating the genetic implications of features that recur in particular sets.


## Contributions

The core of the contributions made by the historical linguistic study of the New World languages is in the ongoing working out of the history of a number of language families in considerable and ever-increasing detail; notable in this regard are Algonquian (reported on by Goddard, this volume), Iroquoian (reported on by Mithun), Mayan (Campbell, this volume), Athabaskan, Miwok-Costanoan, Siouan, Uto-Aztecan, and others. These linguistic histories have provided the basis for studying further questions of diffusion, relations between language and culture (linguistic prehistory), and other topics. The histories of the New World languages also provide many opportunities for investigating a wide range of special questions that are as yet little explored. These include the effect of the transition from an illiterate to a literate society on language change and its documentation; the comparative study of language change in a variety of social and cultural contexts, ranging from hunter-gatherers to complex civilizations with elaborate writing systems; and a wide array of philological questions concerning Mayan and other Mesoamerican hieroglyphic scripts, native literacy and its products, and the evaluation of older materials as sources for descriptive data.

## Distant genetic comparisons

It could be argued that distant genetic comparisons lay outside the scope of the conference — since they rarely involve reconstruction, by any methodology, and hence rarely have anything to tell us about linguistic history, properly speaking. Nevertheless, because distant comparisons have been such a prominent part of work on American Indian languages, it seems advisable to address this question in some way.

The history of American Indian linguistic study is characterized by attempts to reduce the vast diversity in the Americas to manageable genetic schemes. Many hypotheses of remote relationship were proposed initially as hunches, or longshots, to be more fully tested in subsequent research. An example is Hokan, of which Sapir (1925: 526) wrote:

> Such a scheme [Hokan] must not be taken too literally. It is offered merely as a first step toward defining the issue, and it goes without saying that the status of several of these languages may have to be entirely restated.

Unfortunately, such preliminary proposals were too often taken as demonstrated and subsequently became frozen in the literature. This means that many of these widely accepted but poorly founded claims for remote affinity are in need of reassessment. Kroeber and Dixon's Hokan and Penutian hypotheses were among the first reductions proposed, becoming widely known at an early point; later scholars attempted to relate unaffiliated languages to these more familiar groupings, heaping ever greater numbers of languages onto either the Hokan or Penutian pile. Unsurprisingly, many of these rough-and-ready proposals have not panned out — several are demonstrably wrong; several others are seriously challenged (cf. Campbell 1973; Campbell—Mithun 1979; Campbell—Kaufman 1981, 1983; Shipley 1980).

Such proposals of distant genetic relationship, most recently those of Joseph Greenberg (1987 a), have been found unpersuasive, not because we are unsympathetic, but because the evidence offered was weighed against standard techniques for investigating potential distant relationships and was found wanting. These methods for establishing the plausibility of remoter relationships are quite clear and are well-known (see Bright 1984, 1985; Callaghan—Miller 1962; Campbell 1973, 1978; Campbell—Kaufman 1981, 1983; Campbell—Mithun 1979; Chafe 1987; Goddard 1975, 1987; Teeter 1964).

Distant comparisons have, from the beginning, been of interest primarily as a way of developing hypotheses regarding the ethnic history of the New World. It is not clear, however, how a linguistic history of the languages spoken in the New World in 1492 would in principle be related to the ethnic history of the New World since 14,000 before the present. The difficulties here are well-known. Americanists are particularly aware of the lack of correlation between language and culture in the New World. One could, in principle, work out a linguistic history of the known languages of the New World without regard to the biological or cultural history of their speakers. To achieve the goal of elucidating the ethnic history of the people speaking these languages, a way must be found to judge the correlation of the different sources of information on the prehistory of the New World, and this undertaking is likely to involve detailed work of the sort that has hardly been begun. The chances of success are obviously uncertain. The recent claims by Greenberg—Turner—Zegura (1986) of a correlation between physical anthropological traits and linguistic affiliation in the case of Eskimo-Aleut and Athabaskan (with its relatives) are hardly surprising and provide no real demonstration that anything similar could be done for the great majority of the New World languages or for the mass of the total history of the New World that remains to challenge us after these two most recent arrivals are explained (cf. Hamp 1987). It should also be noted that the claimed correlations are not all that precise, modest as they are (see, for example,

Campbell 1986). Much of the prehistory of the New World must have involved speakers of languages with no known descendants, and there is no basis for assuming that only a negligible number of languages would have had this fate. In fact the problem gets larger as the number of accepted distant relationships increases, as true progress in this direction has the effect of reducing the number and time depth of the families that can be documented.

Besides the ethnic history of the New World, distant genetic comparisons ought by rights to shed some light on the linguistic history of the languages compared. In fact, if such comparisons do not lead to hypotheses on linguistic history they are obviously of no use to historical linguistics. Here the inadequacy of most distant genetic work is evident. Direct equations imply linguistic history but are rarely used productively as part of a hypothesis about what the linguistic history actually was. This failing is particularly evident in Greenberg's (1987 a) recent book. What Greenberg calls etymologies are actually sets of word equations. The history that they might be assumed to imply is not discussed. That is to say, the subject matter that is the entire point of historical linguistics is essentially absent from the book. Even established facts about the linguistic history of the languages and forms discussed are generally ignored (Chafe 1987; Goddard 1987; Campbell 1988). Greenberg's point that sound correspondences are not necessary to demonstrate genetic relationship is correct (Greenberg 1987a: 1 ff.), but the comparative method, in the broad sense (see above), is required, and Greenberg makes no use of any variety of the comparative method. That Greenberg's undescribed criteria of similarity produce incorrect equations is shown by cases in which a single form is equated to two forms that are not even equatable to each other (Chafe 1987; Goddard 1987; Campbell 1988). The reason the comparative methodology that Greenberg spurns is needed is precisely to permit us to distinguish between genuine and spurious equations. Effectively, then, Greenberg has produced a book-length example of why historical linguistics must be based on systematic principles that go beyond similarity. Greenberg (1987a: 29) asserts that his "method of multilateral comparison" produces "reliable" classifications, but the fact is that any method of classification based on the tabulation of similarities will produce a classification out of whatever judgments of similarity are assumed, and this outcome alone cannot be taken to indicate that a classification produced in

this way has empirical, historical validity, or "reliability" of any
kind (except as a transposition of the judgments of similarity that
are in question). "The method of multilateral comparison" is the
problem rather than the solution.


## Questions concerning change

We now turn our attention more specifically to the thematic questions addressed by the conference in general and in particular by
the American Indianist participants.

What are the patterns of linguistic change in the Americas? As
indicated above, because of the extensive genetic and typological
diversity among American Indian languages, virtually all known
patterns of linguistic change are found here, although none is unique
to the Americas, and none forces us to reject or modify the basic
assumptions of historical linguistics or the axioms of linguistic
reconstruction, though some situations call for caution, and in some
cases certain questions will probably never be answerable.

What factors affect linguistic change in the Americas? For most
Americanists, historical linguistic practice is "business as usual": we
do regular historical linguistics, though with differing emphases
dictated in part by the nature of the languages and the data available
(see above). Nevertheless, the very diversity in American Indian
languages forces us to become adept at dealing with changes of all
sorts in varying social situations. Moreover, frequently American
Indianists do the fieldwork, collect the data, and do both the
descriptive and historical work on a language, or a group of languages. The resulting feedback contributes to quality control, care
for detail, and rigor, in both description and historical analysis.

Among factors that affect change, we mention some specifics.
With respect to morpho-syntax, there is general agreement among
us that there is no autonomous or independent grammatical change.
The proper study of morpho-syntactic change should include a
variety of factors, e. g., concomitant phonological changes, which
can require grammatical adjustments; perception or processing;
discourse functions; influence from other languages, etc. There are
some excellent studies of grammatical change and syntactic recon-

struction for certain New World languages which are worthy of special attention as models of rigor, for their methods, and for the results in languages with typologies not well known in historical linguistic work as conducted in other parts of the world. Just a few representative examples are: Derbyshire (1981), Haas (1977), Hale — Laverne — Platero (1977), Hinton (1980), Jacobs (1975), Jacobsen (1983), Langacker (1977), Langdon (1977), Mithun (1980), Munro (1984), Muysken (1977), Norman — Campbell (1978), and Weir (1986).

With respect to grammatical reconstruction, Margaret Langdon (this volume) asks a fundamental question: How does one determine what are comparable items, particularly in remoter, less obvious relationships, or in face of the frequent difficulty that basic grammatical morphemes may be quite short (CV, V, or C in shape)?

Another factor affecting change is contact and diffusion. Perhaps more so than elsewhere, scholars in the Americas have developed a healthy respect for contact and diffusion. In the last twenty years areal linguistics has become a high-visibility agenda item in American Indian historical linguistic practice; it should become part of the regular equipment of historical linguistics generally. It is of major importance to attempt to determine the history of what really happened, be it due to descent from a common ancestor or to diffusion across linguistic boundaries. Areal linguistics is important for checks and balances on proposals of remote genetic affinity, since too often evidence that has been put forward on behalf of certain proposals of distant kinship has proved to be due to diffusion (cf. Campbell 1978; Campbell — Kaufman 1981, 1983).

In connection with language contact, we mention language death, of which, unfortunately, examples abound in the Americas. The question has been raised in the case of both language obsolescence and areal diffusion that sound changes may not necessarily prove to be regular or natural (Campbell — Muntzel, in press; Campbell 1985). While we suspect this to be the case, we raise it here only in footnote fashion, since we feel it unwarranted to exaggerate uncertainties — we hasten to add that otherwise sound change in American Indian languages is regular, i. e., not different from elsewhere. In fact, American Indian studies have helped to confirm and sharpen this tenet of historical-comparative linguistics (see above).

Also with respect to diffusion, the potentially complicating issues of dialect mixture (borrowing within a language) and native linguistic traditions for borrowing were discussed. Krauss and Leer have asked (cf. Leer, this volume): How can we know what is cognate, or, what is borrowed? And, if we do not know, how can we trust the comparative method? Other potential explanations in addition to Leer's proposed dialect mixture for the Tlingit circumstances were also raised at the conference, e. g., conditioned changes internal to Tlingit for which the conditioning factors are now lost, with general agreement that in any case the assumption of regular sound change allows us to recognize such special situations.

Finally, save for a sporadic misfire of no real impact here and there in the linguistic literature, it is safe to say that certain issues have now been put to rest, e. g., that unwritten languages exhibit regularity of sound change and do not change at highly accelerated rates as compared with other languages (cf. Bloomfield 1928; Sapir 1931).

## Acknowledgments

This overview was forged with the help and inspiration of the panel members of the American Indian linguistic section: Victor Golla, Michael Krauss, Margaret Langdon, Jeff Leer, Marianne Mithun, and Kenneth Whistler. Ives Goddard was the unannounced, but official, section co-leader, together with Lyle Campbell.

## References

Bloomfield, Leonard
    1925        "On the sound-system of Central Algonquian", *Language* 1: 130 – 156.
    1928        "A note on sound change", *Language* 5: 99 – 100.
Bowen, Thomas
    1983        "Seri", *Handbook of North American Indians* 10: 230 – 249.
Bright, William
    1984        "The classification of North American and Meso-American Indian languages", *American Indian linguistics and literature* (Berlin: Mouton de Gruyter), 3 – 30.
    1985        "La clasificación de los idiomas indígenas de Norteamérica y de Mesoamérica", *Anales de antropología* (México) 20: 173 – 204.
Callaghan, Catherine A. – Wick R. Miller
    1962        "Swadesh's Macro-Mixtecan hypothesis and English", *Southwestern Journal of Anthropology* 18: 278 – 285.
Campbell, Lyle
    1973        "Distant genetic relationships and the Maya-Chipaya hypothesis", *Anthropological Linguistics* 15: 113 – 135.

1978          "Distant genetic relationship and diffusion: A Mesoamerican per-
              spective", *Proceedings of the International Congress of Americanists*
              52: 595 — 605.
1985          "Areal linguistics and its implications for historical linguistic theory",
              in: Jacek Fisiak (ed.), *Proceedings of the Sixth International Confer-
              ence of Historical Linguistics,* (Amsterdam: Benjamins), 25 — 56.
1986          "Comments on the settlement of the Americas: A comparison of the
              linguistic, dental, and genetic evidence", *Current Anthropology* 27:
              488.
1988          Review article on *Language in the Americas,* by Joseph H. Greenberg,
              *Language* 64: 591 — 615.
In press a.   "Philology and Mayan languages", in: Jacek Fisiak (ed.), *Historical
              linguistics and philology* (Berlin: Mouton de Gruyter).
Campbell, Lyle — Terrence Kaufman
1981          "On Mesoamerican linguistics", *American Anthropologist* 82: 850 —
              857.
1983          "Mesoamerican historical linguistics and distant genetic relationship:
              Getting it straight", *American Anthropologist* 85: 362 — 372.
Campbell, Lyle — Marianne Mithun
1979          "North American Indian historical linguistics in current perspective",
              in: Lyle Campbell — Marianne Mithun (eds.), *The languages of Native
              America: A historical and comparative assessment* (Austin: University
              of Texas Press), 3 — 69.
Campbell, Lyle — Martha Muntzel
In press      "The structural consequences of language death", in: Nancy Dorian
              (ed.), *Investigating obsolescence: Studies in language death* (Cam-
              bridge: Cambridge University Press).
Chafe, Wallace
1987          Review of *Language in the Americas,* by Joseph H. Greenberg.
              *Current Anthropology* 28: 652 — 653.
Darnell, Regna — Joel Sherzer
1971          "Areal linguistic studies in North America: A historical perspective",
              *International Journal of American Linguistics* 37: 20 — 28
Delbrück, Berthold
1888          *Altindische Syntax* (Syntaktische Forschungen, 5) (Halle an der
              Saale: Niemeyer) (Reprinted 1968, Darmstadt: Wissenschaftliche
              Buchgesellschaft).
1893          *Vergleichende Syntax der indogermanischen Sprachen* 1. Part III
              (1900) (= Karl Brugmann — Berthold Delbrück, *Grundriss der ver-
              gleichenden Grammatik der indogermanischen Sprachen* III) (Strass-
              burg: Trübner).
Derbyshire, Desmond C.
1981          "A diachronic explanation for the origin of OVS in some Carib
              languages", *Journal of Linguistics* 17: 209 — 220.
Goddard, Ives
1975          "Algonquian, Wiyot, and Yurok: Proving a distant genetic relation-
              ship", in: M. Dale Kinkade — Kenneth L. Hale — Oswald Werner
              (eds.), *Linguistics and anthropology in honor of C. F. Voegelin* (Lisse:
              de Ridder), 249 — 262.

1987      Review of *Language in the Americas,* by Joseph H. Greenberg. *Current Anthropology* 28: 656 – 657.

Golla, Victor
1987      Review of *Language in the Americas,* by Joseph H. Greenberg. *Current Anthropology* 28: 657 – 659.
1988      Review of *Language in the Americas,* by Joseph H. Greenberg, *American Anthropologist* 90: 434 – 435.

Greenberg, Joseph H.
1987a     *Language in the Americas* (Stanford: Stanford University Press).
1987b     Reply. *Current Anthropology* 28: 664 – 666.

Greenberg, Joseph H. – C. H. Turner – S. Zegura
1986      "The settlement of the Americas", *Current Anthropology* 27: 477 – 497.

Haas, Mary R.
1977      "From auxiliary verb phrase to inflectional suffix, in: Charles Li (ed.), *Mechanisms of syntactic change* (Austin: University of Texas Press), 525 – 537.

Hale, Kenneth – Jeanne LaVerne – Paul Platero
1977      "Three cases of overgeneralization", in: P. Culicover – T. Wasow – A. Akmajian (eds.), *Formal syntax* (New York: Academic Press), 379 – 416.

Hamp, Eric
1987      "On the settlement of the Americas: The linguistic evidence", *Current Anthropology* 28: 101.

Hinton, Leanne
1980      "When sounds go wild: Phonological change and syntactic re-analysis in Havasupai", *Language* 56: 320 – 344.

Jacobs, Roderick A.
1975      *Syntactic change: A Cupan (Uto-Aztecan) case study* (University of California Publications in Linguistics 79.) (Berkeley: University of California Press).

Jacobsen, William H., Jr.
1983      "Typological and genetic notes on switch-reference systems in North-American Indian languages", in: John Haiman – Pamela Munro (eds.), *Switch reference* (Typological studies in language 2.) (Amsterdam: Benjamins), 151 – 186.

Jakobson, Roman
1931      "Über die phonologischen Sprachbünde", *Travaux du Cercle Linguistique de Prague* 4: 234 – 240.
1938      "Sur la thèorie des affinités phonologiques entre les langues", *Actes du quatrième congrès international de linguistes tenu à Copenhague du 27 août – 1 septembre, 1936:* 48 – 58. (Reprinted and translated: "On the theory of phonological associations among languages", in: Allan R. Keiler (ed.), *A reader in historical and comparative linguistics* (New York: Holt, Rinehart and Winston, 1972), 241 – 252.
1944      "Franz Boas' approach to language", *International Journal of American Linguistics* 10: 188 – 95.

Langacker, Ronald W.
1977      *An overview of Uto-Aztecan grammar* (Studies in Uto-Aztecan grammar 1) (Arlington: Summer Institute of Linguistics, University of Texas at Arlington Press).

Langdon, Margaret
1977    "Syntactic change and SOV structure: The Yuman case", in: Charles
        Li (ed.), *Mechanisms of syntactic change* (Austin: University of Texas
        Press), 255–290.
Longacre, Robert
1967    "Systematic comparison and reconstruction", in: Norman A.
        McQuown (ed.), *Handbook of Middle American Indians* 5 (Austin:
        University of Texas Press), 117–159.
McQuown, Norman
1955    "The indigenous languages of Latin America", *American Anthropologist* 57: 501–570.
Meillet, Antoine
1926–1936  *Linguistique historique et linguistique générale* 1–2 (Paris: Champion/Klincksieck).
Mithun, Marianne
1980    "A functional approach to syntactic reconstruction", in: E. C. Traugott–R. La Brum–S. Shepherd (eds.), *Papers from the 4th International Conference on Historical Linguistics* (Amsterdam: Benjamins), 87–96.
Munro, Pamela
1984    "Auxiliaries and auxiliarization in Western Muskogean", in: Jacek
        Fisiak (ed.), *Historical syntax* (Berlin: Mouton), 333–362.
Muysken, Pieter
1977    *Syntactic developments in the verb phrase of Ecuadorian Quechua,*
        (Studies in Generative Grammar 2) (Dordrecht: Foris).
Norman, William–Lyle Campbell
1978    "Toward a Proto-Mayan syntax: A comparative perspective on grammar", in: Nora England (ed.), *Papers in Mayan linguistics* (Columbia,
        Missouri: Department of Anthropology, U. of Missouri), 136–156.
Sapir, Edward
1913, 1914  "Southern Paiute and Nahuatl, a study in Uto-Aztekan, 1–2",
        *Journal de la Sociètè des Américanistes de Paris* 10: 379–425, 11:
        443–488.
1925    "The Hokan affinity of Subtiaba of Nicaragua", *American Anthropologist* 27: 402–435.
1931    "The concept of phonetic law as tested in primitive languages by
        Leonard Bloomfield", in: Stuart A. Rice (ed.), *Methods in social
        science,* (Chicago), 297–306.
Seler, Eduard
1887    *Das Konjugationssystem der Maya-Sprachen* (Berlin: Unger).
Shipley, William F.
1980    "Penutian among the ruins: A personal assessment", *Berkeley Linguistics Society* 6: 437–441.
Slotkin, J. S. (ed.)
1965    *Readings in early anthropology* (Viking Fund Publications in Anthropology 40) (New York: Wenner-Gren).
Stoll, Otto
1884    *Zur Ethnographie der Republik Guatemala* (Zürich: Orell Füssli).

1885            "Supplementary remarks on a grammar of the Cakchiquel language
               of Guatemala", *Proceedings of the American Philosophical Society*
               22: 255–268.
Teeter, Karl
1964            "Algonquian languages and genetic relationship", *Proceedings of the
               9th International Congress of Linguists* (The Hague: Mouton), 1026–
               1033.
Voegelin, Carl F.
1942            "Sapir: Insight and rigor", *American Anthropologist* 44: 322–324.
1965            "Classification of American Indian languages", *Anthropological Lin-
               guistics* 7.7: 121–150.
Weir, E. M. Helen
1986            "Footprints of yesterday's syntax: Diachronic developments of cer-
               tain verb prefixes in an OSV language (Nadëb)", *Lingua* 68: 291–
               316.

# The role of typology in American Indian historical linguistics[1]

*Marianne Mithun*

Linguistic reconstruction in North America has generally followed the same lines of development as reconstruction in other parts of the world. Work has normally proceeded from the establishment of regular sound correspondences among closely related languages, to the investigation of those among more distantly related groups. Once phonological correspondences have been understood, grammatical systems have been compared. Steady progress has been made in the grouping, subgrouping, and reconstruction of most of these languages, and most of the over fifty language families established by the end of the nineteenth century are still recognized today.

Throughout this period, however, scholars engaged in traditional comparative work have been struck by pervasive structural resemblances among many of these languages. Early in the nineteenth century, Peter Stephen Duponceau, secretary to the American Philosophical Society, commented on the grammatical resemblances among the lexically diverse North American languages he had examined. In his essay *Mémoire sur le système grammatical des langues de quelques nations indiennes de l'Amérique du nord*, he noted their polysynthetic nature, the high numbers of morphemes contained in single words.

> Le caractère général des langues américaines consiste en ce qu'elles réunissent un grand nombre d'idées sous la forme d'un seul mot; c'est ce qui leur a fait donner par les philologues américains le nom de langues *polysynthétiques*. Ce nom leur convient à toutes (au moins à celles que nous connaissons), depuis le Groenland jusqu'au Chili, sans qu'il nous ait été possible d'y découvrir une seule exception, de sorte que nous nous croyons en droit de présumer qu'il n'en existe point. (Duponceau 1831: 89)

The pervasiveness of polysynthesis in America was the source of much discussion throughout the nineteenth century and into the twentieth. Some of the philologists engaged in establishing relationships on the basis of demonstrable sound correspondences began to wonder whether such structural unity might be indicative of deeper genetic ties. It was proposed on several occasions that all American languages "descended from a single parent language, for, whatever their differences of material, there is a single type or plan upon which their forms are developed and their constructions made" (Whitney 1867: 348). (A history of nineteenth-century views on the relative value of lexical and grammatical correspondences in genetic classification can be found in Haas 1969.)

Daniel Brinton, a contemporary of Powell, further described the characteristics of polysynthetic languages as follows:

> The psychic identity of the Americans is well illustrated in their languages. There are indeed indefinite discrepancies in their lexicography and in their surface morphology; but in their logical substructure, in what Wilhelm von Humboldt called the "inner form", they are strikingly alike. The points in which this is especially apparent are in the *development of pronominal forms,* in the abundance of generic particles, in the overweening *preference for concepts of action (verbs), rather than concepts of existence (nouns),* and in the consequent subordination of the latter to the former in the proposition. This last mentioned trait is the source of that characteristic called *incorporation* ... I have yet to find one of which we possess ample means of analysis, in which it does not appear in one or another of its forms, thus revealing the same linguistic impulse. (Brinton 1891, cited in Haas 1969)

Considerations of structural similarity were first applied formally to the classification of North American languages by Edward Sapir in 1929. Although he was both an experienced field worker and a rigorous historical linguist, Sapir felt that due to the limited documentation of many North American languages, as well as the tremendous time depths separating them, the traditional comparative method could be of little use in establishing deeper ties. On the basis of purely structural characteristics, he proposed an overarching scheme that conflated the fifty-some families into six superstocks: Eskimo-Aleut, Algonkin-Wakashan, Nadene, Penutian, Hokan-Siouan, and Aztec-Tanoan. He did specify that the results were meant to be only suggestive:

> It is impossible to say at present what is the irreducible number of linguistic stocks that should be recognized for America north of Mexico, as scientific comparative work on these difficult languages is still in its infancy. (Sapir 1929)

Some of Sapir's new combinations have since been confirmed by further documentation of the languages and comparative work. Others remain hypotheses, due to the great time depths involved, sufficient to obscure almost all cognates, and the antiquity of language contact, particularly in such areas as the Northwest and California. In some cases, resemblances across superstock boundaries now appear as strong as those within them. Yet Sapir himself was sufficiently careful in specifying the degree of confidence he was willing to accord his various proposals that this work has proven useful in pointing the way to areas inviting special investigation.

Nevertheless, the reliability of structural resemblances as indicators of deeper genetic relationship has not yet been clearly established. Among the grammatical features most often cited as typical of North American languages are the following:

 i) polysynthesis
 ii) pronominal affixes
 iii) incorporation
 iv) the preference for concepts of action (verbs) rather than concepts of existence (nouns) and the consequent subordination of the latter to the former in the proposition.

# 1. Polysynthesis

The morphological elaboration exhibited by many North American Indian languages is familiar to most of those who have been exposed to them. Words like those below are not at all uncommon in North America. In fact, they can be found in languages in each of Sapir's superstocks. (Hyphens indicate morpheme boundaries; periods within interlinear translations do not: the English gloss 'think.that' in the first example thus corresponds to a single Greenlandic morpheme.)

(1)        Greenlandic Eskimo (Eskimo-Aleut) (Fortescue 1984: 315):
           *an-niru-lir-sin-niqar-sinnaa-suri-nngik-kaluar-pakka*
           be.big-more-begin-cause-PASSIVE-can-think.that-not-
               but-1.SG/3.PL.INDICATIVE
           'I don't think that they can be made any bigger, but ...'

(2)        Ojibway (Algonkin-Wakashan) (Richard Rhodes, personal communication):
           *daa-gii-biid-wewe-ganzhy-e-bah-d-oo-w-ag*
           MODAL-PAST-coming-making.repeated.noise-hoof-
               VERBALIZER-cause.to.run-INANIMATE-LOCA-
               TIVE-3-PL
           'they should have come running up making the sound of hoofbeats'

(3)        Chipewyan (Nadene) (Li 1946: 419):
           *bɛ-γá-yɛ́-n-i-ł-tĩ*
           3.OBJ-to-3.OBJ-MOMENTANEOUS-1.SUB-
               CLASSIFIER-handle.a.living.being
           'I have given her to him'

(4)        Takelma (Penutian) (Sapir 1922: 65):
           *gwãn-ha-yaxa-t.'ülü^ulg-á^εn*
           road-in-continuously-follow-1.AORIST
           'I keep following the trail'

(5)        Cayuga (Hokan-Siouan) (Reginald Henry, personal communication):
           *h-ẽ-yõk-w-ak-ya?t-anú-hst-õhõ:-k*
           TRANSLOCATIVE-FUT-1.PAT-PL-
               SEMI.REFLEXIVE-body-cool-CAUS-
               STATIVE-CONT
           'we will be cooling off there'

(6)　　　　Cora (Aztec-Tanoan) (Casad 1984: 214):
*nʸe-tʸíʔi-n-kɨye-tʸ-e*
I-DISTRIBUTIVE-REFLEXIVE-stick-make-
　APPLICATIVE
'I am making my wooden sword'

Yet polysynthesis is far from universal in North America. While there are no extreme isolating languages comparable to those found in Asia, there are numerous languages roughly equivalent in synthesis to many Indo-European languages. Note the low number of morphemes per word in (7), for example, the beginning of a tale from a California language.

(7)　　　　Wikchamni Yokuts (Gamble 1978: 132):
*hiya·m̓u　xo·-ʔoxʔoš*
long.ago　live-DUR.AORIST
'Long ago, when the world was made,

*ʔaŋaʔš-aña　　　　huhtʰutu　xi*
packbasket-ATTRIB　owl　　　this
there lived an owl

*ʔo·ma　p̓aʔañ　tíʔĩs-n-aš*
when　world　make-MEDIOPASS-DUR.AORIST
'with a burden basket on its back.

*ʔama　ʔan　ʔaŋaš　　meṭʰ.*
and　her　packbasket　big
Her basket was big.'

Furthermore, polysynthesis is not restricted to North America. Long words can be found in many areas of the world. Note the morphological structure of the verbs below from Africa, Australia, Siberia, South America, and Austronesia.

(8)　　　　Turkana (Nilo-Saharan, Nigeria) (Dimmendaal 1983: 462):
*pɛ-ɲ-ɛ-ɪt-a-kɪn-i-à-tà*
TOPICALIZED.NEGATION-not-3-plant-EP-
　DATIVE-ASPECT-VERB-PLURAL
'they are not planting'

(9)        Tiwi (Australia) (Osborne 1974: 47):
           *ji-məni-ŋilimpaŋ-alipi-aŋkina*
           he-me-sleeping-meat-steal
           'he stole my meat while I was asleep'

(10)       Kamchadal (Chukotko-Kamchatkan, Siberia) (Bogoras
           1922: 833):
           *tı-maiñı-ḷauˊtı-pıˊkt-ik-ın*
           I-much-head-suffer-I-ASPECT
           'I have a bad headache'

(11)       Nomatsiguenga Campa (Arawakan, Peru) (Wise 1986:
           624):
           *na-kant-a-kag-ant-a-bi-t-ak-a-ri*
           1-tell-EP-COMITATIVE-INSTRUMENTAL-
               EP-FRUSTRATIVE-EP-PERFECT-NONFUT-
               REFLEXIVE-3.M
           'I explained it to him, but'

(12)       Selayarese (Austronesian, Indonesia) (Hasan Basri, per-
           sonal communication):
           *la-mu-paka-ta-s-suŋké-aŋ-i*
           FUTURE-2.-SG.ERGATIVE-CAUSATIVE-
               BENEFACTIVE-PATIENT-INTRANSITIVE-open-
               BENEFACTIVE-3.ABSOLUTIVE
           'you (familiar) will open it for him/her/them'

The polysynthesis found in North America is neither universal nor
unique.

There is good evidence that the degree of synthesis characteristic
of a language can change radically over a very short period of
reconstructible time. Selayarese, the Austronesian language cited in
(12) above, is polysynthetic, but few Austronesianists would reconstruct a polysynthetic parent language. Many Austronesian languages are still relatively analytic, and in the more synthetic languages, the recent origins of affixes are often transparent. Those
languages with more complex morphologies often do not show
parallel morphological structures, suggesting that their affixes are
the result of independent developments.

Compare the Selayarese sentence below to a similar expression
in Yapese, another Austronesian language, spoken in Micronesia.
The Yapese version requires several separate words:

(13)    Selayarese (Austronesian, Indonesia) (Hasan Basri, personal communication):
*la-ku-pa-ɲ-jamá-ʔaŋ-ko*
FUTURE-1.SG.ERGATIVE-BENEFACTIVE-
   INTRANSITIVE-work-BENEFACTIVE-
   2.SG.ABSOLUTIVE
'I will work for you.'

(14)    Yapese (Austronesian, Micronesia) (Jensen 1977: 277):
*raa  gu  marweel  ni  faan      ngoom*
will  I   work      for  purpose  to-you
'I will work for you.'

The two languages exhibit quite different grammatical structures, but the tense, case, and pronominal morphemes are transparently cognate. Further examination of other grammatical markers reveals more cognates, although many are no longer precisely equivalent in function in the two languages.

Similar examples of the recent development of polysynthesis can be found all over the world. In many of the cases, as in Selayarese and Yapese, grammatical structures in related languages differ radically, while phonological correspondences are so transparent that cognates are often easy to spot by naive inspection. Since polysynthesis is neither universal nor unique in North America, and since it can develop in such a short period of time, it cannot be considered a reliable indicator of deep genetic relationship.

## 2. Pronominal affixes

Many polysynthetic languages, like most of those cited above, contain bound pronominal affixes within verbs. The affixes refer to primary arguments of the verb.

1)    Greenlandic
*annirulirsinniqarsinnaasurinngikkaluarpakka*
'*I* don't think that they can be made any bigger, but'

2)    Ojibway
*daagiibiidweweganzhiiptoowag*
'they should have come running ...'

3)      Chipewyan
        *bɛγáyénił̃tĩ*
        '*I* have given <u>her</u> to <u>him</u>'

4)      Takelma
        *gwãnhayaxat:ülü<sup>u</sup>lgá<sup>ɛ</sup>n*
        'I keep following the trail'

5)      Cayuga
        *hẽy̆õkwakya<sup>ʔ</sup>tanúhstõhõ:k*
        '<u>we</u> will be cooling off there'

6)      Cora
        *n<sup>y</sup>et<sup>y</sup>í<sup>ʔ</sup>inkiye-t<sup>y</sup>e*
        '<u>I</u> am making my wooden sword'

The pronominal affixes are obligatory in most languages, whether or not additional nominal phrases are present. The Cayuga verb in (15), for example, still contains the pronominal prefix *kon-* 'they' even though a separate nominal 'someone' appears in the same clause.

(15)    Cayuga (Reginald Henry, personal communication):
        *A:yẽ<sup>ʔ</sup>   <u>sõkwan<sup>ʔ</sup>áht</u>*
        seems   <u>someone</u>
        'It looks like some

        <u>kon</u>-ẽ-nat-íny<sup>ʔ</sup>õ-t-õh.
        <u>3.PL.PAT</u>-S.RFL-site-enter-CAUS-STAT
        people have moved in'

The pronominal affixes are more than simple agreement markers: they are the actual arguments of their verbs. Verbs containing such affixes constitute complete clauses in themselves. Associated nominals, like the word for 'someone' in (15), are appositives to the affixes, further identifying them, but they are not necessary for grammaticality.

Pronominal affixes appear in languages throughout North America, but they are by no means universal. Many languages have only first and second person pronominal affixes. Many others have no pronominal affixes at all. All pronouns in Central Pomo, for example, are free.

(16)       Central Pomo (Pomoan, California) (Eileen Oropeza,
           personal communication):
           *ʔaa  múuṭu  pʰdéenʔkʰe  ʔe  béeṭ'.*
           *I   her   care.for-will  it.is  today*
           'I am going to take care of her today.'

Pronominal affixes are also not limited to North America. Note
the pronominal prefixes in the Turkana, Tiwi, Kamchadal, Campa,
and Selayarese examples cited earlier.

8)         Turkana
           *peɲɛɪtakɪnɪàtà*
           'they are not planting'

9)         Tiwi
           *jiməniɲilimpaŋalipiaŋkina*
           'he stole my meat while I was asleep'

10)        Kamchadal
           *tɪmaiñɪḷau'tɪpɪ'tikin*
           'I have a bad headache'

11)        Nomatsiguenga Campa
           *nakantakagantabitakari*
           'I explained it to him, but'

12)        Selayarese
           *lamupakatassuŋkéaɲi*
           'you will open it for him'

There is ample evidence that pronominal affixes can develop in
a language that previously had none. Selayarese, cited above, now
has a full set of ergative prefixes and absolutive enclitics. Yapese
has developed object affixes, but no subject affixes.

The rapidity with which pronominal affixes can develop is illustrated by a number of Pama-Nyungan languages of Australia.
Among even closely related languages, some have only free pronouns, while others have full sets of transitive and intransitive
pronominal clitics or affixes. The free form sources of the modern
bound forms are still transparent in most cases. Dixon (1980: 246)
notes that the development of bound pronouns is concentrated in
specific areas of Australia, and "this isogloss often does not coincide

with strong genetic boundaries". He provides numerous examples like that below.

> Most of the languages in the Yolŋu subgroup, from north-east Arnhem Land, lack bound pronominals; but these are found in two languages on the edges of the Yolŋu area. Ritharŋu, the southernmost Yolŋu language, has developed pronominal ENclitics under areal pressure from its southerly neighbours Nunggubuyu and Ngandi (which have pronominal PREfixes); these are transparently reduced forms of the Yolŋu independent pronouns. Djinaŋ, in the northwesterly corner of the Yolŋu region, has moved in a different direction, and developed a system of pronominal PROclitics, that can be shown to be historically related — at slightly further remove than the Ritharŋu forms — from free-form pronouns in other Yolŋu languages; this was again due to areal pressure, from the prefixing languages to the west.

In some cases, the process of fusion can be seen in the earliest stages of its development. Yallop (1977: 46) notes that "the personal pronouns of Alyawarra are independent words", but "certain sequences of words may, through vowel elision and loss of primary stress, become phonetically indistinguishable from a single word". The pronouns may still appear in any order, either proclitic or enclitic to verbs.

(17)    Alyawarra (Pama-Nyungan, Australia) (Yallop 1977: 46):
Pronoun — Verb
*athá aríka* or *athárika*
'I saw'

Verb — Pronoun
*aríka athá* or *aríkatha*
'I saw'

Pronoun — Pronoun — Verb
*athá ngínha aráyntiya* or *athánginharāyntiya*
'I'll be seeing you'

Verb — Pronoun — Pronoun
*inpíka athá rínha* or *inpíkathirĭnha*
'I got it'

Breen (1981) reports on a particularly interesting phenomenon. Margany and Gunya are closely related dialects of a (Pama-Nyungan) Mari language, spoken in Queensland, Australia. They are essentially equivalent structurally, except for one feature: "Gunya has a transparent and obviously recent system of pronominal suffixes to the verb, which Margany lacks" (Breen 1981: 275). (Note the pronominal suffixes in the Gunya verb in 18.)

(18)      Gunya (Mari, Pama-Nyungan, Australia) (Breen 1981: 331):
          *yulbiyiŋgiyaṇḍaṇa*
          chase-CONT-FUT-1.SG-3.PL-ACC
          'I'll hunt them away'

Breen points out that the bound forms are highly transparent in origin and variable in use. The singular suffixes are identical to their free counterparts minus the initial syllable (sometimes with vocalic increment).

(19)                                    Free        Bound
          1 Nominative Singular        *ŋaya*       *-ya*
          2 Nominative Singular        *inda*       *-nda*
          2 Accusative Singular        *inaṇa*      *-naṇa*
          3 Nominative Singular        *ṇula*       *-la*
          3 Accusative Singular        *ṇuṇuṇa*     *-ṇa*

Most non-singular free and bound forms are identical.

The pronouns have not fused at all in Margany. Compare the sentences from Gunya and Margany in (20) and (21).

(20)      Gunya (Mari, Pama-Nyungan, Australia) (Breen 1981: 331):
          *wadʸayiṇiya*            *unayiŋgiya*
          go-CONT-PRES-1.SG   lie-CONT-FUT-1.SG
          'I'm going to have a sleep'

(21)      Margany (Mari, Pama-Nyungan, Australia) (Breen 1981: 319):
          *ṇula   wabataŋga   ŋaya   unangu*
          3.SG   go-CJ-LOC   1.SG   lie-PURP
          'As soon as he goes I'm going to have a sleep'

Pronominal affixes are pervasive in North America, but they are neither universal nor unique. Furthermore, they can develop relatively rapidly. The presence of pronominal affixes cannot be considered a reliable indicator of deeper genetic relationship either.

## 3. Incorporation

A number of languages throughout North America exhibit noun incorporation, whereby a noun stem, usually referring to a patient but sometimes to an instrument or location, is compounded with a verb stem to form a derived verb stem. Examples of incorporation can be seen in the Ojibway, Takelma, Cayuga, and Cora examples cited earlier.

2)      Ojibway
        *daagiibiidweweganziiptoowag*
        'they should have come running making the sound of
        hooves'

4)      Takelma
        *gwãnhayaxat.'ülü$^u$lgá$^e$n*
        'I keep following the trail'

5)      Cayuga
        *hẽyõkwakya$^?$tanúhstõhõ:k*
        'we will be cooling off (our bodies) there'

6)      Cora
        *n$^y$et$^y$í$^?$inkiyet$^y$e*
        'I'm making my wooden sword'

Incorporation is by no means universal throughout North America, however. Numerous languages show no incorporation at all.

   Noun incorporation is also not confined to North America. Note the examples cited earlier from Tiwi and Kamchadal.

9)      Tiwi (Australia)
        *jimaniŋilimpaŋalipiaŋkina*
        'he stole my meat while I was asleep'

10)      Kamchadal (Siberia)
         *tımaiñılau'tıpıktikin*
         'I have a bad <u>headache</u>'

There is considerable evidence that noun incorporation can develop relatively quickly. The presence of incorporation is often not consistent within language families. Within the Mayan family, for example, certain languages have no incorporation at all, such as Ixil and Aguacatec. Some others, such as Kanjobal, Mam, and Chuj, have the beginnings of incorporation. A transitive verb and unmodified noun may be juxtaposed to indicate a conceptually unitary activity. Although they remain separate words, the verb and noun form a syntactic unit equivalent to an intransitive verb. The noun, no longer a syntactic argument of the clause, does not refer to a specific, countable entity; it simply narrows the scope of the verb semantically to an activity directed at a certain type of patient. The Kanjobal verb in (22) is grammatically intransitive, as shown by the use of an absolutive case pronoun for 'you'.

(22)     Kanjobal (Mayan) (Robertson 1980):
         *š-<u>at</u>-lo-w-i*                    *<u>pan</u>*
         PAST-<u>2.ABS</u>-eat-AF-AF   <u>bread</u>
         'you bread-ate'

Compare: *š-∅-<u>a</u>-lo-t-oq*                  *in-pan*
         past-3.ABS-<u>2.ERG</u>-eat-go-OPT   1.ERG-bread
         'you ate my <u>bread</u>'

In Yucatec, incorporation can function in a similar way, but the incorporated noun is further integrated into the host verb, usually appearing before several suffixes.

(23)     Yucatec Mayan (Bricker 1978):
         *č'ak-<u>čeʔ</u>-n-ah-en*
         chop-<u>tree</u>-ANTIPASS-PRF-1.ABS
         'I wood-chopped'

Compare: *t-in-č'ak-ah*                      *čeʔ*
         COMP-1.ERG-chop-PRF          tree
         'I chopped a tree'

The absence of incorporation in many Mayan languages, the transparency of the incorporated structures in the others, and the lack of relic forms, indicate that incorporation is a new development within this family, rather than an earlier trait that is decaying. (For more on the nature, development, and distribution of noun incorporation see Mithun 1984.)

Since noun incorporation is neither universal nor unique to North America, and since it can develop relatively rapidly, it cannot be considered a reliable indicator of deep genetic relationship either.

## 4. The predominance of verbs over nouns

The predominance of verbs in natural discourse is a striking feature of many North American languages. A typical example of this can be seen in (24), a passage from a Tuscarora legend. We are told that long ago the Indians were bothered by a flying head that used to kill people and take children away. (All morphological verbs are underlined.)

(24)    Tuscarora (Iroquoian, New York State) (Elton Green, personal communication):

U:nə̃ hésnə̃: kyení:kə̃: ə́:tsi tyahwáhe:t kyení:kə̃:
now  then  this  one  so it carries  this
'Now then, one time,

kahstra?níhrə̃ ə́:tsi
she sits  one
a woman was sitting

yə̃tsù:ri unə́he kanə̃hakə̃rí?nahw,
she eats  corn  it corn-roasted is
eating roasted corn.

Yú:?neks uhə̃?nə? tisnə̃?
it burns  ahead  and
A fire was burning before her, and

neyu?nə̃tá:kə̃ ha? kə̃? yé?rə̃?,
it open is  the  there she dwells
the door to her log cabin

_nekarɔ̃ʔnuʔnáhrhɔ̃h._
it log layered is
was open.

_Twɔ̃ʔnyerɔ́:tsih,   héʔthuh   thruʔnaʔníhrɔ̃h,_
she astonished is there        there he stood
All of a sudden she was surprised by a flying

_kunɔ̃hrayɔ́hnɔ̃h.   WaʔakɔhréːΘrɔ̃ʔ._
it head flies       she afraid became
head standing there. She became afraid.

_Waíhrɔ̃:ʔ   "U:nɔ̃   héh   nɔ̃kwhe_
she said    now      Q     also
She said, "Now will he

_héʔiʔ   ɔ̃hrakhɔ́:reːt?"          Yɔ̃tsùːrih_
me      will he me carry off    she eats
carry me off too?" As she ate,

_heníːkɔ̃:   tsyakyehyáhraʔ_
that        she remembered
she remembered that

_kayɔ̃ʔnaʔnatkahríʔΘeh    haʔ   katéhraʔΘ_
they her storytold have   the   it fears
she had been told that it was afraid

_haʔ   utsɔ́heh._
the   fire
of fire.

_U:nɔ̃   hésnɔ̃:   waʔéːkɔ̃ʔ   nahràːyɔ̃ʔ._
now    then      she saw     it came in
And then she saw it come in.'

This passage contains twenty morphological verbs but only two nouns. All other words are particles.

The predominance of verbs is of course not unrelated to the three other features mentioned earlier. As in other polysynthetic languages, the productive morphological complexity in Tuscarora is centered within its verbs. Much of the information conveyed by other words in less synthetic languages is conveyed in Tuscarora by verbs. The pronominal prefixes obviate the need for separate noun phrases iden-

tifying the arguments of each clause. Noun incorporation also elim-
inates the need for many free noun phrases. The above passage contains incorporated nouns for 'corn', 'log', and 'head'. Finally, morphological verbs in this language can function syntactically not only
as predicates and clauses, but also as nominals, with no additional
marking. The fire, the log cabin, and the flying head, are identified
by morphological verbs in the passage above.

Although many North American languages do show a prepon-
derance of verbs, many others do not. The text in (25) comes from
a Central Pomo legend. (Tuscarora and Central Pomo were classified together by Sapir in the Hokan-Siouan superstock.) Again,
verbs are underlined.

(25)     Central Pomo (Pomoan, California) (Frances Jack, per-
         sonal communication):
         *Bel mačí ʔdóma, ʔúdaaw.. čʰé  múl.*
         this day   QUOT lots       rain fall
         'On this day, it was told, it was raining a lot.'

         *Muul ʔdóma bal.. šaqóot' máaṭa, ʔélya,*
         that   QUOT this   mouse   woman  the-TOPIC
         At that time, it seems, the mouse lady

         *dálqʰač' pʰwíw, ṭíikʰe čá     ʔmii  hṭow.*
         outward look    her   house there from
         was looking out from her house.

         *ʔúdaaw qʰač' daaw    maa     tʰabám.*
         really   wet   outside ground laying
         The ground was very wet outside.

         *Méen ʔíba ʔdóma, ṭíikʰeṭ' qanémač',*
         so    and  QUOT her       relative
         And so she had a relative,

         *qʰálʔts'a ʔmúuṭu,*
         weasel    him
         a weasel,

         *muul mída qóyow, múuṭu ṭéṭeenʔkʰe,*
         that   there here.go her    tell to
         who came by to tell her,

"*Bal qʰá ʔel ʔdoo ʔúdaaw ʔúyuu néyqʼkʰe.*"
this water the QUOT really high rise will
"This water is going to rise up high." '

The proportion of verbs in Central Pomo differs consistently from that in Tuscarora. The above passage contains only six verbs but nine nouns. It also expresses several things in separate words that would be expressed by verbal morphology in Tuscarora, such as the pronouns, possessives, directional adverbs, and the adjective 'wet'.

A predominance of verbs is pervasive in North America, but it is neither universal nor unique. In itself, it cannot be considered a reliable indicator of deep genetic relationship.

## 5. The value of typology in historical linguistics

None of the major typological features most commonly associated with North American languages, polysynthesis, bound pronouns, incorporation, nor a predominance of verbs over nouns, provides a reliable indicator of deep genetic relationship. Nevertheless, typology has much to contribute to accurate reconstruction and to an understanding of language change.

The primary goal of typology is the identification of clusters of structural features that cooccur in languages. The more we know about language typology, the better equipped we are to reconstruct typologically coherent proto-languages. At this point, for example, few linguists would happily reconstruct a proto vowel system consisting solely of two front rounded vowels and four back vowels. Such repertoires of front and back vowels are not known to cooccur. Similarly, few would propose a system of bound pronouns containing only first and third person forms, although most would confidently reconstruct a system containing first and second person forms with no third.

The more we learn about clusters of features in different areas of language structure, the more effective we can be in uncovering comparable material. The discovery of one feature shared by related languages can stimulate the pursuit of others that are usually associated with it. A basic understanding of phonological systems should immediately prompt the search for evidence of front unrounded vowels in the case above. The discovery of a reconstructible dual number suffix should stimulate the quest for a reconstructible plural suffix. The reconstruction of ergative case marking might encourage a search for traces of antipassive constructions. At the same time, when systems of interacting features are well understood and familiar, we can discern their patterns from less evidence than if each piece is unexpected.

Typological sophistication can also permit finer evaluation of the evidence for particular genetic relationships. If four structural features are generally known to cooccur in languages, for example, the fact that they are shared by particular languages may constitute a single piece of evidence in support of their relationship, rather than four.

Typology can, furthermore, serve as a preliminary step toward a richer understanding of language change. Once clusters of cooccurring features are identified, the functional interrelationships responsible for their cooccurrence can be investigated. Often one trait creates a predisposition for the development of others. The discovery of this effect can be important in reconstructing the sequence of events involved in the evolution of language families. If several languages share a set of structural features, they may have inherited all of these from a common ancestor, or they may have inherited only one, which subsequently motivated the development of the others individually in the various daughter languages.

If the motivating trait is borrowable, languages sharing the resulting complex of features may not even be genetically related at all. As discussed earlier, areal studies in Australia indicate that the development of bound pronouns can be stimulated by contact. Bound pronouns tend to cooccur with a number of other structural characteristics in languages. If bound pronouns can arise from contact alone, and if their presence does in fact motivate the subsequent development of the other characteristics, then languages might share a major complex of features for geographical rather than genetic reasons.

Finally, typological investigation is crucial to diachronic linguistics in another way. Much of the traditional comparative work on Indo-European has, appropriately, been based on an understanding of Indo-European systems of grammar. Certain categories are traditionally isolated and compared, and developmental interrelationships are expected among particular parts of grammars. As has been shown, many North American languages differ typologically from Indo-European languages in important ways. In many cases, the grammatical categories to be investigated differ subtly from those in Indo-European languages, and various areas of grammatical structure function and interact differently.

In fact, the typological features discussed earlier have major effects on the nature of many of the categories that are grammaticized in North American languages and on the general kinds of grammatical systems that result. Perhaps the most salient characteristic is their elaborate verb morphology, often combined with relatively limited noun morphology. Many distinctions expressed in European languages by nominal morphology or by separate words appear to be conveyed in North America by verbal morphology. Most European languages contain obligatory number inflection on nouns, for example. By contrast, many North American languages exhibit no number marking on nouns, or very limited marking, but extensive number marking on verbs. Compare the commands in (26) from Central Pomo. (Number markers are underlined.)

(26)     Central Pomo (Frances Jack, personal communication):
qʰabé ʔnée-la-m
rock   throw.one-down-*SG.IMPV*
'Throw a rock down!'

qʰabé mča-la-ṭa-m-meʔ
rock   throw.sev-down-*MULT.EVENT-COLL.AGENCY-PL.IMPV*
'Throw some rocks down, everybody!'

Such verbal affixes have often been interpreted as agreement markers, copies of nominal number markers. A closer examination of their use, however, indicates that they are not precisely equivalent to the inflectional number suffixes of European languages. Their primary function is not to quantify persons and objects, but rather to describe aspects of events and states. In Central Pomo, throwing several objects is categorized as a different kind of action from throwing a single object, so a different verb root is used. Multiple eventhood, such as several different throws, are specified by a verbal suffix. If several participants act jointly, this cooperation is signaled by another verbal suffix. If a command is directed at several people, a special imperative suffix is used. Each of these markers describes the action, although the participation of multiple people and the involvement of multiple rocks may be inferred.

In many European languages, all nouns are obligatorily inflected for case. In most (not all) North American languages, nouns are not inflected for primary case, but verbal morphology can convey similar information.

(27)      Takelma (Sapir 1922: 68):
          *lōbō´xade*[ε]
          pound-I
          'I pound'

          *noxwa` yana-wa-lobobi*[ᵚ]*n*
          pestle   acorn-with.it-pound-I
          'I pound acorns with a pestle.'

Morphemes like the Takelma instrumental prefix have sometimes been interpreted as misplaced case markers. In fact, their primary function is not to modify the associated noun ('pestle') but rather to characterize the action, pounding with an instrument. Of course the role of an accompanying noun may be inferred. An accompanying noun is not necessary for grammaticality, however.

Both of these examples illustrate a general characteristic of the verbal morphology of many North American languages. Just as the affixes on nouns in European languages tend to modify persons and objects, indicating such things as their number, their role in events (case), and their gender, the affixes on verbs in North American languages tend to characterize events and states. The results are sometimes similar, like the effects of number and case morphemes described in (26) and (27), but they are not equivalent. What one asserts the other only implies.

The distinction is subtle but it can have an important effect on the development of morphological systems. Inflectional affixes like the number and case affixes of European languages are normally specified obligatorily on all nouns. All nouns can thus be expected to have singular and plural forms. They can be expected to have forms in all cases. Inflectional categories must accordingly be sufficiently general in meaning to be applicable to all entities. Since objects referred to by count nouns can usually be enumerated, and participants usually serve an identifiable role in clauses, this is feasible. The same is not necessarily true of verbal number and case markers in North American languages. Such distinctions as joint agency may be highly pertinent to some events (carrying), but inapplicable to others (being sick). Some actions can be done with instruments, but many cannot. For this reason, verbal affixes of these kinds rarely become inflectional. Instead, they remain derivational and are used to create new lexical items only when needed. An understanding of such differences is certainly pertinent to a reconstruction of the history of these languages.

Similar typological differences can be found in syntax. As noted earlier, many North American languages contain obligatory bound pronouns in verbs referring to core aguments. Associated noun phrases or complements in many of these languages function more as appositives to the pronominal arguments than as arguments themselves. The syntactic bonds between such constituents are accordingly subtly different from those in Indo-European languages. Often in these languages, syntactic relations such as complementation or relativization are not as tightly grammaticized as in Indo-European languages. A sensitivity to possible differences in degrees of grammaticization is crucial to an understanding of language change.

# 6. Conclusion

Typological resemblances alone are not reliable indicators of deep genetic relationship. Typological investigations can be crucial to the comparativist, however, as a guide not only to the reconstruction of typologically coherent proto-languages, but also to a sound understanding of the interrelationships among structural factors in languages, and the motivations and sequences of change involving them. The pressing need in diachronic work with non-Indo-European languages is not a new set of comparative techniques, but rather richer models of language structures.

*Notes*

1. An earlier version of some of these ideas was presented at the IREX Conference on Comparative Linguistics, held at the University of Texas at Austin, in November of 1986.

2. I am grateful to the following speakers who have graciously shared their expertise on their native languages: Hasan Basri, of Palu, Indonesia, on Selayarese; the late Elton Green, of Lewiston, New York, on Tuscarora; Reginald Henry, of Six Nations, Ontario, on Cayuga; Eileen Oropeza, of Point Arena, California, on Central Pomo; and Frances Jack, of Hopland, California, on Central Pomo. I also appreciate material on Ojibway contributed by Richard Rhodes.

## References

Bogoras, Waldemar
    1922     "Chukchee", in: Franz Boas (ed.), *Handbook of American Indian languages* (Bureau of American Ethnology Bulletin 40.1) (Washington: Government Printing Office), 631 – 903.
Breen, J. G.
    1981     "Margany and Gunya", in: R. M. W. Dixon – Barry J. Blake (eds.), *Handbook of Australian languages* 2 (Canberra: The Australian National University Press), 275 – 394.
Bricker, Victoria
    1978     "Antipassive constructions in Yucatec Maya", in: Nora C. England (ed.), *Papers in Maya linguistics* (Columbia: University of Missouri), 3 – 24.
Brinton, Daniel G.
    1891     *The American race* (Philadelphia: David McKay).
Casad, Eugene
    1984     "Cora", in: Ronald Langacker (ed.), *Studies in Southern Uto-Aztecan grammar* (Arlington: Summer Institute of Linguistics), 151 – 459.
Dimmendaal, Gerrit Jan
    1983     *The Turkana language* (Dordrecht: Foris).
Dixon, R. M. W.
    1980     *The languages of Australia* (Cambridge: Cambridge University Press).
Duponceau, Peter Stephen
    1838     *Mémoire sur le système grammatical des langues de quelques nations indiennes de l'Amérique du nord* (Paris).
Fortescue, Michael
    1984     *West Greenlandic* (London: Croom Helm).
Gamble, Geoffrey
    1978     *Wikchamni grammar* (University of California Publications in Linguistics 89) (Berkeley: University of California Press).
Haas, Mary R.
    1969     "Grammar or lexicon? The American Indian side of the question from Duponceau to Powell", *International Journal of American Linguistics*, IJAL-NATS 35: 239 – 255.
Jensen, John Thayer
    1977     *Yapese reference grammar* (Honolulu: University Press of Hawaii).
Li, Fang-Kuei
    1946     "Chipewyan", in: Harry Hoijer (ed.), *Linguistic structures of native America* (Viking Fund Publications in Anthropology 6) (New York: Wenner-Gren), 398 – 423.

Mithun, Marianne
1984        "The evolution of noun incorporation", *Language* 60: 847—894.
Osborne, C. R.
1974        *The Tiwi language* (Australian Aboriginal Studies No. 55) (Canberra: Australian Institute of Aboriginal Studies).
Robertson, John S.
1980        *The structure of pronoun incorporation in the Mayan verbal complex* (New York: Garland Press).
Sapir, Edward
1922        "The Takelma language of southwestern Oregon", in: Franz Boas (ed.), *Handbook of American Indian languages* (Bureau of American Ethnology Bulletin 40.1) (Washington: Government Printing Office), 1—296.
1929        "Central and North American languages", *Encyclopaedia Britannica* 14 (London and New York: Encyclopaedia Britannica Company), 5: 138—141. Reprinted in: David G. Mandelbaum (ed.), *Selected writings of Edward Sapir* (Berkeley: University of California Press, 1951), 169—178.
Whitney, William Dwight
1867        *Language and the study of language* (New York: Scribner).
Wise, Mary Ruth
1986        "Grammatical characteristics of PreAndine Arawakan languages of Peru", in: Desmond C. Derbyshire—Geoffrey K. Pullum (eds.), *Handbook of Amazonian Languages* 1 (Berlin: Mouton de Gruyter), 567—642.
Yallop, Colin
1977        *Alyawarra: An aboriginal language of central Australia* (Canberra: Australian Institute of Aboriginal Studies).

# Algonquian linguistic change and reconstruction

*Ives Goddard*

The Algonquian languages are closely enough related for their relationships to be obvious on inspection, yet differentiated enough to give work to historical linguists. The framework of the comparative phonology was formulated in some detail by Leonard Bloomfield in 1925, on the basis of four languages that turned out to be sufficiently conservative to have permitted the reconstruction of most of the contrasts of Proto-Algonquian (Bloomfield 1925).[1] Comparative Algonquian lexicography and grammar had begun even earlier, as Algonquianists got into the habit early on of trying to elucidate lesser known languages by using the available descriptive materials on others, notably the extensive grammars and dictionaries of Ojibwa and Cree by nineteenth-century linguists who worked as missionaries (Cuoq 1886, 1891 – 1894; Lacombe 1874; Baraga 1850, 1853, 1878 a, 1878 b, 1880). Before Bloomfield's first paper, Truman Michelson (1917: 55 – 56, 1919, 1920) had pointed out several widespread morphophonemic alternations and the relative chronology of some phonological developments.

To a considerable extent the reconstruction of Proto-Algonquian (PA) has provided a basis for the reconstruction of the history of the phonology and morphology of the separate languages. A good number of treatments of individual historical phonologies have appeared, and extensive segments of the historical morphology of the family are understood (Michelson 1935; Bloomfield 1946; Voegelin 1941; Siebert 1941, 1975; Hockett 1942; Miller 1959; Silver 1960; Goddard 1974 a, 1979 b, 1981 a; Pentland 1979 b).[2] The resulting reconstruction of Algonquian history has provided a framework for the description of the Algonquian languages, in which the reconstructed protolanguage has served as a point of reference for the identification of morphemes and other features (Bloomfield 1927, 1941; Goddard 1974 b, 1979 a).

## Reconstruction

Generally speaking the similarity of the Algonquian languages re-
duces the problem of determining the shape of reconstructed systems
and elements. Only a few details of Proto-Algonquian phonology
have resisted explicit formulation. In some cases competing reconstructions may be the result of an indeterminacy in the relative
chronology or scope of morphophonemic rules. For example, there
is evidence that an original or underlying sequence PA *awe* might
be realized as *awe*, *a ˙*, or *o ˙*, and PA *aye* as *aye*, *a ˙*, or *e ˙*,
but the detailed distribution and history of these treatments has not
yet been completely worked out.[3] Reconstructions are arrived at by
the usual comparative methodology: evidence from languages preserving each given opposition or contrast is combined to formulate
a proto-segment or proto-element that forms the best starting point
for the subsequent divergent histories of the separate languages. It
is this implied subsequent linguistic history that validates the reconstruction, as the examples given in this paper will demonstrate.

## Linguistic change

In general, linguistic change in the Algonquian languages can be
characterized as conservative. This goes for the phonology, morphology, and lexicon. Blackfoot and Micmac, on the most isolated
western and eastern extremes, respectively, appear to have the most
divergent lexicons, and the Plains languages, Blackfoot, Arapaho-
Atsina, Nawathinehena, and Cheyenne, are most likely to have the
Algonquian affinities of inherited forms obscured by sound changes.

The Proto-Algonquian system of four short and four long vowels
is usually reflected in recognizable form. Fox retains the protosystem
with very few changes in distribution:

(1)        Proto-Algonquian and Fox
           *i   o    i˙  o˙*
           *e   a    e˙  a˙*

The Eastern Algonquian languages shared a reduction to six vowels;
the Proto-Eastern Algonquian (PEA) system is retained best by

Eastern Abenaki, which has one phonetic shift and a few changes in distribution:

(2)        PEA                    Eastern Abenaki
            *i·  o·*                 *i  o*
        *ə  a    e·  a·*        *ə  a    e  α*

Micmac and the Delaware languages, Munsee and Unami, expanded the Proto-Eastern Algonquian roster by reintroducing length contrasts.[4] Cheyenne, Nawathinehena, and Common Arapaho-Atsina[5] share a falling together of the Proto-Algonquian high (or mid) back rounded vowels with the high front vowels; Arapaho reintroduces, via vowel harmony, a fourth vowel quality, in the form of a pair of high back unrounded vowels (Goddard 1974a: 104, 106–107, 111; Pentland 1979a: 107–109):[6]

(3)        Arapaho-Atsina    Arapaho
        *i      i·*              *i  u    i·  u·*
        *e  a    e·  a·*        *e  o    e·  o·*

Blackfoot collapses the unrounded short vowels to *i* (preserving some different effects on consonants) and emerges with new vowel lengths and sequences that, like much in this language, remain to be fully explained. Potawatomi collapses the unrounded short vowels to *ə*. Other losses of contrast are found here and there. Most languages drop all or most final vowels, and some drop certain secondarily final syllables or semivowels as well. Fox and Shawnee, and apparently Illinois and Cheyenne, retain final vowels in all independent words (the Proto-Algonquian pattern), though Shawnee and Cheyenne lose some final CV syllables.

No prosodic features can be reconstructed for Proto-Algonquian, but the prosodic systems of several languages can be explained taking as the starting point reconstructed forms consisting entirely of segmental phonemes. These developments should clearly be taken into account in the formulation of general hypotheses regarding tonogenesis. In Cheyenne, underlying high tone reflects Proto-Algonquian vowel length (Frantz 1972), and from an underlying high-low contrast tonal interactions have produced four distinct level tones (Leman 1981). The contrasting tones appear clearly in the first syllables of disyllables, which have devoiced and hence toneless ultimas (Leman 1981):[7]

(4)       Cheyenne
*šé?šE*  | xé?xé |  < PA *\*ši· ?ši·pa* 'duck'       (> Fox *ši·ši·pa*)
*hē?E*  | he?e |  < PA *\*eθkwe·wa* 'woman'       (> Fox *ihkwe·wa*)
*mèsE*  | mése |  < PA *\*mi·čikwe* 'eat it       (> Fox *mi·čiko*)
              (you pl.)'
*he?E*  | he?e |  < PA *\*weθkweni* 'liver'       (> Fox *ohkoni*)

A bi-valent pitch-accent system emerges in Maliseet-Passamaquoddy as a consequence of final syllable loss (Goddard 1976):

(5)       Maliseet
          *épit* < *PEA \*e·pi·t* 'one who is sitting'
          (′ = stressed high)

          *èpit* < *PEA \*e·pi·te·* 'when he was sitting'
          (ˋ = stressed low)

A similar system emerges in Eastern Abenaki in the wake of vowel contractions.[8] The Kickapoo mono-valent pitch-accent system arose with the loss of most intervocalic semivowels (Voorhis 1971: 243)

(6)       Kickapoo
          *poohkamáaki* < *\*po·hkama·waki* 'peaches'
          (′ = pitch drop on following vowel)
          *poohkámaaki* < *\*po·hkama·ki* 'in a peach'

The relatively complex Arapaho system is not yet well understood, but it pretty clearly reflects perturbations induced by the loss of certain final syllables and of pre-consonantal glottal stop (Goddard 1974 a: 115, 1982 b: 49).

The Proto-Algonquian consonant system had a single series of stops and fricatives ($*p$, $*t$, $*č$, $*k$; $*s$, $*š$, $*h$), two nasals ($*m$, $*n$), two semivowels ($*w$, $*y$), and two phonetically indeterminate continuants conventionally reconstructed $*l$ and $*θ$. All the languages reduce the number of contrasts in the original system, but some acquire additional consonants from conditioned reflexes or clusters. All languages undergo contraction or loss of post-consonantal semivowels in some or all positions. In most languages *$l$ and *$\theta$ fall together to a voiced lateral (written $r$ in 17th-century recordings of several languages), which in a number of cases is subsequently reflected as $n$, $y$, or $t$. Common Cree-Montagnais and some dialects originally kept *$l$ distinct from all other segments (though some dialects merge it with $n$ or $y$), and collapsed *$\theta$ with $t$. Arapaho collapsed *$l$ with $n$ and collapsed *$\theta$ and *$č$ to $\theta$. A number of languages merge *$s$ and *$š$.

A limited number of consonant clusters occurred intervocalically. In the case of a number of these, even though they are shown to be distinct by their divergent histories, the phonetic or phonemic identity of the first member cannot be established from its reflexes. These uncertain preconsonantal segments are traditionally reconstructed algebraically (*$ʔ$, *$x$, and *$ç$);[9] there are enough phonemes available to account for them, but the difficulty is determining which is which and what neutralizations may already have taken place in the protolanguage. All the languages reduce the contrasts in the system of clusters.

Less typical, although apparently, like some innovations already mentioned, partially shared by diffusion, are the consonantal developments in the Arapahoan languages and Cheyenne. Arapaho-Atsina reduced the Proto-Algonquian system of thirteen consonants to eight, plus a glottal stop arising in certain clusters. The more disruptive innovations were the loss of *$k$; the shift of *$p$ to a new *$k$; the falling together of *$w$ and *$y$ to *$y$; the shift of this intermediate-stage *$y$ to $n$ if not originally post-consonantal; and some banalities like the falling together of medial *$s$ and *$h$ to $h$, which drops word-finally. (The shift of initial *$s$ to $n$ is noticeable but, owing to the paucity of words exhibiting it, not particularly disruptive.) On top of this Arapaho and Atsina each underwent separate patterns of conditioned consonantal splits that built up new inventories of consonants once more; the new intermediate-stage *$k$, for example, splits in Arapaho into $k$ and $č$. The effects of the Arapaho consonant shifts are seen in the following examples:

(7)        Arapaho
*hóuu* 'crow'                       < PA *$ka\cdot ka\cdot kiwa$ 'raven'
*nóóku* 'rabbit, hare'              < PA *$wa\cdot poswa$ 'hare'
*henééčeenóʔ* 'buffalo bulls'       < PA *$aya\cdot pe\cdot waki$
                                        'male ungulates'[10]

Cheyenne, though in some ways less transformed than Arapaho, shows one intriguing development that is not yet explained: *p and *k are both dropped, but only, it would seem, optionally; where doublets can be compared, the form with retention has a diminutive meaning beside the form with loss:

(8)      Cheyenne
         *éma?eta* 'he is red' < prefix + PA *meçkweθe-
            'be red (animate)'
         *éma?keta* 'he is red (diminutive)'

Such doublets appear to point to the negative semantic conditioning of a sound law, surely not a very common type of sound change.[11] The situation is, however, obscured by the existence of words and even single morphemes showing a mixture of retention and loss (Goddard 1978: 75). It is possible that an original phonetic conditioning of the two types of reflexes has been obscured by a redistribution of the variants in accordance with, or as a mark of, a semantic opposition. Other Algonquian languages occasionally show irregularities in diminutives and the like, but these seem clearly to be cases of diminutive or imitative consonant symbolism, or other marked surface patterns, superimposed on regular sound laws.[12]

The phonological history of Blackfoot has not been worked out in detail, but the scattered observations that have been made show that it has undergone at least some quite disruptive sound changes. For example, Thomson (1978) has shown that at least some Blackfoot geminates arise from consonant assimilation after vowel syncope:

(9)      Blackfoot
         *kimm-* 'poor' < PA *ketem-
         *inno-* 'long' < PA *kenw-

The extensive and sometimes extreme phonological changes in the Plains languages raise an obvious question. Can it be an accident that the languages with the most divergent phonological histories are precisely those spoken by the Algonquian peoples with the most divergent cultural histories? Perhaps in the Plains Algonquian languages the accelerated linguistic change correlates with the accelerated cultural change. No direct causation need be assumed, only that social and cultural change introduces generational and factional diversification that provides a fertile ground for linguistic innovations to become established in segments of a community.

Morphological change in the Algonquian languages generally involves the reshaping or loss of existing elements and paradigms. Where a particular formation has a restricted distribution, it is often difficult to say (or at least a matter of controversy) whether it is a residue of something old or an innovation. It is clear, though, that the Algonquian languages provide the opportunity for a great deal of work to be done on historical morphology.

The starting point for the study of the historical morphology of the Algonquian languages is a protolanguage for which a large part of the morphology has been reconstructed. Not only are a great many specific morphemes known with considerable confidence, their syntagmatic patterns of combination and paradigmatic patterns of contrast are also in remarkably clear focus (Bloomfield 1946; Goddard 1974 b, 1979 a, 1979 b, 1983).

The morphological changes found in the history of Algonquian languages are of the familiar varieties. Categories or categorial contrasts are sometimes lost; new shapes and sequences of morphemes arise by proportional analogy; paradigms undergo leveling; new paradigms emerge from the detritus of old material. A unique creation is the new Arapaho theme sign -ee- for action by first plural on second person:

(10)          Arapaho

| Intransitive subject | | | First plural subject with various objects | | | | |
|---|---|---|---|---|---|---|---|
| -t | 3sg | < PA *-ta | -éét | 1pl — 3sg | < PA *-akenta | | |
| -n | 2sg | < PA *-yani | -een | 1pl — 2sg (NOT | < | PA | *-eθa˙nke |
| | | | | 1pl — 2sg/pl) | | | |
| -nee | 2pl | < PA *-ye˙kwe | -eenee | 1pl — 2pl (NOT | < | PA | *-eθa˙nke |
| | | | | 1pl — 2sg/pl) | | | |

In these Arapaho forms inherited -éét (1pl — 3sg) has been reanalyzed as consisting of a theme sign -ee- followed by the productive third singular ending -t; on this new theme sign the forms for first plural on second person have been built using the inherited second person endings.[13]

The Algonquian languages all retain a rich inflectional morphology and complex patterns of stem derivation, and no cases have been noted in which phonological change has led to an extensive morphological or syntactic overhaul. The loss of the contrast between singular and plural in the obviative category in Cree may result from the falling together of the common singular and plural endings by sound law, but other languages show the same loss of contrast with no phonological impetus. Some languages that do this generalize the singular ending, and some generalize the plural ending:

(11)

| | Proto-Algonquian | Fox | Cree | Menominee | Massachusett |
|---|---|---|---|---|---|
| obv. sg. | *-ali | -ani | -a | -an | -oh |
| obv. pl. | *-ahi | -ahi | -a | -an | -oh |

Some changes in morphology have consequences for syntax. The Proto-Algonquian negative inflection on verbs was lost or functionally displaced in most languages, with the consequence that new lexical and syntactic means of indicating negation are widespread. In Eastern Algonquian, morphology used to mark secondary objects is extended to form a new mode of the independent order, the subordinative, which takes over from the conjunct order the major burden of forming complement phrases (Goddard 1974 b, 1983). In Arapaho, Illinois, and Micmac the Proto-Algonquian participle (a mode of the conjunct order used to make relative clauses) has become the normal indicative form of the verb; the old indicative (a mode of the independent order) is lost in Micmac, retained with some sort of a differentiated function in Illinois, and relegated to providing the inflection for the negative, interrogative, and narrative modes of Arapaho. Preverbs, phonologically independent words that are part of compound verb stems, have an old and widespread use as independent particles, and in some languages these particles develop a use as emergent prepositions:[14]

(12)    Fox

a) *we·ta·paniki    e·h=išiweneči*
east-obv.        lead/to-3/pass./narr.
'it [flute] was blown to the east'

b) *we·ta·paki    iši-anwe·we·hta·pi*
east            to blow-inan./pass./indic.
'he was led to the east'

c) *si'po'ki*      *iši*
river-loc.      to
'to the river'

d) *ayo'hi=*      *'ši wi'kiya'peki*
this-loc.      to house-loc.
'to this house'

(13)      Cree
         *natimihk*      *isi*
         west-loc.      to
         'to the west'

In (12 b) *iši* 'to' is a preverb, identical except in morphological class to the initial in the verb stem *išiwen-* 'lead to' in (12 a). In (12 c) and (12 d) *iši* is an independent particle, used as a preposition; its Cree cognate in the same function is seen in (13). Such prepositions have become so common in Massachusett that they must be recognized as a separate, full-fledged part of speech, and the locative is no longer obligatory with them:

(14)      Massachusett[15]
     a)    *en [w]ekit*
         to his-house-loc.
         'to his house'

     b)    *en [w]etu*
         to house
         'to the house'

     c)    *en kennau*
         'to you (pl.)'

The Algonquian languages have remained in contact throughout their histories, and the diffusion of innovations across language boundaries has evidently not been uncommon. So far, however, borrowing has been used as an ad hoc explanation but has not been the subject of a systematic, comprehensive investigation. The impact of non-Algonquian languages (before recent contacts with English and French) has been very slight. Areal influences may be present in the shaping of the phonologies of the Plains languages[16] and in the emergence of a nasalized vowel in the phoneme inventories of the southern New England languages and Mahican, which form a geographical continuum with Iroquoian languages in which nasalized vowels are an old feature (Goddard 1971: 140; Sherzer 1972).

## Distant relatives

Algonquian is known to be related to Wiyot and Yurok, two languages of northern California. Wiyot and Yurok may form a subgroup, Ritwan (Berman 1982), but even so the divergence between them is nearly as great as the divergence between them and Algonquian.

Algonquian, Wiyot, and Yurok form a genetic grouping that is at, or very close to, the maximum depth at which it is possible to reconstruct features of the protolanguage that retain any appreciable degree of resolution.[17] The comparisons that constitute the demonstration of the relationship, of course, imply the existence of corresponding ancestral features. But it is methodologically instructive to note that this is a case in which the comparative method produces a proof of genetic relationship without there being a reconstructed phonology or phonological history beyond what is implied by a handful of equations of identity, or near identity.

Still, it is possible to recover some coherent information on the history of these languages. For example, a loose end in the well-known equation of the pronominal prefixes of the three branches (Goddard 1975: 250−254, 1986: 193) is that the Yurok prefixes are glottalized on nouns and verbs, but not as part of the independent pronouns:

(15)      Pronominal prefixes (and Yurok pronouns)

|  | Proto-Algonquian | | Yurok | | Wiyot[18] |
|---|---|---|---|---|---|
| first person | *ne-, | *ne(t)- | ʔne- | (nek 'I') | d- |
| second person | *ke-, | *ke(t)- | k'e- | (keʔl 'you (sg.)') | kh- |
| third person | *we-, | *we(t)- | ʔwe- | | w- |

Berman (1982: 418) has made the very attractive proposal that the glottalization reflects the intercalated *t* that is inserted after the prefixes before vowel-initial non-dependent stems in Wiyot and Algonquian but is not found in Yurok. The assumption would be that the glottalized variants originating before vowel-initial stems were generalized for all occurrences of the prefixes, while the independent pronouns, as frozen formations, remained unaffected. There are other etymologies that appear to support the equation of Yurok glottalized consonants with Algonquian and Wiyot sequences of consonant plus *t*:

(16)      Cognates of Yurok glottalization

|  | Proto-Algonquian | Yurok | Wiyot |
|---|---|---|---|
| a) third person (PA conjunct order) | *-t- | glottalization of final consonant[19] | |
| b) 'spruce root'[20] | *watapya | ʔwohpeɣ | tòp |

The equations in (15) and (16) suggest the hypothesis that the Yurok glottalized consonants, which have no counterparts in Wiyot or Algonquian, are secondary. The emergence of glottalized consonants in Yurok could presumably be correlated with the movement of the speakers of pre-Yurok from the pre-Algonquian area, which lacked such consonants, into California, where glottalized consonants are a feature of the languages of several families. On a more general level, this case illustrates how, even at the limits of our perception, where only dispersed fragments of the protolanguage can be perceived, the comparative method is the key to unraveling linguistic prehistory.

*Notes*

1. The four languages were Fox, Cree, Menominee, and Ojibwa. For the particular dialects and sources used, see Goddard (1987: 179—180).
2. There are also extensive unpublished treatments of Blackfoot (Taylor 1960) and Maliseet (Sherwood 1981). Tabulations of sound correspondences are better represented in the Algonquian literature than full-fledged historical phonologies. For Cheyenne the basic correspondences have been known since Michelson (1935), with steady refinement accompanying the gradually perfected understanding of the synchronic phonology (Frantz 1982; Leman 1980a, 1980b, 1981); a synthesis is in Goddard (1988). Recent years have seen the appearance of a number of innovations in the transcription of Proto-Algonquian forms, some of which imply new interpretations of linguistic history; a discussion of

these new interpretations, beyond the remarks in notes 3 and 9, lies outside the scope of this paper, not least because they have generally only been hinted at rather than comprehensively formulated.

3. The decision to reconstruct no contractions in the protolanguage in these and other cases (e. g. Pentland 1979 b: 407) ignores Michelson's insight that some shared contractions have such idiosyncratic distributions that they must be common inheritances (Michelson 1920: 300). Goddard (1981 b) argues for old contractions against the proposals of Proulx (1980); more remains to be said on this topic, as there are examples of Proulx's correspondence (Fox [etc.] *a* ˙ : Menominee *i* ˙ : Eastern Algonquian *\*e* ˙) not noted in these papers that remain to be accounted for, but I am still of the opinion that irregular correspondences among contracted vowels generally result from perturbations of the original distribution of inherited treatments.

4. The inventory and distribution of the Proto-Eastern Algonquian vowels is quite directly reflected by the underlying forms of morphemes showing vowel alternations in Maliseet-Passamaquoddy (Sherwood 1986: 13), Eastern Abenaki (Siebert 1980: 124), and Delaware (Goddard 1979 a: 11, 1982 a: 30).

5. Common Arapaho-Atsina is the shallow-level protolanguage of Arapaho and Atsina, which are considered to be, or to have been, mutually intelligible dialects of one language.

6. In the transcription of Arapaho established by Salzmann (1956) two-vowel and three-vowel sequences were written; subsequent analysis has shown the advisability of analyzing some two-mora sequences as unit-phoneme long vowels (Goddard 1982 b: 49; Salzmann 1983: 28 − 31). Arapaho *o* ranges from [a] to [ɔ], *o* ˙ is [ɔ ˙], *u* is [ɨ], and *u* ˙ is [ɨ ˙].

7. The tones in order from high to low are high (*é*), raised low (*ē*), lowered high (*è*), and low (*e*); there is also a raised high tone (*ê*), but it does not contrast phonemically with the high tone.

8. This is shown by the examples of accentual contrast cited by Frank T. Siebert in an oral report to the Conference on Algonquian Linguistics held in Ottawa in 1964.

9. In the case of these algebraic segments and *\*θ*, phonetic and phonemic indeterminacy has led some Algonquianists to make various substitutions in the symbols conventionally used to represent the protolanguage; popular are *\*t* for *\*x* (despite the counterevidence in Goddard 1979 a: 130, 199), *\*s* for *\*ç*, and *\*l* for *\*θ*. Those engaging this practice have not dealt with the arguments that have been expressed against it (Goddard 1979 b: 72 − 78), even when seeming to do so (Proulx 1984: 168 − 69).

10. All three forms reflect vowel-harmony assimilations. Vowel sequences are reduced to three moras, and a quantitative metathesis shifts *\*V ˙ V to VV ˙*. Word-initial *h* always results from the addition of *h* before primary or secondary initial vowels, and *ʔ* is added after a single final short vowel.

11. At the conference at Stanford, where this paper was originally presented, examples of the irregular retention of consonants in expressive or imitative words were cited by John Whitman (from Japanese) and Bob Dixon (from Australian languages).

12. Diminutive consonant symbolism in Munsee is treated in Goddard (1982: 20 − 21, 29). The recognition that diminutives can be marked by surface ablaut

prompts the rejection of the new correspondence postulated by Proulx (1976) to account for the irregular or unexpected vowel length found with the diminutive endings of several languages.

13. The endings given are from the Arapaho indicative mode, which continues the Proto-Algonquian participle of the conjunct order. The new theme sign is also extended to the non-indicative modes of Arapaho that reflect the Proto-Algonquian independent order.

14. I use the term preposition, long accepted as having no reference to word order, in preference to the ill-formed adposition.

15. The Massachusett examples are from the writings of native speakers. (14a) and (14b) are in successive sentences in the same document, which is a copy; the brackets indicate emendations.

16. For the remarks on Arapaho-Atsina in Goddard (1974a: 110), see the important qualification in Goddard (1982b: 49).

17. The careful work of Berman (1982) makes it clear how few reconstructions can be established when the task is approached with rigor and realism; the exuberant etyma of Proulx (1984, 1985) are almost completely unconvincing because of the extent to which they depend on the postulation of multiple reconstructed variants and of unmotivated complex clusters that simplify in different ways in the descendant languages, among other reasons.

18. These are the prefixes used on dependent stems (stems that are always prefixed) before vowels; before a consonant, first-person *d-* and third-person *w-* drop and second-person *kh-* is realized as the aspiration of the consonant.

19. E. g., stem *ma?epet-* 'to tie up': *ma?epet* 'he ties up' (Robins 1958: 33).

20. The equation and the Wiyot form (stem *tóph-*) are from Proulx (1984: 191), who points out the important use of spruce roots for sewing; Proulx's analysis, however, is unnecessarily contorted and ad hoc. The vowel correspondence is one of those tabulated by Berman (1982: 413, 414). The correspondence of PA *\*y* to Yurok $\gamma$ is well established; perhaps the underlying Wiyot *ph* is from *\*p* plus this segment. The PA form could be from pre-PA *\*\*wetapya*, with the widespread assimilation of *\*e* to *\*a* before an *\*a(ˊ)* in the following syllable; the first syllables would then exactly match the correspondence in the third person prefix under the present hypothesis. This equation is clearly one of the very best there is for Algonquian-Ritwan.

## References

Baraga, Frederic
1850        *A theoretical and practical grammar of the Otchipwe language* (Detroit: Jabez Fox).
1853        *A dictionary of the Otchipwe language* (Cincinnati: Jos. A. Hemann).
1878a       *A theoretical and practical grammar of the Otchipwe language* (2nd edition) (Montreal: Beauchemin & Valois).
1878b       *A dictionary of the Otchipwe language* part 1 (2nd edition) (Montreal: Beauchemin & Valois).
1880        *A dictionary of the Otchipwe language* part 2 (2nd edition) (Montreal: Beauchemin & Valois).

Berman, Howard
    1982        "Two phonological innovations in Ritwan", *IJAL* 48: 412—420.
Bloomfield, Leonard
    1925        "On the sound-system of Central Algonquian", *Lg.* 1: 130—156.
    1927        "The word-stems of Central Algonquian", *Festschrift Meinhof* (Hamburg), 393—402.
    1941        "Proto-Algonquian -*i˙t*- 'fellow' ", *Lg.* 17: 292—297.
    1946        "Algonquian", in: *Linguistic structures of Native America* (Viking Fund publications in anthropology 6) (New York: Viking Fund), 85—129.
Cuoq, Jean-André
    1886        *Lexique de la langue algonquine* (Montreal: J. Chapleau et fils).
    1891—1894  "Grammaire de la langue algonquine", *Memoirs of the Royal Society of Canada* 9 (1): 95—114, 10 (1): 41—119, 11 (1): 137—179.
Frantz, Donald G.
    1972        "The origin of Cheyenne pitch accent", *IJAL* 38: 223—225.
Goddard, Ives
    1971        "More on the nasalization of PA *a˙ in Eastern Algonquian", *IJAL* 37: 139—145.
    1974 a      "An outline of the historical phonology of Arapaho and Atsina", *IJAL* 40: 102—116.
    1974 b      "Remarks on the Algonquian independent indicative", *IJAL* 40: 317—327.
    1975        "Algonquian, Wiyot, and Yurok: Proving a distant linguistic relationship", in: M. Dale Kinkade—Kenneth L. Hale—Oswald Werner (eds.), *Linguistics and anthropology: In honor of C. F. Voegelin* (Lisse: Peter de Ridder Press), 249—262.
    1976        *Preliminary informal statement on Malecite prosodics* (2nd edition) . Dittoed report on deposit in papers of R. H. Ives Goddard III, National Anthropological Archives, Smithsonian Institution, Washington, D.C.
    1978        "The Sutaio dialect of Cheyenne: A discussion of the evidence", in: William Cowan (ed.), *Papers of the Ninth Algonquian Conference*, 68—80.
    1979 a      *Delaware verbal morphology: A descriptive and comparative study* (New York: Garland).
    1979 b      "Comparative Algonquian", in: Lyle Campbell—Marianne Mithun (eds.), *The languages of Native America: Historical and comparative assessment* (Austin: University of Texas Press), 70—132.
    1981 a      "Massachusett phonology: A preliminary look", in: William Cowan (ed.), *Papers of the Twelfth Algonquian Conference*, 57—105.
    1981 b      "Against the linguistic evidence claimed for some Algonquian dialectal relationships", *Anthropological Linguistics* 23: 271—297.
    1982 a      "The historical phonology of Munsee", *IJAL* 48: 16—48.
    1982 b      "Addenda and corrigenda", *Algonquian and Iroquoian Linguistics* 7: 47—54.
    1983        "The Eastern Algonquian subordinative mode and the importance of morphology", *IJAL* 49: 351—387.

1986        "Sapir's comparative method", in: William Cowan—Michael K.
            Foster—Konrad Koerner (eds.), *New perspectives in language, cul-
            ture, and personality* (Amsterdam: John Benjamins), 191—210.
1987        "Leonard Bloomfield's descriptive and comparative studies of Al-
            gonquian", *Historiographia Linguistica* 14(1/2): 179—217.
1988        "Pre-Cheyenne *y", in: William Shipley—Margaret Langdon—Wick
            R. Miller (eds.), *In honor of Mary Haas* (Berlin: Mouton de Gruyter),
            345—360.
Hockett, Charles F.
1942        "The position of Potawatomi in Central Algonquian", *Papers of the
            Michigan Academy of Science Arts and Letters* 28: 537—542.
Lacombe, Albert
1874        *Dictionnaire et grammaire de la langue des cris* (Montreal: Beau-
            chemin & Valois).
Leman, Wayne
1980 a      "Evidence for a PA *k: Cheyenne n correspondence", *IJAL* 46: 316—
            318.
1980 b      "Some Cheyenne consonant alternations: Synchronic and diachronic
            views", in: William Cowan (ed.), *Papers of the Eleventh Algonquian
            Conference*, 262—273.
1981        "Cheyenne pitch rules", *IJAL* 47: 283—309.
Michelson, Truman
1917        "Notes on Algonquian languages", *IJAL* 1: 50—57.
1919        "Two proto-Algonquian phonetic shifts", *Journal of the Washington
            Academy of Sciences* 9: 333—334.
1920        "Two phonetic shifts occurring in many Algonquian languages",
            *IJAL* 1: 300—304.
1935        "Phonetic shifts in Algonquian languages", *IJAL* 8: 131—171.
Miller, Wick
1959        "An outline of Shawnee historical phonology", *IJAL* 25: 16—21.
Pentland, David
1979 a      "Causes of rapid phonological change: The case of Atsina and its
            relatives", *Calgary Working Papers in Linguistics* 5: 99—137.
1979 b      *Algonquian historical phonology*, [Ph. D. dissertation in Anthropol-
            ogy, University of Toronto].
Proulx, Paul
1976        "A new Algonquian correspondence", *IJAL* 42: 71—73.
1980        "The linguistic evidence on Algonquian prehistory", *Anthropological
            Linguistics* 22: 1—21.
1984        "Proto-Algic I: Phonological sketch", *IJAL* 50: 165—207.
1985        "Proto-Algic II: Verbs", *IJAL* 51: 59—93.
Robins, R. H.
1958        *The Yurok language: Grammar, texts, lexicon* (University of Califor-
            nia, Publications in Linguistics 15) (Berkeley: University of Califor-
            nia Press).
Salzmann, Zdeněk
1956        "Arapaho I: Phonology", *IJAL* 22: 49—56.

1983            *Dictionary of contemporary Arapaho usage* (Arapaho language and culture instructional materials series 4) (Wind River Reservation: Arapaho Language and Culture Commission).

Sherwood, David
1981            *An outline of Maliseet historical phonology,* [Manuscript].
1986            *Maliseet-Passamaquoddy verb morphology* (Canadian Ethnology Service Paper No. 105) (Ottawa: National Museums of Canada).

Sherzer, Joel
1972            "Vowel nasalization in Eastern Algonquian: An areal-typological perspective on linguistics [!] universals", *IJAL* 38: 267—268.

Siebert, Frank T., Jr.
1941            "Certain Proto-Algonquian consonant clusters, *Lg.* 17: 298—303.
1975            "Resurrecting Virginia Algonquian from the dead: The reconstituted and historical phonology of Powhatan", in: James M. Crawford (ed.), *Studies in southeastern Indian languages* (Athens: University of Georgia Press), 285—453.
1980            "The Penobscot Dictionary Project: Preferences and problems of format, presentation, and entry", in: William Cowan (ed.), *Papers of the Eleventh Algonquian Conference,* 113—127.

Silver, Shirley
1960            "Natick consonants in reference to Proto-Central Algonquian", *IJAL* 26: 112—119, 234—241.

Taylor, Allan
1960            *Blackfoot historical phonology: A preliminary survey* (With one-page addendum dated 1978). Manuscript on deposit in the Survey of California and Other Indian Languages, University of California at Berkeley.

Thomson, Gregory
1978            "The origin of Blackfoot geminate stops and nasals", in: Eung-Do Cook—Jonathan D. Kaye (eds.), *Linguistic studies of Native Canada* (Vancouver: University of British Columbia Press) 249—254.

Voegelin, C. F.
1941            "Proto-Algonquian consonant clusters in Delaware", *Lg.* 17: 143—147.

Voorhis, Paul
1971            "Notes on Kickapoo whistle speech", *IJAL* 37: 238—243.

# Mayan languages and linguistic change

*Lyle Campbell*

## I. Introduction

The linguistic history of Mayan languages is very well known. Since there are a number of recent overviews (cf. Campbell – Kaufman 1985; Campbell 1979, in press a; Justeson – Norman – Campbell – Kaufman 1985; Kaufman 1976, etc.), I will present in this paper only a very brief summary of Mayan historical linguistics, concentrating on the family's potential contribution to the concerns of historical linguistics in general.

## 2. Summary of Mayan historical linguistics

The Mayan family consists of 31 languages spoken in Guatemala, southern Mexico, and Belize. Mayan subgrouping is quite advanced; the most widely accepted classification is

Huastecan: Huastec, Chicomuceltec [extinct]
Yucatecan: Yucatec, Lacandon; Mopan, Itzá
Cholan-Tzeltalan (or Greater Tzeltalan):
    Cholan: Chol, Chontal; Chortí, Choltí [extinct]
    Tzeltalan: Tzeltal, Tzotzil
Kanjobalan-Chujean (or Greater Kanjobalan):
    Kanjobalan: Kanjobal, Acatec, Jacaltec; Motocintlec (and Tuzantec)
    Chujean: Chuj, Tojolabal
Quichean-Mamean (or Eastern Mayan):
    Quichean: Kekchí; Uspantec; Pokomchí, Pokomam; Quiché, Cakchiquel, Tzutujil, Sacapultec, Sipacapeño
    Mamean: Teco, Mam; Aguacatec, Ixil (cf. Campbell – Kaufman 1985)

There is general agreement on these five major branches, but there is less consensus concerning more inclusive groupings. Most

Mayanists believe that Huastecan was the first to split off, followed later by the Yucatecan branch, and then finally the remaining groups diversified. Refinements in the subgroup classification may be expected only when grammatical innovations come to be better understood.

Reasonably extensive descriptive materials (grammars and dictionaries) exist for most Mayan languages; the most underrepresented are Chontal, Motozintlec, Acatec, Kanjobal, Uspantec, Sipacapeño, Aguacatec, and Teco.

The most widely accepted proposed phonemic inventory of Proto-Mayan is

| $p$ | $t$ | $t^y$ | $\phi$ | $\check{c}$ | $k$ | $q$ | $\ʔ$ | | $i$ | | $u$ | V: |
|---|---|---|---|---|---|---|---|---|---|---|---|---|
| $b\ʼ$ | $t\ʼ$ | $t^{yʼ}$ | $\phi\ʼ$ | $\check{c}\ʼ$ | $k\ʼ$ | $q\ʼ$ | | | | $e$ | $o$ | |
| $m$ | $n$ | | | | $\ŋ$ | | | | | $a$ | | |
| | $s$ | | | $\check{s}$ | $x$ | | | | | | | |
| | $l$ | | | | | | | | | | | |
| | $r$ | | | | | | | | | | | |
| $w$ | | | | $y$ | | | $h$ | | | | | |

Some important differences from earlier proposed reconstructions include the absence of retroflexed consonants, tones, schwa, $p\ʼ$, and $k^y$, with *$r$ added (cf. McQuown 1955, 1956 a; Kaufman 1964 a; Campbell 1977).

Reconstruction of portions of Proto-Mayan syntax have been made (Norman – Campbell 1978; Kaufman 1986). Proto-Mayan was ergative with the usual ergative typological traits, including the antipassive. Ergative alignment was signaled by cross-referencing pronominal clitics or affixes on the verb. There were three morphologically distinct verb classes, transitives, intransitives, and positionals (e. g., 'sit, squat, lie, stand', etc.). Proto-Mayan seems to have had VOS basic word order when S was higher than O in "animacy", but VSO order when both S and O were equal in animacy. Proto-Mayan nominal possession was of the form, "his-dog the man" for "the man's dog"; prefixes (equivalent to the ergative markers) signaled pronominal possession. Proto-Mayan had relational nouns in locative functions (i. e., in construction a possessed noun root, e. g., the equivalent of "my-head" for "on me", "his-stomach" for "in him").

Distant genetic relationships have been proposed between Mayan and Araucanian, Yunga, Chipaya-Uru, Penutian, Hokan, Lenca,

Tarascan, Huave, Mixe-Zoquean, and Totonacan, among others (Brown – Witkowski 1979; Hamp 1967, 1970, 1971; Kaufman 1964 b; McQuown 1942, 1956 b; Olson 1964, 1965; Stark 1970, 1972; Swadesh 1966; Witkowski – Brown 1978, 1981; etc.). None, however, has been demonstrated, while most have been seriously discredited. The initially promising Chipaya-Uru (Olson 1964, 1965) proposal has not held up under closer scrutiny (Campbell 1973 a). The Macro-Mayan hypothesis, in which Mayan, Mixe-Zoquean, and Totonacan are grouped together, has received much attention (Brown – Witkowski 1979; Kaufman 1964 b; McQuown 1942, 1956 b; Witkowski – Brown 1978, 1981; etc.), but much of the evidence presented proves to involve diffusion and other explanations; still, this hypothesis bears more investigation (Campbell – Kaufman 1976, 1980, 1983). None of the other proposals is convincing. Thus, the Mayan family has no known relatives beyond the 31 languages named in the classification above.

Mayan languages also reflect membership in the Mesoamerican linguistic area, sharing with the other languages of Mesoamerica these traits: a vigesimal numeral system; nominal possession of the form, e. g. 'his-dog the man'; relational nouns; non-verb-final basic word order; and several semantic calques (loan-translated compounds), among others (Campbell – Kaufman – Smith-Stark 1986).

Linguistic prehistory links the findings of historical linguistics with archaeology, ethnohistory, ethnographic analogy, and other sources of historical information for a fuller picture of prehistory. It is hypothesized that Proto-Mayan was spoken in the Cuchumatanes Mountains of Guatemala, around Soloma, Huehuetenango, at ca. 2200 B. C., where its speakers exploited both highland and lowland ecological zones. Reconstructed vocabulary shows Proto-Mayan speakers to have been highly successful agriculturalists, having a full range of Mesoamerican cultigens, with the maize complex at its core. Proto-Mayan diversified and groups ultimately migrated to the areas of the present-day languages (Kaufman 1976, Campbell 1978 a). The principal bearers of Classic Lowland Maya culture (300 – 900 A. D.) were first Cholan speakers, later joined by Yucatecans (Kaufman 1976, Campbell 1984 a). The Lowland Maya linguistic area was formed during this period, contributing many loan words both internally among these Mayan languages and to neighboring non-Mayan languages (Justeson – Norman – Campbell – Kaufman 1985; Campbell 1978 a).

Recently great progress has been made toward full decipherment of Mayan hieroglyphic writing and towards adequate reading of the texts. The hypotheses of historicism and phoneticism are oft-cited breakthroughs. Historicism refers to the historical content of the texts, many of which contain dynastic histories of the births, kinship, offices, marriages, and deaths of rulers. Mayan writing is a mixed script. It began with logographic signs, which have the value of whole morphemes. The use of rebuses made it more phonological, where something easier to depict could be employed for similar-sounding morphemes more difficult to represent graphically, e. g., a picture of an "eye" to represent English "I". Phonetic complements (or determiners) arose from logograms for morphemes of the form CVC, where the final C was "weak" (i. e., *h*, *ʔ*, rarely also *y* or *w*) and ignored in reading. Such phonemic determiners could be used to distinguish different semantic values of logograms. For example, most Mayan languages have two words for 'house' (e. g., *nah* and *-otot*). The HOUSE logogram (T 614) sometimes bears as a phonetic complement T 59, in origin a representation of a "torch", cf. Chol *tah*, with weak final C (T numbers from Thompson's 1962 catalogue of Mayan hieroglyphs.) The HOUSE sign plus the phonetic determiner *ta* specified that the value ending in final *t*, i. e., *-otot*, was intended, rather than *nah*. Later, the use of phonetic complements was expanded to contexts independent of the semantic value of logograms, employed in combinations solely for their phonetic value to spell words syllabically. Mayan words could be written either partly or totally with signs whose value is CV. Since Mayan roots are typically monosyllabic of the form CVC, they could be spelled with two CV signs, where the vowel of the second is silent, but chosen to match the vowel of the root, e. g. Yucatecan /ku:¢/ 'turkey' was spelled *ku-¢u* in the codices. The Cholan hypothesis is also a breakthrough. The script originated with speakers of Cholan (or Cholan-Tzeltalan) and was later passed on to Yucatecan speakers. Many of the monuments are demonstrably Cholan; the codices are in Yucatec. The development of phonetic values can be understood only through Cholan. Many aspects of glyph grammar are also clear now, corresponding to Cholan grammar. Glyphic word order is Verb-Object-Subject, often preceded by a date. It reflects split ergativity, gapping, and conjunction reduction, Mayan verb classes, and the paired couplets so typical of Mayan ritual discourse. These "breakthroughs" converge to facili-

tate decipherment. For example, T 644, th
the historical event of rulers being "seated" in
bears the suffixes T 130.116, read phonetically as
Mayan positional verbs (of which 'seating' is a prime exa
special morphology, and only in Cholan do we find -*wan* 'com
aspect' of positional verbs plus -*i* 'intransitive', exactly matchin
the glyphic spelling of these Cholan suffixes (Campbell 1984 a,
1984 b; Justeson — Norman — Campbell — Kaufman 1985; Fox —
Justeson 1984; Kelley 1976, Thompson 1962, etc.)

## 3. Mayan contributions to historical linguistics in general

With this brief general overview of the historical linguistics of the
Mayan family in mind, we can now turn to the questions of what
it may contribute to the practice of historical linguistics generally.
I will address the questions which the American Indianists considered at the conference from which this volume is derived.

1) What are the patterns of linguistic change in the various
language families or groups? Work in Mayan linguistics has emphasized phonological change; it is seen to be regular, though
occasionally subsidiary principles come into play, e. g., analogy,
onomatopoeia, etc. A few morphologically conditioned sound
changes have been identified, and there are some diffused sound
changes (Campbell 1971, 1977, 1978 a; Kaufman 1964 a; Kaufman —
Norman 1984). However, there is nothing unusual or bizarre in
Mayan historical phonology. Given the number of languages, their
rich phonological inventories, and the rather large quantity of well-
understood sound changes, Mayan provides considerable ammu-
nition for studies of universal and typological properties of sound
changes in general. Reconstruction of morphology and syntax is
well underway (Norman — Campbell 1978; Kaufman 1986).

2) What factors affect linguistic change: tabu, geography, size, social patterns, typology, etc.? The answer is: none in particular. Mayan
sound changes illustrate neogrammarian regularity for the most part.
Known morphological and syntactic changes generally are typolog-

itterns of word-order uni-
ypology, etc.

in are most useful? The an-
storical linguistic handbooks;
s here. While totally normal,
some special characteristics. In
vith many other language families,
World, a family-framework, i. e., a
guide both historical and descriptive
(family typology) constrains work on
econstruction, and interpretation of
nanges, perhaps intrafamilial diffusion is
so than borrowing in other known families
(Kaufm.            , Justeson — Norman — Campbell — Kaufman
1985).

4) How does hi. orical linguistic practice vary among different American Indian families or regions, and to what extent is this conditioned by the structure of the languages in question? Mayan practice is much like that in other areas; I am aware of no unique features. There are occasional disputes over the value or role of glottochronology among Mayanists, but there is general agreement otherwise on historical linguistic methods, evidence, and standards of reconstruction.

Mayan does have some special features. Mayanists are in the privileged position of having a wealth of written documentation, extensive texts for over 450 years in Spanish-inspired orthographies, and hieroglyphic texts from ca. 300 A. D. until after the Spanish Conquest. The philological investigation of these has paid off, helping to resolve issues concerning past contrasts now merged, subgrouping, diffused sound changes, and even the linguistic iden-tity of now lost languages (see Campbell 1973 b, 1974, 1977, 1978 b, in press b; Kaufman 1980, see below).

5) What is the role of typological considerations? In essence, typology plays the same role in work on Mayan as it has played elsewhere. Mayan has ergative typology, which helps guide historical work on Mayan morphosyntax, but the study of ergativity in Mayan languages has also contributed to the understanding of ergativity in general (cf. Larsen — Norman 1979). Changes in case marking among the various Mayan languages provide a rich laboratory for the study of change in ergative languages. However, Mayan, with

a variety of passive constructions, provides no passive-to-ergative changes. In phonology, typology has had a similar role. For example, the series of glottalic consonants in most Mayan languages has imploded *b'*, but others in the series are mostly ejectives (*t'*, *ȼ'*, *č'*, *k'*, *q'*). While formerly this was thought somehow to be aberrant — some even insisted on reconstructing Proto-Mayan with *\*p'* instead of *\*b'* —, typological studies have shown this to be an expected pattern, labials favoring implosion (Greenberg 1970), and at the same time the Mayan examples have served to refine this typology (Campbell 1973 d). Thus Mayan historical work has both benefitted from, and contributed to, linguistic typology.

6) What can Mayan contribute to historical linguistics generally? Mayan historical linguistics offers strong examples confirming the general principles of historical linguistics. While Mayan holds no special problems for traditional and standard methods of historical linguistics, some aspects give it a special character.

First, the philological study of Mayan languages, documented for more than 450 years, has much to contribute, in spite of the stereotype that in American Indian languages there is little written documentation, with shallow time depths. For example, documented changes in Huastec have been useful in resolving issues in the reconstruction of Proto-Mayan phonology. McQuown (1955, 1956 a) had proposed that Proto-Mayan had contrastive labiovelars, *\*k^w* and *\*k^{'w}*, based on correspondences involving Huastec *k^w* and *k^{'w}*. However, forms preserved in Tapia Zenteno (1767 [written 1727]) show that the Huastec sounds are the result of a more recent change:

$$ k(') \begin{Bmatrix} o \\ u \end{Bmatrix} \begin{Bmatrix} w \\ y \\ h \\ \text{\textglotstop} \end{Bmatrix} \quad V > k(')^w V $$

(Kaufman 1980: 106).

Some examples of uncontracted forms attested in Tapia Zenteno are:

1) ⟨*tzanaco*⟩ 'bean'; cf. *ȼanak^{'w}* (Potosí dialect), *čanak^{'w}* (Veracruz dialect) [PM *\*kenaq*].

2) ⟨*cuyx*⟩ 'vulture'; cf. *k$^w$i:š*.

3) ⟨*coyen*⟩ 'masa' [mass]; cf. *k$^w$en* 'grouped, piled together' (both Potosí and Veracruz).

4) ⟨*cohuych*⟩ 'fresh corn tamale'; cf. *k$^w$i:č* (Potosí), *k$^w$i:ȼ* (Veracruz).

This philological information shows Huastec *k(')$^w$* to be secondary and helps to refine the reconstruction of Proto-Mayan.

Modern Cakchiquel has verb tenses, although its Quichean close relatives and other Mayan languages lack tense, having only aspectual systems. Old Cakchiquel also had only aspect markers, and the change to tenses is attested philologically. Colonial grammars (and other materials) unanimously present Cakchiquel with the aspect system:

> *x*- (/š-/) 'completive aspect (perfect)'
> *t*- 'transitive incompletive aspect'
> *c-/qu*- (/k-/) 'intransitive incompletive aspect'

A "present" sense could be indicated in the incompletive aspects by the particle *tan* 'now', e. g. ⟨*tan t-in-ban*⟩ [now Asp-lErg-do] 'now I am doing it', ⟨*tan ti-v-oqueçeh*⟩ [now Asp-lErg-believe] 'I presently believe it'. This combination of particle and incompletive aspect marker underwent changes which resulted in the modern tense system:

> *tan* + *t*-Verb > *tan* + *d*-Verb > *nd*-Verb > (*n*-Verb in some dialects)
> *tan* + *k*-Verb > *tan* + *g*-Verb > *ng*-Verb > ((*n*)*y*-Verb in some dialects)

That is, the *t*- and *k*- aspect markers were voiced after the final *-n* of the *tan* particle, which itself was cliticized to the verb, abbreviated, and the result ultimately was grammaticalized as present-tense markers, *nd*- or *n*- and *ng*-, *ny*-, or *y*. The old completive aspect marker, *š*-, was left with the meaning 'past', since actions that are completed typically occur in the past. The former incompletive *k*- with no particle came to be reinterpreted as 'remote past'. Without the philological information, one could not completely recover this sequence of changes or understand how the aspect system came to be transformed into tense. (See Campbell 1974, 1977, 1978 b.)

Colonial sources of Pokomam and Pokomchí, closely related Quichean languages, and of Kekchi, show that they had not yet changed *$\phi$ ([ts]) fully to *s*. For example, Zúñiga's (c.1608) Pokomchí dictionary presents entries such as:

> *azbez, atzbez; vatz, vaz* 'older brother' (modern *(w-)as* '(my-)older brother') (PM *$a\phi$ 'elder brother')
> *azeh, azih, atzih, atzeh* 'hermanear, tomar un hermano mayor' [to treat as a brother, to take an older brother]

Of these, Zúñiga said: "some say it with *tz* [i. e. [$\phi$]] *atzeh*, and others with only *z, azeh, azih*, or *atzih*; say it as you please. Most say *azeh*, with *z* [i. e. [s]], and some, with *tz*".

> *litzlotic, lizlotic* ('better with *tz*') 'sparkle'
> *tzab*, or more common *zab* 'addition, balancing weight'
> *tzinuh*, 'more common than' *zinuh* 'oak'
> *tzototzic, zotozic*, ('better the latter') 'round, circular, like a rainbow'
> *tzub; zub* ('*zub* is better') 'the profit from what is sold'

Similar data are found in Pokomam and Kekchi sources (cf. Campbell 1974). The philological evidence that the *$\phi$ > *s* change in these three languages was completed after the writing of these early documents has consequences for Mayan subgrouping. Scholars had previously grouped Pokomam-Pokomchí and Kekchi together as members of a single subgroup, based on the assumption of a shared *$\phi$ > *s* innovation. However, the documentation shows that the change diffused after the three had split up into separate languages; this change is not evidence for a closer classification (Campbell 1973 b, 1974, 1977).

The contribution of Mayan philology is seen in a) documentation of former contrasts now lost, b) evidence for resolving Proto-Mayan phonological reconstruction, c) evidence that sound changes can and have diffused across language boundaries, d) correction of subgrouping, etc. The rewards to historical linguists who exploit the philological resources in Mayan languages are great.

A second particularly valuable feature of Mayan historical linguistics is that it is extremely fertile ground for the investigation of linguistic prehistory and has made many contributions to the understanding of Mesoamerican prehistory and to the Mayan past (see above; Campbell 1978 a; Campbell — Kaufman 1976; Kaufman 1976).

A third feature is the loan words. Mayan languages have both donated and received many loans; the investigation of these has contributed much to an understanding of prehistory, chronology of changes, reconstructions, Mesoamerican areal linguistics, and proposals of distant linguistic kinship (Campbell 1973 a, 1977, 1978 a, 1978 c; Campbell — Kaufman 1976, 1983; Campbell — Kaufman — Smith-Stark 1986; Justeson — Norman — Campbell — Kaufman 1985; Kaufman 1964 a, 1980).

A fourth significant feature of Mayan historical linguistics is its own little-known but impressive history. The study of Mayan languages has been up-to-date and in tune with major developments in linguistics almost from the beginning. Grammars of several Mayan languages were written before those of a number of European languages; for example, we can contrast the early Mayan grammars of Cakchiquel 1550, Quiché 1550, Kekchi 1554, Huastec 1560, Tzeltal 1560, 1571, Mam 1644, Pokomchí 1648, Yucatec Maya 1684, Cholti 1685, and Tzotzil 1688 (cf. Campbell, Ventur et al. 1978) with the earliest of European languages, i. e., German 1573, Dutch 1584, English 1586, Danish 1688, Russian 1696, and Swedish 1696 (Rowe 1974). Relationships among the languages were recognized already in the sixteenth century (cf. for example Diego de Landa 1560 [Tozzer 1941: 30]; see also Fox 1978). Ximénez's (1952 [ca. 1792]: 1) vision of the family relationship, though lacking modern terminology, was particularly clear:

> ... all the languages of this Kingdom of Guatemala, from the languages *tzotzil, zendal* [Tzeltal], *chañabal* [Tojolabal], *coxoh* [Southeastern Tzeltal?], *mame* [Mam], *lacandon, peten* [Itzá], *ixil, q'aq'chiquel* [Cakchiquel], *q'aq'chi* [Kekchí], *poq'omchi* [Pokomchí], to many other languages ... were all a single one, ... it is no miracle, since we see it in our own Castilian language — the languages of Europe being daughters of Latin, which the Italians have corrupted in one way, the French in another, and the Spanish in another ... (Fox 1978: 4).

Johann Severin Vater (1810) recognized the relationship between Huastec and Yucatec, and later other Mayan languages, publishing correct cognates (Adelung 1970 [1816]; Vater 1810).

Otto Stoll was a contemporary of the Neogrammarians and in tune with their movement; he published a number of Mayan "sound laws", saying:

... it is to be hoped ... that we shall be able not only to define the difference between the Quiché languages and the classic Maya, but even to trace out the laws, according to which these differences have realized themselves. (Stoll 1885: 256)

These changes follow regular phonetic laws and bear a strong affinity to the principle of "Lautverschiebung" (Grimm's law), long ago known as an agent of most extensive application in the morphology of the Indo-European languages. (Stoll 1885: 257)

Mayan studies were also inspired by, and contributed to, early work in comparative syntax. Edward Seler, the most celebrated Mesoamericanist of all time, wrote his dissertation in linguistics on Mayan historical grammar (Seler 1887); it was squarely in the tradition of Indo-Europeanists of the time, under their direction, actually predating Delbrück's (1888, 1893) extremely famous studies of Indo-European historical syntax in some of its ideas. Seler is still read with profit to this day. It may be worth reemphasizing that Mayan studies in the last century were both up-to-date with comparative linguistic developments in Europe and contributed to them. They are not the Johnny-come-lately stepchild of modern American anthropology that some may be prone to believe.

Finally, as mentioned above, Mayan contributes much to the stock of natural changes, valuable for testing proposed universals and refining typological considerations.

7) How are remote genetic proposals to be treated? Answer: with distrust and with emphasis on assessment of proposed evidence. No language or group beyond the Mayan family proper has been shown to be related to Mayan; some hypotheses should definitely be discarded; a few others are still worthy of attention. (Campbell 1978 c, 1979; Campbell — Kaufman 1980, 1983; see above.)

8) What is the (proper) role of language contact and areal linguistics? An important lesson from the study of Mayan contacts and the Mesoamerican linguistic area is that much evidence offered in support of several proposed distant genetic relationships is actually the result of borrowing. Thus, attention to borrowing and areal linguistics is important for maintaining a balanced perspective on proposals of distant kinship. Also, as seen above in the case of Pokomam-Pokomchí and Kekchi, an understanding of diffused sound changes is important for checks on the interpretations of shared innovations as evidence for subgroupings.

9) In general, what do Mayanists have to say to other historical linguists? The main message of Mayan historical linguistics is that Mayanists do real historical linguistics successfully with standard methods in a business-as-usual manner and without the need of any special or unique concepts. Mayan studies offer an excellent model from which others can learn; they provide abundant, clear examples of changes, which should not be ignored in any attempts at broader theoretical or methodological claims about language change in general.

## *References*

Adelung, Johann C.
   1970 [1816]   *Mithridates, oder allgemeine Sprachenkunde* 3. (Hildesheim: Georg Olms).
Brown, Cecil H. — Stanley R. Witkowski
   1979      "Aspects of the phonological history of Mayan-Zoquean", *IJAL* 45: 34 – 47.
Campbell, Lyle
   1971      *Historical linguistics and Quichean linguistic prehistory* (Ph. D. dissertation, UCLA).
   1973 a    "Distant genetic relationships and the Maya-Chipaya hypothesis", *Anthropological Linguistics* 15: 3: 113 – 135.
   1973 b    "The philological documentation of a variable rule in the history of Pokom and Kekchi", *IJAL* 39: 44 – 46.
   1973 c    "On glottalic consonants", *IJAL* 39: 44 – 46.
   1974      "Quichean palatalized velars", *IJAL* 40: 132 – 134.
   1977      *Quichean linguistic prehistory* (University of California Publications in Linguistics 81) (Los Angeles: University of California Press).
   1978 a    "Quichean prehistory: Linguistic contributions", in: Nora C. England (ed.), *Papers in Mayan linguistics* (Columbia: Department of Anthropology, University of Missouri), 25 – 54.
   1978 b    "Quichean linguistics and philology", in: William C. McCormack — Stephen A. Wurm (eds.), *World anthropology: Approaches to language, anthropological issues* (The Hague: Mouton), 223 – 233.
   1978 c    "Distant genetic relationship and diffusion: A Mesoamerican perspective", *Proceedings of the International Congress of Americanists* (Paris: Presses Universitaires de Paris), 52: 595 – 605.
   1979      "Middle American languages", in: Lyle Campbell — Marianne Mithun (eds.), *The languages of Native America: Historical and comparative assessment* (Austin: University of Texas Press), 902 – 1000.
   1984 a    "The implications of Mayan historical linguistics for glyphic research", in: John S. Justeson — Lyle Campbell (eds.), *Phoneticism in Mayan hieroglyphic writing* (Institute for Mesoamerican Studies, Publication 9) (Albany: SUNY), 1 – 16.

1984 b  Review of "Mayan glyphs: The verb", by Linda Schele. *Language* 60: 621 – 624.

In press a  "Mayan languages", *Oxford International encyclopedia of linguistics* (Oxford: Oxford University Press).

In press b  "The philological documentation of changes in Mayan languages", in: Jacek Fisiak (ed.), *Historical linguistics and philology* (Berlin: Mouton de Gruyter).

Campbell, Lyle – Terrence Kaufman

1976  "A linguistic look at the Olmecs", *American Antiquity* 41: 80 – 89.

1980  "On Mesoamerican linguistics", *American Anthropologist* 82: 850 – 857.

1983  "Mesoamerican historical linguistics and distant genetic relationship: Getting it straight", *American Anthropologist* 85: 362 – 372.

1985  "Mayan linguistics: Where are we now?", *Annual Review of Anthropology* 14: 187 – 198.

Campbell, Lyle – Terrence Kaufman – Thomas Smith-Stark

1986  "Meso-America as a linguistic area", *Language* 62: 530 – 570.

Campbell, Lyle – Pierre Ventur – Russell Stewart – Brant Gardner

1978  *Bibliography of Mayan Languages and Linguistics* (Institute for Mesoamerican Studies, Publication 3) (Albany: SUNY).

Delbrück, Berthold

1888  *Altindische Syntax* (Syntaktische Forschungen, 5) (Halle an der Saale) [Reprint 1968, Darmstadt: Wissenschaftliche Buchgesellschaft.]

1893  *Vergleichende Syntax der indogermanischen Sprachen* 1 [Part III of Brugmann and Delbrück's Grundriss der vergleichenden Grammatik der indogermanischen Sprachen.] (Strassburg: Karl J. Trübner).

Fox, James Allan

1978  *Proto-Mayan accent, morpheme structure conditions, and velar innovations* [Ph. D. dissertation, University of Chicago].

Fox, James A. – John S. Justeson

1984  "Polyvalence in Mayan hieroglyphic writing", in: Justeson – Campbell (eds.), 17 – 76.

Greenberg, Joseph H.

1970  "Some generalizations concerning glottalic consonants, especially implosives", *IJAL* 36: 123 – 145.

Hamp, Eric P.

1967  "On Maya-Chipayan", *IJAL* 33: 74 – 76.

1970  "Maya-Chipaya and the typology of labials", *Chicago Linguistic Society* 6: 20 – 22.

1971  "On Mayan-Araucanian comparative phonology", *IJAL* 37: 156 – 159.

Justeson, John S. – Lyle Campbell (eds.)

1984  *Phoneticism in Mayan hieroglyphic writing* (Institute for Mesoamerican Studies, Publication 9) (Albany: SUNY).

Justeson, John – William Norman – Lyle Campbell – Terrence Kaufman

1985  "The foreign impact on lowland Mayan language and script", (Middle American Research Institute, Publication 53) (New Orleans: Tulane University).

Kaufman, Terrence S.
1964a    "Materiales lingüísticos para el estudio de las relaciones internas y externas de la familia de idiomas mayanos", in: Evon Vogt (ed.), *Desarrollo cultural de los mayas* (Special publication of the Seminario de Cultura Maya.) (Mexico: Universidad Nacional Autónoma de México), 81–136.
1964b    *Evidence for the Macro-Mayan hypothesis* (Microfilm collection of manuscripts on Middle American cultural anthropology, 55) (University of Chicago Library).
1976    "Archaeological and linguistic correlations in Mayaland and associated areas of Meso-America", *World Archaeology* 8: 101–118.
1980    "Pre-Columbian borrowing involving Huastec", in: K. Klar – M. Langdon – S. Silver (eds.), *American Indian and Indo-European studies: Papers in honor of Madison S. Beeler* (The Hague: Mouton), 101–112.
1986    "Outline of comparative Mayan grammar 1: Morphology and particles", [Paper presented at the First Spring Workshop on Theory and Method in Linguistic Reconstruction, University of Pittsburgh].
Kaufman, Terrence – William Norman
1984    "An outline of Proto-Cholan phonology, morphology, and vocabulary", in: Justeson – Campbell (eds.), 77–166.
Kelley, David
1976    *Deciphering the Maya script* (Austin: University of Texas Press).
Larsen, Thomas W. – William M. Norman
1979    "Correlates of ergativity in Mayan grammar", in: Frans Plank (ed.), *Ergativity: Towards a theory of grammatical relations* (London: Academic Press), 347–370.
McQuown, Norman A.
1942    "Una posible síntesis lingüística macro-mayence", *Mayas y olmecas* (Segunda Mesa Redonda) (México: Sociedad Mexicana de Antropología), 37–38.
1955    "The indigenous languages of Latin America", *American Anthropologist* 57: 501–569.
1956a    "The classification of the Mayan languages", *IJAL* 22: 191–195.
1956b    "Evidence for a synthetic trend in Totonacan", *Language* 32: 78–80.
Norman, William – Lyle Campbell
1978    "Toward a Proto-Mayan syntax: a comparative perspective on grammar", in: Nora C. England (ed.), *Papers in Mayan linguistics* (Columbia: Department of Anthropology, University of Missouri), 25–54.
Olson, Ronald D.
1964    "Mayan affinities with Chipaya of Bolivia, I: Correspondences", *IJAL* 30: 313–324.
1965    "Mayan affinities with Chipaya of Bolivia, II: Cognates" *IJAL* 31: 29–38.

Rowe, John Howland
1974          "Sixteenth and seventeenth century grammars", in: Dell Hymes (ed.),
              *Studies in the history of linguistics: Traditions and paradigms* (Bloo-
              mington: Indiana University Press), 361 – 379.
Seler, Eduard
1887          *Das Konjugationssystem der Mayasprachen* (Berlin: Unger [Th.
              Grimm]). (Also in Seler's *Gesammelte Abhandlungen zur Amerika-
              nischen Sprach- und Altertumskunde* 1.65 – 126 [Berlin: A. Ascher].)
Stark, Louisa
1970          "Mayan affinities with Araucanian", *Chicago Linguistic Society* 6:
              57 – 69.
1972          "Maya-Yunga-Chipayan: a new linguistic alignment", *IJAL* 38:
              119 – 135.
Stoll, Otto
1885          "Supplementary remarks on a grammar of the Cakchiquel language
              of Guatemala", *Proceedings of the American Philosophical Society*
              22: 255 – 268.
Swadesh, Morris
1966          "Porhé y maya", *Anales de Antropología* (México: Universidad Na-
              cional Autónoma de México), 3: 173 – 204.
Tapia Zenteno, Carlos de
1985 [1767[   *Paradigma apologético y noticia de la lengua huasteca: con vocabu-
              lario, catecismo y administración de sacramentos,* edited by René
              Acuña. (Instituto de Investigaciones Filológicas, Gramáticas y dic-
              cionarios 3) (México: Universidad Nacional Autónoma de México).
Thompson, J. Eric S.
1962          *A catalogue of Maya hieroglyphics* (Norman, Oklahoma: University
              of Oklahoma Press).
Tozzer, Alfred M.
1941          "Landa's Relación de las cosas de Yucatán: a translation", *Papers
              of the Peabody Museum of American Archaeology and Ethnology* 4.3
              (Cambridge, Mass.: Peabody Museum, Harvard University).
Vater, Johann Severin
1810          *Untersuchungen über Amerika's Bevölkerung aus dem alten Kontinente*
              (Leipzig: Friedrich Christian Wilhelm Vogel).
Witkowski, Stanley R. – Cecil H. Brown
1978          "Mesoamerica: A proposed phylum", *American Anthropologist* 80:
              942 – 944.
1981          "Mesoamerica: Historical linguistics and distant genetic relation-
              ship", *American Anthropologist* 85: 905 – 911.
Ximénez, Fr. Francisco
1952 [ca. 1702] *Arte de las tres lenguas Cakchiquel, Quiche y Tzutuhil* (Microfilm
              collection of manuscripts on Middle American cultural anthro-
              pology, 36) (University of Chicago Library).
Zúñiga, Dionysio de
ca. 1608      *Diccionario Pocomchi* (Gates collection) (Provo, Utah: Brigham
              Young University Library).

# Summary report:
# Linguistic change and reconstruction methodology in the Austronesian language family

*Robert Blust*

## 1. Introduction

The following survey is intended to provide a bird's-eye view of progress to date in Austronesian comparative linguistics, and to draw attention to some of the outstanding problems that remain to be solved. As such it briefly reviews major developments in the history of this field, and attempts to place the present contributions in a context that will be more meaningful to the general reader. Each of these contributions is accordingly mentioned in the appropriate section. Since Indo-European is the best-studied of all language families, it will serve as a yardstick when general comparisons are sought to provide perspective.

## 2. The use of documentary evidence

Ruhlen (1987) lists some 144 Indo-European languages, of which 93 are Indo-Iranian and 16 are Romance. Yet these 109 languages are represented in the basic Indo-European handbooks by two, or at the most three witnesses: Sanskrit (with occasional references to Avestan) and Latin. Moreover, the oldest Sanskrit texts carry us back over three millennia. Together with Greek documents of over 3,500 years and Latin documents of over 2,000 years age the Sanskrit material has enabled Indo-Europeanists to directly compare languages that were spoken over two millennia ago. Not only is the material old, but following the earliest attested stages it is relatively abundant.

By comparison Ruhlen lists some 959 Austronesian languages, or about 6.66 times the Indo-European total.[1] Documentary material on these languages predating the period of European colonialism is found only rarely, and under special circumstances. The principal cases are as follows:

1) Old Cham.   Modern Cham is spoken in south-central Vietnam and Kampuchea. It is descended from the language spoken in the Indianized state of Champa, which was destroyed by the Vietnamese in 1471. According to Maspéro (1928), the earliest Cham dynasty arose in 192 A.D. in reaction to the colonial ambitions of Han China. Champa was already at that time "une dynastie hindoue ou hindouisée" and the stone inscription of Võcanh which records its ascent was composed entirely in Sanskrit. The earliest dated inscription in Cham bears the date 829 A.D. (Dyen 1971). All told, earlier stages of Cham are recorded in some 75 inscriptions, most of them terse formulaic accounts of dynastic changes and the like.

2) Old Malay.   Modern Malay is spoken in (generally coastal regions of) the Malay peninsula, with dialect variations in eastern Sumatra, several coastal enclaves in Borneo, in the port of Jakarta and in scattered locations throughout the Indonesian archipelago. When the first Dutch sailors arrived in Java in 1596 they found that Malay was the lingua franca of the major entrepôts, and vocabularies recorded by Antonio Pigafetta during the voyage of Magellan show that Malay had already penetrated the central Philippines as a trade language by the early sixteenth century.

The Indianized kingdom of Śrīvijaya, which flourished in southeast Sumatra from about the seventh to tenth centuries, generally is regarded as Malay-speaking. This view is perhaps supported by three stone inscriptions (Kedukan Bukit, Talang Tuwo, and Kota Kapur) from the region which bear the dates 683, 684, and 686 A.D., respectively (Coedès 1930). The language of these inscriptions shows strong resemblances to modern Malay dialects, and is accordingly called "Old Malay". A stone inscription from the site of Gaṇḍasuli in central Java, dated at 832 A.D., appears to be composed in the same, or a very similar, language (de Casparis 1950).

Some Malay inscriptions from the Muslim period dating as far back as the end of the thirteenth century are also known (Teeuw 1961). Beginning around 1500 a number of manuscripts of some literary merit composed in "Classical Malay" have been preserved and studied.

3) Old Javanese. Modern Javanese is spoken over all but the western third of the island of Java, where it yields to Sundanese. With 65 million speakers it is by far the largest of all Austronesian languages.

The term "Old Javanese" is applied to "a language known from texts of a rich variety in form and content and of considerably different periods. They have in common that they were all written in the pre-Moslem era of Javanese history, mainly emanating from the culture of Indianized kingdoms of East Java which existed there at least from about the 9th century to the 15th century" (Uhlenbeck 1964: 108). An extensive Old Javanese-English dictionary is now available (Zoetmulder 1982).

Epigraphic and textual materials dating back several centuries are also available for Old Sundanese, Old Balinese and the languages of a few other ethnic groups in western Indonesia which were strongly affected either by Hinduism or Islam, but on the whole the material is later and/or less extensive than that for Old Cham, Old Malay or Old Javanese.

To summarize, the earliest datable written materials in Austronesian languages owe their existence entirely to Indian cultural influence, and are composed in some version of the Devanagari script. One salient consequence of this fact is the heavy admixture of Sanskrit with native lexical material in the inscriptions and texts. Zoetmulder (1982: IX) notes that "Of the more than 25,500 entries in [the Old Javanese] dictionary, over 12,600, that is almost half the total number, go back, directly or indirectly, to a Sanskrit original." Much the same can be said for the Old Malay material brought together by Coedès. Given this fact, their general brevity and their limited thematic range, the Old Cham and Old Malay materials are of only marginal interest in comparative Austronesian linguistics. The Old Malay data show certain morphological differences from modern Malay which are noteworthy, but they appear to add nothing that is not already richly attested in many other modern languages. The Old Javanese materials are far fuller, and some early researchers such as Kern (who not insignificantly had been trained as a Sanskritist) tended to treat Old Javanese as though it had changed little from Proto-Austronesian. We now know that this view is erroneous. Old Javanese had already changed more than many modern Austronesian languages, and the study of Old Javanese texts, valuable in its own right, contributes little to higher-level reconstruction that cannot be gained from the study of modern Javanese. The one area in which we might find an exception to this statement is that of word-order typology: both modern Malay and modern Javanese are SVO, but earlier stages of both languages tend increasingly toward the verb-initial typology that almost certainly characterized Proto-Austronesian.

In short, the comparative enterprise in Indo-European linguistics was significantly simplified through the use of attested ancestral stages of the modern languages (particularly Indo-Iranian and Romance), while nothing of the kind can be said for Austronesian. As will be noted below, Dempwolff was able to reconstruct a phonological system for "Proto-Austronesian" based only on three languages. However, this was a consequence of patterns of sound change in the Austronesian languages which are quite different from those in Indo-European, rather than of the use of ancient written documents. Particularly for lexical and semantic reconstruction all of the modern Austronesian languages are relevant and important. This is very different from Indo-European, where one can ignore, e. g., Hindi or Italian in higher-level reconstruction, since everything of comparative interest in these languages is found more clearly preserved in Sanskrit or Latin. As a practical consequence the data-processing task in Austronesian comparative linguistics is of an order far exceeding the 6.66 times greater magnitude suggested by the number of modern Indo-European and Austronesian languages.

# 3. Reconstruction methodology

I will take "reconstruction" in the broadest sense to mean historical inferences of any kind, including subgrouping inferences. The major areas to be surveyed in this section are thus: 1) phonological reconstruction, 2) lexical reconstruction, 3) semantic reconstruction, 4) morphological and syntactic reconstruction, and 5) subgrouping. I will use the neutral term "early Austronesian" when it is desirable to avoid commitment to a specific proto-language.

## 3.1 Phonological reconstruction

Despite some important pioneering work among the languages of western Indonesia by the Dutch scholar H. N. van der Tuuk in the 1860s and 1870s, the first attempt at a systematic reconstruction of early Austronesian (called "Original Indonesian") phonology was that of the Swiss linguist Renward Brandstetter (1916).[2] Brandstetter's attention was, however, confined to the languages of island Southeast Asia, arbitrarily excluding the Oceanic region. Moreover, Brandstetter never produced a comparative dictionary with explicit lexical reconstructions.

The first relatively complete reconstruction of early Autronesian phonology that incorporated data from (almost) all major geographical regions was that of the German linguist Otto Dempwolff. In a series of publications that culminated in his *Vergleichende Lautlehre des austronesischen Wortschatzes* (VLAW), Dempwolff laid the foundations for all future work in the phonological comparison of Austronesian languages. To accomplish this task it was necessary for Dempwolff to find some way to conflate the evidence without distorting it. As we have already seen, he could not do this through reference to classical written languages in the way that Indo-Europeanists could use Sanskrit to represent all 93 of the modern Indo-Iranian languages or Latin to represent all 16 of the modern Romance languages. Some other strategy was needed.

Dempwolff found his methodological inspiration in Hans Vaihinger's (1911) philosophy of the "as if". Vaihinger documented the common use of idealizations in the physical sciences to facilitate the recognition of underlying regularities that would often be obscured by a literal account of the facts (e. g., Galileo's laws of terrestrial motion apply only in a complete vacuum, yet he formulated them without access to such an ideal condition and hence without empirical verification). After surveying certain critical aspects of the historical phonology of over 100 Austronesian languages prior to attempting the reconstruction of Proto-Austronesian, Dempwolff concluded that Tagalog (Philippines), Toba Batak (Sumatra), and Javanese (Java) could represent all Austronesian languages for purposes of reconstructing an adequate ancestral phonology. In Vaihinger's terms, the use of three languages to reconstruct the phonology of a prehistoric language with hundreds of attested descendants was a fiction. Dempwolff actually used hundreds of witnesses, but for practical reasons he carried out the reconstruction as if it were based only on Tagalog, Toba Batak and Javanese.

Putting aside Dempwolff's treatment of the "laryngeals" and his omission of the Formosan languages (to which we will return below), his phonological reconstruction was remarkably successful: in volume I (1934) he proposed an "inductive" reconstruction of Proto-Austronesian phonology based ostensibly on just three languages; in volume 2 (1937) he tested his reconstruction "deductively" with data from eight other languages, including five from Melanesia and Polynesia; finally, in volume 3 (1938) he proposed some 2,215 lexical reconstructions. One perhaps ineluctable consequence of Dempwolff's "as if" approach is that no three languages which were considered to be adequate for phonological reconstruction could be expected to be adequate as well for grammatical reconstruction. This shortcoming is not apparent in Dempwolff's work, as he confined himself to the reconstruction of phonology and lexicon. However, Dempwolff's reconstructed lexicon was limited to cognate sets which are represented in at least two of the six languages he called "Indonesian", or in at least one "Indonesian" language and at least one "Melanesian" or Polynesian language. As a result many other widely distributed cognate sets were neglected.

As intimated by the use of double quotes with "Indonesian" and "Melanesian" Dempwolff worked without a well-established subgrouping of the languages he compared. In place of a linguistically justified subgrouping he substituted the geographical labels "Indonesian", "Melanesian" and "Polynesian". Of these only the last corresponds to a linguistically justifiable subgroup. Some of his comparisons are restricted to closely related languages in western Indonesia. Many of these involve Malay and a language (Toba Batak, Javanese, Ngaju Dayak, in some cases Tagalog) which has borrowed fairly extensively from some Malay dialect. Dempwolff's lexicon thus contains reconstructions of widely varying timedepth, some based on cognate sets which probably are the products of borrowing from Malay (an important trade language throughout Indonesia for centuries).

Two of the hallmarks of Dempwolff's phonological reconstruction are his implicit appeal to an "independent evidence" requirement, and his sometimes bothersome preoccupation with symmetry. The independent evidence requirement, though not discussed explicitly, was followed with great consistency. Dempwolff reconstructed a phonological distinction only if it was attested in at least two geographically separated languages. Thus the proto-phoneme now written *j has merged intervocalically with *D in Tagalog, Javanese, Malay, Ngaju Dayak and Malagasy (five of the six "Indonesian" languages he considered in VLAW), but is distinguished by Toba Batak (*j > g, but *D > d), and by the "Melanesian" and Polynesian languages as a whole. Irregularities that were confined to a single language were listed *in extenso*, but never projected into reconstructions.

The only exception to this procedure was made in connection with Proto-Austronesian *T. Javanese, unlike the other languages compared by Dempwolff, has a separate series of retroflex stops /ṭ/ and /ḍ/. In cognate forms all other languages show the regular reflex for *t or *d, but Javanese unpredictably exhibits /t/ or /ṭ/, /d/ or /ḍ/. To account for these facts Dempwolff posited separate Proto-Austronesian retroflex stops now written *T and *D. He believed that Tagalog also distinguishes non-final *d and *D (as d-, -r-; l-, -l- respectively), and thus provides independent evidence for the distinction based most directly on Javanese. However, for *T only Javanese has a distinctive reflex. In this one case Dempwolff posited a proto-phoneme based on a distinction maintained by a single language. His argument for doing so was based on symmetry: since he believed that *D was independently supported and since Javanese has both voiced and voiceless retroflex stops which presumably derive from phonetically parallel sources, it was necessary that he reconstruct *T alongside *D.

Dempwolff's appeal to symmetry in the preceding example illustrates a more general concern with symmetry as an organizing principle in phonological reconstruction. Despite the fact that all of the languages he compared permit initial and final vowels and medial vowel sequences Dempwolff recognized only two disyllabic canonical shapes in reconstructed forms: CVCVC and CVCCVC. He justified this imposition of symmetry on the data by supplying 1. a phonetically vacuous consonant, the "spiritus asper" (written *ʿ), or 2. a homorganic semivowel in reconstructions that would otherwise violate the established canonical shape: e. g. *ʿijaʿ for what is today written *ia '3rd sg.' Largely as a result of such artifices, Dempwolff failed to cope with the "laryngeal" correspondences (glottal stop, h, and zero) in his data. To tie up loose ends in the phonology he was forced to resort to other solutions in the lexicon: the reconstruction of a number of doublets which show parallel differences (e. g., one beginning with *h, the other with *ʿ).

Two major advances have been made over Dempwolff in the reconstruction of phonology. First, Dyen (1953) offered a far more consistent interpretation of the laryngeal correspondences that needed no support from ad hoc devices in the lexicon (this set of Dempwolff's doublets was therefore eliminated). Second, the incorporation of Formosan data in comparisons made it clear that certain distinctions which are widely reflected in the fourteen surviving Formosan languages are old, and probably have been lost through merger elsewhere. The first researchers to recognize the importance of Formosan evidence for phonological reconstruction in Austronesian were Ogawa and Asai (1935). Dyen (1965 a) provides a more exact treatment of the data. Other researchers, most notably Dahl (1976, 1981) have since suggested other interpretations of the Formosan material.

Methodologically Dyen's work differs from that of Dempwolff in certain pivotal respects. Most central to their differences is Dyen's disregard for the independent — evidence requirement. In its place accountability for the correspondences is elevated to a supreme position. The result is a dramatic growth in the number of proto-phonemes recognized by Dyen, as against Dempwolff. Where Dempwolff reconstructed 23 "Proto-Austronesian" consonants Dyen has introduced symbols for over 55, many of them supported by irregularities in only one or two forms in a single language or close-knit subgroup.

In reaction to this "labelling = explanation" approach Wolff (1974, 1982, 1988) has proposed not only that Dyen's phonological addenda be ignored, but that the Proto-Austronesian consonant inventory be reduced through the elimination of at least five distinctions which Dempwolff recognized. The addition of well-supported distinctions based on Formosan evidence brings the total consonant inventory in Wolff's system up 20 phonemes (Wolff 1988: 138).

In addition to phonological reconstruction at the highest levels, reconstructions have, of course, been attempted for various lower-level proto-languages (Proto-Philippines, Proto-Oceanic, Proto-Polynesian, etc.). Space does not permit these to be considered here apart from a single passing remark. With over 450 members, the Oceanic subgroup comprises at least one half of all Austronesian languages. The lexically most conservative Oceanic languages (Motu, the languages of the southeastern Solomons and parts of northern Vanuatu, Trukic, Fijian and Polynesian) have lost original final consonants, but a geographically contiguous chain of languages in western Melanesia which is lexically much less conser-

vative preserves them. It thus not uncommonly happens that a
CVCVC form in western Indonesia or the Philippines is cognate
with a CVCV form in one or more of the lexically more conservative
Oceanic languages, but lacks a known cognate in any of the Oceanic
languages which preserve final consonants. Yet in reconstructing
the Proto-Oceanic form it is clear that a final consonant must be
posited. To do otherwise would imply that final consonants were
lost in Proto-Oceanic only in certain morphemes: to wit, in those
morphemes which failed to survive in an Oceanic language which
preserves final consonants. Such a set of relationships requires a
special extension of the Comparative Method which I have called
"reconstruction from the top down" (Blust 1972 a), and which
Anttila (1972) has called "inverted reconstruction". Inverted reconstruction, to use Antilla's more felicitous alternative, raises an
interesting issue in general scientific method, as it requires the
justification of an inference not primarily by observation, but by
reference to the presumed validity of a predetermined principle (in
this case the regularity of sound change).

## 3.2 Lexical reconstruction

As noted already, Dempwolff's method for coping with a phonological reconstruction involving hundreds of languages imposed an
artificial limitation on lexical reconstruction. Despite this limitation
he posited over 2,200 reconstructed forms. Dempwolff's comparative dictionary remains today the major collection of reconstructions
with supporting evidence available in the Austronesian field. It is
nonetheless badly out of date. Throughout the 1940s, 1950s, and
much of the 1960s the prevailing attitude appeared to have been
that Dempwolff had found most of the interesting comparisons.
Remarkably little effort was made to find new ones. Dyen's work
in comparative phonology, for example, relied almost exclusively
on Dempwolff comparisons.

Beginning in the late 1960s, this situation began to change. Reconstruction on lower levels, particularly work on Proto-Oceanic by
Milke (1968) and Grace (1969) stimulated a renewed search for widely
distributed cognate sets. The first fruit of this effort was a set of 443
new "Proto-Austronesian" etymologies (Blust 1970). In the absence
of a generally accepted subgrouping of the Austronesian languages

no distinctions of time-depth in reconstructions were suggested. Several other publications in the early 1970s increased the number of addenda to Dempwolff to over 770. At about the same time Zorc (1971) compiled an extensive list of Proto-Philippine reconstructions without supporting evidence. Mills (1975) proposed a large number of reconstructions which he attributed to Proto-South Sulawesi (the immediate ancestor of some half dozen languages in central Indonesia) and a smaller number which he attributed to chronologically earlier proto-languages, while Tsuchida (1976) suggested several score new reconstructions based on Formosan: non-Formosan comparisons. The 1980s have seen another surge of activity, most notably Mills (1981), Zorc (1981, 1982, 1985) and Blust (1980a, 1983/84b, 1986, in press). As a result the size of Dempwolff's "Proto-Austronesian" lexicon has grown dramatically (Blust 1980a, 1983/84b and 1986 each contain 443 new reconstructions, while Blust [in press] contains over 700). The composite comparative dictionary that can now be compiled by integrating Dempwolff's comparisons with those proposed more recently stands at well over 5,000 entries, one of the largest for any reconstructed language.

One of the innovations in Blust (1980a) and subsequent publications is the explicit marking of time-depth for every etymon. As a result of closer attention to subgrouping and borrowing it now appears that a number of Dempwolff's reconstructions, perhaps several hundred, will have to be discarded as products of borrowing, or as late innovations in western Indonesia. Dempwolff himself included a number of non-Austronesian loanwords, mostly from Sanskrit, in his comparative dictionary. He marked these as loans, and justified their inclusion on the grounds that they are fully assimilated, and so can be used to illustrate the correspondences found in native material. This convention was adopted also in Blust (1970), but has been abandoned in subsequent publications.

In looking at the reconstructed lexicon for Austronesian languages two things catch one's attention rather soon. One is the large number of doublets that seem to be unavoidable (e. g., *bitaquR, *bitaŋuR 'a tree: Calophyllum inophyllum', *kambiŋ, *kandiŋ 'goat', *nasuk, *Nasu 'cook by boiling', *Rataq, *Ratas 'milk', *tiDuR, *tuDuR 'sleep', etc.). Unlike the doublets that Dempwolff proposed to reconcile irregularities in his treatment of the laryngeals, these doublets in general do not exhibit parallel differences and cannot easily be eliminated by an appeal to early borrowing or to errors in the reconstructions. Whatever the cause of this phenomenon, it is widespread in attested Austronesian languages. The frequency of doublets in Austronesian proto-languages does not therefore necessarily indicate methodological error in reconstruction.

The second noteworthy feature of reconstructed Austronesian lexical material is somewhat more subtle. As early as 1911, the Swiss linguist Renward Brandstetter (1916) recognized that the vocabulary of many languages in Indonesia and the Philippines shows patterns of recurrent association between the last syllable of many morphemes (usually the last -CVC) and a global meaning. These patterns of sound-meaning association are submorphemic, as they are based not on paradigmatic contrast, but entirely on recurrent association. Brandstetter referred to the submorphemic element in question as a "root" (Wurzel). The issue of roots was neglected by Dempwolff, and not treated seriously again until the appearance of Blust (1988), where Brandstetter's central claim is vindicated, though his methods are found wanting. Zorc has capably taken up the matter of the root in his contribution to this volume. His paper touches, albeit schematically, on most of the important issues. Because space limitations prevented him from providing background information for the general reader, however, his discussion may be difficult to follow.

The recognition of roots creates a set of relationships that allows an unorthodox approach to lexical reconstruction. Because of its general methodological interest this approach should be mentioned at least in passing.

In Blust (1988) care is taken to segregate cognate forms which contain a common root from non-cognate forms which contain the same root (e. g., numerous reflexes of *gilap* 'lustre, shine' vs. such isolated forms as Tagalog *kisláp* 'sparkle' or Malay *relap* 'glint, flash'). Of 2,561 etymologically independent root attestations cited in that source, more than 1,800 are morpheme isolates ( = non-cognate forms which share a common root). This still growing corpus of material invites comparison, as many morpheme isolates in the past have eventually turned out to be members of previously unrecognized cognate sets. Conventional methods call for the comparison of at least two languages simultaneously. With the recognition of a relatively small number of roots, however, this situation is changed fundamentally.[3] A dictionary can be scanned for morphemes which contain a known root, and when these are found they can be checked immediately against the corpus of roots collected to date. If the newly recognized

form belongs to an established cognate set, it provides no new etymologically independent support for the root in question. If the newly
recognized form does not belong to an established cognate set and is
not cognate with any previously recognized morpheme isolate, it does
provide etymologically independent support for the root in question
but does not increase the corpus of established reconstructions that
contain a root. If, however, the newly recognized form does not belong
to an established cognate set, and is cognate with a previously recognized morpheme isolate, a new cognate set must be recognized and
a reconstruction provided. In other words, the recognition of roots
creates the possibility of applying the Comparative Method for purposes of reconstruction to one language at a time. This is not simply
an abstract possibility, but one which has already yielded rich results,
especially in Blust (in press). Alongside the increased reconstructional
power which root theory allows, however, is an inescapable increase
in the role that convergence must play in creating recurrent correspondences. The balance of gains and losses in applying this extension
of the Comparative Method is discussed in Blust (1988).

## 3.3 Semantic reconstruction

Under the heading "semantic reconstruction", I will include any
comparative work in which a reconstructed form is assumed and
the primary research task is the determination of its meaning.
Moreover, to distinguish more clearly semantic reconstruction from
morphological or syntactic reconstruction, I will restrict my use of
the term to lexical semantics. If the Austronesian language family
is representative, interest in semantic reconstruction would seem to
develop later than interest in phonological reconstruction. Brandstetter and Dempwolff paid scant attention to the reconstruction of
meaning, and in Dyen's work reconstructed forms typically are not
glossed at all. Capell (1938/1939) is perhaps the earliest publication
in Austronesian linguistics which is concerned with the original
meaning of a widely distributed form with varied semantic reflexes.

Virtually all work concerned with semantic reconstruction in the
Austronesian language family has appeared within the past 20 years.
Blust (1972 b, 1980 b, 1987), and Pawley (1982, 1985) are the principal
publications which take the reconstruction of meaning as their pri-

mary focus. Lichtenberk (1986) challenges the conclusions of Pawley (1982) and raises some points of general methodological interest.

With regard to method Blust (1972 b) addresses the issue of how to justify the combination of disparate meanings under a single reconstructed gloss. Reflexes of *qa(R)ta* mean 'human being' in a number of widely separated Austronesian languages; in a number of other widely separated languages reflexes of an identical form mean 'slave'. Should the comparativist reconstruct two homophonous forms or a single polysemous form? Arguments are presented for the latter alternative, among them the recurrence of a similar semantic variation with an etymologically unrelated base *qulun*.

Other publications, as Pawley (1985) and Blust (1987), are concerned with establishing what might be called a "semantic field" approach to the reconstruction of meaning. Details cannot be discussed further here.

## 3.4 Morphological and syntactic reconstruction

Dempwolff (1934) maintained that the Austronesian languages lack a common grammatical structure, and he implied that grammatical reconstruction would therefore prove fruitless. It is not surprising, then, that the earliest work in the comparative syntax of Austronesian languages concentrated on the Polynesian subgroup, where a similar syntactic type is found throughout, and the languages on the whole are exceptionally well-documented. The differences of detail between Polynesian languages which have tended to attract theoretical attention have to do with the nature of subject marking: some languages are ergative, others accusative (cf., e. g., Hohepa 1969).

The major contributions to Polynesian comparative syntax are Pawley (1970), Clark (1976), and Chung (1978). Methodologically the contributions of Pawley and Clark can be seen as extensions of the Comparative Method: essentially they take as their point of departure the comparison of cognate grammatical forms. The work of Chung, on the other hand, is concerned primarily with the comparison of structures, with little reference to the cognation or non-cognation of the morphemes that manifest them.

The major publications on Proto-Austronesian syntax are Wolff (1973, 1979) and Starosta—Pawley—Reid (1982). Wolff reconstructs a Proto-Austronesian system of verbal affixation which functioned to mark grammatical "focus", much as is found in Tagalog and other Philippine languages today. Starosta, Pawley and Reid, on the other hand, argue that the affixes in question originally permitted several types of nominalization, and were only later reinterpreted as verbal affixes in Philippine languages. The present contribution of Gibson and Starosta takes up the issue of ergative/ accusative originally developed in the context of Polynesian comparative linguistics and later in the context of Philippine linguistics (Starosta 1987). It concludes that Polynesian ergativity continues an unbroken tradition from Proto-Austronesian to such modern languages as Samoan and Maori. Methodologically it shares far more with the work of Chung than with that of Pawley or Wolff in that it is primarily concerned with the comparison of structures, with only tangential regard to the grammatical morphemes that manifest them.

### 3.5 Subgrouping

As noted earlier, Dempwolff began his *magnum opus* without a linguistically justified subgrouping of the languages he compared. Nonetheless, one of the major conclusions to emerge from vol. 2 of VLAW (1937) was that the Polynesian languages constitute a subgroup with most of the languages of Melanesia and Micronesia. Dempwolff called this collection of over 450 languages "Melanesisch".

Dempwolff's subgrouping conclusion was supported by Milke (1958 and subsequent publications), who renamed the group in question "Oceanic", and by Grace (1955, 1969). In more recent years a number of other scholars, including Pawley (1972, 1973), Blust (1972 a, 1978) and Ross (1988) have contributed to the establishment of the Oceanic subgroup of Austronesian languages. The Oceanic hypothesis is justified by a uniquely shared set of phonological innovations (merger of *$*b$* and *$*p$*, *$*g$* and *$*k$*, *$*d$* and *$*r$*, *$*s$*, *$*c$* and *$*z/Z$*, and *$*e$* and *$*-aw$*, prenasalized reflexes of initial stops in certain morphemes), and by some exclusively shared grammatical characteristics which are assumed to be innovations.

In 1965, Isidore Dyen published the most comprehensive classification of the Austronesian languages ever undertaken, and at the same time the most significant test of the value of lexicostatistics as a tool of historical linguistics. On the basis of his interpretation of a matrix of computer-generated pair-wise lexicostatistical percentages for some 245 Austronesian languages, Dyen found that the Austronesian language family divides into 40 primary branches, of which 34 are located in or near Melanesia. He concluded, contrary to all previous research in linguistics and ethnology, that the Austronesian homeland was near New Guinea, and that Austronesian speakers had spread thence both eastward into Polynesia and westward into Indonesia, the Philippines and Taiwan.

Grace (1966) quickly drew attention to the conflict between Dyen's lexicostatistical results, which assigned many languages in Melanesia to primary branches of Austronesian, and the qualitative evidence which indicated that these same languages were Oceanic.

In the 1970s, several linguists began to assemble qualitative evidence for subgrouping the Austronesian languages on the highest levels. Dahl (1976) and Blust (1977) both argue that the first split was between one or more subgroups in Taiwan and the rest of Austronesian. In Blust (1977), the non-Formosan languages are collectively designated "Malayo-Polynesian". Harvey (1982) adopts a similar view, but believes that one Formosan language (Amis) belongs in the Malayo-Polynesian group.

Both phonological and grammatical evidence supports a Formosan: Malayo-Polynesian dichotomy. Phonologically, all Malayo-Polynesian languages merge Proto-Austronesian $*C$ and $*t$, $*N$ and $*n$. In addition, $*S$ evidently weakened to [h] in final position in all Malayo-Polynesian languages, subsequently disappearing in final position in all languages except Itbayaten (geographically one of the two closest Malayo-Polynesian languages to Taiwan). Grammatically, certain differences in the formal relationship of subject and possessive pronouns between Formosan and Malayo-Polynesian languages can be shown to be almost certain innovations in the Malayo-Polynesian group (Blust 1977).

The goal of Dyen's contribution to the present volume is ostensibly to show that the distribution of exclusively shared cognates is likely to correspond to valid linguistic subgroups. He coins the term "homomery" for a collection of cognate sets "distributed over exactly the same set of languages", and applies the procedure both to Austronesian and to Indo-European languages in an effort to establish higher-level subgroupings. It is noteworthy that "the same set of languages" is defined intuitively in at least the Austronesian case, since the existence of both Formosan and Philippine subgroups is simply assumed, and few if any of the cognate distributions Dyen decribes involve exactly the same languages (as opposed to the same "set of languages"). Moreover, he dismisses significant evidence which is contrary to his position with a wave of the hand. Nonetheless, Dyen has assembled an interesting corpus of data in his paper which is valuable and deserving of further study.

In Dyen's view, traditional subgrouping on the basis of exclusively shared innovations begs the question as to whether a given diagnostic feature is an innovation or a retention. The advantage of working with "homomeries" is that they allow the comparativist "freedom from the necessity of identifying the innovations on which a subgrouping hypothesis is based." But in reality Dyen has simply shifted the probabilism which all good comparativists have traditionally associated with the retention:innovation distinction from putative exclusively shared innovations to putative exclusively shared distributions. One can only wonder why he has taken such pains to reinvent historical linguistics with a terminology that few can be expected to adopt.

## 4. Studies of change

There have been many studies of change in Austronesian languages, and only a few of these can be mentioned here.

One of the earliest studies of phonological change in a typologically aberrant Austronesian language is that of Dyen (1949), which derived the nine vowel system of Trukese (Micronesia) from Dempwolff's reconstructed four vowel system through a series of conditioned changes. Another is that of Blust (1969), where an attempt was made both to document and to explain the origin of a series of phonemic voiced aspirates in Kelabit (northern Sarawak).

At least since Codrington (1885) the Austronesian languages of Melanesia have been roughly divided into two groups: "typical" languages (viz., those with a relatively high concentration of widely-distributed characteristics), and "aberrant" languages (those with a relatively low concentration of widely-distributed characteristics). The characteristic most commonly used to distinguish typical from aberrant languages is cognate vocabulary, though typological features both in phonology and in grammar have also figured in the often impressionistic distinction.

Grace's paper in the present volume focuses on some of the more extreme examples of "aberrant" Melanesian languages. His conclusion that the rate of linguistic change can, and does, vary widely is well supported both by documentary and by inferential evidence. But unquestionably the most original and theoretically significant contribution of his paper is the extraordinary comparative picture he presents for Canala and Grand Couli, two "closely related" languages of southern New Caledonia, and the explanation he proposes for the correspondences between them. This is a paper which truly challenges some of our basic assumptions about language change, and which will force some of us to rethink important aspects of our discipline.


# 5. Conclusion

Every language family can contribute to the development of a general historical linguistics, but each undoubtedly will present certain problems which are distinctive, if not unique to it. Apparent violations of the scientific paradigm of historical linguistics such as those described by Grace may indicate that traditional formulations of the Comparative Method have not been sufficiently general to accommodate the description of language change in small-scale multilingual societies. The papers in the present section can only sample some of the variety of comparative work in progress on the Austronesian languages. Hopefully they give a faithful picture of the distinctive problems of this large and challenging field, and at the same time strike an occasional note of familiarity for comparativists working with other language families.

*Notes*

1. My own estimate is about 825 languages, or 5.73 times the Indo-European total.
2. The essays in Brandstetter (1916) were originally published in German between 1910 and 1915.
3. The 2,561 root attestations in Blust (1988) are assigned to just 231 roots.

## References

Anttila, Raimo
1972        *An introduction to historical and comparative linguistics* (New York: Macmillan).
Blust, Robert
1969        "Some new Proto-Austronesian trisyllables", *Oceanic Linguistics* 8: 85—104.
1970        "Proto-Austronesian addenda", *Oceanic Linguistics* 9: 104—162.
1972 a      "Proto-Oceanic addenda with cognates in non-Oceanic Austronesian languages: A preliminary list", *Working Papers in Linguistics* 4.1: 1—43 (Honolulu: Department of Linguistics, University of Hawaii).
1972 b      "Note on PAN *qa(R)(CtT)a 'outsiders, alien people'", *Oceanic Linguistics* 11: 166—171.
1977        "The Proto-Austronesian pronouns and Austronesian subgrouping: A preliminary report", *Working Papers in Linguistics* 9.2: 1—15 (Honolulu, Department of Linguistics, University of Hawaii).
1978        *The Proto-Oceanic palatals* (The Polynesian Society, Memoir 43) (Wellington: New Zealand).
1980 a      "Austronesian etymologies", *Oceanic Linguistics* 19: 1—181.
1980 b      "Early Austronesian social organization: The evidence of language", (with comments and reply) *Current Anthropology* 21: 205—247.
1983/1984 a "More on the position of the languages of eastern Indonesia", *Oceanic Linguistics* 22/23: 1—28.
1983/1984 b "Austronesian etymologies II", *Oceanic Linguistics* 22/23: 29—149.
1986        "Austronesian etymologies III", *Oceanic Linguistics* 25: 1—123.
1987        "Lexical reconstruction and semantic reconstruction: The case of Austronesian 'house' words", *Diachronica* 4.1-2: 79—106.
1988        *Austronesian root theory: An essay on the limits of morphology* (Studies in Language companion series 19) (Amsterdam: John Benjamins).
in press    "Austronesian etymologies IV", *Oceanic Linguistics*.
Brandstetter, Renward
1916        *An introduction to Indonesian linguistics* [translated by C. O. Blagden] (London: The Royal Asiatic Society).
Capell, Arthur
1938/1939   "The word 'mana': A linguistic study", *Oceania* 9: 89—96.
Casparis, J. G. de
1950        *Inscripties uit de Çailendra-tijd* [Inscriptions from the time of Śailendra] (Jakarta).
Chung, Sandra
1978        *Case marking and grammatical relations in Polynesian* (Austin: University of Texas Press).
Clark, Ross
1976        *Aspects of Proto-Polynesian syntax* (Auckland: Linguistic Society of New Zealand).
Codrington, Robert H.
1885        *The Melanesian languages* (Oxford: Clarendon Press).

Coedès, Georges
1930        "Les inscriptions Malaises de Śrīvijaya", *Bulletin de l'École Française d'Extrême Orient* 30: 29—80.
Dahl, Otto
1976 [1973]   2nd, rev. ed. *Proto-Austronesian* (Scandinavian Institute of Asian Studies monograph series 15) (Lund).
1981        *Early phonetic and phonemic changes in Austronesian* (Oslo: Universitetsforlaget).
Dempwolff, Otto
1934—1938   *Vergleichende Lautlehre des austronesischen Wortschatzes.* 1. *Induktiver Aufbau einer indonesischen Ursprache* (Zeitschrift für Eingeborenensprachen, Suppl. 15 [1934]). 2. *Deduktive Anwendung des Urindonesischen auf austronesische Einzelsprachen* (Zeitschrift für Eingeborenensprachen, Suppl. 17 [1937]). 3. *Austronesisches Wörterverzeichnis* (Zeitschrift für Eingeborenensprachen, Suppl. 19 [1938]). (Berlin: Reimer).
Dyen, Isidore
1949        "On the history of the Trukese vowels", *Language* 25: 420—436.
1953        *The Proto-Malayo-Polynesian laryngeals* (Baltimore: Linguistic Society of America).
1965 a      "Formosan evidence for some new Proto-Austronesian phonemes", *Lingua* 14: 285—305.
1965 b      "A lexicostatistical classification of the Austronesian languages", *International Journal of America Linguistics, Memoir* 19 (Vol. 31, No. 1).
1971        *The Chamic languages*, in: Thomas A. Sebeok (ed.), *Current Trends in Linguistics* 8: *Linguistics in Oceania* (The Hague: Mouton), 200—210.
Grace, George W.
1955        "Subgrouping of Malayo-Polynesian: A report of tentative findings", *American Anthropologist* 57: 337—339.
1966        "Austronesian lexicostatistical classification: A review article", *Oceanic Linguistics* 5: 13—31.
1969        "A Proto-Oceanic finder list", *Working Papers in Linguistics* 1(2): 39—84 (Honolulu: University of Hawaii).
Harvey, Mark
1982        "Subgroups in Austronesian", in: Amran Halim et al. (eds.), *Papers from the Third International Conference on Austronesian Linguistics* 2 (Pacific Linguistics C 75) (Canberra, Australian National University), 47—99.
Hohepa, Patrick W.
1969        "The accusative-to-ergative drift in Polynesian languages", *Journal of the Polynesian Society* 78: 295—329.
Lichtenberk, Frantisek
1986        "Leadership in Proto-Oceanic society: Linguistic evidence", *Journal of the Polynesian Society* 95: 341—356.
Maspéro, Georges
1928        *Le royaume de Champa* (Paris & Bruxelles: G. van Oest).

Milke, Wilhelm
1958        "Zur inneren Gliederung und geschichtlichen Stellung der ozea-
            nisch-austronesischen Sprachen", *Zeitschrift für Ethnologie* 82: 58 –
            62.
1968        "Proto-Oceanic addenda", *Oceanic Linguistics* 7: 147 – 171.
Mills, Roger F.
1975        *Proto-South Sulawesi and Proto-Austronesian phonology* 1 – 2 (Ann
            Arbor: University Microfilms International).
1981        "Additional addenda", in: Robert A. Blust (ed.), *Historical linguistics
            in Indonesia* 1 (NUSA: Linguistic studies in Indonesian and languages
            in Indonesia 10) (Jakarta), 59 – 82.
Ogawa, Naoyoshi – Erin Asai
1935        *The myths and traditions of the Formosan native tribes* (Taipei).
Pawley, Andrew
1970        "Grammatical change and reconstruction in Polynesia and Fiji", in:
            Stephen A. Wurm – Donald C. Laycock (eds.), *Pacific linguistic
            studies in honour of Arthur Capell* (Pacific Linguistics C 13) (Can-
            berra: Australian National University), 301 – 367.
1972        "On the internal relationships of eastern Oceanic languages", in: R.
            C. Green – M. Kelly (eds.), *Studies in Oceanic Culture History* 3
            (Pacific Anthropological Records 13) (Honolulu: Bernice P. Bishop
            Museum), 1 – 142.
1973        "Some problems in Proto-Oceanic grammar", Papers of the First
            International Conference on Comparative Austronesian Linguistics,
            1974 – Oceanic. *Oceanic Linguistics* 12: 103 – 188.
1982        "Rubbish-man commoner, big-man chief? Linguistic evidence for
            hereditary chieftainship in Proto-Oceanic society", in: Jukka Siikala
            (ed.), *Oceanic Studies: Essays in honour of Aarne A. Koskinen* (Hel-
            sinki: The Finnish Anthropological Society), 33 – 52.
1985        "Proto-Oceanic terms for 'person': A problem in semantic recon-
            struction", in: Veneeta Z. Acson – Richard L. Leed (eds.), *For Gordon
            H. Fairbanks* (Oceanic Linguistics Special Publication No. 20) (Hon-
            olulu: University of Hawaii Press), 92 – 104.
Ross, Malcolm David
1988        *Proto-Oceanic and the Austronesian languages of western Melanesia*
            [unpublished Ph. D. dissertation] (Canberra: Pacific Linguistics C
            98, Australian National University).
Ruhlen, Merritt
1987        *A guide to the world's languages* (Stanford: Stanford University
            Press).
Starosta, Stanley
1987        *Three views of Tagalog ergativity* (Calgary: Department of Linguis-
            tics, University of Calgary).
Starosta, Stanley – Andrew K. Pawley – Lawrence A. Reid
1982        "The evolution of focus in Austronesian", in: Amran Halim et al.
            (eds.), *Papers from the Third International Conference on Austronesian
            Linguistics* (Pacific Linguistics C 75) (Canberra: Australian National
            University), 145 – 170.

Teeuw, A.
1961        *A critical survey of studies on Malay and Bahasa Indonesia* (Koninklijk
            Instituut voor Taal-, Land- en Volkenkunde, Bibliographical Series
            5) (The Hague: Nijhoff).
Tsuchida, Shigeru
1976        *Reconstruction of Proto-Tsouic phonology* (Studies of Languages and
            Culture of Asia and Africa, monograph No. 5) (Tokyo: Institute for
            the Study of Languages and Cultures of Asia and Africa).
Uhlenbeck, E. M.
1964        *A critical survey of studies on the languages of Java and Madura*
            (Koninklijk Instituut voor Taal-, Land- en Volkenkunde, Biblio-
            graphical Series 7) (The Hague: Nijhoff).
Vaihinger, Hans
1911        *Die Philosophie des Als Ob. System der theoretischen, praktischen und
            religiösen Fiktionen der Menschheit auf Grund eines idealistischen
            Positivismus* (Berlin).
Wolff, John U.
1973        "Verbal inflection in Proto-Austronesian", in: Andrew B. Gonzalez
            (ed.), *Parangal kay Cecilio Lopez: Essays in honor of Cecilio Lopez
            on his seventy-fifth birthday* (Philippine Journal of Linguistics, special
            monograph issue no. 4) (Quezon City: Linguistic Society of the
            Philippines), 71—94.
1974        "Proto-Austronesian *r and *d", [First International Conference on
            Comparative Austronesian Linguistics, 1974 — Proto-Austronesian
            and Western Austronesian], *Oceanic Linguistics* 13: 77—121.
1979        "Verbal morphology and verbal sentences in Proto-Austronesian",
            in: Paz Buenaventura Naylor (ed.), *Austronesian Studies: Papers from
            the Second Eastern Conference on Austronesian Languages* (Ann
            Arbor: Center for South and South-east Asian Studies, University
            of Michigan), 153—168.
1982        "Proto-Austronesian *c, *z, *g and *T", in: Amran Halim et al.
            (eds.), *Papers from the Third International Conference on Austronesian
            Linguistics* (Pacific Linguistics C 75) (Canberra, Australian National
            University), 1—30.
1988        "The PAN consonant system", in: Richard McGinn (ed.), *Studies in
            Austronesian linguistics* (Ohio University Monographs in Interna-
            tional Studies, Southeast Asia Series, 76) (Athens, Ohio), 125—147.
Zoetmulder, P. J.
1982        *Old Javanese-English dictionary* 1—2 (Koninklijk instituut voor
            taal-, land- en volkenkunde) (The Hague: Nijhoff).
Zorc, R. David Paul
1971        *Proto-Philippine finder list* [typescript].
1981        *Core etymological dictionary of Filipino* 2: *k.* (Manila: De La Salle
            University).
1982        *Core etymological dictionary of Filipino* 3: *d,g,h.* (Manila: De La
            Salle University).
1985        *Core etymological dictionary of Filipino* 4 (Manila: De La Salle
            University).

# The "aberrant" (vs. "exemplary") Melanesian languages

*George W. Grace*

Otto Dempwolff's *Vergleichende Lautlehre des austronesischen Wortschatzes* (Dempwolff 1934 — 38) has long been recognized as the cornerstone of comparative Austronesian linguistics. One rather remarkable feature of this work is that Dempwolff reconstructs the phonemic system of Proto-Austronesian as well as a substantial amount of Proto-Austronesian vocabulary from the data of just three languages: Tagalog, Toba-Batak, and Javanese. This fact has frequently been commented upon. However, it is customary to point out that his reason for working from just three languages was that it simplified the presentation of his argument, that he had done extensive previous research in which he examined the available evidence for a very large number of Austronesian languages, and that in fact he had anticipated most of the details of the reconstruction in earlier works. He himself made it clear that it was only on the basis of this extensive prior research that he was able to choose three languages which, among them, provided all of the phonemic distinctions required for the proto-language.

All of these qualifications are valid, but still there is another significant fact here. Whether or not Dempwolff actually did make a reconstruction of Proto-Austronesian which was adequate to account for the several hundred Austronesian languages — or at least what was known of them at the time — from the evidence of only three of them is beside the point. What is so remarkable is that he demonstrated that it would have been possible to do so. That is tantamount to saying that if all of the Austronesian languages except three had disappeared without a trace, he would still have been able to make as complete and accurate a reconstruction of Proto-Austronesian phonology as he was able to make with the evidence of hundreds of them — provided, of course, that the three which had survived had been the right three.

On the other hand, it is easy to think of sets of three Austronesian languages which would have provided virtually no information on the characteristics of the proto-language. To design just one ex-ample, consider Yapese of Micronesia, any language of southern New Caledonia, and (in order not to stack the deck by picking three languages all of which might belong to the same subgroup of Austronesian), the Atayal language of Taiwan. I doubt very seri-ously that any significant start whatever toward the reconstruction of Proto-Austronesian could have been made from those three languages. It is doubtful, indeed, that if these had been the only surviving Austronesian languages, anyone would ever have imag-ined that they were even related to one another.

The point is that some languages provide much better testimony as to the nature of their ancestral stages than do others. I used to refer to the languages which provide the best testimony as "well-behaved" languages and those which provide the poorest testimony as "badly-behaved", but I later decided that those terms might sound flippant. Since then, I have been using the terms "exemplary" and "aberrant".

In a family such as Austronesian, with hundreds of member languages, it is probably not surprising that there are a large number of languages which could be counted as exemplary and a large number which could be counted as aberrant. In Austronesian, we can find enough exemplary languages to enable us to do a rather gratifying amount of reconstruction at several levels, which we do by relying almost exclusively on the exemplary languages and pretty much ignoring the aberrant ones. But unless aberrant languages are a peculiarly Austronesian phenomenon, it would seem that the reconstructability of the proto-languages of language families or subgroups consisting of small numbers of languages must be a matter of luck — a matter of whether an adequate sample of exemplary languages are included among the languages which have survived.

But what are aberrant languages? What is the nature of their aberrancy, and under what conditions does it arise? I have for some time been proclaiming that if we are serious about understanding the processes of linguistic change and of providing an adequate foundation for diachronic linguistics, we must take the behavior of aberrant languages as well as that of exemplary languages into account.

Actually, to suggest that every Austronesian language falls into one of two types is certainly an oversimplification. It would be somewhat more accurate to speak of aberrancy as a matter of degree and to imagine a scale such that every Austronesian language could in principle have its degree of aberrancy plotted on the scale. In fact, I have no doubt that when we know enough, we may well find that there are many different kinds of aberrancy and that it may be difficult or fruitless to attempt to reduce them all even to one scale. However, since I do not know how to subclassify aberrant languages either by degree or by kind, I will for the moment speak of aberrancy as if it were a single phenomenon which was either present or absent in a language.

My title specifies aberrant *Melanesian* languages. Although the aberrant Austronesian languages are not limited to Melanesia, it is generally acknowledged that they are more numerous there than in any other Austronesian area. In addition, one of the two principal explanations offered for the Melanesian languages which I am labelling "aberrant" is not applicable to any other Austronesian languages. According to that explanation the Melanesian languages are mixed languages.

But what is it for a language to be aberrant? Well, what I have in mind is aberrancy from the point of view of comparative-historical linguistics: a language whose history does not conform to the expectations of comparative-historical linguistics is an aberrant language. However, before entering into the question of what particular expectations might be involved, I will use the term loosely here to refer to languages whose history either does not conform to these expectations or has proven sufficiently difficult to reconstruct that we do not know whether or not it conforms to them. The difficulties may concern either the changes which the language has undergone since it separated from its nearest relatives or the problem of which languages in fact *are* its nearest relatives. Indeed one of these kinds of difficulty is likely to lead to the other.

In one sense, all of the Melanesian languages might be said to be aberrant if certain scholars — I have in mind particularly Sidney Ray and Arthur Capell, who believed that they were all mixed languages — were right. But before going on, I had better take a moment to explain that the term "Melanesian languages" is customarily used to refer to those languages of geographical Melanesia which belong to the Austronesian language family, but not to the Polynesian subgroup (or sub-subgroup, or sub-sub-subgroup, etc.) of that family.

This may require a bit of additional explanation for anyone who is not familiar with the historical background. An important part of the background is an assumption that the original human inhabitants of Melanesia belong to a different race (a race often described as "Negroid") from the inhabitants of Indonesia, Micronesia, and Polynesia. This assumption may be traced back at least as far as the eighteenth century. Some people suppose these Melanesian peoples originally to have spoken Papuan languages, with the languages which are now called Melanesian having been introduced by invaders from Indonesia. Accordingly, the term "Melanesian language" would apply to all of the Austronesian languages of geographical Melanesia if it were not for the fact that there are also some Polynesian languages spoken in that area whose speakers seem to have arrived more recently from geographical Polynesia. These languages are the so-called "Polynesian Outliers".

The prevailing view among Austronesianists today is that there is no genetic grouping comprising just those languages which we call Melanesian. Rather, according to this view, there is a subgroup of Austronesian called "Oceanic" which includes all of the Melanesian languages but also includes all of the Polynesian languages and most of the languages of Micronesia. However, as we have seen, some influential earlier scholars believed that the Melanesian languages represented a fundamentally distinct historical phenomenon — that they were mixed languages, the result of contact between indigenous Papuan languages and the Austronesian languages of Indonesian colonists. They were regarded as having some Austronesian "content", but this content was always small in comparison with that of Indonesian languages.

I said above that if those scholars who believed that they were all mixed languages were right, all of the Melanesian languages might be said to be in some sense aberrant. However, even they saw some as more aberrant, or as they would put it, as having less Austronesian content, than others. Their perception of the nature of these "mixed" languages is worth reviewing here. I believe that the following propositions (based particularly upon Ray 1926) fairly represent what they perceived to be the facts:

1. Only a small part of the vocabulary of any Melanesian language is shared with any other languages.

2. Virtually all of the vocabulary that any Melanesian languages share with one another they also share with Indonesian languages.

3. The reverse is not true: there is much vocabulary which is widely shared among Indonesian languages which they do not share with any Melanesian language.

4. Some Melanesian languages have significantly more cognates with other Austronesian languages, both those spoken in Melanesia and those spoken elsewhere, than do others.

5. These cognates — i. e., the vocabulary items which have been retained from Proto-Austronesian or subsequent proto-languages — tend to exhibit more straightforward sound correspondences in some languages than in others, and it is generally the languages which show the smallest numbers of retentions which also show the most complex sound changes.

Ray does not say specifically that the sound changes in the languages of the last category also tend to show the greatest numbers of apparent irregularities, but others would be willing to add that judgment.

To the extent that the first three claims are valid, we might be justified in regarding all of the Melanesian languages as aberrant. However, the first two claims, at least as I have worded them here, seem overstated, although not entirely false. In any case, it is mainly the other claims that will concern us — those which suggest that different Melanesian languages are aberrant in different degrees.

I defined an "aberrant" language as one that does not conform to our expectations — i. e., to the assumptions of comparative-historical linguistics. But what are these assumptions that have been disappointed?

One assumption which I believe is implicit in many of our decisions, though rarely made explicit, is that there is some degree of regularity in the rates at which languages change. But I think it is apparent that languages change at significantly different rates (cf. Grace 1985 for further discussion), or at least that some aspects of them do, and that these differences raise serious concerns about the reconstruction of proto-languages.

Lexicostatistical glottochronology is the one linguistic approach which explicitly makes the assumption that at least one kind of linguistic change proceeds at a constant (within limits) rate. There is a well-known genetic classification of the Austronesian languages made by Isidore Dyen (1965) entirely on the basis of lexicostatistics. The results of this classification differ very conspicuously from the prevailing view of Austronesian internal relations which I referred to above. If the prevailing view is right, the most likely explanation for the discrepancy of the lexicostatistical results is significant differences in the rates at which the languages involved have changed — at least in the aspect measured by lexicostatistics.

Let us consider the conclusions of Dyen's study as they concern us here. The relevant conclusions were that, according to the cognate percentages for the lexicostatistical test list, Austronesian has 40 branches, of which 24 consist of a single language each, and of which 29 consist only of "Melanesian" languages (as we have been using the term). An additional eight branches are represented only in areas adjacent to Melanesia (Western New Guinea, the Moluccas, and Micronesia). Only two are restricted to areas distant from Melanesia (namely, a group of two languages on Taiwan and Enggano, off the coast of Sumatra).

The largest of the branches, called "the Malayopolynesian Linkage", consists of 129 languages. It includes almost all of the Austronesian languages outside the Oceanic area as well as all of the Polynesian languages, but only eight of the 72 Melanesian languages used in the study.

Thus, of the Melanesian languages, while eight belong to this largest branch, the remaining 64 Melanesian languages in the study constitute 29 of the 40 branches of Austronesian. These 29 branches have from a minimum of one to a maximum of seven members each.

Now I mentioned above that in the prevailing view there is a subgroup of Austronesian called "Oceanic" which includes all of the Melanesian languages as well as all of the Polynesian languages and most of the languages of Micronesia. In fact, according to Robert Blust's (1977) classification, which appears to be accepted at least as a working hypothesis by the majority of Austronesianists, Oceanic is at most a subgroup of a subgroup of a subgroup of Austronesian.

Thus, the subgrouping picture produced by lexicostatistics may be described as exactly the reverse of what would have been expected. Whereas it was to be expected that the relationship of any Melanesian language to any other one would show up as relatively close, while the relationship of one Indonesian language to another often would be measured as considerably more remote, lexicostatistics came up with almost precisely the opposite results. (It is noteworthy, however, that the distribution of higher and lower cognate percentages on which the lexicostatistical classification is based appears to conform quite closely to what those earlier scholars, such as Ray and Capell, who believed the Melanesian languages to be mixed languages, would have predicted).

From the foregoing it may be seen that there is something of a consensus that, at least according to some criteria, there is greater diversity among the Melanesian languages than among the other Austronesian languages. The explanation offered by the mixed-language school is that their non-Austronesian component is different from language to language. According to this school, they are not Austronesian languages in the full meaning of the term, and it was clearly implied that the evidence of the Melanesian languages did not deserve to be given as much weight in the reconstruction of Proto-Austronesian as the evidence of other Austronesian languages.

The lexicostatistical explanation seems quite straightforward; namely, that the greater diversity among the Melanesian languages simply reflects greater genetic diversity. However, there is evidence that this is incorrect. There is one piece of direct evidence that the cognate percentages obtained for the lexicostatistical test list reflect different rates of change rather than true genetic differences. This evidence is provided by a study of retention rates in 216 Austronesian languages by Robert Blust (1986). Blust's approach is to reconstruct as precisely as possible the lexicostatistical test-list equivalents for Proto-Austronesian, and then to determine which of the original list have been retained in each of the daughter languages. The study showed that the retention rates of Indonesian languages clustered at the high end of the scale and those of Melanesian languages at the low end. Thus, the average retention rates for Melanesian languages were much lower than those for Indonesian languages.

A second kind of evidence that the lexicostatistical classification is wrong comes from the fact that the prevailing view of Austronesian internal relationships rejects it. The question is: is there an adequate basis for this rejection?

The basis for the prevailing view, in particular for the key hypothesis that the Oceanic subgroup includes all of the languages which we are calling Melanesian, is not as neat as we might wish. There is, however, what I consider a quite strong case that an Oceanic subgroup exists. Proto-Oceanic appears to reflect a number of phonemic unifications, the most easily documented of which is the unification of Proto-Austronesian *p* and *b*. There has also been considerable work on the reconstruction of Proto-Oceanic syntax, and the results at this stage indicate a system distinctly different from the Proto-Austronesian system.

Now, it has generally been assumed that all of the Melanesian languages are members of the Oceanic group — of course along with all of the Polynesian languages and all but a few Micronesian languages. In the case of the more exemplary languages, the evidence of membership appears quite unambiguous; it is with the more aberrant Melanesian languages that the trouble begins.

The sheer number of Melanesian languages, probably over 400, would make it difficult to deal with them individually even if sufficient information were available. Therefore, some have been hypothesized to belong to the Oceanic subgroup on the basis of skimpy linguistic evidence combined with indirect indications that membership is plausible. In the case of languages which are sufficiently aberrant that their sound correspondences cannot be worked out in much detail, it may still be possible to find some minimal indications of Proto-Oceanic characteristics. For example, it may be possible to work out enough of the sound correspondences to determine that Proto-Austronesian *p* and *b* have been unified, or that some initial consonants are reflected as nasal clusters, or one might even give some weight to such characteristically Oceanic features as the distinction between alienable and inalienable possession, which is not made by most Indonesian languages.

A major indirect indication would be geographical relations. Although linguistic classifications are not supposed to consider such non-linguistic considerations, it is nevertheless obvious that the closest relatives of a language are more often than not spoken in relatively close geographical proximity (I discussed this matter somewhat in Grace 1986). Therefore, when a language on which we have little information appears, from what information we do have, to share what are probably common innovations with languages spoken nearby, it seems reasonable to hypothesize that they are relatively closely related. In fact, as long as no Austronesian language which can be shown not to be Oceanic has been found anywhere in the Melanesian area, the fact that a language is located in that area will make it easy to get people to assume — at least as a working hypothesis — that it is Oceanic.

The uncertainty of the placement of some of the more aberrant Melanesian languages poses a problem, however. Lexicostatistics would deny that many of the aberrant Melanesian languages are descendants of Proto-Oceanic. (Of course, lexicostatistics does not recognize the existence of a Proto-Oceanic, but it would deny that these languages have a closer relationship to one another and to the more exemplary Melanesian languages than the latter do to Indonesian languages). And as I have just pointed out, the connection between the specific characteristics of these languages and those of Proto-Oceanic, as it has been reconstructed, are very tenuous. These languages contribute almost nothing to the specification of the characteristics of Proto-Oceanic, and, on the other side of the same coin, very few of the characteristics of the reconstructed Proto-Oceanic seem to be required in an ancestor of these languages. Let me be more specific and talk about the languages of the south of New Caledonia (to which I will return below). Proto-Oceanic could presumably be their ancestor; in fact, I presume that it is. However, in that case, they have undergone very fundamental (and, therefore, presumably rapid) changes since the breakup of Proto-Oceanic.

That is all very well, but is Proto-Oceanic in fact the last ancestor shared by these New Caledonian languages with any languages outside of New Caledonia? If we make no assumptions about any regularity in the rate at which linguistic change occurs, some much later proto-language might qualify as well as Proto-Oceanic does. As we just saw, Proto-Oceanic may be said to have some vague, general suitability to serve as an ancestor of these New Caledonian languages. However, as far as I can see, the last ancestor which the Polynesian languages share with any non-Polynesian languages — what is generally called Proto-Central-Pacific — would be equally suitable as an ancestor of these particular New Caledonian languages. (I should point out that there is some limit — Proto-Polynesian, for example, appears to have undergone innovations which the New Caledonian languages have not).

Obviously, there is much that is uncertain where these languages are concerned. However, there can be little doubt that they have undergone very fundamental, and consequently very rapid, changes. We have no way of knowing how rapid, or of reconstructing the changes in any detail. However, my colleagues have shown a noticeable tendency to put their separation from other Oceanic languages as early as possible — which means at the initial breakup of Proto-Oceanic. One cannot blame them; I believe that there are two considerations which make this assumption attractive. First, the more time we allow for the aberrant characteristics of these languages to have developed, the more comfortable we feel. And second, by giving them a separate history since the breakup of the earliest proto-language available, we free ourselves of any obligation to take them into account in the reconstruction of any proto-languages except that one. But any decision we make is a guess, and there is no way for us to obtain any significant assistance from these languages in the task of reconstructing the history of the family, a state of affairs which leaves us in the uncomfortable position of having to ignore the evidence of some languages.

So much for the assumption of regularity in the rates at which languages change. The other main question which I want to raise about our assumptions concerns the assumption that sound change is regular. There are some Melanesian languages whose sound correspondences appear not to meet the expected standards of regularity. I can best illustrate this problem from some of my own research on languages of the south of New Caledonia.

I should explain that I chose the southern (more accurately, southeastern) end of New Caledonia as a site for research for two reasons. First, the languages of that area have quite generally been recognized as among the most problematic, or to stick to the term I have been using, among the most aberrant of all Melanesian languages. Their phonologies are quite atypical of Oceanic languages: the number of phonemes is unusually large; the canonical forms are unusual, with numerous monosyllables; there are very few apparent cognates with other Austronesian languages; and sound correspondences are not self-evidently regular. Second, the languages of that area all seem to be quite closely related to one another, a fact which should, I thought, make possible a strategy of reconstructing their history back from a very recent stage to successively earlier stages. In fact, I hoped to discover that a sufficiently careful analysis of sound correspondences between neighboring languages would reveal that the sound changes had been quite regular, even though, no doubt, quite complicated, and that once the correspondences were understood, many cognates would be found to exist.

In 1955 and again on several occasions in the early 1970s, I went to the island to collect data, hoping that I would be able to find a key to the mystery. I wound up collecting sizable vocabularies for two neighboring languages (cf. Grace 1975, 1976), which may be referred to here as the languages of Canala and Grand Couli.

It should be noted that these languages do show evidence of being quite closely related. For example, texts can to a great extent be translated morpheme for morpheme (including grammatical morphemes). I was able to compile a list of over 900 possible cognate sets — i. e., lexical items in the two languages which were well matched in meaning and which resembled each other phonetically sufficiently to justify, in my opinion, an initial hypothesis that they were cognate. With the help of my colleague, Bob Hsu, I entered these hypothetical cognates into computer storage in such a format that the sound correspondences upon which each hypothesis depended could readily be identified by the computer. We then listed all of the correspondences so hypothesized and counted the number of occurrences of each.

My expectations were: 1) that the number of valid correspondences for any phoneme in either language would almost always be quite small — probably one or two in most cases, but 2) that any correspondence which was found in more than a few items would either be a valid one or would reflect a pattern of heavy borrowing from a single source. In short, I thought most of the valid correspondences would stand out conspicuously, and that almost all of the invalid hypotheses would be so infrequent as to be clearly implausible. It was true, of course, that borrowing might be expected to complicate the picture somewhat, but I expected the number of problematic correspondences to be quite small.

In sum, I expected that there would be a number of valid correspondences not much greater than the number of phonemes in either language, and that most of these would be pretty self-evident. Then I expected that there would be a sizable, but random, collection of invalid correspondences which had been included simply because they had appeared plausible on purely phonetic grounds. The invalidity of these I supposed also would generally be self-evident. Finally, I anticipated that there might be a few problematic correspondences: correspondences appearing frequently enough not to be discarded out of hand, and yet doubtful because they were in competition with other correspondences purporting to account for the same phoneme in each language. Some of these would be due to borrowing and some to phonemic splits whose conditions had been obscured by subsequent developments.

That is what I expected, but I found nothing of the kind. Each language has 26 consonants (not counting probably borrowed ones in Grand Couli); each also has 18 vowels (10 are oral and 8 nasalized in each language; however, it should also be noted that two of the 18 in Grand Couli are rare and probably to be regarded as suspect). What I found was 140 consonant correspondences (counting 24 in which a consonant in one language corresponded with zero in the other) and 172 vowel correspondences (counting 26 in which a vowel in one language corresponded with zero in the other). Of course, many of these correspondences occurred only once, and others only two or three times, but there were 56 consonant correspondences and 67 vowel correspondences which occurred at least five times. It was remarkably difficult to find even the approximate place to draw the line between clearly valid and clearly invalid correspondences.

Actually, what was most discouraging in my results was that I failed to find any obvious conditioning — any indications of complementation — among all of these correspondences.

There are some regularities that could be pointed out — notably that for consonants point of articulation seems to correspond more regularly than manner. In fact, it would certainly be possible to make a start toward reconstructing the last common proto-language of these two languages. We could begin by accepting the most frequently occurring correspondences as valid and assigning a symbol to represent each (or if complementary distribution could be found between any, to represent each complementary set). It would probably be possible to reconstruct some vocabulary items and grammatical morphemes using these reconstructed phonemes (or allophones). And there are various criteria which we might use for then accepting additional correspondences and reconstructing further vocabulary items. In fact we might be able to reconstruct a fair number of vocabulary items if we were willing to disregard the vowels. However, I cannot imagine that this would ever lead to my being able to carry out my original program. That is, I cannot imagine that I would ever be able to reconstruct such recent proto-languages in enough detail that they could be used as the basis for reconstructing the next earlier stage in a process that would lead eventually back to Proto-Oceanic.

And what makes this particularly discouraging is that these languages appear on other criteria to be very closely related.

Of course, it is impossible for me to prove that a more perceptive analysis of the data which I have, or some crucial information which I lack, might make everything fall into place. In such a case, obviously, this example would lose its validity. But then, there are numerous other languages which might be substituted as examples of seeming irregularity. (Quite a few other Melanesian examples come to mind, but also such languages of Micronesia as Yapese, Kosraean, or Nauruan).

But assuming that this example or some other one is valid — i. e., assuming that there are related languages whose sound correspondences are irregular — what kind of explanation can be proposed?

I see two possible explanations for an irregularity of this kind. The most obvious one would be that the sound changes which the language has undergone have not been regular as we understand that term, by which I mean that the changes, or at least some of them, have been morphologically conditioned. I will return to this possibility below, but first I would like to discuss another possible source of irregular sound correspondences — the possibility that the linguistic tradition whose changes we have been observing is the wrong unit.

What I mean by that is that there might be a situation in which it is not so much the case that the linguistic change (or, specifically, the sound change) within a particular linguistic tradition has not been regular as that we have been looking at the wrong synchronic unit as the manifestation of the tradition. More specifically, it may be that we have assumed that the tradition is always manifested synchronically as an individual language (I do not mean to suggest that we know what that is, but that is a different problem), but that sometimes it may not be.

Linguistics has generally assumed that a theory of linguistic change will attempt to explain changes, or the possibility of particular changes, in terms of the prior state of the system which undergoes them. And we usually think of individual languages as being those systems which undergo the changes, and therefore, of course, as the systems which should exhibit regularity of changes. However, in the light of recent research on sound change in progress it seems clear that the system which undergoes the changes, or at any rate sound changes, is often very much smaller than a language as a whole. If English is the language spoken in such places as Martha's Vineyard and New York City, one could not say that it is the system which has undergone the recent changes reported in those places. If the English language was changed by the centering of the *ay* and *aw* diphthongs on Martha's Vineyard, I am not at all clear on how that change is to be expressed in a description of English.

But of course the same fact is apparent from the earlier history of English. At any point in its history English has consisted of a number of different dialects, each responding in its own way to its own peculiar phonological system. The phonological history of English is a resultant of the changes which occurred in the various dialects plus the effects in terms of dialect prominence and intensified dialect contact produced by the complex social, political, and economic factors that have existed at different times in that history. It would seem perfectly possible, then, that the sound changes reported for some language might appear to be chaotic, but that they had in fact been perfectly regular within the sound systems that were actually undergoing the changes — that is, the dialects.

There is an opposite kind of situation. The Numbami language of Papua New Guinea is spoken in only one village. Yabem and Tok Pisin are also widely known and frequently used in the village. Since almost everyone speaks all three languages, much code-switching and ad-hoc word borrowing occurs. When Joel Bradshaw was studying Numbami, the speakers found it very difficult to produce pure Numbami (cf. Bradshaw 1978). One might say that although the language is still alive, although it still exists in the minds of its speakers, it has ceased, or very nearly ceased, to have a separate existence — in isolation from the other languages in their repertoire.

Of course, the Numbami situation which I have just been talking about may well be simply the last stage in the death of the Numbami language. This particular situation would certainly not have come about if New Guinea had been spared contact with the outside world. But there are indications that similar situations probably existed, and probably were more stable, in parts of Melanesia in pre-contact times.

Someone once compared the situations in which many Melanesian societies lived, and in which many Melanesian languages were spoken, with that of border areas in other parts of the world. There seem to have been numerous villages, in New Caledonia and else-where, where wives were brought in from villages speaking different languages. The children sometimes learned their mother's language earlier than their own. Sometimes there were a substantial number of wives speaking the same outside language. In fact, several cases have been reported of a village abruptly changing its "official" language.

Maurice Leenhardt, who was for many years a missionary in New Caledonia, attributed such shifts to the in-marrying women (cf. Leenhardt 1930, 1946). However, there were many other sources of contact with speakers of other languages, such as ceremonial events, trade networks, and warfare. Leenhardt also emphasized that there was much multilingualism, and that for speakers of one New Caledonia language to learn another was much easier than to learn French, because the words in each corresponded to identical representations in the minds of the speakers. Equivalent words in different languages were like synonyms, and in fact were used as such in oratory. The knowledge of many languages was, therefore, a great advantage in oratory. Although the situations which I have been describing have ceased to exist, and we therefore cannot investigate them, these accounts suggest that the individual lan-guages spoken in such circumstances may have been quite compa-rable to Numbami in lacking a truly separate existence in the minds of their speakers.

There are, then, two kinds of possible problems concerning the synchronic manifestation of the tradition which undergoes the changes, even when the changes themselves are regular. First, it seems possible that the system which underwent each may have been smaller than a whole language, and, since the inventory of systems — of dialects — existing at different times may not have been identical, it is also possible that the system which underwent a particular earlier change may not even have had an exact descen-dant at the time of a particular later change.

Second, it is possible that the language as a whole had no truly separate existence in the minds of its speakers. In Grace (1981: 263—264) I made the following very speculative suggestion about the earlier state of affairs in New Caledonia:

> In the situation which I have described we may imagine that each individual conceives of the immediate linguistic reality in terms of pools of linguistic resources ...

In the final analysis, each individual would have his/her own pool consisting of those resources known to him/her. However, we may imagine that to some extent the pools of the individuals of a particular village might overlap enough to permit us to speak loosely of the pool of linguistic resources accessible to the particular village. In fact, in some degree the linguistic resources of the whole island would have constituted a single pool. Although I would presume that a modern linguist would have been able at any stage of the history of this island to have divided up the linguistic resources with a normal degree of success into a number of different languages, I would imagine that the language boundaries would have had somewhat less significance for the people of the island than we would be inclined to attribute to them.

Certainly it would be very difficult to determine how much validity such a speculative picture might have, but it does serve to emphasize how completely linguistics has been committed to the idea that all linguistic phenomena can be understood in terms of individual languages. But if changes are to be described in terms of how they affect the system (as we have repeatedly been told they should be), and if we are to seek the causes of changes in the prior state of the system (as established practice dictates), we are in some difficulty if we mistake what the system is.

One possible source of apparent irregularity in sound changes, then, is that we have looked for regularity in the wrong place — within the wrong entity. The other possibility which we were going to consider was that the sound changes which the language has undergone have actually not been regular according to acceptable standards — i. e., that the changes, or at least some of them, have been morphologically conditioned.

Aside from the absence of linguistic differentiation in the area in which the language in question is spoken, it is difficult to know what kind of evidence would point to irregularity of sound change rather than misidentification of the synchronic manifestation of the relevant tradition as the explanation for irregular sound correspondences. However, it seems appropriate to point out here that regularity of sound change does not have the plausibility that it once had and to suggest that the evidence supporting it deserves to be re-examined.

The assumption that sound change is regular is associated particularly with the late nineteenth century Neogrammarians. Their extremely strong claim of *Ausnahmslosigkeit der Lautgesetze* gained its initial plausibility from the fact that explanations had been discovered for what had previously appeared to be irregularities. However, it also gained plausibility from the fact that there was an apparent explanation for this regularity. The explanation was the "mechanism" (in Hockett's terms) which was supposed to cause sound change. Briefly, the explanation was that speakers had articulatory targets for phonemes (or more exactly for positional allophones), and that through the accumulation of errors too small to be perceived, these targets sometimes gradually shifted. Since the targets pertained uniformly to all instances of an allophone, changes were inevitably regular (differently put, the concept of regularity in changes is precisely definable in terms of positional allophones). A consequence was that any phonological change which was not regular was by definition not the result of "sound change" but of some other process.

However, there is now serious doubt that any such mechanism exists. Henry M. Hoenigswald (1964, reprinted in Baldi—Werth 1978: 164—165) said of it: "So far as I know it has always been an entirely speculative picture whose best feature is a surface plausibility which it once possessed but does not possess any more. Are there any data that would bear it out?"

It has become quite unclear, and recent studies of lexical diffusion and of sound change in progress make it even more unclear why sound change should be regular. It seems that, at the least, the question of how much regularity there really is, and under what circumstances, deserves to be re-examined on the basis of the evidence.

I suppose the final conclusion here should be that historical linguistics is based on a metaphor in which individual languages are thought of as (analogous to) physical entities, and that the inaccuracies of the metaphor are beginning to exact a price. Languages exist only by virtue of the people who speak them. They do not exist in exactly the same form for all of their speakers, and they do not have clear boundaries — some people speak them more nearly alike than others, but whether or not two people speak the same language is not a simple question. In any case, it is not clear that what we might choose to mark off as one language necessarily corresponds to what will change as a unit in diachronic perspective.

Also, some people speak more than one language. It is not at all clear that monolingualism is more natural, or has been more common in the human experience, than multilingualism. The degree to which multilinguals keep their languages separate varies.

A language exists in the people who speak it, but people do not live very long, and the language goes on much longer. This continuity is achieved by the recruitment of new speakers, but it is not a perfect continuity. Children (or adults) learning a language learn it from people who already speak it, but these teachers exercise considerably less than total control over the learning process. They may not be the only influence on the language development of the learner.

To speak of "aberrant" languages suggests that the question to be asked is: What can go wrong in the processes of linguistic change? I suggest that we might do well to turn our attention to the exemplary languages, and ask the opposite question: What goes right that has permitted us to get as far as we have with our traditional assumptions?

## References

Baldi, Philip — Ronald N. Werth (eds.)
  1978        *Readings in historical phonology: Chapters in the theory of sound change* (University Park and London: The Pennsylvania State University Press).
Blust, Robert
  1977        "The Proto-Austronesian pronouns and Austronesian subgrouping: A preliminary report", *University of Hawaii Working Papers in Linguistics* 9 (2): 1 — 15.
  1986        "Why lexicostatistics doesn't work", Talk given to the University of Hawaii Tuesday seminar (March 4, 1986).
Bradshaw, Joel
  1978        "Multilingualism and language mixture among the Numbami", *University of Hawaii Working Papers in Linguistics* 10 (1): 85 — 100.
Dempwolff, Otto
  1934 — 38   *Vergleichende Lautlehre des austronesischen Wortschatzes* 1 — 3 (Beihefte zur Zeitschrift für Eingeborenen-Sprachen, 15, 17, 19).
Dyen, Isidore
  1965        *A lexicostatistical classification of the Austronesian languages* (International Journal of American Linguistics, Memoir 19).

Grace, George W.
1975        *Canala dictionary (New Caledonia).* (Pacific Linguistics C-2).
1976        *Grand Couli dictionary (New Caledonia)* (Pacific Linguistics C-12).
1981        "Indirect inheritance and the aberrant Melanesian languages", in:
            Jim Hollyman — Andrew Pawley (eds.), *Studies in Pacific languages
            and cultures in honour of Bruce Biggs* (Auckland: Linguistic Society
            of New Zealand), 255—268.
1985        "Oceanic subgrouping: Retrospect and prospect", in: Andrew Paw-
            ley — Lois Carrington (eds.), *Austronesian linguistics at the 15th Pa-
            cific Science Congress* (Pacific Linguistics C-88), 1—18.
1986        "Further thoughts on Oceanic subgrouping", in: Paul Geraghty —
            Lois Carrington — Stephen A. Wurm (eds.), *FOCAL II: Papers from
            the Fourth International Conference on Austronesian Linguistics.* (Pa-
            cific Linguistics C-94), 1—12.
Hoenigswald, Henry M.
1964        "Graduality, sporadicity, and the minor sound change processes",
            *Phonetica* 11: 202—215. [Reprinted in Baldi — Werth 1978].
Leenhardt, Maurice
1930        *Notes d'ethnologie néocalédonienne* (Travaux et Mémoires de l'Institut
            d'Ethnologie, 8).
1946        *Langues et dialectes de l'Austro-Mélanésie* (Travaux et mémoires de
            l'Institut d'Ethnologie, 46).
Ray, Sidney H.
1926        *A comparative study of the Melanesian island languages* (Cambridge:
            Cambridge University Press).

# Patterns of sound change in the Austronesian languages[1]

*Robert Blust*

## 1. Introduction

In any language family, many patterns can be discerned within the general phenomenon of sound change. Such patterns can relate to the regularity of sound change, to the naturalness of sound change, or to more specific details such as the relative stability of consonants as against vowels, of particular consonants or vowels as against others, the proportion of conditioned as against unconditioned changes, of mergers as against splits, and so on.

My initial intention was to conduct a large-scale statistical investigation of sound change in Austronesian (AN), providing fairly complete accounts of the major phonological developments in perhaps 50 of the more than 800 Austronesian languages.[2] Limitations both of space and of time, however, have forced me to retreat from this plan. In the following pages I will briefly discuss the subgrouping of the Austronesian languages, the phoneme inventories of Proto-Austronesian (PAN) and Proto-Malayo-Polynesian (PMP), some salient types of sound change in the descendants of these reconstructed languages, and two topics of general theoretical import: 1) the correlation of sound change and geography; 2) the Regularity Hypothesis as heuristic and as truth.

## 2. Subgrouping

The higher-level subgrouping of the Austronesian languages has been a subject of considerable controversy. Dyen (1965 a) proposed an Austronesian family tree with some 40 primary branches, most of them located in Melanesia. Virtually all Austronesianists today reject this view. In its place a number of scholars, including Haudricourt (1965), Dahl (1976), Blust

(1977 a), and Harvey (1982) recognize an early split that separated the aboriginal languages of Taiwan (21 or 22 within recorded history) from the approximately 800 Austronesian languages spoken elsewhere. In a series of publications (Blust 1974 a, 1977 a, 1978, 1982 a, 1983/84) I have argued for the following major divisions: 1) Austronesian splits into at least one Formosan subgroup and Malayo-Polynesian (MP = all extra-Formosan Austronesian languages). The Formosan languages fall into three widely divergent groups, and may comprise more than one primary subgroup of Austronesian; 2) Malayo-Polynesian splits into Western Malayo-Polynesian (WMP), with approximately 200 members in the Philippines, western Indonesia, mainland Southeast Asia, Madagascar, and western Micronesia (Palauan, Chamorro), and Central-Eastern Malayo-Polynesian (CEMP), with approximately 600 members; 3) Central-Eastern Malayo-Polynesian splits into Central Malayo-Polynesian (CMP), with approximately 120 members in eastern Indonesia exclusive of the northern Moluccas, and Eastern Malayo-Polynesian (EMP), with approximately 480 members; 4) Eastern Malayo-Polynesian splits into South Halmahera-West New Guinea (SHWNG), with approximately 30 members in the northern Moluccas and coastal areas of the Vogelkop Peninsula of New Guinea, and Oceanic (OC), with approximately 450 members. The internal subgrouping of the Oceanic languages need not concern us further, but it should be noted that Proto-Oceanic probably was spoken in the region of the Bismarck Archipelago of western Melanesia and that Austronesian speakers apparently migrated through the Solomon Islands to Micronesia, Vanuatu, southern Melanesia, Fiji, and Polynesia.

# 3. Proto-Austronesian phonology

The first systematic reconstruction of early Austronesian phonology was that of Dempwolff (1934—1938) who, however, did not consider Formosan evidence. A number of revisions of Dempwolff's work have been proposed in the past half century, most of them based on material from the Formosan languages. The most impor-

tant and widely accepted revision of Dempwolff (which is not based
on Formosan evidence) is Dyen (1953 a).

As in the study of other language families, there is some disagreement among scholars concerning the phonological system of
Proto-Austronesian. Since my paramount concern in this paper is
with the evolution of that system over the past six millennia rather
than with its reconstruction, I will confine myself to the most widely
accepted distinctions. Other possible proto-phonemes will be mentioned only in passing, as these will contribute little to our understanding of the broad patterns of change within the Austronesian
language family as a whole. I will begin with the consonants, treating
them in classes defined by manner of articulation.

## 3.1 The voiceless stops

Proto-Austronesian probably had six voiceless stops (including affricates): *p, t, C, c, k, q*.[3] As a matter of convenience all phonetic
statements concerning these phonemes will be made in absolute
terms, though it should be understood that these are statements of
probability.

All stops were unaspirated. *\*p* was bilabial and *\*t* was dental or
alveolar. A number of Western Malayo-Polynesian languages and
perhaps some others contrast a dental /t/ with an alveolar /d/ and /n/
. The antiquity of this phonetic difference is unknown, but a similar
distinction is found in a number of the non-Austronesian languages
of mainland Southeast Asia (Henderson 1965). *\*C* and *\*c* were alveolar and palatal affricates respectively. *\*C* is distinguished from *\*t*
only by certain of the Formosan languages. *\*c* is distinguished from
*\*s* only by certain of the languages of western Indonesia. Unlike the
other voiceless stops it had a clear positional restriction: *\*c* did not
occur syllable-finally. *\*k* was velar and *\*q* back velar (probably uvular), though outside Taiwan it is widely reflected as a glottal stop.

## 3.2 The voiced stops

Proto-Austronesian probably had five voiced stops (including affricates): *b, d, z, j, g*. *\*b* was bilabial, *\*d* alveolar, and *\*g* velar.
*\*z* was a palatal affricate, written as a palatalized *\*d* by Demp-

wolff. *$j$ was a palatalized velar stop [gʸ]. It had no voiceless counterpart, and in other respects appears to have been an "island" within the phoneme inventory. Although Dempwolff treated *$j$ as a palatal, its distribution differs from that of *$c$ and *$z$: whereas the latter did not occur word-finally, *$j$ did not occur word-initially.

## 3.3 The nasals

Proto-Austronesian probably had four nasals: *m, n, ñ* and *ŋ*. All nasals were voiced: *$m$ was bilabial, *$n$ alveolar, *$ñ$ palatal and *$ŋ$ velar. Like *$c$ and *$z$, *$ñ$ did not occur in final position. In addition *$N$ (distinguished from *$n$ only by certain Formosan languages) has been reconstructed, but its phonetics remain problematic (see "liquids").

Since we have now reviewed the reconstruction of stops and nasals, this is perhaps an opportune juncture to mention as well the proposals of Haudricourt (1951) and Goodenough (1962) that Proto-Austronesian had a labiovelar series which included *$p^w$, *$k^w$ and *$m^w$. Problems with these proposals are discussed in Blust (1981 b).

## 3.4 The fricatives

Proto-Austronesian probably had three fricatives: *$s$, *$S$ and *$h$. All three were voiceless, but beyond this general statement phonetic details are unclear.

Based on morphophonemic behavior Dempwolff considered *$s$ to be a palatal stop. His arguments for this interpretation have their merits, but the majority of Austronesian languages in all major subgroups reflect *$s$ as a dental sibilant. *$s$ may have been a voiceless palatal fricative, though even its palatal character must always be inferred from indirect evidence. *$S$ probably was an alveolar or alveo-dental fricative and *$h$ a glottal fricative. The former has weakened to /h/ or zero in most attested languages, including virtually all Malayo-Polynesian languages; the latter survives only vestigially in Taiwan, the Philippines and western Indonesia.

## 3.5 The liquids

Proto-Austronesian probably had four liquids: *l*, *L*, *r* and *R*. *\*l* was a voiced alveolar lateral, *\*r* an alveolar tap and *\*R* an alveolar or uvular trill. *\*L* probably was a voiceless alveolar lateral.

Proto-Austronesian *\*n* and *\*L* were not distinguished by Dempwolff, but were labelled *\*n₁* and *\*n₂* by Ogawa and Asai (1935). Dyen (1965 b) rewrote these symbols as *\*n* and *\*N*, later suggesting that *\*N* may have been a voiceless lateral. Following up this suggestion Dahl (1976) writes Dyen's *\*N* as *\*l̥*.

## 3.6 The semivowels

Proto-Austronesian probably had only the two semivowels *\*w* and *\*y*, each with its expected phonetic value.

## 3.7 The vowels

In contrast to the consonants there has been little controversy surrounding the reconstruction of the Proto-Austronesian vowels. Since Dempwolff there has been general agreement that Proto-Austronesian had four vowels: *\*a*, *\*i*, *\*u* and shwa (written *\*e*). Brandstetter (1916) suggested that marginal mid-front and mid-back vowels may also have been part of the "Original Indonesian" sound system, but the evidence is slight. More recently Dyen (1978) has proposed on the basis of double reflexes in certain languages of the central Moluccas that Proto-Austronesian had two additional mid vowels. There is, however, no independent support for Dyen's proposal, and for the present the four-vowel view predominates.

## 3.8 The diphthongs

Apart from the consonants and vowels, researchers in Austronesian linguistics from Dempwolff onward have reconstructed a set of diphthongs, which often behave differently in historical change than their constituent elements in other positions. Proto-Austronesian probably had four diphthongs: *\*ay*, *\*aw*, *\*uy* and *\*iw*. In Austronesian linguistics the term "diphthong" generally is restricted to word-final sequences of vowel plus semivowel. For reasons of syllabification the similar sequence word-internally usually behaved differently, and is analyzed as a VC sequence like any other.

## 3.9 Prenasalization

In addition to various series of simple stops Dempwolff reconstructed parallel series of homorganically prenasalized stops. His reason for doing so was that prenasalized stops became unit phonemes in many daughter (especially Oceanic) languages, and such reflexes contrast with the reflexes of the simple stops. Such differences in Oceanic languages are often described as differences of "consonant grade".

## 3.10 Stress/accent

Between one third and one half of the more than 100 languages of the Philippines have contrastive accent, and many of these agree in the accentuation of cognate morphemes. Dempwolff and most subsequent writers have treated this phenomenon as historically secondary, but explanatory conditions are notoriously difficult to find. As a consequence Zorc (1978) reconstructed contrastive accent for "Proto-Philippines" (PPH), noting (p. 99) that "Philippine accent primarily involves vowel length or shortness in the penultimate syllable." Because the alternative is to derive Proto-Philippine accent *ex nihilo* Zorc suggests that similar accent contrasts "must then be posited for Proto-Hesperonesian, possibly for Proto-Austronesian as well" (where "Hesperonesian" = Western Malayo-Polynesian). As external support for this inference he attempts to explain rules of accent shift, consonant gemination and some other phenomena in non-Philippine Western Malayo-Polynesian languages as reflexes of earlier accent contrasts. Zorc's proposals are well-argued, important, and likely to be widely accepted in time, although a number of problems remain in relating the accent contrasts of Philippine languages to non-accentual phenomena in other areas.


## 3.11 Summary

In summary, the following Proto-Austronesian phoneme inventory probably represents a "majority view" among Austronesianists in the sense that a majority of scholars would support these individual phonemes (and not others), though no scholar would necessarily accept the lot: 24 consonants (*p, t, C, c, k, q, b, d, z, j, g, m, n, ñ, ŋ, S, s, h, l, L, r, R, w,* and *y*) and four vowels (*a, e, i, u*), plus diphthongs *ay, aw, uy,* and *iw*. The Proto-Malayo-Polynesian inventory differed in two or three details: 1) *\*C* merged with *\*t*; 2) *\*L* merged with *\*n*; 3) *\*S* may have shifted to some kind of glottal spirant (at least word-finally), but without merging with *\*h*. Some scholars would recognize additional phonemes not included here, while some others, most notably Wolff (1974, 1982, 1988), reject some of the distinctions proposed by Dempwolff and widely accepted by other researchers.


## 3.12 Canonical shape

In his pioneering reconstruction of the Proto-Austronesian lexicon Dempwolff (1934—1938) recognized only two word shapes: CVCVC and CVCCVC, the latter subdivided into words with a homorganically prenasalized medial stop and reduplicated monosyllables. Dyen (1953a) corrected Dempwolff's methodological bias against initial and final vowels and medial vowel sequences, thereby admitting a canonical shape CVCCVC, where all of the consonants are optional. As noted by Chrétien (1965), some 90% of Dempwolff's reconstructions are disyllabic. Some trisyllables are found in the general vocabulary, but monosyllables appear to be restricted to grammatical particles and onomatopoetic interjections. Prenasalized initial obstruents are found in some Western Malayo-Polynesian languages of Sulawesi, some Central Malayo-Polynesian languages of the Lesser Sunda Islands and many Oceanic languages, but Dempwolff treated all of these (where he discussed them) as historically secondary.


## 3.13 Reduplication

Reduplication has been an ongoing process in the history of the Austronesian languages, subsuming many functions in both nouns and verbs. However, the many reduplicated monosyllables that must be posited for Proto-Austronesian and the majority of its descendants appear to have been lexicalized at the earliest inferrable period. As noted already, all securely reconstructed monosyllables in Austronesian are either grammatical particles or onomatopes. Reduplicated monosyllables such as *butbut* 'pluck, uproot' or *kaŋkaŋ* 'spread apart (legs, fishhook)' thus cannot be attributed to morphological processes which operated after the dispersal of Proto-Austronesian.

Reduplicated monosyllables often exhibit sound changes which set them apart from other word-forms. These generally involve the first of the medial consonants, which may undergo partial or complete assimilation, or disappear altogether. Other changes that appear to be confined to reduplicated monosyllables will be discussed under "canonical targets".


## 3.14 Distributional limitations

Some of the distributional limitations of Proto-Austronesian phonemes have been discussed above, and it will be convenient to summarize the full set of limitations here.

The palatals *c, *z and *ñ did not occur syllable-finally (whereas *s, *j and *y did). Proto-Austronesian *j did not occur syllable-initially, and Proto-Austronesian *y did not occur word-initially.

With two possible exceptions there appear to have been no distributional limitations on vowels. First, *e (shwa) did not occur word-finally. Second, in words of more than two syllables *e has not yet been reconstructed in prepenultimate position. This may be an accidental consequence of the limited number of trisyllabic etyma, or it may reflect a real morpheme structure constraint.

# 4. Changes

In approaching the description of a language family the size of Austronesian, one must be selective. To avoid an "Old Curiosity Shoppe" aproach, I have attempted to impose some sort of order on the data through generalization. The organization I have adopted is justified solely by convenience in ordering a large corpus of data under tight constraints of manuscript length.

## 4.1 Canonical changes

Under "canonical changes", I include changes which affected the canonical shape of lexical items by operating on entire classes of phonemes (generally consonants or vowels). Consonants and vowels will be referred to as follows: $C_1$ = initial, $C_2$ = intervocalic, $C_3$ = final, $C_4$ = preconsonantal, $C_5$ postconsonantal; $V_1$ = final, $V_2$ = penultimate, $V_3$ = prepenultimate.

### 4.1.1 Loss of consonants

Consonants as a group have been lost in a number of languages in either of two positions: 1) as $C_3$ and 2) as $C_4$. We will consider only the former.

Final consonants have been lost in one Western Malayo-Polynesian language (Nias, of the Barrier Islands west of Sumatra), although other Western Malayo-Polynesian languages show severe reduction of the consonant inventory in final position (e. g. Minangkabau, which allows only /ʔ/, /m/, /n/, /ŋ/, /h/, /w/ and /y/, Buginese, which allows only /ʔ/ and /ŋ/, or the west Toraja language Uma, which allows only glottal stop in addition to vowels in final position. Several Central Malayo-Polynesian languages, including Bimanese, have lost all final consonants, but in general the rarity of final consonant loss in Central Malayo-Polynesian and especially Western Malayo-Polynesian languages contrasts markedly with the situation in the Oceanic subgroup. So widespread is the loss of final consonants in Oceanic languages that many Proto-Oceanic etyma were initially reconstructed without them, though it is now clear that this was an error. In a number of widespread Oceanic languages the historical final is preserved as the "thematic" consonant of suffixed forms, e. g. POC *qutup* 'submerge a vessel to fill it' > Wuvulu *uʔu* 'idem', *uʔuf-ia* 'fill it!', POC *inum* 'drink' > Samoan *inu* 'idem', *inum-ia* 'was drunk'.

### 4.1.2 Loss of vowels

Vowels as a group have been lost in a number of languages in one of three positions: 1) as $V_1$, 2) as $V_3$ and 3) in the environment VC_CV.

All of the 40 or more languages of Borneo have lost initial *a, or *a preceded by *q or *S (which disappeared) in prepenultimate position, thereby reducing a number of original trisyllables to disyllables. A similar change has taken place in Malay and some other Western Malayo-Polynesian languages. As a result, Dempwolff (1934 — 1938) reconstructed some items that we now know were trisyllabic (*qasawa* 'spouse', *SabaRat* 'northwest monsoon') without the initial syllable. Comparative evidence shows that the loss of prepenultimate *a was a by-product of the merger of pretonic vowels: first *a, then the high vowels merged as shwa in prepenultimate syllables, and this shwa dropped if it came to be initial. It is possible that this drift-like tendency to lose pretonic vocalic distinctions initiated the transformation of the Proto-Austronesian "focus" system in western Indonesia through eliminating the instrumental passive marker *Si-.

The loss of final vowels, like the loss of final consonants, is most common in the Oceanic group. In some languages, including those of the eastern Admiralties, parts of northern Vanuatu, and much of Micronesia, both the final consonant and the last vowel have been lost, thus eliminating an entire syllable: POC *qudaŋ* > Sori (western Manus) *guh* 'lobster', *kudon* > *uh* 'cooking pot', *kuluR* > *uŋ* 'breadfruit', *apaRat* > *japay* 'northwest monsoon'. In such languages an entire thematic syllable reappears in suffixed forms: POC *mpulut* 'bird lime' > Mota (Banks Islands) *pul* 'gum of trees, bird-lime', *mpulut-i* > *pulut* 'make to stick, make sticky', *tasik* > *tas* 'sea, saltwater', *tasik-i* > *tasig* 'pour saltwater into an earth oven'.

Finally, in a number of the languages of Taiwan and the Philippines *e (and occasionally other vowels) disappeared in the environment

VC_CV, giving rise to historically secondary heterorganic medial consonant clusters (e. g. *ta-telu* > Tagalog *tatló* 'three', *baqeRu* > Bunun *baqlu*, Aborlan Tagbanwa *bag?ú*, Cebuano 'new'). In a number of languages including Tagalog, Cebuano, and Chamorro this change resulted in synchronic alternations triggered by the addition of a suffix. In either case these clusters sometimes underwent secondary change (as the metathesis in Cebuano *bag?ú* and the various changes for Tagalog and Cebuano reported in Blust 1971, 1979). Malay and many other languages of western Indonesia evidently underwent a similar syncope, with subsequent reduction of most resulting heterorganic clusters (Blust 1982 b). Similar to the foregoing, but historically independent, was the loss of any unstressed vowel in the environment VC_CV in most languages of the eastern Admiralty (EA) Islands: PADM *papanako* > Aua (western Admiralties) *fafanao*, Nali (EA) *pahana*, Kuruti (EA) *pahna*, Ere (EA) *panna* 'to steal'.

### 4.1.3 Addition of vowels

Canonically altering vowels have been added in Malagasy, in Rukai and the three Tsouic languages of central Taiwan (Tsuchida 1976), and in a number of the Oceanic languages occupying a more-or-less continuous block from Mussau (St. Mathias Archipelago) to the western Solomons. In Malagasy the added vowel was always /a/: Proto-Malayo-Polynesian *anak* > *(z)anaka* 'child', *enem* > *enina* 'six', *laŋit* > *lanitra* 'sky'. It has been suggested that the Malagasy development is a product of Bantu substratum (Dahl 1954). In western Melanesia, an echo vowel was added to the reflex of Proto-Oceanic forms with a final consonant, thereby preserving the consonant, but altering the predominant CVCV(C) canonical form of Proto-Oceanic morphemes to CVCVCV (e. g., Proto-Oceanic *salan* > Mussau *salana* 'path, road', *ŋkiñit* > *kiniti* 'to pinch', *pulan* > *ulana* 'moon, month').

### 4.1.4 Addition of consonants

Consonant addition rules are on the whole less widely appreciated than rules of vowel epenthesis or rules of segment deletion. Yet many examples of consonant epenthesis can be seen in the historical phonology of the Austronesian languages. For convenience, changes that affect overall canonical shape and changes that affect only the canonical shape of particular morphemes will be conflated.

In a number of widely separated Austronesian languages, the reflex of a Proto-Austronesian or Proto-Malayo-Polynesian final vowel is followed by a fully predictable glottal stop. Languages that show such a presumably secondary segment include Atayal, Sediq and many of the "Paiwanic" languages of Taiwan, Ivatan and Kalamian Tagbanwa in the Philippines, and Sundanese in west Java. In some Kayan dialects of Borneo the sequences *-V and *-Vq are reflected respectively as -V? and -V. A clearly secondary final glottal stop is found in a number of the languages of Manus (Admiralty Islands), where the sequences -/i/ : -/iy/, -/e/ : -/ey/, -/u/ : -/uw/ and -/o/ : -/ow/ contrast phonetically as -V? : -V:, the glottal closure presumably serving to enhance an inherently unstable distinction (although glottal stop was also added after -/a/).

Several languages which occupy a much more restricted area (Tausug of the southern Philippines, Kelabit, the Berawan dialects and various "Lower Baram" languages of northern Sarawak) have added a final /h/. A particularly noteworthy set of final consonant additions is found in Singhi and some other Land Dayak languages of southwest Borneo. In these languages *-a and *-u generally are reflected with epenthetic final /x/ (voiceless velar fricative), while *-i quite consistently (exclusive of recent loans) appears as -/is/: *besi 'iron' > Singhi bosis 'small axe, hatchet' (cf. the Malay loan bosi 'iron'), *kali > karis 'dig', *iti > itis 'this', etc. This change strikingly parallels one reported by Burling (1966) for the Tibeto-Burman language Maru, and together with certain other observations these facts suggest the need for a unified set of vowel and consonant features in phonological theory.

Apart from final consonant accretion, initial consonants have been added in some languages. In pre-Chamorro, *w evidently was added before all initial vowels. The subsequent development of this glide will be discussed below under "fortitions". In Palauan, a velar nasal appears before the reflex of all Proto-Malayo-Polynesian initial vowels (*anak > ŋalek 'child', *ikan > ŋikel 'fish', *uRat > ŋurd 'vein, artery'). The suggestion that these developments are due to the fossilization of old grammatical markers is superficially attractive, but since the epenthetic consonant is associated with all grammatical classes in both languages there appears to be little reason to consider it a product of anything but phonological change.[4]

One of the most intriguing drifts in Austronesian languages is the addition of /y/ before the reflex of Proto-Austronesian initial *a. This change is most widespread in the Oceanic subgroup, but also appears in eastern Indonesia. In some languages, /y/ prothesis occurred early enough for the glide to undergo subsequent changes that affected inherited *y, as in Motu of southeast New Guinea, where both became /l/, some of the languages of the southeast Solomons, where both became /s/ (Sa'a, Arosi), /r/ ('Are'are), or a voiceless interdental fricative (Kwara'ae), and in Fijian (Bauan), where all instances of inherited *y became a voiced interdental fricative. That this is a recurrent change is clear from differences of detail among the languages which share it: in Motu, for example, POC *qa-, *ka- and *a- are reflected respectively as /a/, /a/ and /la/ (*qasawa > adava 'spouse', *qanse > ade 'chin', *kani > ani-a 'eat', *kau > au 'wood, tree', *ajan > lada 'name', *api > lahi 'fire', *aku > lau 'I'), while in Fijian *qa- and *a- have become / ya/ or /ca/, and *ka- has become /ka/.

In a number of the Oceanic languages, including some of the languages of Manus, northern Vanuatu and Micronesia glides /w/ and /y/ have been added before initial /u/ and /i/ respectively, in some cases whether this vowel was originally initial or whether it came to be initial through consonant loss.

## 4.1.5 Canonical targets

Some of the preceding developments raise the issue of teleology in sound change. Three general developments in Austronesian historical phonology are best seen as teleological: (1) areal adaptation in the Chamic languages; (2) the widespread disyllabic canonical target of Austronesian languages; (3) the open-syllable canonical target of most Oceanic languages.

There are some six or seven members of the Chamic group of Western Malayo-Polynesian languages, located in Vietnam, Kampuchea, and southern China. Because of their typological similarity to other languages of mainland Southeast Asia, Schmidt (1906) misclassified the Chamic languages as Austroasiatic, an error that persisted in some quarters for decades (Sebeok 1942). Schmidt's error derives in large part from the consequences of a single sound change: penultimate vowels were weakened to shwa, and where this shwa could be dropped to produce a pronounceable consonant cluster it was. The result was a basic change of canonical shape. In words that began with a consonant, the only vowel that could occur in a non-final syllable was shwa (PMP *mata* > PC *məta* 'eye', *qudaŋ* > *hədaŋ* 'shrimp'). Many disyllables were reduced to monosyllables and a range of initial consonant clusters was introduced (*bulan* > *blaan* 'moon, month', *malem* > *mlam* 'night', *taqun* > *thuun* 'year'). Length distinctions developed in the vowels, and depending upon one's synchronic analysis, separate series of voiced preglottalized and voiceless aspirated stops arose. Finally, Cham proper developed two tonal registers and Jarai developed an allophonic short rising pitch before final glottal stop. With the possible exception of the last change, all of the resulting typological traits are fairly common among neighboring Mon-Khmer languages (Henderson 1965). There can be little doubt that this resemblance is the product of generations of multilingualism in which the Austronesian languages have become assimilated in various features of phonology, canonical shape, morphology, and syntax to the speech of their numerically superior Mon-Khmer neighbors. In short, the adaptive changes in the Chamic languages exemplify the kind of teleology seen in the formation of linguistic areas.

Other instances of teleology are perhaps best treated under the rubric "drift". Brandstetter (1916), Blust (1976, 1977 b) and some others have noted a disyllabic canonical target in Austronesian historical phonology. As noted already, more than 90% of the vocabulary in Dempwolff (1934—1938) is disyllabic. Where an original disyllable has been reduced to a monosyllable through regular sound change, an otherwise inoperative vowel epenthesis (with shwa or /a/) sometimes takes place to restore the disyllable (Javanese, Tiruray, Kelabit, Sesayap). Where an original disyllable has been made longer by reduplication or affixation, the preferred disyllabism is often restored through changes that would not otherwise occur: e. g., in the reduplicated forms of many bases (and also in unaffixed trisyllables), Tagalog loses /h/ or /ʔ/ between like vowels which then coalesce, and many Oceanic languages reduce the suffixed forms of reduplicated monosyllables by haplology (Blust 1976, 1977 b).

Many Oceanic languages have lost original final consonants; others occupying a more-or-less continuous block in western Melanesia have added echo vowels. In terms of syllable shape (but not word shape) the result in the two cases is the same: closed syllables are eliminated. A superficially similar development is seen over much of Sulawesi in central Indonesia. Languages as distinct as Bare'e (central), Mori (central-east), Wolio and Muna (southeast) have lost all final consonants, whereas Sangir of extreme north Sulawesi has added a supporting vowel. However, there are important differences of detail between the situation in Sulawesi and that in Oceanic languages. Other languages of Sulawesi also show phonological erosion from the right, but still permit one final consonant (Uma), two (Buginese), or sometimes more.[5] Moreover, Sneddon (1984) has shown that although Sangir and Bantik have added supporting vowels in certain contexts these are followed by glottal stop (PMP *pusej* > Sangir *puidəʔ* 'navel', *teRas* > *tihasəʔ* 'hard'). Unlike the monosyllabic target of the Chamic languages or the disyllabic target of most other Austronesian languages, the open syllable canonical Austronesian target of most Oceanic languages and of many languages in Sulawesi cannot easily be explained as an areal adaptation or a response to inherited structural pressures. Perhaps it is simply an expression of the universal tendency of human languages to favor open syllables, but if so it is puzzling that this tendency in Austronesian is far more strongly expressed in Oceanic than in non-Oceanic languages.

## 4.2 Segmental changes

Segmental changes are changes that affected individual phonemes or classes of phonemes without altering canonical patterns. These will be discussed under the headings: 1) phonetically unnatural changes; 2) phonetically natural changes; 3) feature transfers; and 4) fortitions and lenitions.

### 4.2.1 Phonetically unnatural changes

Two methods of assessing phonological naturalness are known to me: 1) feature counting and 2) cross-linguistic distribution. Since little information is yet available on universals of sound change, the latter method is for the present impracticable. Whether it is true or not, our expectation as linguists is that most sound change is phonetically natural. It is thus surprising — sometimes very surprising — when we encounter sound changes which appear to be phonetically arbitrary. The following is a sampling of sound changes that to my knowledge are both cross-linguistically uncommon and difficult to express simply in terms of feature matrices.

PMP *t* unconditionally shifted to /k/ in Enggano (Western-Malayo-Polynesian) of the Barrier Islands west of Sumatra; in Kisar (Central-Malayo-Polynesian) and sporadically in Hoti (Central-Malayo-Polynesian) of eastern Indonesia; in Numfor and Ron (South-Halmahera-West New Guinea) of western New Guinea; in Iaai (Oceanic) of the Loyalty Islands; and independently in three Polynesian languages: Luangiua (Ontong Java), Samoan and Hawaiian. It is clear in the latter two cases that this was a single-step change. In Hawaiian, the change has not yet taken place in the dialect of Ni'ihau Island, and /t/ and /k/ evidently varied freely (or under unrecorded sociolinguistic constraints) in other Hawaiian dialects at the time the missionary-based orthography was established early in the nineteenth century. In Samoan, the change is in progress, and is correlated with speech registers: /t/-forms are used in formal, /k/-forms in informal speech. A conditioned change of *t* to /k/ is found in northern New Caledonia (word-initially in Gomen, Pabwa, Koumac and Nenema), and on the island of Manus in northwest Melanesia, where after the loss of final syllables Proto-Oceanic medial *t* (which had become final) shifted to /k/ in Bipi, Likum, Levei, Lindrou, Pelipowai, Ahus, Ndrehet and Mondropolon: *kutu* > Lindrou *kuk* 'louse', *qatop* > *kak* 'roof thatch', *putun* > *buk* 'a tree: *Barringtonia asiatica*'.

Although *t* > /k/ is a recurrent change in Austronesian languages, it appears to be rare in human languages generally.[6] Moreover, it has tended to occur more often in the more easterly areas of Austronesian. The change is unknown in Taiwan, and, apart from Enggano, no Western Malayo-Polynesian shows an unconditioned change *t* > /k/, although the derivative cluster -/tl/- is sometimes unmarked by a similar conditioned change in the Philippines and in Chamic: *qiteluR* > Tagalog *itlóg*, but, e. g., Agta *iklug* 'egg'; *telu* > Jarai *klew* 'three'.

The Berawan languages of northern Sarawak (Borneo) have unusual historical phonologies. One of the most peculiar features distinguishing the group is the change *-b-* > /k/ in Long Terawan, Batu Belah, Long Teru and Long Jegan. Since PAN *R* has fallen together with *b* intervocalically and is reflected as /g/ in other environments, it is possible that both proto-phonemes changed to *g* before devoicing. While this may enable us to account for the change of *-b- to /k/ in two steps, the first of which is phonetically comprehensible (at least acoustically), we still must admit against all phonetic sense that *g* devoiced intervocalically.

Two other phonetically unnatural changes for which it is difficult to conceive of plausible intermediate steps are 1) the unconditioned change of Proto-Polynesian *l to Rennellese (Solomon Islands) [ŋg] (further evolved to [ŋ] in the dialect of Bellona Island), and 2) the conditioned change of earlier *w (from PAN *w and *b) to Sundanese /c/-, -/nc/- in many forms (Nothofer 1975).

Two changes which are peculiar more for the condition under which they occur than for the phonetic differences of the segments involved are: 1) the merger of voiced stops with the homorganic nasals (Karo Batak of northern Sumatra, certain Kayan dialects of central Borneo, as Long Atip), and 2) the merger of *l and *n (Bintulu, Kiput, Long Terawan Berawan, some Kayan dialects and most [perhaps all] Kenyah dialects of northern Sarawak; Loniu, Bipi, Likum, Lindrou, Levei, Ndrehet and Sori of Manus in western Melanesia). Each of these changes occurs in the stated languages only in word-final position. The result in all cases is a nasal consonant (*-b and *-m merging as /m/, *-d and *-n as /n/, *-l and *-n as /n/, etc.). In Levei, Ndrehet, Sori, and perhaps other languages of western Manus which lost Proto-Oceanic final syllables, the resulting alveolar nasal later merged with *ŋ: POC *salan> Levei *soŋ*, Sori *saŋ* 'path, road', *kuluR > Levei *kuŋ*, Sori *uŋ* 'breadfruit', *mpaluj > Levei *pʷaŋ*, Sori *baŋ* 'fruit pigeon'.

Somewhat more subtle are certain vowel changes. In Mukah and other members of the Melanau dialect chain of coastal Sarawak, *i and *u developed a mid-central offglide before certain final consonants. In Mukah, these final consonants include /k/ and /ŋ/, but not /g/, thus destroying the possibility of describing the environment in terms of any felicitous set of feature values.

In a basically synchronic analysis, Bender (1969) noted that sequences of /aCa/ (generally if the first /a/ was in an initial syllable) dissimilated to [eCa] in Marshallese (eastern Micronesia): e. g. *maj* 'eye', *meja-n* 'his eye'. Since /a/ is the least marked vowel, this change might be seen as increasing markedness, and hence as unnatural. Yet a very similar change occurs in Ere of eastern Manus (*mata > mat* 'eye', *mira-n* 'his eye', *kamaliR > kimal* 'men's house'). In both languages, the change appears to be blocked by intervening /h/. Examples such as this remind us that intuitive or aprioristic notions of naturalness may in some cases mask interesting and still poorly understood language universals.

Finally, Maddieson (1987) provides an excellent phonetic description of the linguo-labial stops, nasals, and fricatives of certain languages in northern Vanuatu. In all cases for which an etymology is known, these typologically unusual segments appear to have developed through an unconditioned change from simple labials.

### 4.2.2 Phonetically natural changes

Because they appeal to a shared understanding, there will be no need to document phonetically natural sound changes at great length. Recurrent sound changes in Austronesian which will occasion no surprise are: 1) the devoicing of final stops (Malay, Toba Batak, Chamorro, Manggarai); 2) the devoicing of all or some final vowels (Malagasy, Samoan, Sonsorol-Tobi); 3) the merger of final *p, *t, *k as /ʔ/ (Minangkabau, Uma, Buginese); 4) the change of *t to /s/ before *i (Isneg, Kelabit, Ma'anyan, Bola'ang Mongondow, Buli, Numfor and other South Halmohera-West New Guinea languages, Motu, Dobuan, Tongan); 5) *p > /f/ (many languages; see below); 6) *k > /h/ or /ʔ/ (many languages; see below); 7) *s > /h/ (Atayal, Ifugao, Botolan Sambal, Murik, Sika, Lamaholot, Kisar, Tongan); 8) *l > /r/ and *r or *R to /l/ either as an unconditioned change, or in dissimilations of sequential liquids (many languages); 9) *-ay > /e/ and *-aw > /o/ (many languages). One apparently unnatural sound change which turns out to be natural is POC *t > Rotuman /f/ (through a voiceless interdental fricative recorded by Horatio Hale in 1845).

### 4.2.3 Feature transfers

Under the heading "feature transfers", I will group sound changes which appear to involve a movement of feature values from one segment to another, adjacent segment. The material is organized into four categories: 1) nasality, 2) rounding, 3) tone, and 4) nasal-oral timing.

Phonemically nasalized vowels are rare in Austronesian, but have developed occasionally under either of two conditions: 1) adjacent to earlier nasals which disappeared, 2) adjacent to laryngeals. Keraf (1978) describes a number of Lamaholot dialects in eastern Indonesia with word-final nasalized vowels that reflect *-VN. In some dialects (as Lamalera) only *a* was nasalized. A typologically unusual language with vowel nasality is Seimat of the western Admiralty Islands, where phonemically nasalized vowels occur only after /w/ and /h/. The former reflect Proto-Oceanic vowels that followed *m*ʷ:POC *dam*ʷ*a* > /kawã/- 'forehead', but *qawaŋ* > /awa/- 'mouth'. The latter are enigmatic. Earlier *p* and *d* (which may have first become *r*) merged as /h/, but are still distinguished in some cases by the nasality of the following vowel. Vowels following /h/ from *p* are invariably oral (*puaq* > /hua/ 'fruit', *patu* > / hatu/ 'stone'), but in the few available examples vowels following / h/ from *d* are nasalized: *dua* > /hũa/ 'two (in counting trees)', / hũohũ/ 'two (in serial counting)', *wada* > /wahã/ 'root', *matiduR* > /matihũ-en/ 'slept'. The latter examples support Matisoff's (1975) insightful and entertaining defense of the phenomenon of "rhinoglottophilia", an "affinity between the feature of nasality and the articulatory involvement of the glottis." Other Austronesian data provide additional confirmation of Matisoff's claim. Narum of northern Sarawak has the minimal pair /hãw/ (< *kasaw*) 'rafter' : /haw/ (< *kaSu*) '2nd sg.', but distinctively nasalized vowels otherwise apparently do not occur in the language. Similarly, in the Kedah dialect of Malay /r/ has two allophones: a uvular trill before vowels and a pharyngeal stop before word boundary. Before the pharyngeal stop high vowels are pronounced with a mid-central offglide and nasalized. Finally, in Rennellese, a Polynesian Outlier of the Solomon Islands vowels (most noticeably /a/) are predictably nasalized after /h/.

A number of the Oceanic languages occasionally reflect PAN *p*, *m*, and sometimes *k* as the corresponding labiovelars (with different phonetic realizations in different languages). This is often, but by no means always, conditioned by a rounded vowel in an adjacent syllable. Where conditioning is apparent the rounding feature is quite commonly transferred from vowel to consonant: POC *Rumaq* 'house' > Nali (eastern Manus) *yim*ʷ*a-n* 'its nest', Mota (Banks Islands) *im*ʷ*a* 'house', Trukese (Caroline Islands, Micronesia) *iim*ʷ 'house, building'; *pulan* > Levei (western Manus) *p*ʷ*iŋ* 'moon'; *kudon* > Levei *k*ʷ*iŋ* 'cooking pot'. In some cases, the transfer of rounding carries over more than one syllable, and is perhaps best described as a "prosody": Loniu (eastern Manus) /lo kaman/ > [lo kom ʷan] 'in the men's house' (where the syllable break is *ka.man*).[7]

Contrastive lexical tone is known to occur only in certain of the Chamic languages, a few languages on or near New Guinea and some of the languages of New Caledonia. In Jarai of central Vietnam, all vowels are pronounced with a short rising pitch before final glottal stop (< *t*). Cham proper distinguishes low and high registers, continuing earlier voiced-voiceless contrasts which have been lost through merger (Lee 1966). Quite exceptionally in Austronesian, Huihui (or Utset), a Chamic language spoken on Hainan Island off the coast of southern China, may have as many as five tone contrasts (Benedict 1984, Keng-fong Pang, personal communication).

Tones are tentatively reported for Mayá and some other South Halmahera-West New Guinea languages spoken around the northwest extremity of New Guinea (Robert van der Leeden, personal communication), in Mor, a South Halmahera-West New Guinea language of Sarera Bay, New Guinea (Laycock 1978) and in several languages of the south of New Caledonia (Haudricourt 1971). In general, the origin of these tonal distinctions is obscure, although Haudricourt attributes high tone in the New Caledonian cases to the influence of adjacent aspirated consonants which may have arisen from earlier geminates.

Finally, Yabem (in the German sources: Jabem) and Bukawa, two neighboring languages of the Huon Gulf region of New Guinea, distinguish two registers (Capell 1949). Although the history of this development is complicated by considerations of tone/consonant harmony, Bradshaw (1979) has argued that the low tone of Yabem developed next to a voiced obstruent.

Apart from the New Caledonian cases, all Austronesian tone languages are spoken near tonal languages belonging to other families. It thus appears likely that contact has been a significant factor in the acquisition of tone by Austronesian languages.

Two distinct nasal-oral timing phenomena are found in a number of the languages of Borneo, Sumatra, and mainland Southeast Asia. These probably should not be conceived as involving feature transfers, but are otherwise difficult to place in our classificatory scheme. The first, which McGinn (1982) and Coady—McGinn (1982) incorrectly associate with an ingressive airstream, involves the reflexes of prenasalized voiced obstruents. In Iban, Narum, and some other languages of Sarawak, as well as in Rejang and Acehnese of Sumatra, such sequences differ from their normal phonetic value in that the velum is closed only an instant before the oral release, producing what is often misheard as a simple nasal. Scott (1957), who first reported the phenomenon for Iban, contends that the distinction between underlying medial nasals and prenasalized voiced obstruents is realized phonetically as contrastive nasality on the following vowel. A similar analysis is adopted for Acehnese by Durie (1985). In such analyses nasalized vowels have the peculiarity of generally contrasting with oral vowels only after nasal consonants.

The second nasal-oral timing phenomenon is that of "preploded" final nasals. In certain Land Dayak languages of southwest Borneo (Scott 1964; Court 1967), final nasals are often combined with a preceding obstruent, voiced in some languages, voiceless in others: Mentu *ciupm* 'kiss' (Malay *cium*), Bukar-Sadong *kaidn* 'cloth' (Malay *kain*). Simple nasals occur in final position if the final syllable begins with a nasal consonant: Bukar-Sadong *teŋan* 'hand, arm'. A similar phenomenon occurs in Banggi, spoken between north Borneo and the Philippine island of Palawan; in Tunjung of southeast Borneo; and in some dialects of Mentawai, spoken in the Barrier Islands west of Sumatra (Bernd Nothofer, personal communication). Northern Roglai, a Chamic language of Vietnam, reflects Proto-Austronesian final nasals as the homorganic voiceless stop. If the final syllable begins with a nasal, however, the final nasal is preserved — a clear indication of the former presence of preploded nasals in that language as well. A similar evolution of preploded final nasals to homorganic voiceless stops is found in some Kendayan Dayak languages in southwest Borneo, and in the Mentawai dialect described by Morris (1900). Since preploded final nasals have also been reported in the Austroasiatic languages of the Malay Peninsula, they appear to be an areal feature in western Indonesia. However, within this area the distribution is discontinuous, skipping over hundreds of miles and dozens of languages in some cases.

## 4.2.4 Fortitions and lenitions

If we take free breathing to be the weakest possible articulation, then a continuum from weaker to stronger phonation types is defined by 1) increasing constriction of the airstream; 2) increasing duration of constriction; and 3) any increase of markedness (e. g., devoicing of intervocalic obstruents, voicing of word-final obstruents). Any historical movement in this direction will be called a fortition.

Apart from some marginal phenomena such as *l > /d/ before *i in Malagasy, *l > /d/ before any high vowel in Tonsea, and the frequent reflex *R > /g/ in the Philippines and occasionally elsewhere, fortitions in Austronesian are confined by and large to the semivowels. Although both *w and *y have disappeared in some languages, in many others they have been strengthened, sometimes singly and sometimes together. The most interesting fortitions involve the conversion of *w to a labiovelar stop and *y to a coronal affricate or fricative. The change *w > /g$^w$/ is attested in Chamorro before non-rounded vowels, in Lindrou, Likum, and some other languages of western Manus, and in late nineteenth century Bintulu (Ray 1913), where it has since become /b/. The change *w > /b/ in Miri and Long Terawan Berawan of northern Sarawak, and *w > /g/ in Tunjung of southeast Borneo; in Chamorro (before rounded vowels); in most of the languages of the Aru Islands (Collins 1982); and in Sori of northwest Manus also appears to be through intermediate *g$^w$. In Alune of Seram (central Moluccas), and Lau of the southeast Solomons *w changed to /k$^w$/. In many of the same languages *y underwent a parallel strengthening (Chamorro /dz/, Lindrou, Long Terawan, Tunjung, Sori /j/, Bintulu /z/, Lau /s/). That this was not invariably the case, however, is clear from cases like Alune, where *w > /k$^w$/, but *y disappeared (Collins 1983).

Most intriguingly, the non-phonemic transitional glide that is unavoidable between a high vowel and a following unlike vowel is also strengthened in some languages. Thus PAN, *duSa > Bintulu ba, Miri dəbeh, Long Terawan ləbih, Tunjung rəga, Chamorro hug$^w$a 'two' shows fortition of a glide which clearly is secondary, since it could form only after *S was lost. In many languages of northern Sarawak, as Bintulu, Miri and Long Terawan a high vowel (but not *a) which preceded a strengthened glide shifted to shwa: the foregoing and *quay > Bintulu, Miri bay 'rattan', *abuat > Bintulu bat, Miri bet, Long Terawan kəbəiʔ 'long', *buaq > Miri beʔ 'fruit', *diaq > Bintulu dəzaʔ, Miri jeʔ 'good', *siaw > Bintulu (sə)zaw 'chicken'. In such cases the entire first syllable usually was lost in Miri (the word for *two* is an exception), and sometimes was lost in Bintulu. Thus, Bintulu, Miri bay reflect only the diphthong of *quay (preceded by the non-phonemic transitional glide [w]). In Long Terawan, the syllable preceding a strengthened glide was not lost, but the first syllable of a trisyllable that contains a strengthened glide before the last vowel was. Together with other innovations, this change produces some remarkable etymologies, as *baRuaŋ > kəbiŋ 'the Malayan honey bear' and *duRian > kəjin 'durian' (from *Ruaŋ and *Rian, with *R > /k/, strengthening of the non-phonemic glide, centralization of the high vowel before the strengthened glide, and last-syllable *a > /i/).

Perhaps to be noted here as well is the development of geminate consonants and implosive stops. The former have several sources. In many Western Malayo-Polynesian languages, most consonants are predictably geminated following shwa. This can be viewed as a tendency to maintain a constant unit of length over adjacent VC sequences: since the duration of *e typically is less than that of other vowels the consonant that follows shwa undergoes a kind of 'compensatory' lengthening. Where the vowel system remained unchanged, this phonetic relationship produced no phonemic change. However, in Isneg and some other languages of the Philippines in which *e > /a/, these phonetic differences became phonemic: cf. PMP *enem > annám 'six', but *anak > aná? 'child'.

In other languages geminates developed through the complete assimilation of a medial nasal to the following homorganic voiceless obstruent. Such cases include Kiput of northern Sarawak (*matay > mataay 'die', *mantis > mattay 'kingfisher', *rantay > lattaay 'chain'), and Toba Batak of northern Sumatra (*mp > /pp/, *nt > /tt/, *ns > /ts/, *ŋk > /kk/).

It can also be noted here that the Berawan languages of northern Sarawak have a pervasive set of fortis:lenis distinctions in which the fortis consonant appears (to the unaided ear) to be of normal duration and the lenis consonant to be extra short (*Ratus > Long Terawan gitoh 'hundred', *batu > bit!oh 'stone'). The origin of this distinction is totally baffling.

Preglottalized and implosive stops have developed in several parts of the Austronesian world, most notably in Chamic; parts of central and western Borneo (Kenyah dialects, Bintulu); southern Sulawesi; and geographically adjacent parts of the Lesser Sunda Islands. In general these reflect earlier consonant clusters (for details see Blust 1980). The appearance of implosive stops in central and western Borneo is the result of an unusual historical development which

produced a set of true voiced aspirates in Bario Kelabit (Blust
1974b) and a synchronic alternation of /b/ and /s/ in Kiput (Blust
1974c).

Finally, a prenasalized voiced bilabial trill occurs in many of the
languages of central and eastern Manus, where it is paralleled by a
prenasalized voiced alveolar trill. Catford (1988) describes a very
similar pair of phonation types in Nias of the Barrier Islands west
of Sumatra, and a similar alveolar trill (written *dr*) is found in
standard Fijian. In all examples for which an etymology is known
the segments in question derive from prenasalized stops or continuants.

If fortition tends to be the exception in phonological change,
lenition is the normal course of things. PAN *p* has some 17 known
reflexes in Austronesian languages, and the great majority of these
(apart from *p* > /p/) can be characterized as lenitions, /f/, /h/,
zero, /v/, and /w/ being particularly common. Much the same can
be said for *k*, where /h/, /ʔ/, and zero are common reflexes (*s* is
more problematic, as it is both weakened to /h/ or zero, and
strengthened to /t/ in a number of languages). Developmental sequences such as *p* > *f* > *h* > zero can be characterized as
erosion sequences. Both canonical erosion sequences (e. g., erosion
"from the right") and segmental erosion sequences (as from *p* to
zero) are clearly present in Austronesian. Because they sometimes
present interesting and previously unexplored correlations with geography, erosion sequences will be the subject of a separate, if brief,
discussion in the following section.

## 5. The mapping of linguistic change

Dialect geographers have long made use of maps to plot the distribution of linguistic features over space, but historical linguists have
paid scant attention to the geographical distribution of diachronic
data on a larger scale. Preliminary impressions suggest that the
Austronesian material may yield very interesting results when this
is done.

Let us for the moment consider only PAN *p*, and assign a
numerical value to reflexes as follows: /p/ = 1, /f/ = 2, /h/ = 3,

zero = 4. Such values define the degree of erosion of *p, since in general all higher-numbered reflexes are likely to have passed through lower-numbered intermediate stages. It must also be recognized that more than one erosion path is possible. Next to the sequence sketched above, for example, we might also recognize: /p/ = 1, /f/ = 2, /v/ = 3, /w/ = 4. Questions about the equivalence or non-equivalence of similarly numbered stages in such alternative paths cannot be dealt with here. If we plot the results on a map of the Austronesian world, the results are quite remarkable: (1) all of the 21 or 22 Austronesian languages of Taiwan are at stage 1; (2) all of the 100-odd languages of the Philippines except Buhid of Mindoro (Zorc 1974) and the South Mindanao languages (a genetic unit consisting of Tiruray, Tagabili, and Bilaan) are at stage 1; the exceptions are at stage 2, except that *p generally became Tagabili /h/ (stage 3) word-initially; (3) in western Indonesia the degree of erosion increases, with Banggi, Miri, Nias, and Malagasy (ultimately from southeast Borneo) all independently arriving at stage 2, and Simalur of the Barrier Islands at stage 3 (/h/) medially and stage 4 (zero) initially; (4) in eastern Indonesia stage 2 is fairly common, being found in Bimanese and Mambai of the Lesser Sunda Islands, Yamdena of the Tanimbar Archipelago, Kola of the Aru Islands, Kei and a number of languages in the central and northern Moluccas; stage 3 (/h/) is seen in Roti, Atoni, and Tetun of the Lesser Sundas, in Hoti, Manusela, Kayeli and some other languages of the central Moluccas, in Soboyo of the Sula Archipelago, and in Kayoa, East Makian, and the Wosi and Saketa dialects of Gimán (Gane) in extreme southern Halmahera (Dik Teljeur, personal communication); stage 4 (zero) is attested in Helong, Kemak, and Kisar of the Lesser Sunda Islands, in Ujir of the Aru Islands (Collins 1982), and in a number of languages in the central Moluccas; (5) within Oceanic *p is retained as a stop only in a few languages in western Melanesia, /f/ or /v/ being more nearly the norm, with /h/ and zero as not infrequent reflexes.

If we were to use the suggested numerical values to compute an 'erosion index' for *p, it is clear that the average numerical value would increase significantly in moving south from Taiwan into the Philippines and western Indonesia, and particularly in moving from western Indonesia into eastern Indonesia and the Pacific. In computing any such index we would need to pay close attention to "Galton's problem" (the issue of the historical independence of sample units). However, even without a detailed investigation it is clear that much of this erosion was independent and parallel. Ross (1988), for example, reconstructs POC *p as a voiceless bilabial stop, implying that the widespread erosion of PAN *p in Oceanic languages was independent of that in eastern Indonesia and, moreover, occurred independently in many Oceanic languages. To a very large extent this pattern can be generalized to reflexes of PAN *k, and probably to some other erosion sequences. It would seem to follow that the greater the distance travelled from the probable Austronesian homeland (on or near Taiwan) or from the probable Oceanic homeland (in or near the Bismarck Archipelago), the greater the average degree of phonological erosion encountered (at least for *p and *k). Why this correlation of phonological change and geography should exist, is still unknown. The correlation itself, however, appears to be beyond dispute, and agrees closely with global features of syntactic change (Wolff 1973; Starosta — Pawley — Reid 1982).

## 6. The Regularity Hypothesis

There can be little doubt that the Regularity Hypothesis has exerted a salutory influence since it was first vigorously asserted some 112 years ago. It is nevertheless worth keeping in mind that the heuristic value of the Regularity Hypothesis and the truth of its claims are separate issues. As a matter of sound method, the investigator in historical linguistics should make every reasonable effort to find explanations for apparent irregularities through 1) phonological conditioning, 2) borrowing, or 3) etymological error. However, where these efforts prove fuitless, artificial attempts to contrive conditions, vacuous references to borrowing, or the reconstruction of typologically bizarre proto-languages can only obscure what should be viewed as legitimate problems for scientific inquiry. The Regularity Hypothesis is not a divine dictum nor a fact of Nature: it is a scientific hypothesis, and like any other hypothesis, it is in need of relentless scrutiny and testing.

The data of Austronesian comparative linguistics strongly support the Regularity Hypothesis in the sense that application of the

Comparative Method yields a limited number of well-attested, widely supported correspondences. These correspondences in turn permit the reconstruction of a phoneme inventory which exhibits a fairly high degree of internal coherence and natural language plausibility. At the same time, many languages exhibit unexplained diachronic irregularities. In some cases, these irregularities may be due to changes in progress; in others, they may be due to undetected borrowing or obscure phonological conditions. But in a significant percentage of cases, it appears that we should seriously consider the possibility of true irregularity. Four types of apparently irregular phonological change in Austronesian come readily to mind: 1) sporadic prenasalization, 2) multiple reflexes of *R, 3) fronting of back vowels, especially *u, and 4) voicing cross-over in the velar stops.

Disagreements in the prenasalization of medial obstruents were noted by Dempwolff (1934—1938), who symbolized them by the reconstruction of "facultative" nasals: *tu(m)buq 'grow' (some languages reflecting *tubuq, others *tumbuq), etc. In medial position, the problem is endemic in languages of the Western Malayo-Polynesian group. In the Oceanic languages, the problem is even more pervasive in the sense that "oral grade" and "nasal grade" reflexes are found both in initial and in medial position, and cross-linguistic disagreements of consonant grade occur in at least 10% of the available etymologies.[8] Various proposals have been made concerning the cause of these irregularities, but none has yet succeeded in dealing with the problem as a whole.

As noted earlier, PAN *R probably was an alveolar or uvular trill. Its most common reflexes are /g/, /l/, /r/, and zero, with /h/, /s/, and /y/ also occurring in at least two widely separated languages. This proto-phoneme has long been a source of comparative problems. Some languages have a single reflex, but many others exhibit two or more reflexes without clear conditions. In some cases (Ngaju, Dayak, Tiruray) the split of *R is almost certainly due to borrowing, but in others (Bisaya of Brunei, the Melanau languages of Sarawak, the languages of Manus, Nuclear Micronesian), no straightforward hypothesis of borrowing is available. As a first step in dealing with this problem, Dyen (1953 b) subdivided *R into four subscripted varieties, each representing a distinct correspondence class. Dahl (1976) has argued that Dyen's proposal fails to take account of borrowing. In any case, it is clear that as more languages with multiple reflexes of *R are incorporated into the comparative picture, Dyen's approach will require the recognition of an ever-increasing number of subscripted varieties of *R, each supported by an ever-diminishing data base. The further this line of analysis proceeds, the less plausible it becomes, and the more one feels compelled to seek other types of explanation (cf., e. g., Geraghty no date).

The sporadic fronting of back vowels, particularly *u in Oceanic languages, was first noted by Blust (1970). Although other types of vocalic irregularity occur in the same set of languages, the irregular change *u > /i/ seems especially common. In some cases, doublets result (POC *qumun > Hawaiian *imu, umu* 'earth oven'), while in others only a form with front vowel survives (POC *tamanu > Hawaiian *kamani* 'a shore tree: *Calophyllum inophyllum*'). Although this phenomenon is most apparent in Oceanic languages, a similar sporadic fronting of *u has been observed in Chamorro (western Micronesia) and in Singhi (southwest Borneo), both Western Malayo-Polynesian languages.

Dempwolff (1934 – 1938) reconstructed some 2,215 lexical items which he attributed (somewhat optimistically, given the limited geographical distribution of some of his proposed cognate sets) to the common ancestor of the Austronesian languages. In this corpus of reconstructed forms, word-initial *g is found 106 times and word-initial *k 214 times. Among the 11 languages that Dempwolff compared, five retain the *g/k distinction. For around 5% of all Dempwolff reconstructions that begin with a velar stop, at least one reflex exhibits an unexpected value for voicing. Many other examples of voicing cross-over in the velar stops can be cited from languages not considered by Dempwolff, and a number of previously overlooked Tagalog-Malay comparisons can be assembled once the cross-over phenomenon is recognized.

Several observations about these correspondences are worth making. First, the voicing cross-over in velar stops is not paralleled by voicing cross-over in the labial or dental stops. Second, the irregularities in velar reflexes almost exclusively involve voicing crossover. Third, voicing cross-over does not occur in final position, and is rare intervocalically or medially following a nasal. Fourth, although other kinds of irregularities are more common in individual languages, the voicing cross-over in velar stops is a) one of the most common types of irregularity noted, b) evenly distributed over all of the diagnostic languages, and c) works in both directions. In short, there appears to be an inherent instability in the voicing distinction for velar stops that is not matched by stops of other orders.

When this comparative problem first became apparent to me in 1973, I had an opportunity to ask Chin-wu Kim (then visiting in Hawaii) if he knew any phonetic reason why the voicing value for velar stops should be inherently less stable than the voicing value for pre-velar stops. He provided the following explanation. Voiced stops are produced by allowing egressive pulmonic air to pass through the narrowed vocal cords into a closed supraglottal cavity. Once the cavity is filled the pressure differential across the vocal cords is neutralized, thus suppressing vocal cord vibration (= voicing). The oral cavity volume available for continued expansion of the airstream before release of the closure is greater for labials than for dentals, and greater for dentals than for velars.

Without entering into more than minimal detail here, it is worth noting that this difference in potential duration of voicing has been confirmed as a difference in actual duration of voicing for English stops (Smith 1977). The facts in English (with labials having the greatest voicing duration and velars the least) do not necessarily establish the same relations for other languages, but it is likely that they point in the same direction.

Although the phonetic information at our disposal for Austronesian languages is limited, the suggestion of Kim and the study of Smith do raise interesting prospects for matching phonetic theory with historical data. If the *$g/k$ distinction is inherently unstable in Austronesian languages because of general articulatory properties of stops, it will be unstable in other language families as well. In other words, the analysis suggested here predicts that in many language families voicing cross-over will be found in the correspondences holding between velar stops, but not in those holding between pre-velar stops.

More generally still, our analysis raises questions about the regularity of sound change. In the Neogrammarian position as epitomized by Hermann Paul sound change is unconscious, gradual, and mechanical. Its regularity is a function both of communicative need and of the independence of sound from meaning. The speaker does not single out individual words in aiming at an articulatory target, and if the target drifts, it will drift without respect to semantic considerations. In an important sense, then, Paul maintained that the regularity of sound change is a by-product of the physiology of speech.

The experience of comparativists working in many different language families has shown that sound change does, indeed, appear to be overwhelmingly regular. Its general regularity may even be in part physiologically motivated. However, the analysis of velar stop correspondences in Austronesian suggests that the physiology of the speech organs may also be responsible for certain types of universal exceptions to the regularity of sound change. These types of exceptions need not be limited to voicing cross-over in the velar stops. More generally, wherever a phonemic contrast involves a perceptually difficult distinction there is a greater likelihood that the phonemes in question will be interchanged in some lexical items, probably by first passing through a stage in which the problematic items have variant pronunciations.

Why variants might develop in some morphemes but not in others, is unclear. It is possible that regular sound change is basically a matter of production: consciously or otherwise speakers alter a phonetic form either unconditionally or in a given environment. The examples of voicing cross-over discussed above probably have nothing to do with production. Rather, frequent mishearing raises doubts for some speakers as to the correct voicing value for a velar stop in a particular lexical item. By their nature, errors of perception are more likely to be random than errors of production, a fact observable in loanwords, which often undergo random phonetic substitutions. In a sense, one might even wish to exclude changes such as those discussed here from the category "sound change": what is involved is not a change of articulatory norms nor of phonemes, but a change in the phonemic composition of morphemes based on a high incidence of mishearing and consequent reinterpretation. Given this position, however, not all phonetic change is sound change, and the regularity of sound change would become little more than a matter of definition.

## 7. Summary

In summary, various kinds of patterns can be discerned in the historical phonology of Austronesian languages. Some of these are basically canonical, while others are segmental. Some show noteworthy correlations of phonological erosion with geography. Others raise important questions about the Regularity Hypothesis. Much remains to be done in almost every area. Indices of phonological erosion could be compared with indices of lexical erosion (Blust 1981 a) and a search made for possible correlations. Stability indices could be computed for individual proto-phonemes, and the relative frequency of types of sound change (conditioned vs. unconditioned, splits vs. shifts vs. mergers, etc.) determined. Although many sound changes in Austronesian doubtless remain undocumented, a great deal of material is available, and much will be learned by matching the data from this large and internally diverse language family with the expectations derived from general theories of language change.

## Notes

1. This paper is an abbreviated version of a 65-page manuscript which itself was incomplete at the time of presentation. As such it represents a rather serious compromise between my intentions and the requirements of the present volume. Much is left out, and much that could be treated in greater detail is covered only schematically.
2. Ruhlen (1987) lists 941 Austronesian languages, a figure which comes to 19.8% of his world total of 4,741. The lower number is based on a compilation of areal estimates made by various Austronesian specialists, and is conservative.
3. In writing Proto-Austronesian phonemes, I use the orthography introduced by Dyen in the 1940s and since widely employed in Austronesian linguistics. As will be seen, this does not imply that I accept all of his interpretations of the sound correspondences.
4. In Kadazan of northwest Borneo, on the other hand, all Proto-Austronesian nouns that began with a vowel are reflected as *t* V-. This consonant is a better candidate for a fossilized grammatical marker.
5. See Mills (1975) for an overview of South Sulawesi languages, where much erosion "from the right" seems to postdate the break-up of Proto-South Sulawesi, and Sneddon (1978) for a comparative account of the Minahasan languages in north Sulawesi, where almost no erosion has occurred.
6. According to D. C. Laycock, the correspondence *t* : *k* is not uncommon in Papuan languages; once systematic comparative work is undertaken on a larger scale, it may be determined that a similar change is found in one or more non-Austronesian language groups of the New Guinea area.
7. Hamel's (1988) description of these facts as instances of "vowel harmony" is misleading and inaccurate.
8. Blust (in press). The "nasal grade" consonants of Oceanic languages are not always prenasalized, and it is a legitimate question whether the phenomenon of sporadic prenasalization in Western Malayo-Polynesian languages and the phenomenon of "oral-nasal cross-over" in Oceanic languages is historically the same. Some oral-nasal alternations and cross-linguistic disagreements in Oceanic languages appear to stem from the fossilization of grammatical markers (Lynch 1975, Crowley 1988).

## References

Bender, Byron W.
1969        "Vowel dissimilation in Marshallese", *Working Papers in Linguistics*
            1.1: 88−96 (Honolulu, Department of Linguistics, University of
            Hawaii).
Benedict, Paul K.
1984        "Austro-Tai parallel: A tonal Chamic language on Hainan", *Com-
            putational Analyses of Asian and African Languages* 22: 83−86.
Blust, Robert
1970        "*i* and *u* in the Austronesian languages", *Working Papers in Lin-
            guistics* 2.6: 113−145 (Honolulu, Department of Linguistics, Uni-
            versity of Hawaii).
1971        "A Tagalog consonant cluster conspiracy", *The Philippine Journal of
            Linguistics* 2.2: 85−91.
1974 a      "Eastern Austronesian: A note", *Working Papers in Linguistics* 6.4:
            101−107 (Honolulu, Department of Linguistics, University of Ha-
            waii).
1974 b      "A double counter-universal in Kelabit", *Papers in Linguistics* 7.3/4:
            309−324.
1974 c      *The Proto-North Sarawak vowel deletion hypothesis* (Ph. D. disser-
            tation, unpublished, Honolulu, Department of Linguistics, Univer-
            sity of Hawaii).
1976        "Dempwolff's reduplicated monosyllables", *Oceanic Linguistics* 15:
            107−130.
1977 a      "The Proto-Austronesian pronouns and Austronesian subgrouping:
            A preliminary report", *Working Papers in Linguistics* 9.1: 1−15
            (Honolulu, Department of Linguistics, University of Hawaii).
1977 b      "A rediscovered Austronesian comparative paradigm", *Oceanic Lin-
            guistics* 16: 1−51.
1978        "Eastern Malayo-Polynesian: A subgrouping argument", in: Stephen
            A. Wurm−Lois Carrington (eds.), *Second International Conference
            on Austronesian Linguistics: Proceedings, Fascicle* 1 (Pacific Linguis-
            tics C61) (Canberra: Australian National University), 181−234.
1979        "Coronal-noncoronal consonant clusters: New evidence for marked-
            ness", *Lingua* 47: 101−117.
1980        "More on the origins of glottalic consonants", *Lingua* 52: 125−156.
1981 a      "Variation in retention rate among Austronesian languages" [Paper
            presented at the Third International Conference on Austronesian
            Linguistics, Denpasar, Bali, January, 1981].
1981 b      "Some remarks on labiovelar correspondences in Oceanic lan-
            guages", in: Jim Hollyman−Andrew Pawley (eds.), *Studies in Pacific
            languages and cultures in honour of Bruce Biggs* (Auckland, Linguistic
            Society of New Zealand), 229−253.
1982 a      "The linguistic value of the Wallace Line", *Bijdragen tot de Taal-,
            Land- en Volkenkunde* 138: 231−250.
1982 b      "An overlooked feature of Malay historical phonology", *Bulletin of
            the School of Oriental and African Studies* 45: 284−299.

1983/1984   "More on the position of the languages of eastern Indonesia",
            *Oceanic Linguistics* 22/23: 1—28.
in press    "Toward an adequate theory of consonant grade in Oceanic lan-
            guages", *Proceedings of the Fifth International Conference on Austro-
            nesian Linguistics* (Te Reo, New Zealand).

Bradshaw, Joel
1979        "Obstruent harmony and tonogenesis in Jabem", *Lingua* 49: 189—
            205.

Brandstetter, Renward
1916        *An introduction to Indonesian linguistics* [translated by C. O. Blagden]
            (London, The Royal Asiatic Society).

Burling, Robbins
1966        "The addition of final stops in the history of Maru", *Lg.* 42: 581—
            586.

Capell, Arthur
1949        "Two tonal languages of New Guinea", *Bulletin of the School of
            Oriental and African Studies* 13: 184—199.

Catford, John C.
1988        "Notes on the phonetics of Nias", in: Richard McGinn (ed.), *Studies
            in Austronesian Linguistics* (Ohio University Monographs in Inter-
            national Studies, Southeast Asia Series, no. 76), 151—172.

Chrétien, C. Douglas
1965        "The statistical structure of the Proto-Austronesian morph", *Lingua*
            14: 243—270.

Coady, James—Richard McGinn
1982        "On the so-called implosive nasals of Rejang", in: Rainer Carle et
            al. (eds.), *GAVA':* Studies in Austronesian languages and cultures
            dedicated to Hans Kähler (Berlin, Reimer), 437—449.

Collins, James T.
1982        "Linguistic research in Maluku: A report of recent field work",
            *Oceanic Linguistics* 21: 73—146.
1983        *The historical relationships of the languages of central Maluku, In-
            donesia* (Pacific Linguistics D47) (Canberra: Australian National
            University).

Court, Christopher
1967        "Some areal features of Mentu Land Dayak", *Oceanic Linguistics* 6:
            46—50.

Crowley, Terry
1988        *Southeast Ambrym, Paama and Lopevi verb initial mutation.* Ms.

Dahl, Otto Chr.
1954        "Le substrat Bantou en malgache", *Norsk Tidsskrift for Sprogviden-
            skap* 17: 325—362.
1976 [1973] *Proto-Austronesian* 2nd rev. ed. (Scandinavian Institute of Asian Stud-
            ies, Monograph Series no. 15) (Lund).

Dempwolff, Otto
1934—1938   *Vergleichende Lautlehre des austronesischen Wortschatzes* 1: *Induk-
            tiver Aufbau einer indonesischen Ursprache* (= *Zeitschrift für Einge-
            borenensprachen, Supplement* 15) (1934); 2: *Deduktive Anwendung des*

162    *Robert Blust*

Urindonesischen auf austronesische Einzelsprachen (= *Zeitschrift für Eingeborenensprachen, Supplement* 17) (1937); 3: *Austronesisches Wörterverzeichnis* (= *Zeitschrift für Eingeborenensprachen, Supplement* 19) (1938). (Berlin, Reimer).

Durie, Mark
1985    *A grammar of Acehnese on the basis of a dialect of North Aceh* (Verhandelingen van het Koninklijk Instituut voor Taal-, Land- en Volkenkunde 112) (Dordrecht: Foris).

Dyen, Isidore
1953a    *The Proto-Malayo-Polynesian laryngeals* (Baltimore: Linguistic Society of America).
1953b    "Dempwolff's *R*", *Lg.* 29: 359−366.
1965a    *A lexicostatistical classification of the Austronesian languages* (International Journal of American Linguistics, Memoir 19) (= *IJAL* vol. 31, no. 1).
1965b    "Formosan evidence for some new Proto-Austronesian phonemes", *Lingua* 14: 285−305.
1978    "Proto-Ambonic evidence for additional Proto-Austronesian vowels", in: S. Udin (ed.), *Spectrum: Essays presented to Sutan Takdir Alisjahbana on his seventieth birthday* (Jakarta, Dian Rakyat), 390−399.

Geraghty, Paul
no date    "Proto Eastern Oceanic *R* and its reflexes" [typescript].

Goodenough, Ward H.
1962    Comment on Capell, "Oceanic linguistics today", *Current Anthropology* 3: 406−408.

Hamel, Patricia J.
1988    "Vowel harmony and affixation in Loniu", in: Richard McGinn (ed.), *Studies in Austronesian Linguistics* (Ohio University Monographs in International Studies, Southeast Asia Series, no. 76), 235−249.

Harvey, Mark
1982    "Subgroups in Austronesian", in: Amran Halim et al. (eds.), *Papers from the Third International Conference on Austronesian Linguistics* 2 (Pacific Linguistics C75) (Canberra, Australian National University), 47−99.

Haudricourt, André G.
1951    "Variations parallèles en Mélanésien", *Bulletin de la Société de Linguistique de Paris* 47: 140−153.
1965    "Problems of Austronesian comparative philology", *Lingua* 14: 315−329.
1971    "New Caledonia and the Loyalty Islands", in: Thomas A. Sebeok (ed.), *Current Trends in Linguistics* 8: *Linguistics in Oceania* (The Hague: Mouton), 359−396.

Henderson, E. J. A.
1965    "The topography of certain phonetic and morphological characteristics of South East Asian languages", *Lingua* 14: 400−434.

Keraf, Gregorius
1978        *Morfologi dialek Lamalera* (Ende, Flores: Arnoldus).
Laycock, D. C.
1978        "A little Mor", in: Stephen A. Wurm — Lois Carrington (eds.), *Second International Conference on Austronesian Linguistics: Proceedings* 1 (Pacific Linguistics C61) (Canberra: Australian National University), 285 — 316.
Lee, Ernest Wilson
1966        *Proto-Chamic phonologic word and vocabulary* (Ph. D. dissertation, Indiana University) (Ann Arbor, University Microfilms International).
Lynch, John
1975        "Oral/nasal alternation and the realis/irrealis distinction in Oceanic languages", *Oceanic Linguistics* 14: 87 — 99.
Maddieson, Ian
1987        "Linguo-labials", *UCLA Working Papers in Phonetics* 68: 21 — 45.
Matisoff, James A.
1975        "Rhinoglottophilia: The mysterious connection between nasality and glottality", in: Charles A. Ferguson et al. (eds.), *Nasálfest: Papers from a symposium on nasals and nasalization* (Special publication, Language Universals Project) (Department of Linguistics, Stanford University), 265 — 287.
McGinn, Richard
1982        "Outline of Rejang syntax", *NUSA: Linguistic studies of Indonesian and other languages in Indonesia*, vol. 14. (Jakarta).
Mills, Roger F.
1975        *Proto South Sulawesi and Proto Austronesian phonology* 1 — 2 (Ph. D. dissertation, University of Michigan) (Ann Arbor: University Microfilms International).
Morris, Max
1900        *Die Mentawai-Sprache* (Berlin: Conrad Skopnik).
Nothofer, Bernd
1975        *The reconstruction of Proto-Malayo-Javanic* (Verhandelingen van het Koninklijk Instituut voor Taal-, Land- en Volkenkunde 73) (The Hague: Nijhoff).
Ogawa, Naoyoshi — Erin Asai
1935        *The myths and traditions of the Formosan native tribes* (in Japanese) (Taipei).
Ray, Sidney H.
1913        "The languages of Borneo", *The Sarawak Museum Journal* 1.4: 1 — 196.
Ross, Malcolm David
1988        *Proto-Oceanic and the Austronesian languages of western Melanesia* (Pacific Linguistics C 98). (Canberra: Australian National University).
Ruhlen, Merritt
1987        *A guide to the world's languages* 1: *Classification* (Stanford, CA: Stanford University Press).

Schmidt, Wilhelm
    1906        *Die Mon-Khmer-Völker: ein Bindeglied zwischen Völkern Zentral-
                asiens und Austronesiens* (Braunschweig: Vieweg).
Scott, N. C.
    1957        "Notes on the pronunciation of Sea Dayak", *Bulletin of the School
                of Oriental and African Studies* 20: 509–512.
    1964        "Nasal consonants in Land Dayak (Bukar-Sadong)", in: David Aber-
                crombie et al. (eds.), *In honour of Daniel Jones* (London: Longmans,
                Green and Co.), 432–436.
Sebeok, Thomas
    1942        "An examination of the Austro-Asiatic language family", *Lg.* 18:
                206–217.
Smith, Bruce L.
    1977        "Effects of vocalic context, place of articulation and speaker's sex
                on 'voiced' stop consonant production". Paper presented at the West
                Coast Phonetics Symposium, March 26–28, 1977, Santa Barbara,
                California.
Sneddon, J. N.
    1978        *Proto-Minahasan: Phonology, morphology and wordlist* (Pacific Lin-
                guistics B54) (Canberra: Australian National University).
    1984        *Proto-Sangiric and the Sangiric languages* (Pacific Linguistics B91)
                (Canberra: Australian National University).
Starosta, Stanley–Andrew K. Pawley–Lawrence A. Reid
    1982        "The evolution of focus in Austronesian", in: Amran Halim et al.
                (eds.), *Papers from the Third International Conference on Austronesian
                Linguistics* 2 (Pacific Linguistics C75) (Canberra: Australian Na-
                tional University), 145–170.
Tsuchida, Shigeru
    1976        *Reconstruction of Proto-Tsouic phonology* (Study of Languages and
                Cultures of Asia and Africa Monograph Series, no. 5) (Tokyo, In-
                stitute for the Study of Languages and Cultures of Asia and Africa).
Wolff, John U.
    1973        "Verbal inflection in Proto-Austronesian", in: Andrew B. Gonzalez
                (ed.), *Parangal kay Cecilio Lopez: Essay in Honor of Cecilio Lopez
                on His Seventy-Fifth Birthday* (Quezon City, Linguistic Society of
                the Philippines), 71–91.
    1974        "Proto-Austronesian *r* and *\*d*", *Oceanic Linguistics* 13: 77–121.
    1982        "Proto-Austronesian *\*c*, *\*z*, *\*g* and *\*T*", in: Amran Halim et al.
                (eds.), *Papers from the Third International Conference on Austronesian
                Linguistics* (Pacific Linguistics C75) (Canberra: Australian National
                University), 1–30.
    1988        "The PAN consonant system", in: Richard McGinn (ed.), *Studies in
                Austronesian Linguistics* (Ohio University Monographs in Interna-
                tional Studies, Southeast Asia Series, No. 76), 125–147.
Zorc, R. David
    1974        "Internal and external relationships of the Mangyan languages",
                *Oceanic Linguistics* 13: 561–600.

1978       "Proto-Philippine word accent: Innovation or Proto-Hesperonesian retention?", in: Stephen A. Wurm—Lois Carrington (eds.), *Second International Conference on Austronesian Linguistics: Proceedings* 1 (Canberra: Australian National University), 67—119.

# Etymologies, equations, and comparanda:
# Types and values, and criteria for judgment

*Calvert Watkins*

Language change is a fact. I will not consider here the possible or probable causes of language variation and language change. For our purposes I prefer to stay with the simple Saussurian notion that all things change over time, and there is little reason why we should expect human language to be any different.

The study of etymology represents a pivotal dimension of the response of the science of linguistics to the empirical fact of language change.

Now etymologies, as is well-known, are a good deal older than the science of linguistics, and a great deal more widespread. The making of "etymologies" by that or any other name is part of the metalinguistic techniques or operations of language speakers around the world, and has been since the documentation of human language. The urge to etymologize, like the cognate urge to pun, is deeply rooted in the human psyche; it is part of man's impulse to have power over his language, and thereby over the world it symbolizes. An etymology removes the arbitrary nature from the linguistic sign, and substitutes control. Socrates in the *Kratylos* (409 c, d) is asked to etymologize 'fire' and 'water'. He provides the explanation for 'water', by appeal to meaning, but claims he cannot do the latter. τὸ πῦρ ἀπορῶ he says, 'I give up on "fire"', yet the phonetic figure gives him away: πῦρ ... πορ *is* his etymology, by another route, that of sound.

Small wonder that etymology is enduringly appealing to the popular mind, and enduringly fraught with misunderstanding.

There is no shortage of manuals and handbooks of etymology. To mention only a few, of the postwar period, we have V. Pisani, *L'Etimologia: storia — questioni — metodo* (1947[1], 1967[2], German translation 1975); P. Guiraud, *L'étymologie* (1964[1], 1967[2]); A. S. C. Ross, *Etymology, with especial reference to English* (1958); Y. Malkiel, *Etymological dictionaries: A tentative typology* (1976);

J. Trier, *Wege der Etymologie* (1981); E. Seebold, *Etymologie* (1981); A. Bammesberger, *English etymology* (1984). There have been many article-length discussions, notably the studies, classical and more recent, collected in R. Schmitt (ed.), *Etymologie* (1977) and the later surveys, some by prominent practitioners of the art, assembled in A. Bammesberger (ed.), *Das etymologische Wörterbuch: Fragen der Konzeption und Gestaltung* (1983).

The many contributions of Yakov Malkiel deserve special notice here. Of those writing on the subject on the American scene, he is the most prolific and the most articulate, and probably the wisest. See in particular his "Etymology and general linguistics", and other studies collected in his *Essays on linguistic themes* (1968), as well as "Etymology and modern linguistics", and others in his *From particular to general linguistics* (1983).

Parenthetically, we may note that the Soviet linguist V. N. Toporov has discussed the issues in a series of Russian publications from "On some theoretical foundations of etymological analysis" [Russ.] (1960) through "Vedic *r̥tá*: On the correlation of conceptual structure and etymology" 1979 [1981] and "On some theoretical aspects of etymology" (1984; *non vidi*). Toporov's approach of "polysemous or polysemantic etymology" (*mnogoznačnaja ètimologija*) is fundamentally analogous to Malkiel's approach. It is both productive and insightful when handled with sensitivity and sophistication, as in Toporov's own monumental ongoing and truly paradigmatic Old Prussian etymological dictionary (*Prusskij jazyk*); but as handled by some other Soviet linguists, it has all the potential of Lysenkism in biology.

It should be apparent that the number of those writing on etymology in general is at least comparable in order of magnitude to those writing etymological dictionaries. It is still, one hopes, less than the sum total of those linguists producing etymologies during the last decades.

Still it must be admitted that etymology is hardly an expected activity of today's theoretical linguist, i. e., yesterday's general linguist. Malkiel in *Etymological dictionaries* recalls with some nostalgia William Dwight Whitney's estimation of etymology a century earlier as the cornerstone of any progressive, truly scientific inquiry into language (*The life and growth of language,* 1875). Whitney here echoes his own earlier words of 1867 (*Language and the study of language*): "Etymology ... is the foundation and substructure of all investigation of language; the broad principles, the wide-reaching views, the truths of universal application and importance, which constitute the upper fabric of linguistic science, all rest upon word-genealogies" (from Silverstein (ed.), 1971: 25—26). Today, 120 years later, Whitney's statement retains its pristine elegance and value; we need only delete "etymology" and "word-genealogies" and fill in the blanks with something else. Malkiel continues, happily adapting the resounding words of General de Gaulle: "Etymology has lost a battle but not the war". I was myself not aware of such a stage of belligerency, and the fact is that good etymologies are still being produced. The general decline in prominence of etymology is an obvious function of the decline of history-diachrony in favor of synchrony in linguistics on the one hand, and on the other an equally obvious function of the shift in focus from the word and its meaning to the sentence and its structure. Whitney called attention, with characteristic pungency, to the lack of relevance of etymology to linguistic synchrony, what he calls "the practical purposes of speech", where "etymological reminiscences ... would, if more prominent before our attention, be an actual embarrassment to us" (Whitney 1867: 5).

Yet, if etymologies are still with us — to the degree that historical linguistics is still with us —, I should inject a note of caution. In his recent work *Language in the Americas*, as in his earlier (1963) work on the classification of African languages, *The languages of Africa*, J. Greenberg specifically and intentionally eschews both sound correspondences and asterisked reconstructions, believing neither to be critical in demonstrating genetic classification. He does, however, believe firmly in the value of etymologies — "resemblances involving sound and meaning simultaneously" (1987: 29) — and the presentation of these is the principal thrust of his book. He terms the technique "multilateral comparison", "looking at everything at once", a comparison involving "few words but many languages", and one intended to yield in the first instance an alleged genetic classification. Whether Greenberg's book succeeds in this aim depends crucially then — stands or falls — on the quality of the etymologies he presents. In my opinion, the work fails; but it fails precisely in not adhering to its rightful method. Greenberg states, "The broad approach advocated here does not require the reckless positing of risky and uncertain etymologies ... it is better to start with a relatively small number of first-rate etymologies" (1987: 37). It is the etymologies themselves, the observable similarities in sound and meaning, which turn out to be inadequate to the task.

"Resemblances involving sound and meaning simultaneously" are only a beginning, at best. In particular, they are notoriously vulnerable to accidental similarity. The possibility of accidental similarity among languages results from an overriding condition of language change: the fact that it is bounded. This is a consequence of the fundamental paradox of our discipline: that on the one hand, all human languages are different, but on the other, all human languages are the same. The differences among languages are imputable ultimately to the fact of language change and linguistic diversification. But the set of linguistic universals or constraints on the form of grammars acts as a sort of governor regulating and channeling linguistic change, keeping it within certain bounds. The result is that the number of possible strings of the shape $C_iVC_j$ (for example) in the languages of the world is limited, and overlap in similar meaning in basic vocabulary consequently not unexpected. This after all is why we have and need historical linguistics.

As to the mystique of sound laws on the other hand, Greenberg is quite right to quote with approbation the Africanist Paul Newman (1970): "The proof of genetic relationship does not depend on the demonstration of historical sound laws. Rather the discovery of sound laws and the *reconstruction of linguistic history* normally emerge from the *careful* comparison of languages already presumed to be related" (Greenberg, 1987: 3, emphasis mine). What Newman is saying here, I think, could be restated in the following way: a genetic linguistic relationship is first assumed, or hypothesized, by inspection or whatever. At that point must begin the careful and above all systematic comparison, which will lead, if the hypothesis or supposition of genetic relationship is correct, to the reconstruction of the linguistic history of the languages concerned, including the discovery of the attendant sound laws, which are a part of that history. In other words, systematic comparison requires the postulation, reconstruction, or restoration of a common original, and of a set of rules by which that original is transformed into the later attested languages. That is what we mean by linguistic history. It is the history which is, de facto, the proof of the genetic relation. The implication is clearly that if the careful comparison of such languages does not yield a reconstruction of linguistic history as we know it, then the presumption that the languages are related is at best uninteresting, and at worst, in grave jeopardy.

It is well to remember that our goal is precisely linguistic history: both the history of languages and the history of speech communities. These goals are expressly recognized by Greenberg himself, as lying "at the very heart of linguistics as a scientific enterprise", "the understanding of linguistic change", and "the contribution the comparative method can make to nonlinguistic history".

"Etymology" in this structure or process has in fact at least two, and more realistically three, distinct values. In the sense of noting comparanda, things to be compared, etymology is just the first step. Greenberg discusses his illustration with forms of 'tooth' in Indo-European languages (1987: 26 — 27), "we might note the somewhat vague resemblance between English tooth and Hindi dã:t". That is etymology by inspection — call it E 1. It may be multiplied — this is the point of the Swadesh list, as well as of Greenberg's "multilateral comparison" — but it is still a hypothesis, whose fragility may be grasped by considering a simple and plausible etymological set at this level:

|          | Eng.      | Fr.      |
|----------|-----------|----------|
| 'tooth'  | *tuθ*     | *dã*     |
| 'eye'    | *aj*      | *öj*     |

We would at this stage have no principled way whatsoever of distinguishing the right etymology 'tooth' from the problematic etymology 'eye'.

Greenberg continues his discussion of 'tooth' by introducing further comparanda and exploiting them to arrive at "an approximate source form, *dant* or *dent*", then adding Lithuanian *dantis* and Modern Greek *dondi*: "... within the etymology for the word 'tooth' ... what we have done is the initial step of the comparative method itself. We have compared related forms and posited an approximate original form and subsequent changes" (1987: 27). This etymology we can now call E 2: no longer just an inspectional similarity, it is now a set of forms with a reconstructible history, a valid etymology and a "true" one. It is the E 2 level etymologies which are the foot soldiers of historical linguistics, the etymologies which do the work, the ones we call up in class or to settle an argument. When Meillet said an etymology had no value unless it was obvious, it was the type of "tooth" he had in mind. In any case the initial step, comparison proper, is followed by its systematic exploitation: we make an equation, then work out the history of phonology and morphology, derivational and inflectional where relevant, and come back with a "true" etymology in the context of an established family.

The "purpose" of E 2 level etymologies may vary according to particular circumstances. Thus in the context of a new language or languages added to an established family, we look for forms like *yakwe* and *yuk* respectively, in order to see what happens to PIE *$e\hat{k}uos$ in Tocharian B and A. It is a shorthand history.

The process may continue further, however, to a level we may call E 3, whose distinguishing feature may be simply that the etymology, or the history, is no longer obvious. Here belongs the history of Classical Armenian *atamn* 'tooth' and Classical Greek *odónt*-, the reconstruction *$h^1d$-ont-, and the further etymological connection with the family of English 'eat', via an assumed earlier meaning 'bite', 'take a bite', or the like. What is interesting in E 3 is clearly inappropriate to E 2; etymologies have different functions at different stages of the historical linguistic investigation.

The difference between E 2 and E 3 is only a matter of degree, and varies with the degree of precision and sophistication of the study of the given language, branch, or family. Both are the result, and at the same time the expression, of the systematic comparison which has yielded a linguistic history: the method of comparative historical linguistics. This is the sense of etymology in our best etymological dictionaries — a genre which can only exist in a family which has been established. "In a proper etymology every divergence must be explained by a postulated change consistent with a complete historical hypothesis", as Ives Goddard tellingly puts it. It is this sense of the term "etymology" — whether "E 2" or "E 3" — which I will assume in this paper to be the only one which is linguistically valid. Put another way, this sense of the word "etymology" is the only one which is linguistically interesting.

Interesting, that is, as theory. An etymology like Socrates' πῦρ ἀπορῶ is of course linguistically interesting, but as data. The same is true of a putative "Amerind" or "Nostratic" etymology. The discovery procedure whereby one initially establishes comparanda, is inspection, whether or not termed "multilateral comparison"

(Greenberg, 1987: 27), and whether or not the comparanda arrived at are termed "etymologies" (Greenberg, 1987: ch. 4: "Amerind etymological dictionary"). A comparison of the language groups in Greenberg's "Eurasiatic" family (p. 332, 337) with those in Illič-Svityč and others' "Nostratic" family shows, if nothing else, the perceptual variability — and consequent fragility — of such inspections. Thus, "Eurasiatic" includes not only Korean and Japanese but also Ainu, Gilyak, Chukotian, and Eskimo-Aleut; "Nostratic" excludes some of these but includes Khartvelian, Dravidian, and at least the "Semito-Hamitic" component of Afro-Asiatic, which for Greenberg (and for me) are separate families. Are these just trivial differences, and am I just being nit-picky to point them out?

First comes the inspection, and the isolation of the comparanda, which we may collect and term E 1 etymologies, or first-pass etymologies. We may assert or hypothesize a genetic relation on the basis of them. But the proof of the linguistic pudding remains in the follow-up, the systematic exploitation, the full implementation of the comparative method, which alone can demonstrate not just a linguistic genetic relationship, but a linguistic history. If I believe in an Indo-European, Algonquian, or Austronesian, it is because scholars have done the necessary systematic explanation and produced the requisite historical results. If I do not yet believe in an Amerind, Eurasiatic, or Nostratic, it is because scholars have so far neither done the one nor produced the other. To spell it out: because scholars have neither done the necessary systematic explanation, nor produced the requisite historical results. And there is no other way.

Once the "obvious" (E 2) etymologies are made in a family — for the principal Indo-European languages known or recognized at the time this was done before 1850 — attention can shift to the "non-obvious" sort (E 3). And here are to be found the etymologies whose very contemplation is the purest pleasure, as the distinguished Indo-Europeanist Oswald Szemerényi once said of German *Messer* from *mezzi-rahs*. Here are the etymologies which bear the stamp of their creator: Saussure's *dominus*, Brugmann's σέβομαι, Trubeckoj's and Vaillant's *dъždъ*, Cowgill's οὐ, Sapir's Navaho *nà'dą́'* 'corn' from 'enemy's food'.

In contemporary Indo-European studies most etymologies now being made fall into the E 3 group, perhaps just by default: all the obvious etymologies like 'tooth' were made long ago. (In most cases, incidentally, long before the development of the notion "sound law".) Szemerényi's six "Principles of etymological research in the Indo-European languages" of 1961 (in Schmitt 1977) are all basically in the form of instructions to make the non-obvious obvious. Perhaps the common touchstone of the memorable and venerated etymologies mentioned above, associated with particular linguists, is that they became obvious only once posed; but before the fact neither the solution nor the problem was evident.

Let us look for a moment at those etymologies, to see what it is that makes each special.

In the case of German *Messer* 'knife', the charm lies in the phonological and semantic attrition of a close compound. We have the clear and semantically transparent living compounds Old High German *mezzi-sahs* and Old English *mete-seax*, both 'food-knife, "meat"-knife'. But the more common Old High German form is *mezzi-rahs*, with rhotacism rendering the second member *sahs* totally opaque. From *mezzirahs* comes Middle High German *mezzeres*, modern *Messer.* (English *hussy* 'house-wife' is comparable both in typology and charm.)

Germanic *\*sahsam* 'knife, sword' could be exactly equatable with Latin *saxum* 'stone'. For the 19th century, this fact gave an extra romantic frisson, that the German dinner table would somehow show a linguistic relic of the weaponry of the stone age; later scholars are more cautious, and inclined to derive both from a root *\*sek-* 'to cut'. But any period of linguistic community of Italic and Germanic must fall well within the European neolithic, and neither phonology nor morphology of the derivation from *\*sek-* 'to cut' is without problems; the last word has probably not been said.

Latin *dominus* 'master'. A connection with *domus* 'house(hold)' was apparent already to the Romans. But the derivational pattern *\*dom-e/ono-*, totally isolated in Latin, was for the first time explained by Saussure's[1] (1949 [1965]: 309−310) comparison of an isomorphic structural set of different derivatives with the same suffix in the same semantic field in another branch: Germanic *\*þeudanaz* 'chief of the *\*þeudō* "people"', *\*druhtinaz* 'chief of the *\*druhti-* "host", leader', *\*kindinaz* 'chief of the *\*kindi-* "clan"'. As Saussure saw, it is a scarcely refutable proof of not only a linguistic community but a community of institutions between the Italic and Germanic peoples.

Greek σέβομαι 'feel awe, venerate'. Brugmann (1881: 301 − 303) equated Vedic Sanskrit *tyájati* 'leaves'. The semantics is non-trivial, a basic religious term meaning 'retreat in awe (from someone, something)', but it is anchored by the Greek causative-transitive σοβέω 'scare away (birds), shoo (flies)' (basically meaning 'cause to retreat in awe'). This Greek verb was unrelated in the speakers' consciousness (and therefore old). The Sanskrit causative *tyājáyati* 'causes to quit, leave' (Epic) on the other hand is productively formed and *pace* Brugmann does not make a true equation. The comparison dictates a reconstruction *$tieg^u$-, with a unique initial cluster and an iron-clad Greek phonological rule of which this is the only example. (One may note also that when Brugmann made the etymology, he still noted the Proto-Indo-European root in the old-fashioned way ["*$tjag^2$-"], and had not added the second *n* to the spelling of his own name).

Old Church Slavonic *dъždь* 'rainstorm, rain' (ὄμβρος, ὑετός) and its pan-Slavic cognates (Russ. *dožd'*, Pol. *deszcz* [OPol. gen. *dżdżu*], S.-Cr. *dažd* etc.). Trubeckoj's (1927) and Vaillant's (1927) independent etymological analysis[2] 'bad weather', 'cloudy sky', punningly 'bad Zeus', from *$dus$-$d\!ju$-$s$ is semantically as felicitous as it is phonologically and morphologically unassailable.

The etymology is not accepted by Vasmer on semantic grounds, following Endzelin: 'rain' to the farmer is not 'bad' but beneficial. The argument, however, can be neatly countered by comparative evidence from the texts. The basic meaning of *$dus$-$d\!ju$-$s$ is not just 'rain', but 'storm', 'rainstorm'; OCS *dъždь* translates Greek ὄμβρος. And this is precisely the earliest meaning of the late Vedic parallel *durdinam* adduced by Trubeckoj (*$dus$-$di$-$n$-) and the semantic opposite of the Greek parallel εὐδία 'fair weather' adduced by Vaillant (*$h_1su$-$d\!ju$-). Compare from the Kauśika-sūtra to the Atharvaveda:

*jarāyuja iti durdinam āyan pratyuttiṣṭhati* (KauśS 38.1)
'When one goes against a storm he faces it while reciting AV 1.12.2' (M. Bloomfield)

and from Pindar, εὐδίαν ... μετὰ χειμερίαν ὄμβρον (Pyth. 5.10) 'fair weather after a wintry storm', εὐδίαν ... ἐκ χειμῶνος (Isth. 7.38) 'fair weather after a winter storm'. I cannot overemphasize here that textual evidence such as this serves not just as an embellishment with the trappings of erudition, nor even only to give flesh and blood to our etymological reconstructions; textual evidence can be a welcome and persuasive independent argument for the correctness of the given etymology, and indeed the texts will often dictate the direction of a solution.

Greek οὐ 'not'. The familiar parallel of French (*ne* ...) *pas* and the like combined with his flair for phonology provided Warren Cowgill (1960) an elegant and immediately illuminating explanation of the sentence negation in the dialect group of Greco-Armenian. Internal reconstruction shows the oldest variant in Greek is οὐκί; though Cowgill did not, I would argue here from poetic language, epic technique, and the Homeric verse-final formulas ὅς τε καὶ οὐκί 'and which not', ἠὲ καὶ οὐκί 'or not'. Greek οὐκί and Armenian *oč'* both contain the Indo-European word for 'eternity', in a semantically faded syntagma with the negation and the indefinite pronoun: *(ne* ...) *h₁oi̯u kᵘid* 'never, no way, nohow'.

Navaho *nà·dą́* 'corn' from 'enemy's food', 'Pueblo food'. Sapir's genius here (1936) and in other examples like -*sàs* 'seed lies' from 'snow lies' was to see in the Navaho words exact formal matches − with phonology and morphology carefully worked out − with Northern Athabaskan cognates with culturally significantly different and older semantics. The whole then constituted "Internal linguistic evidence suggestive of the northern origin of the Navaho".

Szemerényi (1962 [1967]) produced an impressive number of original etymologies to illustrate his six principles; obviously the principles were to a greater or lesser extent inferred from the etymologies. In recognition of the fairness of this etymological-theory equivalent of putting your money where your mouth is, I look now briefly at some of my own published etymologies, to see what general types of solutions and approaches were in play. As it turned out, 20 cases could be reduced to just 5 types.
1) Three depend on determining the meaning of a word occurring only in a single text passage; once given the meaning, obvious

cognates are ready to hand, and we have then an E 2 level etymology. Such are Old Irish ˙ *antar* 'distains' (: Greek ὄνομαι); *milchobor* 'bear' = 'honey-desirer' (: *mil* 'honey', *-cobra* 'desires'); Luvian *waar(-sa)* 'water' (: Vedic *vár, váar*) (Watkins, 1962; 1987 b). It is worth pointing out that if you get the meaning wrong, the etymology will be wrong too: the case of my famous misinterpretation of Hittite *kīya* ['these too'!], which does not equal Ved. *śáye* (Watkins 1969 a, 1.85).[3]

2) Two reflect the principle of the transferred epithet, like 'dry (*\*ters-*) land' > Latin *terra* 'land'. Latin (Lucretius) *animalia suppa* 'animals who go on all fours': Hittite *suppala* 'animal'; 'white (*\*albho-*) grain sp.', Hom. ἄλφιτα λευκά 'id.' (*-it-* from *\*sepit-* 'grain sp.') (Watkins, 1973 a; 1978).

3) Three depend critically on the correct determination of the phonology, morphology, or morphophonemics. Lat. *marītus* 'married' < 'having a *\*mari-* "nubile woman"'; Lat. *uegeō* 'incite' < *\*uogéie-*, to Engl. *wake*; Lat. *ceu* 'like' < *\*k̑e-iue* : Skt. *iva* 'like', *\*k̑e-* of Lat. *ce-do* 'gimme', Hittite *ki-nun* 'now' (Watkins, 1957; 1973 b).

4. Six depend on a semantic overlap or intersection of cognates at only one particular point, culturally determined, often in a partly frozen linguistic formula, and discoverable only through texts. Latin *uespillō* 'undertaker for the poor' : Hittite *waspa-* 'clothes' (no Latin lexical expression for the function of dressing the corpse); Hittite *sarnikizi* 'makes restitution' : Lat. *sarciō* 'repair' (previously known as a root etymology, but exactly equatable in the cognate verbal formulas for the legal institution of noxal surrender); Latin *ador* 'spelt' : Hittite *ḫad-* 'dry' (Hittite formula 'dried spelt meal'); Lat. *iouiste* (gloss) : Ved. *yaviṣṭha* 'O youngest' (address to a divinity, frequent in hymns); Hittite *suppi-* 'consecrated, pure, tabu' : Umbrian *supa, sopa* 'consecrated meats' (Hittite ritual formula ᵘᶻᵘ*suppa* 'consecrated meats'); Latin *satie-tas* 'satiety' : Irish *saithe* 'swarm (of bees)' (cognate Homeric formula μελισσάων ἁδινάων 'bees galore, in abundance', a metaphor common to both Greek and Celtic) (Watkins, 1969; 1970; 1973 c; 1975 a; 1975 b; 1979).

5) Finally in six cases it is a cultural feature or nexus, sometimes manifested as a verbal formula and usually only accessible in texts, which provides the semantic rationale for the etymology. Old Irish *-aim* 'washes (hands)' : Greek ἀμάομαι 'draw liquid, gather, pour' (the evidence of the texts is that the Old Irish washed their hands

by pouring water over them); Latin *sōns* 'guilty' (old participle of the verb 'to be') : Hittite *asān-at* 'it [the sin] (is) being, existing' (formula for the confession of sin); Latin *ūsurpō* 'take up' < *ūsu-rup-* 'breaking, interruption of *ūsus*, the acquistion of power over a wife' (legal institution and technical term); Russian dial. *ërga*, a children's game with sexual overtones < *\*ṛgh-ā* : Hittite *arg-* 'mount'; Irish *dúan* 'poem' : Latin *damnum* < *\*dap-no-* 'gift entailing a counter-gift; damage entailing liability' in the archaic gift and exchange system of poet and patron in Celtic and Indo-European society; Greek μῆνις 'wrath', 'divine vengefulness, vigilance, mindfulness' < *\*mnā-nis* (*\*mnā-* 'be mindful, remember, see') by tabu-deformation; the evidence of the texts shows that the word was tabu to the one who entertained the emotion (Watkins, 1967; 1970; 1975 c; 1976; 1977).

The five types are only approximations; others may well interpret these particular etymologies in some other way; and some of the five types, like (4) and (5), have much in common. How the linguist operates is doubtless a question of scholarly personality. In all the five the "trick", if I may call it that, is knowing what to compare: finding the word in the first place, finding the meaning, finding the parallel, getting the phonology and morphology right, finding the spot of semantic overlap, finding the cultural fact. It is, as I have said elsewhere many times, the first law of the comparative method: you have to know what to compare.

In my own way and to the extent of my abilities I have been trying for over 30 years in this area to follow the method of those memorable etymologies we reviewed earlier, and of those great scholars who made them. The list was produced virtually at random, simply what few etymologies came to my mind; others here could each produce his own list, equally valuable, and equally demonstrative of the same points. For what is common to all of them is something rather rare in linguistics today, which Yakov Malkiel characteristically put his finger on in his chapter heading of a quarter-century ago, "Etymology as Art." Malkiel identified four distinguishing features, or 'virtues': 1) an inventive mind, producing the felicitous association of isolated facts; 2) finesse in marshalling phonology, grammar, and semantics; 3) a combination of erudition and delicacy in handling language and culture; 4) a flair for when to stop.

## Notes

1. The absence of this etymology from the manuscript sources is curious, but does not affect its originality.
2. The appearance of these two in 1927 is a remarkable coincidence in itself. The brevity of both articles is notable, and one should note that the structure of the argument in both is virtually identical; both begin with the West Slavic forms, and show that their phonology is secondary, which invalidates the standard etymology.
3. See now H. C. Melchert (1987) on Luv. *ziyari* which is the required form, IE *ḱéịo(r)*.

## References

Arndt, Walter et al. (eds.)
  1967         *Studies in historical linguistics in honor of George Sherman Lane*
               (Chapel Hill: University of North Carolina Press).
Bammesberger, Alfred
  1984         *English etymology* (Heidelberg: Winter).
Bammesberger, Alfred (ed.)
  1983         *Das etymologische Wörterbuch: Fragen der Konzeption und Gestaltung*
               (Regensburg: Pustet).
Brugman, Karl
  1881         "Griechische Etymologien", *KZ* 25: 298–307.
Cardona, George – Henry Hoenigswald – Alfred Senn (eds.)
  1970         *Indo-European and Indo-Europeans* (Philadelphia: University of
               Pennsylvania Press).
Cardona, George – Norman Zide (eds.)
  1987         *Festschrift for Henry Hoenigswald* (Tübingen: Gunter Narr).
Cowgill, Warren
  1960         "Greek *oú* and Armenian *oč́*'", *Lg.* 36: 347–350.
Greenberg, Joseph H.
  1963         *The languages of Africa* (Bloomington: Indiana University Press).
  1987         *Language in the Americas* (Stanford: Stanford University Press).
Guiraud, Pierre
  1964         *L'étymologie* [1] (Paris: Presses Universitaires de France) [1967 [2]].
Malkiel, Yakov
  1968         *Essays on linguistic themes* (Oxford: Blackwell).
  1976         *Etymological dictionaries: A tentative typology* (Chicago: University
               of Chicago Press).
  1983         *From particular to general linguistics* (Amsterdam: Benjamins).
Mandelbaum, David G. (ed.)
  1968         *Selected writings of Edward Sapir* (Berkeley: University of California
               Press).

Melchert, H. Craig
1987        "PIE velars in Luvian", in Watkins, (ed.), 182—204.
Milner, Jean C. (ed.)
1975        *Langues, discours, société. Pour E. Benveniste* (Paris: Editions du Seuil).
Moïnfar, M. Dj. (ed.)
1975        *Mélanges de linguistique offerts à Émile Benveniste* (Louvain: Éditions Peeters).
Newman, Paul
1970        "Historical sound laws in Hausa and in Dera (Kanakuru)", *Journal of West African Languages* 7: 39—51.
Pisani, Vittore
1947 [1967²]  *L'Etimologia: storia—questioni—metodo* [1] (Milano: Renon) [1967²: Brescia: Paideia).
Pulgram, Ernst (ed.)
1957        *Studies presented to Joshua Whatmough on his sixtieth birthday* (The Hague: Mouton).
Ross, Alan S. C.
1958        *Etymology, with especial reference to English* (Fair Lawn, N.J.: Essential Books).
Sapir, Edward
1936        "Internal linguistic evidence suggestive of the northern origin of the Navaho", *American Anthropologist* 38: 224—235. [reprinted in David Mandelbaum (ed.), 213—224].
Saussure, Ferdinand de
1949        *Cours de linguistique générale* [4] (Paris: Payot).
Schmitt, Rudiger (ed.)
1977        *Etymologie* (Darmstadt: Wissenschaftliche Buchgesellschaft).
Seebold, Elmar
1981        *Etymologie: Eine Einführung am Beispiel der deutschen Sprache* (München: Beck).
Silverstein, Michael (ed.)
1971        *Whitney on language* (Cambridge: MIT Press).
Szemerényi, Oswald
1962 [1977]   "Principles of etymological research in the Indo-European languages", in: Johann Knobloch (ed.), II. *Fachtagung für indogermanische und allgemeine Sprachwissenschaft* (Innsbruck, 10.—15. Oktober 1961). *Vorträge und Veranstaltungen* (*Innsbrucker Beiträge zur Kulturwissenschaft, Sonderheft* 15), 175—212. (Innsbruck: Sprachwissenschaftliches Institut der Leopold-Franzens Universität). [reprinted in R. Schmitt (ed.), 286—346].
Toporov, V. N.
1960        "O nekotoryx teoretičeskix osnovanijax ètimologičeskogo analiza [On some theoretical foundations of etymological analysis]", *Voprosy jazykoznanija* Nr. 3: 44—59.
1979 [1981]   "Vedijskoe ṛtá-: K sootnošeniju smyslovoj struktury i ètimologii [Vedic ṛtá-: On the correlation of conceptual structure and etymology]", *Ètimologija* (Moskva: Nauka), 139—156.

1984　　　　　"O nekotoryx teoretičeskix aspektax ėtimologii [On some theoretical aspects of etymology]", in: *Meždunarodnyj simpozium po problemam ėtimologii, istoričeskoj leksikologii i leksikografii.* Tezisy dokladov. [non vidi].

Trier, Jost
1981　　　　　*Wege der Etymologie* (Berlin: E. Schmidt).

Trubeckoj, N.
1927　　　　　"Urslav. *dъždžь Regen", *Zeitschrift für slavische Philologie* 4: 62 – 64.

Vaillant, André
1927　　　　　"Le nom slave de 'la pluie' ", *Revue des Études Slaves* 7: 112 – 113.

Watkins, Calvert
1957　　　　　"Latin *marītus* ", in: Ernst Pulgram (ed.), 227 – 281.
1962　　　　　"Varia II: 1. Ir. *milchobur*; 2. OIr. *-antar* ", *Eriu* 19: 114 – 118.
1967　　　　　"Latin *sōns* ", in: Walter Arndt et al. (eds.), 186 – 194.
1969 a　　　　*Indogermanische Grammatik III: Geschichte der indogermanischen Verbalflexion* (Heidelberg: Winter).
1969 b　　　　"A Latin-Hittite etymology", *Lg.* 45: 235 – 242.
1970　　　　　"Studies in Indo-European legal language, institutions, and mythology", in: George Cardona – Henry Hoenigswald – Alfred Senn (eds.), 321 – 354.
1973 a　　　　"Latin *suppus* ", *JIES* 1: 394 – 399.
1973 b　　　　"Etyma Enniana", *Harvard Studies in Classical Philology* 77: 195 – 206.
1973 c　　　　"An Indo-European agricultural term: Latin *ador*, Hittite *ḫat-* ", *Harvard Studies in Classical Philology* 77: 187 – 193.
1975 a　　　　"Latin *iouiste* et le langage poétique indo-européen", in: M. Dj. Moïnfar (ed.), 527 – 534.
1975 b　　　　"La designation indo-européenne du 'tabou' ", in: Jean C. Milner (ed.), 208 – 214.
1975 c　　　　"La famille indo-européenne de grec ὄρχις: linguistique, poétique et mythologie, *BSL* 70, No. 1: 11 – 25.
1976　　　　　"The etymology of Irish *dúan* ", *Celtica* 77: 270 – 277.
1977　　　　　"À propos de μῆνις", *BSL* 77: 187 – 209.
1978　　　　　" 'Let us now praise famous grains' ", *Proceedings of the American Philosophical Society* 122: 9 – 17.
1979　　　　　"Old Irish *saithe*, Welsh *haid*: Etymology and metaphor", *Études Celtiques* 16: 191 – 194.
1987　　　　　"Two Anatolian forms: Palaic *aškumāuwa*, Cuneiform Luwian *wa-a-ar-ša* ", in: George Cardona – Norman Zide (eds.), 399 – 404.

Watkins, Calvert (ed.)
1987　　　　　*Studies in memory of Warren Cowgill* (Berlin: de Gruyter).

Whitney, William D.
1867 [1971⁶] *Language and the study of language* (New York: AMS Printing) [1971⁶].
1875　　　　　*The life and growth of language* (New York: D. Appleton).

# Is the "comparative" method general or family-specific?

## Henry M. Hoenigswald

There are questions that it should not be necessary to keep asking. There are also questions that refuse to go away. Sometimes we discover to our puzzlement that the two sets intersect. The question whether the "comparative method" is general or family-specific is at that intersection. This may again be a surprise to some of us, which is as good an excuse as any for bringing it up. I propose to deal first with its persistence, then with its worth or worthlessness as the case may be, and finally with the whys and wherefores of the paradox.

Presistence is simply a fact; it would be tedious to illustrate it by accumulating *ex cathedra* pronouncements. However, here are a few samples. Antoine Meillet (Meillet—Cohen 1924: 9) let it be known that

> one may well ask whether the languages of America (which are still for the most part poorly known and insufficiently studied from a comparative point of view) will ever lend themselves to exact, exhaustive comparative treatment; the samples offered so far hold scant promise ...

and that

> it is not even clear that the principle of genealogical classification applies [generally].

From about the same time date Meillet's famous Oslo lectures. Here, in Sommerfelt territory, while we find an almost complete reliance on Indo-European material (albeit of great variety and of very different antiquity), in the preface Meillet (1925: vi—vii) has this to say:

> However slowly, the historical study of non Indo-European languages is progressing. But the procedures that have been suc-

cessful in Indo-European are not feasible everywhere. We must reflect on our methods, examine their validity, see to it — without compromising their rigorousness — that their scope is widened and made more flexible as is required by their application to new areas.

We perceive a mild retreat from the earlier intransigence, but still no great enthusiasm. As for Alf Sommerfelt himself (1938: 187 — 188), he was convinced that

> [o]f course, the comparative grammar of Aranta calls for special methods. While Indo-European comparative grammar is chiefly built on the foundations of grammatical forms more or less devoid of concrete meaning, in A. all the derivational elements are roots with concrete meaning ... .

We note that *grammaire comparée* is here not just what it is so often (and what it generally was to Meillet), namely a word for "reconstruction" with its strong and commonly recognized concentration on phonemic correspondences among morphs. On the contrary, Sommerfelt actually takes it with the literal meaning of the term "grammar" — signifying precisely not phonology but morphology and syntax. To that extent, we gather with some relief, he is at least not talking about the comparative method in the narrow sense as we know it.

Against this background we understand a little better what Leonard Bloomfield was up against when he writes, in 1932 (Hockett 1970: 249):

> ... this exposition [an allusion to Bloomfield's famous "Note on sound change" and to some of Sapir's work] tells him [the hapless author of the work under review by Bloomfield, Eduard Hermann] only that sound-changes occur, forsooth, also in Indian languages, and that *some* sound-changes have no exceptions. Either by the rarest accident or by the use of black magic, then, Sapir and I must have hit upon sound-changes which belonged to this exceptionless type. Of course, Sapir's inferences and mine were only those which scientific men, including Hermann, make at every step ... .

Some of the allusions here would need spelling out. Meanwhile we might be tempted to agree that sound-changes occur, forsooth, also in Indian languages and that there is no point in flogging a dead horse.

However, these are the 1980s, and Norbert Boretzky has appeared on the scene. In 1982 he writes on "Das indogermanische Sprach-wandelmodell und Wandel in exotischen Sprachen", and in 1984, in a translated "revised[,] and expanded" version on "The Indo-Europeanist model of sound-change and genetic affinity in exotic languages". It appears that the horse isn't dead at all or at least that those who don't think he is are alive. It is not our purpose merely to resume the flogging. There is a possibility, however, that a little sober, down-to-earth observation might help — observation of scholarly conduct in the performance of plausible, internally consistent, substantive work which includes the kind of "inferences which scientific men [like Boretzky] make at every step".

Boretzky contrasts the reconstructibility, or lack thereof, of Ar-anta/Arandic (in Australia) and of Georg Pilhofer's Kâte family (in New Guinea) with that of Slavic and Romance — "exotic" with "European". He complains of two extremes, namely that in exotic languages, semantic slots are likely to be filled either by difficult to relate morphs, or, conversely, that the phonological differences are so small (as for instance in Arandic) that there is no scope for reconstruction. On the other hand, "in the European languages, phonetic variation in given etyma is minor to moderate". He illus-trates this with examples from Slavic and from Germanic (not from overall Indo-European itself). He then presents a theory in which the smallness of the individual Arandic and Kâte groups, the limited extent of their primitive vocabulary (which he asserts), their no-madic ways, and other characteristics, real or alleged, play a role. We can leave this particular aspect aside. The basics, however, continue to give us pause.

Clearly, the telltale one of the two extremes in Boretzky's contra-dictory set is the latter — the near-identity he finds in the Australian and in the New Guinea comparative vocabularies. If that is what the dialects exhibit, then they are indeed too close to allow much recon-struction and that is that — most pairs of American English dialects would not yield an interesting phase of English either. The problem is, then, to explain the other extreme: etymologically (probably) unrelated items showing up in such numbers (?) in the corresponding places of word-lists. From the material (which Boretzky handles very casually) one suspects that, in the process of recording, forms with different locations in morphological paradigms appear in corresponding places as though they were grammatical equivalents from dialect to dialect when in fact they carry different affixes. An Africanist comment by Greenberg (1987: 15) which summarizes earlier work, is here mildly apropos:

> I have described the process by which a demonstrative becomes first a definite article, then a combination of definite and indefinite article … and finally an empty marker. In the last stage …, instead of always remaining on the noun or adjective, or always disappearing in a specific language, we may have random survival for each individual word. An example of this is a prefixed *k-* found in random fashion, distributed differently for each word across the languages in all nouns that originally began with a vowel in Nilo-Saharan …. We shall return to this point.

It is of course not true that plausible comparative work exists only for Indo-European languages; it is sufficient to name Dravidian, Algonquian, Austronesian. But before we dismiss as groundless, and as only due to poor data or lack of method, the malaise which Boretzky and others express so vociferously, we must concede that there are degrees, not of amenability to what we call technically the "comparative" method — that goes against the grain — but of yield. Whoever has involved himself in efforts to collect information, will admit to a feeling that there may be less joy in the reconstruction of Turkic, Finno-Ugric, Athabascan, and even Semitic than may be gotten from, say, Indo-European or Algonquian. Moreover, the list just hinted at includes some sub-fields of Indo-European as well. It is hardly an accident that the comparative method and its adjuncts were hammered out by Indo-Europeanists and not by Romance scholars, some of whom still show a surprising lack of appreciation, not only in matters of formulation — that, after all, would not be important — but in the context of execution.

We are in no position to report on anything like a systematic comparison between the relatively rewarding and the relatively barren fields. Therefore, another approach may be a little more congenial. We can start at the other end, as it were, and look at the particular non-"exotic" area in which we happen to be at home.

One topic which does not have to be labored is writing. That written records add to the fullness of our basic knowledge and give us a "free ride" into the past is of course true, but it does not change the uncertainty which hangs over our inferences. That written records allow us direct observation of changes along something that can come rather close to a direct line of descent is also true, but it still does not solve the problem of how to describe, classify, and "explain" the changes. The most interesting use of written records lies in their availability for the task of confirming or disallowing inferences, as in the case of Latin and Proto-Romance. It should, however, be understood that neither the comparative method nor internal reconstruction depend on written records (and our sampling of reconstruction-friendly language families certainly confirms that).

By mentioning, as we just did, the two kinds of reconstruction that we like to distinguish, we have moved closer to the heart of the matter. For what is at issue is not the comparative method in the narrow sense, fundamental though its operations remain. The history of Indo-Europeanist work shows us something else, namely, the de facto dominance of internal reconstruction, sometimes in the adventure of discovery, sometimes in the striving for effective presentation, and sometimes in both. Three Indo-European classics are instructive in this regard. One is the Verner paper of 1876. It is certainly "comparative". The comparanda under observation include such pairs as Vedic Sanskrit/Germanic (1) /ˈt/ : /þ/ and (2) /°t/ : /d/ (as in the words for 'brother' and 'father', respectively), but the more crucial discovery lies in the fact that (1) and (2) are also found to alternate, for instance in the singular as against the plural of the "perfect/preterit" (the further fact being that Germanic /d/ occurs in yet two more correspondences, (3) /ˈdh/ : /d/ and (4) /°dh/ : /d/). By using notations like /ˈt/ ('accent on vowel + [t]') or /°dh/ ('no accent on vowel + [dh]') we have here adopted an entirely unusual ad hoc segmentation on which to base phonological entities; it is more customary to say, separately, that as we go (synchronically) from singular to plural, a) the Vedic accent shifts, and b) the Germanic /þ/ shifts to /d/ (while the Germanic /d/ does not shift). So Verner found it convincing to start his demonstration by putting the alternation (*grammatischer Wechsel*) at the center. Furthermore, since only one of the alternating entities, the Proto-Indo-European *°t (as distinct from *ˈt) is also partner to a merger (with both *°dh

and *'dh) in Germanic, and since a merger is *ipso facto* an innovation, the reconstruction is made to carry (rightly or wrongly, but
still plausibly) the physical properties of the non-innovating language, Vedic Sanskrit. Our traditional Proto-Indo-European, as we
reconstruct it, in this (oversimplified) example, from Vedic Sanskrit
and Germanic, has " $\pm$ accent" (i. e., */'/ and, by implication, */°/
) rather than an additional lenited stop category hovering between
*/t/ and */dh/. Without the alternating paradigms (preterit, etc.)
the investigator could indeed discover the two-language correlation
between accent and lenition — as Verner did, by his own famous
testimony — but it is the intra-Germanic alternation which makes
it persuasive. (Cf. Jespersen in Sebeok 1966: 539 – 542).

The other two classics tell us similar stories. One is Saussure's
*Mémoire* and the other the first volume of Wackernagel's *Altindische Grammatik*. The latter is surely one of the most elegant
pieces of nineteenth century linguistic writing. Without wasting a
word on method in the abstract (which would have to be elucidated
anyway with the help of the very subject-matter under discussion)
almost every argument is openly organized according to whether it
is internal and built on what happens synchronically in paradigms,
or reflects the chronology of the texts, or comparative evidence
from Iranian, or such evidence from farther afield.

Clearly, successful and interesting reconstruction depends greatly
on paradigms of a more than mere syntactic nature — that is,
paradigms with a fair amount of allomorphy. We like to say that
suppletion (as in English *go* and *went*) indicates syncretism; and
that alternation, if conditioned lexically or grammatically (as in
Germanic *grammatischer Wechsel*), indicates "secondary split",
i. e., the disappearance of a conditioning difference in the environment (in this case, the accent); if phonologically conditioned, morphophonemic alternation signifies a primary split (the residue of a
conditioned merger where the environments that once governed the
sound change are preserved as the environments governing the
alternation [as in German *Auslautverhärtung*]). Thus we codify
some of our working procedures, in this case the procedure of
internal reconstruction. But this is not quite good enough. We have
just seen how important internal reconstruction is, within the limits,
say, observed by Wackernagel. However, our codification gives it
too much strength of a particular kind. Take a language with
pervasive vowel harmony — typically a simple and powerfully

regular, phonologically conditioned alternation. Our rules, as just cited, would make us reconstruct a state in which there was no vowel harmony and help us to a finding that vowel harmony came into existence through a system of assimilatory sound changes. Perhaps this is appropriate in cases where affixes started out as "separate words"; perhaps, also, there is, in the last analysis, only a vague difference between a) internally reconstructing such a development, and b) reconstructing, as we did a moment ago for the sake of the argument, a sound change bringing vowel harmony into existence. It depends, among other things, on what "separate words" means in that sort of typology. It also depends on whether we are content to interpret all morphophonemic alternations, including the most settled and stable ones, as the result of earlier sound changes, only to shove these sound changes back into an immemorial past — denying them historical reality that way. This is a useless game.

Apparently the productivity of the comparative method and its adjuncts depends a good deal on an optimal relationship between certain morphophonemic characteristics both in the descendants and in the proto-language at which the reconstruction aims. Extrapolating from the case of vowel harmony — an extremely simple example — we can see that what makes it relatively uninteresting is that here we have an alternation embedded in a stable history. This is not surprising: the basic comparative method (the examination of sound correspondences for complementarity in morphophonemically unstructured morphs) is uninteresting in instances where all the phonemes in corresponding morphs contrast (so that there are as many proto-phonemes as there are correspondences — sometimes a true description of trivial history, and at other times simply a mark of poor work in which complementarity has escaped the investigator); similarly, a stable vowel harmony offers no interest. On the other hand, the recovery of a proto-language with vowel harmony from descendants either all or some of which no longer have it is another matter. Or, to go to another illustration: Old English had a front rounded vowel, *y*, alternating with a back rounded vowel (as in the antecedents of *mice* : *mouse*). In its relative isolation among the many details of English phonological history, this is a fair example of what productive reconstructions are like.

After these groupings, a few maxims and rules of thumb may not be amiss:

1) The comparative method and its adjuncts are in principle general rather than language-specific or family-specific. If it were otherwise we would have to give up the quasi-universal *of double articulation* (into the phonological and the morphemic).
2) If the descendant languages are too "similar", reconstruction is uninteresting. Put diachronically, it is necessary that the ancestor not be too recent — for two related reasons: descendants must differ sufficiently to give the reconstruction some content, and the play of morphological isolation must have had time to develop.
3) If the descendant languages have come to differ typologically from one another or from the proto-language, the reconstruction gains in interest.
4) Morphophonemic processes such as generally (but not exclusively) occur in "morphology" rather than in "syntax" add to the yield of a reconstruction. This yield, then, depends on the typological, and to an extent on the universal, function of the "word". This is the synchronic formulation; to the extent that morphophonemic processes rest on conditioned sound changes a typology of change favoring conditioned sound changes will also favor reconstructibility.

## References

Boretzky, Norbert
   1982      "Das indogermanische Sprachwandelmodell und Wandel in exotischen Sprachen", *Zeitschrift für vergleichende Sprachforschung* 95: 49–80.
   1984      "The Indo-Europeanist model of sound change and genetic affinity and change in exotic languages", *Diachronica* 1: 1–51.
Bloomfield, Leonard
   1932      Review of Hermann 1931. In Hockett (ed.), 240–51.
Greenberg, Joseph H.
   1987      *Language in the Americas* (Stanford: Stanford University Press).
Hermann, Eduard
   1931      *Lautgesetz und Analogie* (Berlin: Weidmann).
Hockett, Charles F. (ed.)
   1970      *A Leonard Bloomfield anthology* (Bloomington, London: Indiana University Press).
Jespersen, Otto
   n. d. [1966] "Karl Verner. Some personal recollections", in: Sebeok (ed.), 538–548.
Meillet, Antoine
   1925      *La méthode comparative en linguistique historique* (Oslo: H. Aschehoug).

Meillet, Antoine — Marcel Cohen (eds.)
1924        *Les langues du monde* (Paris: Champion).
Sebeok, Thomas A. (ed.)
1966        *Portraits of linguists* (Bloomington, London: Indiana University Press).
Sommerfelt, Alf
1938        *La langue et la société* (Oslo: H. Aschehoug).
Verner, Karl
1876        "Eine Ausnahme der ersten Lautverschiebung", *Zeitschrift für vergleichende Sprachforschung* 23: 97—130.

# Summary report: Linguistic change and reconstruction in the Australian language family

*R. M. W. Dixon*

There were probably between 200 and 250 distinct languages spoken in Australia at the time of the invasion by Europeans, in 1788. About half are no longer spoken, and only a couple of dozen are still being learned by children. Work so far indicates that all but a handful of Australian languages belong to one genetic family; further research may well show that the remainder — scattered across the central north — should also be assigned to the same family.

Aborigines have been in Australia for at least 40,000 years. Proto-Australian may well have been spoken that far in the past, or it could have been more recent — we have no way of knowing.

Many phonological, morphological, syntactic, and lexical traits have an areal distribution. The hardest task in Australian comparative linguistics is to distinguish between similarities that come from areal diffusion and those that are due to genetic retention. As grammatical reconstruction has progressed we have been able to recognize certain features as archaic retentions and others as innovations, but in other instances we are still groping to separate the inherited from the borrowed.

## Phonology

There is fairly general consensus that Proto-Australian had a consonant system something like

|            | apical | laminal | dorsal | labial |
|------------|--------|---------|--------|--------|
| stop       | *d*    | *j*     | *g*    | *b*    |
| nasal      | *n*    | *ny*    | *ŋ*    | *m*    |
| lateral    | *l*    | *ly*(?) |        |        |
| rhotic     | *rr, r*|         |        |        |
| semi-vowel |        | *y*     |        | *w*    |

Some languages preserve an inventory close to this. The apical series often have an apico-postalveolar (retroflex) allophone after *u* and an apico-alveolar allophone elsewhere. The laminal series often have a lamino-palatal allophone before *i* and a lamino-(inter)dental allophone elsewhere. In about three-quarters of the languages of the continent, the phonetic distinction between apico-postalveolar and apico-alveolar has developed into a phonological contrast. And in about half of the languages the phonetic distinction between lamino-palatal and lamino-(inter)dental has developed into a phonological contrast. Languages with two series of apicals all lie in one large area while those with two series of laminals fall into two areas (see the map in Dixon 1980: 141). These distributions do not correlate with any parameters of grammatical or lexical variation and do not provide evidence for subgrouping.

It is a characteristic of Australian languages to have a nasal corresponding to each stop, and also a lateral in each stop-nasal series excepting dorsal and labial. There are generally no fricatives, and no voicing contrast for stops (some Australianists write *b, d, j, g* and some *p, t, c, k* — these are simply terminological variants).

Most Australian languages have two rhotic phonemes (although some show three, and a few just one). Phonetic realization varies a good deal, but there is normally one "front rhotic" which has as central allophone an apico-alveolar trill, and one "back rhotic" which has as central allophone an apico-postalveolar continuant.

The majority of modern languages have three vowel phonemes, *a, i* and *u*, but there is a block in the north with a five-vowel system, *a, e, i, o, u*. No definitive work has yet been done on whether Proto-Australian had 3 or 5 vowels, but it is clear that Proto-Australian had contrastive vowel length, at least in the first, stressed syllable of a word. This has been retained in some modern languages (mostly on the coastal fringe) but lost in others, probably as an areal development. Some of the latter group of languages have re-introduced a length contrast, in a variety of ways.

The canonical syllable pattern in Proto-Australian was CV(C); there appear to have been a fair number of monosyllabic words. Some modern languages retain some monosyllabic roots but have a requirement that every word should contain at least two syllables. In other languages both roots and words must consist of at least two syllables. A number of modern languages have every word ending in a vowel, and some have every word ending in a consonant, but most allow both vowel and consonant in final position. Except in areas where an "initial dropping" change has taken place (see below), it is generally the case that every word must begin with a consonant.

Fuller details of phonological variation, reconstruction and change will be found in chapters 6 and 7 of Dixon (1980), which also contains reference to the relevant literature.

# Morphology and syntax

Capell (1956) distinguished between two morphological types — those languages which use prefixes as well as suffixes, and those which only employ suffixes. Hale (see O'Grady — Voegelin — Voegelin 1966) divided Australian languages into Pama-Nyungan and non-Pama-Nyungan. These two isoglosses almost coincide (see the map in Dixon 1980: 20). About 90% of Australian languages are Pama-Nyungan/non-prefixing; they range from the far north-east (where *pama* is the word for 'man') to the far south-west (where *nyuŋa* is 'man'). Pama-Nyungan languages show recurrent similarities and clearly belong to a single language family. There are only a few dozen non-Pama-Nyungan languages, all in a block in the west and central far north. They fall into a number of subgroups which differ — grammatically and lexically — from each other and also from Pama-Nyungan. (But note that the phonological isoglosses, mentioned above, cut right across both Pama-Nyungan and non-Pama-Nyungan areas.)

It is likely that Proto-Australian had a mildly agglutinative morphology. The Pama-Nyungan languages have moved towards a more fully agglutinating structure, while languages in the non-Pama-Nyungan area have developed polysynthetic words (with a certain amount of fusion, sometimes yielding portmanteau affixes). It appears that the development of polysynthetic structures — which characterize the non-Pama-Nyungan languages — is another areal feature.

Non-Pama-Nyungan languages have incorporated pronominal forms as prefixes into the verb, cross-referencing subject, object, or indirect object, and sometimes other clause constituents. Several groups of Pama-Nyungan languages have bound pronominal suffixes or enclitics. In perhaps half of these Pama-Nyungan languages bound pronouns are transparently reduced from free pronouns; in the remainder they differ significantly in form from the free pronouns.

It seems likely that Proto-Australian had a smallish case system on nouns, with perhaps five members; these included ergative, marking transitive subject; and absolutive (with zero realization), marking transitive object and intransitive subject. Modern Pama-Nyungan languages have extended this, individually evolving one or two new cases from things like postpositions. In the non-Pama-Nyungan area there has been a tendency towards losing non-local case inflections, since the information on syntactic function that they would encode is dealt with by cross-referencing within the verb.

In many Australian languages a specific noun is often accompanied by a general noun (or classifier); a typical construction could be, literally 'the person woman dug up the vegetable yam'. In many non-Pama-Nyungan and in a few Pama-Nyungan languages these classifiers have developed into a system of noun classes, marked either by a prefix on the noun (as in Bantu languages), or by a suffix on a co-occurring determiner (reminiscent of French).

The original pronoun system that can be reconstructed over languages of the Pama-Nyungan type had nominative (transitive and intransitive subject) and accusative (transitive object) forms for the non-singulars, but singulars appear to have had different forms for all of transitive subject, intransitive subject, and transitive object. This contrasts with the ergative-absolutive case inflection on nouns. Some modern languages retain this diversity of marking for syntactic function. Others have changed in one or more of several ways: i) singular pronouns, like non-singulars, have a nominative-accusative paradigm (this correlates with the loss of the original monosyllabic root, which was used in intransitive subject function, the disyllabic transitive subject form being extended also to cover intransitive subject); ii) free pronouns inflect on an ergative-absolutive system, like nouns (but bound pronouns retain nominative-accusative); iii) nouns switch to a nominative-accusative pattern, like pronouns.

Switch-reference marking has developed over the genetically diverse languages of a large area in the west and center of the continent. It appears that just the categories of switch-reference have diffused; each language in the area has developed realizations for these categories in a slightly different way, from its own morphological resources (see Austin 1981).


## Factors affecting change

Australian Aborigines have a strong awareness of language, which is looked upon as a principal marker of membership in tribe, and in local group within tribe. Over much of the continent marriage is exogamous — with someone from another local group within the same tribe, or with someone from another tribe. It is common for father and mother to speak different languages. This leads to a good deal of multilingualism, which facilitates the diffusion of all kinds of linguistic features. The paper by Johnson in this volume is a welcome addition to the literature on these topics.

The name of any recently dead person is tabooed, and the taboo often extends to any noun or verb which is phonologically similar to the name. A tabooed word may return to use after a certain period of time, but it would not always have done so; this must have been a factor in lexical replacement. There are even instances of a pronoun being tabooed — in some dialects of the Western Desert language first singular *ŋayu* was proscribed and replaced by *ŋanku* (borrowed from the avoidance language style) — see Douglas (1964: 3). There is a seminal study of the conditions for diffusion of morphological forms over an area of eastern Arnhem Land in Heath (1978).

As already remarked, Aborigines have been in Australia for at least 40,000 years. (There may have been one, or else several, waves of migration; no certain information is available on this.) There is no evidence of contact with languages from any other family. Since there was a common typological profile across most of the continent, and taking into account the fact that diffusion is such a feature of Australian languages, it will be seen that any language which underwent significant linguistic changes would be under considerable areal pressure, from its more conservative neighbors, to shift back into their common typological matrix.

# Methods of reconstruction

It is quite clear that Australian languages change in a regular fashion, in the same way as Indo-European and other families.

Thirty years ago languages in the north-eastern part of Queensland were thought to be rather aberrant, with many short monosyllabic words beginning in consonant clusters (e. g., *mpi, ŋke*), larger vowel systems than other languages, etc. Then, in a masterly piece of reconstruction, Hale (1964, 1976) demonstrated that they had developed by regular changes from a language of the normal Pama-Nyungan type. A sample of the changes Yinwum has undergone is shown in the following:

| proto-Northern-Paman | Yinwum | |
|---|---|---|
| *\*cámpa-* | *mpí-* | 'to give' |
| *\*cúŋku* | *ŋké* | 'black' |
| *\*kúna* | *nwá* | 'feces' |

These forms illustrate the following regular changes (for which there are many more examples): *a* and *u* in the second syllable of a word become *i* and *e* respectively when the word began with a laminal (e. g. *c*); a *u* in the first syllable gives rise (by metathesis) to a *w* between initial C and V of the second syllable; then initial CV dropped.

Most phonological changes in the development of modern Australian languages have been regular. But, as for other language families, there have been some more limited changes in certain areas of grammar, e. g., in the imperative forms of verbs, and in the pronoun paradigm. The first person singular subject pronoun can be reconstructed as *\*ŋaju* (probably relating at an earlier stage to root *\*ŋay* plus ergative inflection *-ju*). Many modern languages retain this form; many others have changed the final *u* to *a*, i. e., *ŋaja*. The same change has applied to the second and third person singular pronouns, but to no other forms. Languages with *ŋaja* (or, with lenition of the *j, ŋaya*) are found in four distinct areas of the continent, separated by languages with *ŋaju* (or *ŋayu*).

This illustrates another common feature of Australian languages — convergent development. Languages in quite different areas tend to change in similar ways. To take another instance, the "initial dropping" that Hale demonstrated for languages in the far north-east has also applied to languages around Alice Springs, in the centre, and to a single language, Nganyaywana, in the New England highlands region of New South Wales. These languages are not closely genetically related, and there is no evidence that they have been in recent contact.

All the familiar varieties of change in other language families are well attested in Australia, e. g., analogic remodelling of pronoun paradigms, and of verbal conjugations. As mentioned before, many languages have eliminated monosyllabic roots. An original root (e. g., *wu-* 'to give') plus an inflection (e. g., *-ga*, imperative) may be reidentified as the new root (*wuga-* 'to give') and assigned to the open conjugational class to which most disyllabic transitive verb roots belong.

Preliminary attempts have been made at reconstruction of case systems, verbal conjugations and inflections, and pronoun systems (see chapters 10 − 12 of Dixon 1980, and Blake's seminal paper in this volume). Heath's paper in this volume is a further contribution to the debate about reconstruction of verbal categories and forms.

# Subgrouping

The first subgrouping of Australian languages was by lexicostatistics (O'Grady − Voegelin − Voegelin 1966); the data on which it was based − or information on what the data were − has not been made available. This recognized 29 "phylic families", one being Pama-Nyungan (with about 90% of the total languages) and the other 28 covering the non-Pama-Nyungan/prefixing region.

My attempts at reconstruction (Dixon 1980) were initially based on Pama-Nyungan languages. Then it became clear that some of the crucial irregular monosyllabic verb roots did have reflexes in most (but not all) of the non-Pama-Nyungan languages. I had begun by assuming that "Proto-Pama-Nyungan" should be a high node on the Australian language tree. But then, on detailed examination of the data, I could find no convincing set of innovations between Proto-Australian and "Proto-Pama-Nyungan" to justify this node. Almost all the features I was able to reconstruct (e. g., contrastive vowel length) appeared to go back to Proto-Australian.

Pama-Nyungan had been first recognized as a typological group and I suggested that it "has not yet been shown to have any genetic significance" (Dixon 1980: 256). It may have, but more work is needed to demonstrate this.

Blake, in his paper in this volume, remarks that my pronominal reconstruction applies only for Pama-Nyungan and sets forth a further set of reconstructions, for non-Pama-Nyungan. This might be taken to imply that Proto-Australian split into two primary branches, proto-Pama-Nyungan and proto-non-Pama-Nyungan. However, the great differences between languages within the non-Pama-Nyungan area make it unlikely (to me, at least) that taken together they could be a single subgroup, on a par with Pama-Nyungan if, indeed, Pama-Nyungan is a valid genetic subgroup. Many Australianists aver stoutly that it must be (and I would agree that it might well be); but adequate justification has yet to be produced.

And if it were, what are the subgroups within the 200 or so Pama-Nyungan languages? I have tried to investigate the whole matter of subgrouping, using the established techniques which have been evolved and proved in the study of other language families. There are many areal traits, which have to be discarded. A number of non-contiguous languages do have points of similarity but almost every one of these is a genetic retention from the proto-language (e. g., cognate monosyllabic roots for some pronouns and verbs, in a number of languages scattered around the coastal periphery of the continent). These are just languages which are conservative in various ways, and that is no evidence for subgrouping. I am still continuing to work on this question, but it does seem that the tree model of genetic relationship, which is so useful for other language families, may not be the appropriate model for the Australian family.

Proto-Australian may well have been spoken some millennia in the past. Although we cannot be certain, it is quite possible that the Australian language family has a considerably greater time depth than Indo-European, Austronesian, or Semitic. Add to this the fact that there has probably been no contact with languages of another family for all or most of this time. This may explain the extensive nature of diffusion, and the many areal traits. (Mapping linguistic parameters across the 200-plus languages of the continent gives a picture that bears a distinct resemblance to the dialect map for a single language.) Languages most probably did split into twos, threes, or fours, as shown in a genetic tree diagram; but it may never be possible to recover more than small fragments of these splits, due to the extensive diffusion that has continually been taking place.

## References

Austin, Peter
1981        "Switch-reference in Australia", *Language* 57: 309−334.
Capell, Arthur
1956        *A new approach to Australian linguistics* (Sydney: Oceania Linguistic
            Monographs).
Dixon, R. M. W.
1980        *The languages of Australia* (Cambridge: Cambridge University Press).
Douglas, Wilfrid H.
1964        *An introduction to the Western Desert language,* revised edition (Syd-
            ney: Oceania Linguistic Monographs).
Hale, Kenneth
1964        "Classification of the Northern Paman languages, Cape York Pen-
            insula, Australia: A research report", *Oceanic Linguistics* 3: 248−
            265. (Another version is in O'Grady−Voegelin−Voegelin (eds.),
            162−176.)
1976        "Phonological developments in particular Northern Paman lan-
            guages", and "Phonological developments in a Northern Paman
            language: Uradhi", in: Peter Sutton (ed.), *Languages of Cape York*
            (Canberra: Australian Institute of Aboriginal Studies), 7−49.
Heath, Jeffrey
1978        *Linguistic diffusion in Arnhem Land* (Canberra: Australian Institute
            of Aboriginal Studies).
O'Grady, Geoffrey N.−Charles F. Voegelin−Florence M. Voegelin
1966        *Languages of the world: Indo-Pacific* 6 (Anthropological Linguistics
            8, 2) (Bloomington, Indiana: Indiana University Press).

# Social parameters of linguistic change in an unstratified Aboriginal society

*Steve Johnson*

The comparative method of reconstruction has been most thoroughly tested with language families that have generally evolved under particular circumstances that are not necessarily universal. Geographical or social conditions have been such that daughter languages have remained out of contact after the separation that led to their initial split. As a result, any correspondences must predate their separation, since there is no way that innovations could have been subsequently shared. Such situations seem to have been the norm in most of the families that have been intensively studied, such as Indo-European and Finno-Ugric, although even there scholars have noticed correspondences that point to some further language contact after separation.

However, not all societies have been sufficiently organized, cohesive and large enough to successfully migrate long distances through hostile or indifferent territory to new living spaces, or to erect strong cultural barriers between them and their erstwhile kin, so as to avoid linguistic miscegenation. Hunter-gatherer societies (being small-scale and often not hierarchically organized) regularly maintain intimate links with their neighbors, including groups with which they have shared a common ancestry. In at least some areas of Australia, this has resulted in quite unusual social conditions, and powerful sociolinguistic mechanisms have affected the way in which languages have changed to an extent that poses problems for both the comparative and internal method of historical reconstruction.

Rather than take a broad view of language relationship in Australia, which would be premature, I intend here to focus on low-level relationships in one small area, so as to highlight some problems involved. No claim is being made that similar circumstances have played a comparable role in language change everywhere in the Australian continent, but the situation that is found in western Cape York has, I feel, been more prevalent elsewhere than is generally recognized. However, because of the massive disruption of traditional life that has taken place in most areas of Australia that have suffered European invasion, it is often impossible to reconstruct the fine details of former sociolinguistic patterns.


## The linguistic situation in the Wik region of Western Cape York

Wik-Mungkan and Kugu Nganhcara are two closely related Wik languages spoken in the middle of the western Cape York region of North Queensland, principally at the settlements of Aurukun and Edward River (for more information about the historical and social relationships of the Wik languages in general, see Hale 1976; Sutton 1978; and Johnson, in press a). While detailed studies have been made of both languages, little is known about the dialects of Wik-Mungkan. My discussion here will therefore concentrate on the situation in Kugu Nganhcara, which Ian Smith and I have researched in depth. We have collected material on six different varieties of this language, one of which, Wik Iyanh, is closer to Wik-Mungkan than the others, so close in fact that in the past it has been regarded as a dialect of Wik-Mungkan. However, comparative evidence shows that Wik Iyanh is clearly part of the Nganhcara complex. The reason for the differences will be discussed below. The other five patrilects are Kugu Uwanh, Kugu Ugbanh, Kugu Yi'anh, Kugu Mu'inh and Kugu Muminh. The language name consists of the classifier for speech followed by the infinitive of the verb 'go'. I will regularly drop the classifier from the language name in what follows, as is the practice in Kugu Nganhcara.

Lexicostatistical evidence for Mungkan — Nganhcara relationships has been compiled by Sutton (1978: 178). Percentages of close cognates shared by Wik-Mungkan and some Nganhcara patrilects, based on a hundred-word list, are:

| Mungkan | | | | |
|---|---|---|---|---|
| 75 | Iyanh | | | |
| 77 | 88 | Mu'inh | | |
| 63 | 74 | 87 | Uwanh | |
| 61 | 74 | 81 | 84 | Muminh |

If it were not for the considerable phonological and morphological differences between Mungkan and the Nganhcara patrilects, it would be tempting to regard them as one language on lexical grounds. Some important features differentiating Nganhcara from Mungkan are

a) phonetic labiovelars are present: *k* and *g* have developed labio-velar allophones following nasals and stops;
b) voiced and voiceless stops contrast following the first syllable;
c) in final open syllables, all five vowels contrast, whereas in Wik-Mungkan vowel contrasts are neutralized;
d) thematic high vowels in verb stems undergo vowel alternation;
e) pronominal enclitics exist, and they attach to the element pre-ceding the verb (see Smith–Johnson 1985).

(a) and (b) are innovations, (c) and (d) retentions, and the evolution of (e) is at present unclear, as no detailed study of Wik-Mungkan clitics has yet been made. The details of both the nominal and verbal suffixes also differ considerably between the two languages, but I am not at present in a position to explain the historical development of these differences. Wik-Mungkan is also intonation-ally and phonotactically very distinctive.

## The Kugu Nganhcara patrilects

Kugu Nganhcara embraces the five closely related language varieties discussed above, which are associated with exogamous patrilineal clans, or patriclans, as well as Wik Iyanh, which, although its speakers are not so closely integrated into Nganhcara society, is definitely related to the Kugu Nganhcara complex, both linguisti-cally and socially. I will refer to these speech varieties as "*patrilects*" (following Smith–Johnson 1986), since there is no other currently appropriate term.

The relationship between territory, language, and speaker is very complex in this part of Australia. For more detailed discussion than I have space for here, the reader should consult Sutton (1978), Sutton–Rigsby (1979), and Rigsby (1980). Ownership of land, as well as patriclan membership and language, is in theory inherited through the father (from the father's father). The patriclan land may consist of non-contiguous parcels surrounded by land owned by other groups. Moreover, the patriclan is not the equivalent of the local band, the actual land-using camp group. Membership of local bands is rather fluid, and may consist of males and females from several different patriclans (and thus different patrilects, and sometimes even other languages) joined by kinship, marriage, or even friendship with a focal adult male.

Sutton and Rigsby (1979) make the point that although patriclans are much more stable entities than local bands, over a long period they too will change. Some clans may become extinct due to warfare, or to lack of male progeny. A larger clan may split into several small ones; a smaller clan may merge with another on a permanent basis, and the two may come to be considered one. These long-term political changes are governed by shifting alliances and antagonisms at the group level. Members of a dying patriclan may even abandon their patrilect in favor of that of another group with which they are politically allied. This process seems to have taken place with the last speakers of Ugbanh.

Within some patrilects different family groups display variation in vocabulary. When expressing an interest in working with another Uwanh informant, I was told that her family, although Uwanh speakers, were different, as they had their own word for 'swamp turtle'. Informants were quick to point out the differences of a particular speaker's Muminh, Yi'anh, or Uwanh from that of their own speech. Such publicly noted differences were nearly always in vocabulary alone. I have sometimes noticed myself that a particular speaker's style of patrilect was somewhat different from that of my main informants. Von Sturmer (1978: 172) has made similar observations.

A number of factors may lead to individual variation. Marriage among the Nganhcara is most frequently between speakers of different patrilects. As children grow up, they first learn their mother's language, and then switch to their father's as they become adults. They regard their father's language as their own, but all speakers of Nganhcara are competent in at least two patrilects. Many have also learnt their mother's mother's language, or that of other people who have been present in the local band. It is common to hear conversations between people each speaking their own patrilect, but at least passively competent in the other patrilects being spoken.

Speakers of Nganhcara sometimes marry outside of their own
immediate culture and are often multilingual in Wik-Mungkan,
Thaayorre, Ngathanh, or other languages of the region.

With such a complex situation forming the background for the
Nganhcara child's acquisition of language, strong pressures exist
to promote borrowings. This results in a vocabulary pool being
available to all Nganhcara speakers, from which they can select
their own words; speakers of the same patrilect sometimes differ
in their preferred vocabulary, and an unmarked word in one
patrilect may be used by the speaker of another for special effect.
Although people generally agree on which patrilect a word belongs to, there is some variation in usage. A further dimension
to this situation is added by respect vocabulary, described in more
detail below.

Equally strong but opposing forces act to maintain patrilect
distinctiveness. Patriclan membership is an extremely important part
of an individual's social identity, if only because it brings with it
ownership and rights to land, essential to physical survival in a
hunter-gatherer society. Land ownership and other consequences of
patriclan membership, such as ownership of sacred places, rights to
perform certain ceremonies, and ownership of songs and dances,
all enhance the personal prestige and political power of the individual. Patrilect is a marker of patriclan membership and thus a symbol
of identity. Given the small size of the patriclans and the hetero-
geneity of local bands, the marking of identity is a major concern.
Despite the variation noted above, there is general community
agreement on the linguistic feature of each patrilect, and considerable trouble is taken to make sure that children acquire appropriate
forms. My first informant, a widow, although regarding herself as
a speaker of Uwanh, has principally spoken her deceased husband's
patrilect since his death in order to provide her children with the
correct model.

Traditionally there would appear to have been approximately
fifty speakers per patrilect. Similar figures are found at the present
time for the more vigorous of the surviving patrilects, Iyanh, Muminh, Uwanh and Mu'inh. Given such small numbers, it is entirely
possible for a politically active adult male to exert significant control
over his patrilect, and to establish features of his own idiolect as
norms for others.

## Diffusion in Wik Iyanh

Jeffrey Heath has documented in great detail the massive amount of diffusion that has taken place in at least one other part of Australia (Heath 1978, 1979 and 1981). Wik Iyanh, while clearly most closely related to the other Nganhcara patrilects (Johnson, in press b), and more distantly to Wik-Mungkan, shows a number of morphological features that have diffused from Wik-Mungkan.

a) It lacks a distinction between dual and plural first person exclusive: in all other patrilects, *ngana* 'we (dual exclusive)' contrast with *nganhca* 'we (plural exclusive)', while Iyanh has the one form *ngana* 'we (exclusive)' for dual and plural.

b) There is only one conjugation for all verbs, compared with two in the other patrilects.

c) Many of the oblique pronoun forms have a unique structure, and show greater regularity than in the other patrilects. The details of Mungkan influence on pronoun morphology are discussed below.

d) The causative suffix is *-nha* instead of *-nga*.

e) The dative forms of the demonstratives, *ikuwu, nhakuwu* and *akawu*, have a *-k-* instead of *-g-*. Wik-Mungkan lacks the voicing distinction of Nganhcara.

These differences are related to the social allegiances of Iyanh speakers, who are somewhat peripheral to the Nganhcara group, and traditionally have had much closer contact with speakers of Wik-Mungkan. Wik-Mungkan influence in the Iyanh pronominal forms is illustrated below. Forms that Iyanh and the other patrilects share are generally left out. As elsewhere, I am using Kugu as a cover term for all the patrilects excluding Iyanh.

|  | Accusative/Dative | | Genitive/Ablative | |
|---|---|---|---|---|
|  | Kugu | Iyanh | Kugu | Iyanh |
| 1 sg |  |  | *ngathurum* | *ngatharam* |
| 2 sg |  |  | *nhingkurum* | *nhingkaram* |
| 3 sg |  |  | *nhingurum* | *nhinganam* |
| 1 dual inclusive | *ngalina* | *ngaling* |  |  |
| 1 dual exclusive | *nganana* | *nganang* | *ngananam* | |
| 2 dual | *nhipana* | *nhipang* |  |  |
| 3 dual | *pulana* | *pulang* |  |  |
| 1 plural inclusive | *ngampara* | *ngampang* |  |  |
| 1 plural exclusive | *nganhcara* | as for 1 dual exclusive | *nganhcaram* | as for 1 dual exclusive |
| 2 pl | *nhiyana* | *nhiyang* |  |  |
| 3 pl | *thaarana* | *thanang* | *thaaranam* | *thananam* |

(Yi'anh and Mu'inh have the following minor but significant differences: 3 sg Gen: *nhingurum* or *nhingunum*, 3 pl Acc: *thanana*, 3 pl Gen: *thananam*.)

In addition to the syncretism of dual and plural exclusive forms, the Iyanh pronoun declension shows a number of other similarities to Mungkan: the accusative/dative suffix *-ng*; the genitive/ablative singular formed with *-aCam*, instead of *-uCum*; and the reflexive forms (Wik-Mungkan has two formations, one in *-akam* [Iyanh *-aama*], and one in *-amang* related to Iyanh *-mang*).

Iyanh also shows signs of having been influenced by at least one other language of the region. The presence of the peripheral nasals *m* and *ng* in final position is areally unexpected in Cape York, although final *ng* is reported for Wik Me'en (Dixon 1980), a neighboring language which is probably the source for its presence in Wik Iyanh. Final *ng* is rare in other Nganhcara patrilects; Iyanh, however, frequently has a final *ng* where the Kugu patrilects have no final consonant: 'grey kangaroo', *kuja* (Iyanh: *kujang*); 'butcherbird', *thopolo* (Iyanh: *thopolong*).

Finally, Iyanh sometimes has long *aa* before *w*, where the other patrilects have short *a*: *kawa* 'south', Iyanh *kaawa*; *thawa* 'say', Iyanh *thaawa*. This would appear to be due to Wik-Mungkan influence.

## Differentiation in the Kugu Nganhcara patrilects

Only a few phonetic, phonological, and morphological features, apart from vocabulary, distinguish Uwanh, Ugbanh, Muminh, Mu'inh and Yi'anh. Iyanh shares some of these features as well.

While laminals contrast dental and palatal points of articulation, apicals are generally articulated in the alveolar region, although in Iyanh and Muminh, the tongue tip is extremely retracted, being in effect retroflexed (a feature which occurs in languages further south as well). Although this retroflection is not distinctive, its presence is characteristic of an Iyanh or Muminh speaker.

Nganhcara has contrasting voiced and voiceless stops:

|                      |                                          |
|----------------------|------------------------------------------|
| lamino-dental        | *watha* 'water rat'; *wadha* 'crow'      |
| (*th* ~ *dh*)        |                                          |
| lamino-palatal (*c* ~ *j*) | *thuci* 'small bird'; *thuji* 'crawl' |
| velar (*k* ~ *g*)    | *aku* 'skin'; *agu* 'place'              |

Historically, the voicing contrast arose via secondary split. A single series of stops had voiced allophones following long vowels and voiceless allophones following short vowels. Then the vowel length contrast was lost, while the voicing distinction was retained (Hale 1976). This innovation distinguishes the Nganhcara patrilects from Wik-Mungkan, which preserves the original vowel length contrast (Wik-Mungkan *ak* 'skin', *aak* 'place'). The voicing contrast in Nganhcara is found in all positions except word initially and following a long vowel. However, in the Muminh patrilect, intervocalic voiced velars are always preceded by a long vowel, and are (non-distinctively) fricative. This feature is a most obvious marker of a Muminh speaker: 'back' *kiga*, Muminh *kiiga*; 'tendon' *yagi*, Muminh *yaagi*.

Some patrilects have an intervocalic *r* in certain words where others have an *n*, for example Uwanh, Ugbanh, Muminh *iiru* 'this', *aara* 'that' versus Mu'inh, Iyanh, Yi'anh *inu* and *ana*. Two causatives display an alternation between *n* and *r*: *thaaranga* 'stand (trans.)', from *thana* 'stand (intrans.)', and *thooronnga* 'join' (optional), from *thono* 'one'. This correspondence is not regular but is seen occasionally elsewhere in the grammar. For example, it exists as an alternation in the third plural pronominal forms in most of the Kugu patrilects: *thana* (nominative) vs. *thaarana* (accusative/dative). Alternation between *n* and *r* without any difference in vowel length is also found in the pronouns. This alternation would appear to go back to the proto-language (Barry Alpher personal communication), but it is interesting that it has been retained as a marker of patrilectal difference.

Yi'anh has one peculiarity of its own. It has lost a nasal before non-coronal voiced stops in some words: thus Yi'anh *muga* 'eat', *kaagu* 'bandicoot', *pibennga* 'float' (Uwanh *mungga, kaanggu, pimbi*), but also Yi'anh and Uwanh *kumbi* 'shift', *nhumba* 'rub', *yinjenga* 'wet', where the nasal is retained.

Initial clusters are not found in the majority of Nganhcara patrilects, but they do occur in Muminh *ndhaa* 'see', and Iyanh *nhyeen* 'fly' and *nhyaara* 'swift, swallow'.

There are a great many idiosyncratic differences in the phonological makeup of the same word in different patrilects (where the patrilect is not indicated, the word occurs in three or more):

'mother' *ngathidhe, ngathadhe* (Muminh), *ngathidha* (Yi'anh), *ngatha* (Iyanh)
'yam' *kungba* (Uwanh, Ugbanh), *kungkuwa* (Muminh), *kungguwa* (Mu'inh)
'knife spear' *cawara, thawara* (Muminh, Iyanh)
'cry' *paabi, paawi* (Muminh), *paayi* (Iyanh)
'red kangaroo' *yakalba, yakalbi* (Muminh), *yakalwa* (Mu'inh)

The formation of causatives involves considerable morphological irregularity as well as some variation among the patrilects. The most common causative suffix, in all patrilects but Iyanh, is *-nga-*.

A few verbs display an intrusive *n* between the stem and suffix (*paabinnga-* 'make cry' from *paabi-* 'cry'). This is more frequent in Yi'anh than in the other patrilects; for verbs with alternating *e~i* stem vowels, *e* occurs before intrusive *n*, where other patrilects have *i*: *pacennga* (Uwanh *pacinga*) 'cause to sing out' from *paci* 'sing out', *unpennga* (Uwanh *umpinga*) 'light [a fire]' from *umpi* 'cut'.

*-nha-* is the usual causative suffix in Wik Iyanh, but it also occurs, especially in the respect register, in the other patrilects (glosses of respect register forms are preceded by 'R'): Iyanh *matanha*, Uwanh *matanga* 'cause to climb', from *mata* 'climb'; Uwanh, Ugbanh, Iyanh *wadhinha* 'R send back', from *wadhi* 'R return'.

Iyanh sometimes uses *-dha-* to form causatives. Most examples are in the respect register. In some cases the *-dha-* is used along with *-nga-*. Often the non-causative itself ends in *-nga-*; in such cases the Uwanh respect register causative and non-causative are often identical: *wagungadha* (Uwanh *wagunga*) 'R cause to climb' from *wagunga* 'R climb', *kuncungadha* (Uwanh *kuncunga*) 'R cause to descend' from *kuncunga* 'R descend'. There are also one or two examples of *-dha-* in the Iyanh plain register, and in the other patrilects; Iyanh *emadha*, Uwanh *emanga* 'grow, raise' from *ema* 'grow (intransitive)'; Uwanh *paladha* 'R call over' from *pala* 'hither'.

In the Iyanh respect register the causative suffix *-ya-* is occasionally used, in particular when the corresponding plain register term has the same root with the suffix *-nha-*. Usually *-ya-* replaces *-nha-* (*emaya* 'R grow, raise' [plain *emadha*] from *ema* 'grow (intrans.)'), but occasionally *-nha-* is retained (*parkanhaya* 'R warm' [plain *parkanha*] from *parka* 'get warm'). Only one example of *-ya-* has been found in another patrilect: Uwanh *ngucaya* (cf. Ugbanh *ngucanha*) 'R cause [fire] to catch' from *nguca* '[fire] catch'.

The overall picture is complicated, and the origins of the different causative markers have not yet been determined. However, their range of occurrence in the different patrilects points to multidirectional diffusion of varying intensity.

One case marker differs considerably within the patrilects. The comitative marker is *-ra* in Uwanh; Iyanh has *-nta*, Ugbanh and Yi'anh *-la*, and Muminh and Mu'inh *-nhja*. For the locative, Uwanh has *-n* and *-ng* (which appear to be in free variation), while Iyanh has only *-ng*. The other case markers show no patrilectal variation.

## Patrilexis

It is in the lexicon that the majority of differences among the patrilects are to be found. For example:

'frog' *waba* (Muminh, Yi'anh, Ugbanh), *thata* (Uwanh, Mu'inh, Iyanh);

'wallaby' *thuthamba* (Muminh), *pangku* (all other patrilects);

'bandicoot' *kaanggu* (Uwanh, Ugbanh), *kaagu* (Yi'anh), *monke* (Muminh, Iyanh), *woyondo* (Mu'inh);

'yellow bat' *woole* (Uwanh), *kopome* (Yi'anh), *wuki* (Ugbanh, Iyanh), *monthe* (Muminh), *matan* (Mu'inh);

'rat' *kupatha* (Uwanh, Yi'anh), *ciici* (Ugbanh, Muminh), *kalu* (Mu'inh, Iyanh);

and of course the verb 'to go', *uwanh, ugbanh, muminh, mu'inh, yi'anh* and *iyanh*, which is the basis for naming the patrilects.

The large majority of vocabulary is common to all patrilects. The figures on cognate lexicon from Sutton quoted above indicate that interlectal differences are on the order of 15% − 25%. These figures would be higher if phonological differences in cognate items, as illustrated in the previous section, were also taken into account, and are much higher in some sections of the lexicon, such as fauna. The greatest overall lexical differences are between Iyanh and the other patrilects; this accords with Iyanh's peripheral status.

For many lexical items there exists an alternative form which may be used in certain styles or registers of language. These styles include what is referred to by Nganhcara speakers in English as "side talk" and "big" language, and in the literature as avoidance or mother-in-law language. Certain kinfolk may be spoken to only indirectly, the extreme case being mother-in-law — son-in-law, and respect vocabulary is used in doing so. In important situations, talking about customs and giving instruction on ceremonial matters, for example, the heightened nature of the speech event is emphasized by the use of respect words. Usually, in these situations, the frequency of respect forms will be higher at the beginning of a discourse, and will decrease as the speaker continues.

Respect forms are morphologically unrelated to their plain counterparts, except for some derivational categories such as the causative, discussed above, and are available to replace a large part of the vocabulary. In general, the more common a word, the more likely there is to be a respect equivalent. Specific respect forms occur infrequently for flora and fauna, but plain register flora and fauna terms are generally used with the appropriate respect register classifier. All classifiers have respect equivalents, for example: *minha*, R *nhangki* 'animal', *yuku*, R *ngunja* 'thing', *waka*, R *mepam* 'grass'.

A word that belongs to the respect style in one patrilect may be the plain register form in another. For example, in Uwanh *nhangki thuthamba* is the respect form of *minha pangku* 'wallaby', while *minha thuthamba* is the plain form for the same animal in Muminh. Muminh and Iyanh both have the plain form *minha monke* 'bandicoot', for which Uwanh has *minha kaanggu*, replaced in respect register by *nhangki monke*. The Iyanh respect form is again different, *nhangki kalbenji.*

Respect language forms part of the larger pool of vocabulary available to the speaker of a Nganhcara patrilect, all of which can be utilized both for marking clan identity and for individualizing speech. A speaker's patrilexis is the totality of distinctive lexical items that identifies a Nganhcara as the speaker of a particular patrilect, and which is recognized as such by all speakers of Nganhcara. However, one's speech will also include items from other patrilects and languages, acquired from one's mother and more distant relatives, husband or wife and their kin, and perhaps from where one frequently resides, as has been discussed above, and these linguistic markers will be employed when necessary to make political and social statements about one's own allegiances. Thus the lexical makeup of a patrilect can change at varying rates, depending on the fortunes and aspirations of the dominant individual speakers.

The result of these social pressures is large-scale diffusion, which in the case of Nganhcara is most obvious in vocabulary, but is also more indirectly present in phonology and morphology. However, a prime motivating factor is often the desire to differentiate one's own language from that of another person, rather than to emulate the source of the borrowing.

## Some implications for language relationships in Australia

The details of the Nganhcara situation support the position of Dixon (1980: 254) that vocabulary is not a reliable criterion for genetic relationships, at least not in Australia. Lexicostatistical analyses could reveal almost as much about cultural as about linguistic relationships. There are clear examples in Australia of languages whose closest relatives are geographically distant. The Yaralde, who live at the mouth of the Murray River in South Australia, have a story of an ancestral being who travelled down the river to their present home. The language most closely related to Yaralde (Yitha Yitha), (Dixon 1980: 46) is five languages distant upriver. It is unlikely, given the structure of their society, that a large group migrated through hundreds of kilometres of potentially hostile territory to reach their present home. The nucleus of the new group was probably only one or two men accompanied by their immediate family. Such a group would quickly have to form allegiances with their new neighbors in order to survive, and inter-group marriage patterns would lead to diffusional pressures on the language. Interestingly, the Yaralde are intimately associated with the Tanganekald of the Coorong, whose language, although often identified with theirs under the rubric of Ngarrindjeri, appears quite distinct in the texts recorded by Norman Tindale in the 1930s (both languages are today extinct). Although Yaralde genetics are still relatively clear, the passage of another thousand years, with its accompanying sociolinguistic pressures, would have made the genetic relationships of this language obscure. I would imagine that similar situations have been common in the history of the languages of Australia, and in many instances it will be forever impossible to disentangle their products. Possible effects of diffusion on genetic relationships can be diagrammed as in figure 1.

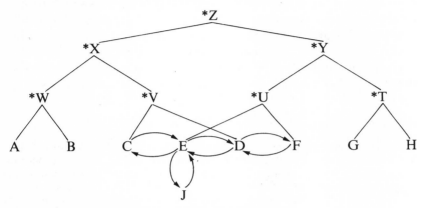

*Figure 1.* Effects of diffusion on genetic relationships

In figure 1 A—H are genetically related languages in spatial relationship, with E and D territorally interchanged, and J a not closely related language now in a close cultural relationship with E. The five central languages will act on each other as shown by the arrows, and diffusion will finally produce a set of languages which could appear to be related as in figure 2.

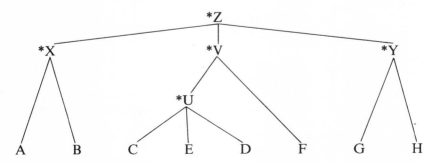

*Figure 2.* Results of diffusion

If only some of the groups involved alter their geographical relationships every five hundred years or so, repeated diffusion would scramble the fine genetic details beyond recovery; the broad genetic relationships of the languages concerned will be obvious, unless other genetically distant languages have been drawn into the situation, but it will be impossible either to carry out internal reconstruction or to ascertain middle-level relationships with any reliability. This unfortunately means that in such cases we will have to continue working directly from present-day languages to the proto-language without the comfort of any intermediate levels. The methods so painstakingly developed and refined by our nineteenth-century predecessors in historical and comparative linguistics are needed more than ever in such circumstances; it is unlikely, however, that they will yield such spectacular results for Australianists.

## Acknowledgments

The details about Nganhcara presented in this paper are as much the work of Ian Smith as of the author. He, Peter Sutton, and Bruce Rigsby have been independently responsible for the development of the sociolinguistic framework I have attempted to present here, and Jeffrey Heath has single-handedly explored virgin territory in studying diffusion in Australian languages. Without their research, I would have nothing to say. Barry Alpher has provided much-needed critical advice. The patience and linguistic sophistication of the many speakers of Kugu Nganhcara who contributed the data is much appreciated. Only they and I are answerable for the contents of this paper.

## References

Dixon, R. M. W.
1980    *The languages of Australia* (Cambridge: Cambridge University Press).
Hale, Kenneth
1976    "Wik reflections of Middle Paman phonology", in: Peter Sutton (ed.), *Languages of Cape York* (Canberra: Australian Institute of Aboriginal Studies), 50–60.
Heath, Jeffrey
1978    *Linguistic diffusion in Arnhem land* (Canberra: Australian Institute of Aboriginal Studies).
1979    "Diffusional linguistics in Australia: Problems and prospects", in: S. A. Wurm (ed.), *Australian Linguistic Studies* (Pacific Linguistics C-54) (Canberra: ANU), 395–418.
1981    "A case of intensive lexical diffusion: Arnhem Land, Australia", *Language* 57: 335–367.
Johnson, Steve
In press a    "From Kugu to Wik — Mungkanization at Aurukun", in: Patrick McConvell (ed.), *Can Aboriginal languages survive?* (St. Lucia: University of Queensland Press).
In press b    "Kugu Uwanh and Wik Iyanh comparative verb morphology".

Rigsby, Bruce
  1980        "Land, language and people in the Princess Charlotte Bay area", in:
              Neville C. Stevens—A. Bailey (eds.), *Contemporary Cape York Pen-
              insula* (Brisbane: Royal Society of Queensland), 89—94.
Smith, Ian
  1986        "Language contact and the life or death of Kugu Muminh", in:
              Joshua Fishman et al. (eds.), *The Fergusonian Impact* 2: *Sociolin-
              guistics and the sociology of language* (Berlin: Mouton de Gruyter),
              513—532.
Smith, Ian—Steve Johnson
  1985        "The syntax of clitic cross-referencing pronouns in Kugu Nga-
              nhcara", *Anthropological Linguistics* 27: 102—111.
  1986        "Sociolinguistic patterns in an unstratified society: The patrilects of
              Kugu Nganhcara", *Journal of the Atlantic Provinces Linguistic So-
              ciety* 8: 29—43.
Sutton, Peter
  1978        *Wik: Aboriginal society, territory and language at Cape Keerweer,
              Cape York Peninsula, Australia* (Ph. D. dissertation, University of
              Queensland).
Sutton, Peter—Bruce Rigsby
  1979        "Linguistic communities and social networks on Cape York Penin-
              sula", in: S. A. Wurm (ed.), *Australian Linguistic Studies* (Pacific
              Linguistics C-54) (Canberra: ANU), 713—732.
von Sturmer, John R.
  1978        The Wik Region: Economy, territoriality and totemism in Western
              Cape York Peninsula (Ph. D. dissertation, University of Queensland).

# The significance of pronouns in the history of Australian languages[1]

*Barry J. Blake*

At the time of the first European intrusions into Australia, the continent was inhabited by an indigenous population speaking over 200 different languages. These languages are generally of an agglutinative character with derivational suffixes followed by inflectional suffixes for case or for tense and aspect. A majority of them have bound pronominal affixes or clitics for subject and object.

Tasmania apart, the languages of Aboriginal Australia afford prima facie evidence for being genetically related, since there is a handful of lexical and functional roots that are very widespread including *nga 'first person', ku 'dative' and *ma which shows up as a lexical verb meaning 'take' or 'get' and as an auxiliary verb or as a verb suffix sometimes with a causative function. However, Australian languages are lexically diverse and the data on many languages meagre, most of them being extinct or on the verge of extinction. Consequently, there has been limited progress in systematic reconstruction.

The lexical diversity of Australian languages is reflected in the 1966 classification of O'Grady and others. This classifies some hundreds of communalects into languages, subgroups, groups, and families according to the percentage of cognates shared. The criterial figures are as follows (O'Grady — Voegelin — Voegelin 1966: 24 — 25):

| | |
|---|---|
| over 71% | dialects of a language |
| 51 – 70 | languages of a subgroup |
| 26 – 51 | subgroups of a group |
| 16 – 25 | groups of a family |
| under 15 [sic] | different families |

Under this system twenty-seven families are recognized (as revised in Wurm 1972).

The most interesting feature of this classification is that one family, Pama-Nyungan, covers about four-fifths of the continent.

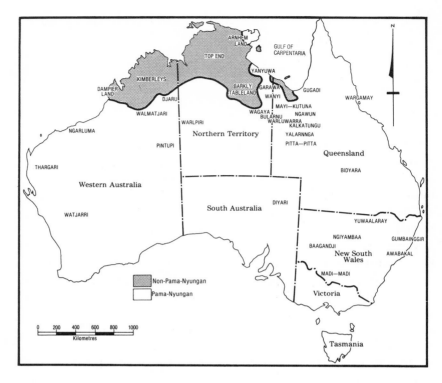

Map 1. Pama-Nyungan Languages

The other twenty-six are concentrated in an area running from Dampier Land in Western Australia to the western coast of the Gulf of Carpentaria (see map 1). More interestingly still, the genetic classification corresponds pretty well with an earlier typological one of Capell's (Capell 1937, 1956). Capell distinguished suffixing languages and prefixing languages. In the former group all affixes are suffixes, in the latter group there are prefixes as well as suffixes, the prefixed morphemes being typically the pronominal elements on the verb and often on the noun where they have a possessive function. The Pama-Nyungan languages are all suffixing (but see the reference to Yanyuwa below), and the other twenty six families are practically all prefixing.

The O'Grady — Voegelin — Voegelin classification has been criticized by Dixon (1980), who points out that the terms used in the classification are not used in the traditional way, i. e., the subgrouping is not based on shared innovations and therefore presents no hypothesis about periods of shared development and subsequent divergence. He points out that establishing a Pama-Nyungan "family" by vocabulary comparison does not enable one to infer that there was ever a proto-Pama-Nyungan. Dixon seems to accept that the Pama-Nyungan languages form a homogeneous group relative to the other "families", but he implies that this homogeneity may be a reflection of their conservatism, i. e., he sees the Pama-Nyungan family as a gigantic relic area.

Dixon (1980) includes a summary of the author's attempts at rigorous reconstruction. In this work he reconstructs a set of pronouns, some case markers, a number of verb roots including a demonstration of how root-final consonants become conjugation markers, plus some other forms such as interrogatives. His reconstructed pronouns are as follows:

(1)　　　Pama-Nyungan Pronouns

|  | singular | dual | plural |
|---|---|---|---|
| 1 | *ngay | *ngali | *ngana |
| 2 | *ngin | *nguNpalV | *nyurra |
| 3 | *nyu (east) | *pula | *tyana |
|  | *ngu (west) | | |
|  | *nyan (east feminine) | | |

The notation employed here uses digraphs to avoid diacritics. Lamino-dentals are marked by *h (th, nh, lh)*, lamino palatals by *y (ty, ny, ly)*, retroflexes by *r (rt, rn, rl)*, the flapped rhotic by *rr* (as opposed to the glide *r*) and the velar nasal by *ng*. Typically there is no phonemic distinction of voicing and I use *t* or *d, p* or *b*, etc., according to the conventions of my sources.

Dixon refers to these forms as 'proto-Australian', but he notes that most of them are reflected only among the Pama-Nyungan languages. Dixon appears to interpret this distribution as an indication of the conservation of Pama-Nyungan as opposed to a variety of innovations among the non-Pama-Nyungan languages. The main thrust of this paper is to point out that another set of proto-pronouns can be established for the non-Pama-Nyungan or northern languages. These northern languages do not reflect a great variety of roots for the various person-number combinations. Rather a small number of roots are quite widespread and the northern languages have a homogeneity with respect to pronouns comparable with that of Pama-Nyungan. On the other hand they do exhibit that great lexical diversity that underlies the twenty-six "families" of the O'Grady classification.

My reconstructed northern forms are displayed in (2). A comparison with (1) shows that the two sets have some forms in common. This is part of the evidence for the ultimate genetic relatedness of Australian languages.

(2)     Northern Pronouns

| | singular | non-singular |
|---|---|---|
| 1 | *ngay* | *nyi-rrV* |
| 1 + 2 | *nya* | *nga-rrV* |
| 2 | *nginy* | (a) *nu-rrV* |
| | | (b) *ku-rrV* |
| 3 | *nu* | *pu-rrV* |
| | *ngaya* (fem) | |

The notation 1 + 2 refers to first and second person, i. e., to an inclusive form. In the north, bare inclusive forms are often opposed to inclusive forms with dual, plural, or non-singular marking, thus they function paradigmatically with singular though referring to two persons. Some linguists use the labels 'minimal' and 'non-minimal' instead of 'singular' and 'plural' in systems of this type.

I will not justify my reconstructions here. Practically all the data are displayed in Blake (1989) and some argumentation is presented. Suffice it to say here that much of the reconstruction is shallow and non-controversial and has been accepted by Australianists. The forms for 1 + 2 and 1 non-singular are problematical, but at least it is accepted that there are forms in *nyi* and *nya* peculiar to the north.

As an example of the reconstruction we would consider the following attested forms for second person singular:

(3)

| | |
|---|---|
| Tiwi | *nginhtha* |
| Gagudju | *nginy* |
| Burarra | *nginyi* |
| Ndjebbana | *nyinydya* |
| Ngalakan | *nginy* |
| Wardaman | *yinyan* |
| Warndarang | *nyinyu* |
| Waray | *nguny* |
| Marengar | *niny* |
| Kuniyanti | *nginytyi* |
| Worora | *ngunytyu* |

If we assume a proto-form *nginy*, then the initial *ny* of forms like Warndarang *nyinyu* can be explained in terms of palatalization and the initial *y* of forms like Wardaman *yinyan* in terms of palatalization followed by denasalization, a commonly attested sound change in initial position in Aboriginal Australia. The second syllable of some of the forms is a reflex of the ergative *-lu* with hardening and assimilation of the *l*. This point is taken up below. The critical point is that forms with a palatal nasal as the third segment are widespread in the northern area whereas among the Pama-Nyungan languages the attested forms all have *n* in this position, e. g., Ngawun *yuntu* and Madi-Madi *nginti*.

Besides *nginy* the forms peculiar to the northern languages are *ngaya* 'she', *nya* 'thou and I', *nyi* 'we (exclusive)' and *ku* 'you'. *pu* 'they' may be peculiar to the northern languages. There is a form *pula* 'two, they two' widely reflected in the Pama-Nyungan area (see (1) above) and it is just possible that the first syllable of this form can be linked with the northern *pu*. The suffix reconstructed as *-rrV* (it occurs as *-rri, -rra, -rru* and *-rr*) is peculiar to the north as an agglutinative element, i. e., as an element combining with a number of person roots, but it may be reflected as the second syllable of Pama-Nyungan *nyurra*.

The third person singular root *nu* can be equated with the corresponding form *nyu* in the Pama-Nyungan table. There are other examples of an initial apical in the northern area corresponding with a laminal in roughly the Pama-Nyungan area, e. g., *na* 'see' in Ngalakan (northern) versus *nhatyi* in Pitta-Pitta (Pama-Nyungan). The second non-singular pronoun root provides another example, although it is possible that this ultimately derives from the same root as the third singular since it is common for third person roots to assume second person reference. However, there are no parallels for the correspondence between *ny* in northern *nginy* and *n* in Pama-Nyungan *ngin*. The palatal-alveolar correspondence may reflect a sound change or the northern palatal may reflect a segment additional to *ngin*. The palatal in *ngay* 'first singular' and its absence in non-singular first person forms is worth noting.

The distribution of the northern forms is shown on maps 2, 3, and 4. Each of the six forms shown has a wide distribution different from that of the others, but remarkably the isoglosses coincide along the margins to produce a well-defined northern area. This is

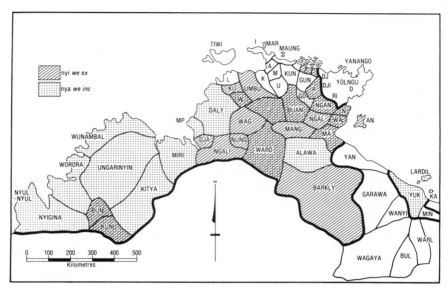

Map 2. Northern 1st Person

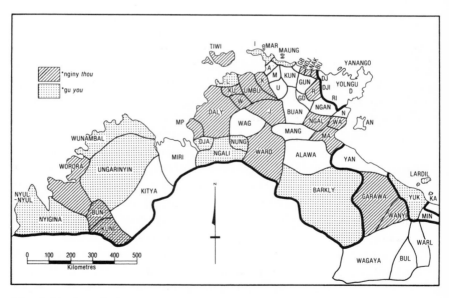

Map 3. Northern 2nd Person

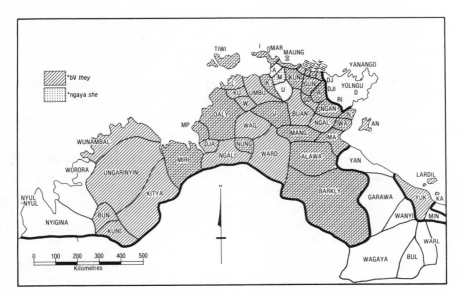

Map 4. Northern 3rd Person

demarcated by a heavy black border on maps 2, 3, and 4 and is shown as a hatched area on map 1. Languages reflect the northern set of pronouns or the Pama-Nyungan set; as a rule, they do not reflect a mixture of the two sets. The only exceptions to this generalization are a pair of relatively closely related languages in the Queensland — Northern Territory border area, namely Garawa and Wanyi. These languages have distinctively Pama-Nyungan forms such as *ngali* 'first dual exclusive', *nimbala* 'second dual', and *bula* 'third dual', see (1), but northern forms such as *ninydyi* 'you singular' — note the palatal third segment; compare (1) and (2) and *nu-* for 'first plural' and first inclusive (the absence of a velar nasal as the first segment suggests that this reflects *\*nya* or *\*nyi*; there are parallels for deriving some instances of Garawa-Wanyi initial *n* from *ny*).

The form *\*-rrV* as an agglutinative element is not shown on the maps. It is practically definitive for the northern area, occurring in virtually every language. In Garawa and Wanyi, it appears in *nurru* 'first plural' and *narri* 'second plural'.

A classification based on the distribution of pronoun roots involves some reassignments of languages between Pama-Nyungan and northern as compared with the O'Grady — Voegelin — Voegelin classification. These reassignments need to be made towards the eastern end of the northern/Pama-Nyungan border:

(i) Yanyuwa, previously classified as non-Pama-Nyungan, has Pama-Nyungan pronouns. In fact, it shares some distinctive forms with Warluwara, Bularnu, and Wagaya, a group of closely related Pama-Nyungan languages.

(ii) Lardil, Kayardilt, Yukulta, and Yanggaal, four closely related languages forming the Tangkic group and located in the southern Gulf area, have northern pronouns. Recent work on old sources by Evans demonstrates that the extinct Minkin language is also northern. In fact it appears to be a member of the Tangkic group. (Evans 1989).

(iii) As mentioned above, Garawa and Wanyi cannot be assigned unambiguously on the basis of their pronouns. They were classified as non-Pama-Nyungan in the O'Grady — Voegelin — Voegelin classification, but in a pronoun-based classification their position becomes ambivalent.

The fact that almost all Australian languages (save those of Tasmania which are discussed briefly below) reflect either the distinctively Pama-Nyungan pronouns or the northern ones is highly significant. Each set contains a number of independent roots and the only reasonable explanation for the consistent co-occurrence of roots from one set or the other in the attested languages is that these languages reflect one of two distinct proto-languages. In other words, the arbitrary association of roots such as *ngin*, *ngali*, and *tyana* must have been a feature of a remote proto-language that underlies the Pama-Nyungan languages. Similarly the association of roots such as *nginy*, *ngaya*, and *-rrV* in the northern languages suggests a common ancestor in which these roots were found. The distribution of languages accords with this hypothesis since the Pama-Nyungan and northern languages occur in blocs with few discontinuities. If the two types had been thoroughly intermingled, it would have defied an explanation in terms of two proto-languages or indeed any other explanation.

The positing of two proto-languages does not, of course, preclude the possibility of a single proto-language of an earlier stage. In fact the occurrence of certain roots among both the northern and Pama-Nyungan languages, such as first singular *\*ngay*, points in that direction. The simplest scenario that would account for the distribution of pronoun roots runs like this: a remote proto-language is reflected over most or all of the continent. A particular language that has accumulated four or five pronoun innovations expands and gives rise to a great number of daughters, granddaughters, and great-granddaughters. In the process it spreads widely and usurps the territory where other languages were previously spoken. These languages could have been conservative ones lacking the innovations entirely, or ones containing any number of innovations.

This scenario could have been realized in two ways, either with the northern languages being the daughters of an innovating proto-northern or with the Pama-Nyungan languages being the daughters of an innovating proto-Pama-Nyungan. The question of where the locus of innovation lay is not easy to answer. The following data are relevant:

(a) the pronouns themselves
(b) the distribution of the northern and Pama-Nyungan languages
(c) other areas of grammar

(a) The pronouns

Since the northern pronouns are agglutinative, they are likely to be innovative with respect to the Pama-Nyungan pronouns which form duals and plurals with a number of "one off" formatives. The agglutinative nature of the northern pronouns is apparent not only in the use of reflexes of *\*-rrV* to form the non-singular, but also in the use of other elements to distinguish dual from plural and in some instances the use of further elements to make masculine-feminine distinctions. In Djamindjung, for instance, the non-singulars are as follows (Cleverly 1968):

(4)

| | Dual | Plural |
|---|---|---|
| 1 | *yirrinyi* | *yirri* |
| 2 | *kurrinyi* | *kurri* |
| 3 | *purrinyi* | *purri* |

Such agglutinative forms certainly look relatively new, but it is not so certain that the roots are relatively new. In fact, the second person non-singular root in Djamindjung, *ku*, reflects one of the two competing northern roots, namely *\*ku*, the other being *\*nu*; see (2). There is evidence to suggest that *\*ku* is an older element. Its distribution is discontinuous (see map 3) and where it co-occurs with reflexes of *\*nu* the *ku* forms are always bound and the *nu* ones free.

The Pama-Nyungan second plural *\*nyurra* looks like a relic of such an agglutinative system and suggests that perhaps the Pama-Nyungan pronouns are newer, but, as Harold Koch has reminded me, there are a number of possible reflexes of *-rrV* in the Pama-Nyungan area. It could be an old element that was taken up by the ancestral northern language for systematic use.

## (b) Distribution

The distribution of the Pama-Nyungan languages involves some discontinuity since there is an enclave in northeast Arnhem Land and perhaps another not so notable discontinuity involving Yanyuwa. Here the situation is ambivalent since the status of Garawa and Wanyi is unclear with respect to the northern versus Pama-Nyungan distinction, although it is clear that Yanyuwa has become cut off from the languages most closely to it, namely Wagaya, Bularnu, and Warluwara. There is a standard argument that discontinuity reflects relic status since the arbitrary relationship between expression and content ensures that separate areas are highly unlikely to have coined the same forms for a particular referent or function. However, this argument assumes no movement of population. In Aboriginal Australia, with the absence of detailed history, we are in no position to talk about movement of population. Moreover, we have no indication of time depth. 17,000 years ago, at the height of the last Ice Age, the Gulf of Carpentaria was dry land, and as recently as 10,000 years ago the coastline was 200 kilometres out to sea from several points on the western coast of the Gulf. It is conceivable that the enclave of Pama-Nyungan in northeast Arnhem Land resulted from the rising sea level along the western shore of the Gulf. Of course, the sea level is relevant only if we are dealing with great time depths. One feature of distribution that is relevant is the homogeneity of Pama-Nyungan. It is less differentiated than the northern languages, which suggests it is younger, and it is so homogeneous with respect to pronouns, case markers, and some other function morphemes that a comparison with Indo-European and Semitic suggests we are dealing with a time depth of some thousands of years rather than one stretching back beyond 10,000 years. There is in fact one small piece of evidence that bears on the question of time depth. Tasmania was cut off from the mainland by a rising sea level about 10,000 years ago, and the re-emerging strait would have proved an insuperable barrier to any subsequent contact between the island and the mainland. The available information on the extinct languages of Tasmania consists almost entirely of word lists notated by amateurs, but the first and second singular pronouns were recorded in some dialects. The first person forms include *mina* and *mang(a)* and the second singular *nina* and *ninga* (Crowley – Dixon 1981: 417). While the *ni* (or *nhi*?) of the latter could be related to proto-Pama-Nyungan *\*ngin*, there is no plausible way to link *mi-* or *ma-* with *\*ngay*. It looks as if Tasmanian could reflect a pre-Pama-Nyungan level or pre-mainland level.

(c) Other areas of grammar

In at least one other domain of grammar the direction in which the northern and Pama-Nyungan languages have diverged is clear and that is case marking. Dixon (1980, building on Dixon 1970; Hale 1976) reconstructs the following proto-Australian case markers:

(5)      ergative-instrumental    *\*-lu*
         locative                 *\*-la*
         dative                   *\*-ku*
         accusative               *\*-nya*

These proto-forms have widespread reflexes among the Pama-Nyungan languages, most languages reflecting most of the forms. Among the northern languages, there are not nearly so many clear reflexes. This is not unrelated to a typological difference. Practically all the northern languages are of the heavily cross-referencing type with the subject and object represented by prefixes on the verb. In such languages, ergative case marking (for the subject of a transitive verb) and accusative case marking do not have a high functional load; in fact, it is unusual in discourse to have a high proportion of noun phrases in subject or object function. Not surprisingly, then, we find that many northern languages lack subject and object case marking. However, bound pronominal markers in object function typically end in *-n*. In Kunwinyku (Gunwinggu) for instance, we find the following contrast (examples based on Oates 1964):

(6)        a. *nga-be-n-bun*        b. *nga-n-di-bun*
              I-them-acc-hit              me-acc-they-hit
              'I hit them'                'They hit me'

This *-n* is a plausible reflex of *-nya* via *-ny*. In Djapu, a Pama-Nyungan language of northeast Arnhem Land, the accusative has *-n* as an alternative to *-nha* (Morphy 1983: 35). Also in Dyirbal two dialects have an accusative *-na* where the third dialect has *-nya* (Dixon 1972: 50).

As Dixon (1977) has demonstrated, the subject form of the singular pronouns in Australian languages very often has a reflex of *-lu* as the second syllable. This reflex does not function as an ergative since it occurs in intransitive as well as transitive subject function. Dixon suggests it was extended to intransitive subject function as an augment to meet an introduced requirement that all words have two syllables. The forms can be illustrated from Ngawun where the first person is *ngayu* ( < *ngay-lu*) and the second person *yundu* from *ngin-lu* with hardening of *l* to *t*, palatalization and denasalization of the initial, and regressive vowel harmony. Forms like these can be found sporadically among the northern languages, see (3). Thus in Worora, the first person singular is *ngayu* ( < *ngay-lu*) and the second person singular is *ngunytyu* ( < *nginy-lu* with hardening and assimilation of *l* to *dy*, and regressive vowel assimilation). Moreover, forms such as *dyu, dya, dyi* and *da* are widespread in the north as second singular roots, usually bound forms and often restricted in their distribution. Bound pronouns are typically reduced forms of free ones and these forms are plausible reflexes of the second syllable of forms like *nginytyu*, i. e., plausible reflexes of ergative *-lu*.

Clear reflexes of the dative *-ku* occur sporadically among the northern languages, though there are few clearly identifiable reflexes of locative *-la* and practically none of *-lu* in instrumental function.

The general picture that emerges is that the proto-case markers belong to a remote proto-language ancestral to both the northern and Pama-Nyungan languages and that they are widely reflected among the latter but only sporadically among the former. This suggests that Pama-Nyungan is conservative with respect to case. Of course a language could be conservative in one area of grammar and innovative in another and indeed is quite likely to be.

If Pama-Nyungan was innovative in its pronouns, then we would have to posit a scenario in which a language that retained a number of proto-Australian case markers acquired a number of pronouns and then spread.

The co-occurrence of bundles of pronoun isoglosses with the prefixing-suffixing boundary is presumably to be explained in terms of the pronouns being bound as proclitics or prefixes in the north and as enclitics or suffixes to the south as the descendants of the innovating language spread. West of the Barkly Tableland, the coincidence is perfect, but towards the eastern end of the boundary, some changes appear to have occurred. Most of these are related to the fact that in this area, prefixing languages came into contact with Pama-Nyungan languages that lacked bound pronouns. Yanyuwa provides a good example. As noted earlier, this language reflects the pronoun roots of the Pama-Nyungan set and shares a number of distinctive forms, pronominal and otherwise, with three closely related Pama-Nyungan languages: Warluwara, Bularnu, and Wagaya. Warluwara, and Bularnu lack bound pronouns; Wagaya has bound suffixed pronouns that are transparent abbreviations of the free forms. Yanyuwa on the other hand has prefixed bound pronouns on the verb and prefixed noun class markers. The bound pronouns on the verb are fairly transparent reductions of the corresponding free forms and the class markers on the nouns show transparent case in concord with the noun to which they are prefixed. For example, the word for 'pandanus palm' is *ma-wukara* with *ma-* being the class prefix for plant nouns. The ergative-allative case of this word is *mungku-wukaralu* where *wukara* exhibits the common Pama-Nyungan variant of the ergative for vowel-final stems of more than two syllables and *ma-* shows the common allomorph for shorter vowel stems, namely *-ngku*. Such transparency is hardly to be found among the other prefixing languages, suppletion and irregular alternants commonly marking case on the class marker. It seems that Yanyuwa was a language without bound pronouns that came into contact with prefixing languages and acquired the prefixing system comparatively recently.

# Conclusion

The main thrust of the present paper is to argue on the basis of the distribution of pronoun roots that two separate proto-languages are widely reflected in Australia and that between them they cover all or nearly all of the continent except for Tasmania. These proto-languages are referred to as proto-northern and proto-Pama-Nyungan. However, there are some forms common to the northern languages and the Pama-Nyungan languages: pronoun roots such as *ngay 'first person singular' and *-ku 'dative'. These provide prima facie evidence that all Australian languages are genetically related. This in turn means that one of my proto-languages should approximate to Dixon's proto-Australian and the other would be innovative.

I have hedged on the question of whether the northern pronouns are older or newer than the Pama-Nyungan ones. The attested northern pronoun sets look newer because of their agglutinative formation, but their roots need not be newer. The idea that the northern languages are innovative is supported by the appearance of vestiges of roots widely reflected in the Pama-Nyungan area such as ergative-instrumental *-lu and by the discontinuous distribution of the Pama-Nyungan languages. Against this there is the relative homogeneity of the Pama-Nyungan languages and the consequent appearance of relative youth. It could be that the Pama-Nyungan languages reflect an older proto-language than the northern ones do and that most of the attested ones are the offspring of a branch that spread comparatively recently.

Positing two very widespread proto-languages is startling since it means that a new language must have been adopted over a wide area. Theoretically this could happen through conquest, but the Australian Aboriginal culture of the recent past is perhaps the least likely of all to have been involved in large-scale organized warfare, invasion, and settlement. It is conceivable that a language was adopted by an ever-increasing circle because of some prestige it had acquired and it is possible that survivors of drought or plague, or a combination of both, spread into what had become unoccupied territory. Even without positing two proto-languages that are reflected over great areas, it is necessary to allow for the spreading of a new language. The relative homogeneity of Pama-Nyungan has already been touched on. There are such great similarities in many of its function roots from one side of the continent to another that it is inconceivable that this is the original language of a land known to have been inhabited by humans for something like 50,000 years.

It remains for future research to find evidence of other roots besides pronominal ones that are widespread among the northern languages and exclusive to them. Such evidence is needed to bolster the idea of a proto-northern. It also remains for future research to examine the meagre material available on the extinct languages of Victoria, where there appear to be some distinctive pronoun roots.

## Acknowledgments

I would like to thank Bob Dixon, Jeffrey Heath, Luise Hercus and Colin Yallop for their advice, Francesca Merlan for access to her unpublished material, Gavan Breen, Neil Chadwick, Nick Evans, Jean Kirton, Harold Koch, Bill McGregor, Alan Rumsey and Tasaku Tsunoda for advice, references and unpublished data. I would also like to thank the participants at the Stanford Symposium for their comments on my presentation.

## Note

1. This paper is abstracted from a long paper entitled "Redefining Pama-Nyungan" (Blake 1989) which contains all the relevant data and references to the sources.

## References

Blake, Barry J.
    1989        "Redefining Pama-Nyungan", in: Evans — Johnson (eds.).
Capell, Arthur
    1937        "The structure of Australian languages", *Oceania* 8(1): 27 — 61.
    1956        *A new approach to Australian linguistics (Oceania Linguistic Monographs* No. 1) (Sydney, University of Sydney).
Cleverly, John R.
    1968        *A preliminary study of the phonology and grammar of Djamindjung* (University of New England, N. S. W., thesis).
Crowley, Terry — Dixon, R. M. W.
    1981        "Tasmanian", in: Dixon — Blake (eds.), 395 — 421.
Dixon, R. M. W.
    1970        "Proto-Australian laminals", *Oceanic Linguistics* 9: 79 — 103.
    1972        *The Dyirbal language of North Queensland* (Cambridge: University Press).

234   *Barry J. Blake*

1977          "The syntactic development of Australian languages", in: Charles Li
              (ed.), *Mechanisms of syntactic change* (Austin: University of Texas
              Press), 365—415.
1980          *The languages of Australia* (Cambridge: University Press).
Dixon, Robert M. W. — Barry J. Blake (eds.)
1979—81       *The handbook of Australian languages* 1—3 vols. (Canberra: A. N. U.
—83           Press; Amsterdam: John Benjamins).
Evans, Nicholas
1989          "The Minkin language of the Burketown region", in: Evans—John-
              son (eds.).
Evans, Nicholas—Steve Johnson (eds.)
1989          *Aboriginal Linguistics* 1 (Armidale, N. S. W.: University of New Eng-
              land).
Hale, Kenneth
1976          "On ergative and locative suffixal alternations in Australian lan-
              guages", in: R. M. W. Dixon (ed.), *Grammatical categories in Austra-
              lian languages* (Canberra: A. I. A. S.; New Jersey: Humanities Press),
              414—417.
Morphy, Frances
1983          "Djapu, a Yolngu dialect", in: R. M. W. Dixon—B. J. Blake (eds.),
              1—187.
Oates, Lynette F.
1964          *A tentative grammar of the Gunwinggu language* (*Oceanic Linguistic
              Monographs* No. 10) (Sydney, University of Sydney).
O'Grady, Geoffrey N. —Charles F. Voegelin—Florence M. Voegelin (eds.)
1966          *Languages of the world: Indo-Pacific* 6 (*Anthropological linguistics* 8,
              2) (Bloomington, Indiana: Indiana University Press).
Wurm, Stephen A.
1972          *Languages of Australia and Tasmania* (The Hague, Mouton).

# Morphological clues to the relationships of Japanese and Korean

*Samuel E. Martin*

0.   The striking similarities in structure of the Turkic, Mongolian, and Tungusic languages have led scholars to embrace the perennially premature hypothesis of a genetic relationship as the "Altaic" family, and some have extended the hypothesis to include Korean (K) and Japanese (J). Many of the structural similarities that have been noticed, however, are widespread in languages of the world and characterize any well-behaved language of the agglutinative type in which object precedes verb and all modifiers precede what is modified. Proof of the relationships, if any, among these languages is sought by comparing words which may exemplify putative phonological correspondences that point back to earlier systems through a series of well-motivated changes through time. The recent work of John Whitman on Korean and Japanese is an excellent example of productive research in this area. The derivative morphology, the means by which the stems of many verbs and nouns were created, appears to be largely a matter of developments in the individual languages, though certain formants have been proposed as putative cognates for two or more of these languages. Because of the relative shortness of the elements involved and the difficulty of pinning down their semantic functions (if any), we do well to approach the study of comparative morphology with caution, reconstructing in depth the earliest forms of the vocabulary of each language before indulging in freewheeling comparisons outside that domain. To a lesser extent, that is true also of the grammatical morphology, the affixes or particles that mark words as participants in the phrases, sentences (either overt clauses or obviously underlying propositions), discourse blocks, and situational frames of reference that constitute the creative units of language use. But the functions of the grammatical morphemes are more easily categorized, and often the looseness of the attachment of a particle or suffix clearly shows that it goes back to an independent element that was "glued on" to perform a specialized task. That is particularly true of the case

markers of Korean and Japanese, less so for those of the other languages in question. But there are examples in each of the languages, I believe, that will show a readiness to discard an old marker for a new, or to use both markers as competing (or distributionally specialized) variants, while retaining the functional category that the marker represents.

One of the functional categories shared by Korean and Japanese but not found in other languages, so far as I can tell, is the particular bundling of features in particles of focus and contrast, essentially features beyond the clause level that are disparately handled in many languages by word order, phonetic salience (phrasal juncture and sentential "stress"), or intonation. Here, too, the actual morphemes representing the bundles of features are subject to replacement by competing morphemes, often loosely attached as specialized uses of independent words. (Semantically complex phrasal postpositions are coming into the grammar all the time, of course, as are phrasal prepositions in languages like English.) The two languages offer virtually identical packages of subtle uses for the subdued focus that often marks old information ('as for ...'), represented by K *un / n(un)< ( $^{u}/_{o}$)n/ $^{\cdot}$n$^{u}/_{o}$n* and J *wa* < $^{\cdot}$ *fa* < $^{\cdot}$ *pa*, and for the highlighted focus that often marks new information ('too; even; ...'), represented by K *to* < $^{\cdot}$ *two* and J *mo* < . *mo* (? < * $^{\cdot}$ *mo . o*). The morphemes are not cognate with each other, but it is possible to find other morphemes in each language which are plausible candidates for at least two or three of the missing cognates.

In this paper, I explore the possibility of Korean and Japanese cognates for some of the more important particles and endings, building on earlier work (in particular, Martin 1968 and 1975), with a very few remarks on Tungusic, Mongolian, and Turkic forms. Unlike the Altaicists and the Nostraticists, I do not start with the premise that these languages (or any others) must be related, but seek, rather, to find ways in which their forms might best be explained as shared inheritance from a common earlier stage.

1.    The genitive-nominative markers enjoy a wide range of functions in Korean and Japanese. Despite the presence of more than one morpheme in each language, all of the functions can be found existing for each of the morphemes in both languages, provided we stop looking merely at the modern standard languages and take into account earlier and dialect forms. The major functions can be roughly described as follows:

*Table 1.* Genitive-nominative markers

|        | Korean                                              | Japanese                         |
|--------|-----------------------------------------------------|----------------------------------|
| (1.1)  | ˙ᵘ/ₒy ? < [G]oy < *ka i                             | ? —                              |
| (1.2)  | ka ? < ˙ka (/ˈkwo) 'question'                       | ga < n ka (? < ka 'question')    |
| (1.3)  | ˙i ? < postadnom ˙i 'one/fact/person' ? < ˙i/ywo 'this (one)' | (i)[2]                 |
| (1.4)  | s ? < postadnom ˙so/to 'fact' NUMERAL -s[3]         | tu NUMERAL -tu                   |
| (1.5)  | —                                                   | no ? < [mo]no[4]                 |
| (1.6)  | ? —                                                 | n / n tu > -zu-; n ka > ga       |
| (1.7)  | —                                                   | na                               |

(1) Marking a noun, noun phrase, or nominalized sentence as adnominal to an overt noun.

(2) Forming a nominalization. This can be regarded as an ad-nominalization to an unstated noun of the type that I have described for Japanese as a postadnominal, either summational ('the fact that …') or extruded ('the one [thing, person, time, place, …] that …').

(3) Marking the subject of a clause. This is the normal subject marker, but it is suppressed when the antithetical particles of focus (Japanese *wa* and *mo*) are attached, leading to the illusion that the particle of subdued focus (Japanese *wa*) is the subject marker except in subordinate clauses. In a sense, all clauses of Korean and Japanese are subordinate; the independent clause or traditional "sentence" is a higher-level unit of discourse.

(4) Marking the affective (cathectic) object of expressions of emotion ('liking wine', 'afraid of ghosts', 'ashamed of the child') and, very occasionally, other kinds of objects.

(5) Marking the complement of a mutative or putative structure ('[so as] to be …'), or of a variety of copular structures that include such meanings as identification (' = ') and propredication ('[it] is [an instance of]'). More commonly in Japanese these are marked by the essive *ni* that underlies the copula structures themselves.

The forms are shown in table 1. With reference to the Korean notations, those unfamiliar with the language should bear in mind that ᵘ/ₒ represents the minimal vowel, usually either a reduction from one of the stronger vowels (*e a wo wu i*) or, typically for grammatical morphemes, inserted by epenthesis. The higher/lower articulation of this "shwa" is either determined by the vowel of the preceding syllable ("vowel harmony") or, at times, freely variable. For other features of the notation, see note 1.

The distribution of the Japanese particles *no* and *ga* varies with dialect and period, but each is attested in identical functions. The distribution of Korean $^u/_o$y and *i* overlaps with respect to marking the subject of adnominal clauses but in other subordinate clauses, I believe, only *i* marks the subject. It should be noted that the modern Seoul pronunciation of the particle *uy* is identical with that of the allative/locative/dative *ey*, though we expect /i/; that pronunciation occurs in dialects, but it is unclear whether the dialect /i/ is a raising of /ey/ or the direct development expected, non-initial *uy* > *i*, or possibly even a survival of the particle *i* itself. I have toyed with the notion that the two particles differed in tightness of attachment: Middle Korean normally contracts the particle *i* to *y* after a vowel, while *uy* seems to be so contracted less often, though there are examples (one being *. na ˙ oy* → *:nay* 'my'), and I now suspect that the two particles differed less than has been generally assumed. (Yet it must be noted that there are no Middle Korean examples of "*i*" for a clearcut genitive, *\*N i N = N oy N*.) For the origin of the particle *oy* we offer the hypothesis that it is a reduction of *\*[G]oy < \*ka i*, just the opposite of the later (pleonastic) ... *i ka* → *y ka*, as in *nay ka < na i ka* 'I'. The *-G-* represents a voiced laryngeal or velar fricative which was only indirectly written by the fifteenth-century orthography. The sound vanished early but left traces by blocking an expected liaison in the spelling of *l* followed by *i, y,* or *z*; those are the only environments for which *-G-* is generally hypothesized, though I have reconstructed it also for other environments (Martin 1982/1983). But reconstructing the pleonastic string of particles *\*ka i* presumes the existence of the particle *ka*, and that is poorly attested in the early texts. In modern Korean the two particles stand in a suppletive relationship: *i* after a consonant, *ka* after a vowel. The origin of the suppletion is a perplexing question; spelling ... *i* (or "*y*") after a vowel obviously continued long beyond the period in which that was the spoken norm. It seems unlikely that the substitution of ... *ka* was influenced by the language spoken by Hideyoshi's invaders at the end of the fifteenth century, who would have used a nasal velar (*ŋa* or *ŋga*), in any event, nor by later contacts with Japanese. Kim Hyengkyu

(1954) imputes two instances to the Koryŏ songs (*sok . ka*) "Twong-twong" and "Sekyeng pyelkwok", but this has not been confirmed. There is but a single clear example in the early Hankul texts: ˙ *qilq-˙chyey˙ka* 'all [believe]' (1463 Pep-hwa 1:120), explicating a Chinese passage. The next examples are a few attested from the latter half of the seventeenth century, such as *poy ka ol kes in i* 'the boat will probably come' (1676 Chep-hay sin-e 1:8, translating a Japanese sentence). I am inclined to think that ... *ka* was there all along, perhaps as a colloquial emphatic. Modern *-uni-kka* (*n*) = *-uni* 'because' is thought to be a semantic extension of *-ni-s-ka* (question), and *-ta-ka* = *-ta* 'and then; only when' is said to be a direct attachment of the infinitive of *taku-* 'bring near', but maybe we should take another look. Compare the development of the meaning 'but' for Japanese *ga* and the antithetical uses of the nominative-marked and accusative-marked nominalizations in both languages. On the Korean *i/ka* see Kim Panghan (1957); Nam Kwangwu (1957); LSN (1958); Kim Hyengkyu (1954, 1964), who attributes the modern rise of *ka* to avoidance of hiatus; Hamada (1970); Hong Yuncak (1975); and ˡYi Sunguk (1981), who would derive *ka* from the verb *ka-* 'go'. See also Se Cengmok (1982) on subject-marking in Middle Korean subordinate clauses; and, on the genitive particles, An Pyenghuy (1968) and Kim Sungkon (1971). The widespread attachment of *-i* to nouns ending in consonants in the northern provinces, especially Hamkyeng, is thought to be an accretion of the same etymon (either by way of the nominative or directly), which is often taken to be the postadnominal meaning 'person', though I view that as a special case of a more general pronominal meaning 'one (= person/thing); fact' just like the postadnominal use of Japanese *no* (and in dialects *ga*). The favorite sentence type of Middle Korean was adnominalization + *i*, either as a bare nominalization or one predicated by a copular form; the perfect/imperfect endings are analyzed as ... *-n/-l i* (*[i]la*), a formal analog of modern J ... *no da* 'It is that ...'. That accretion of *-i* (after vowels *-y*) by nouns may well have encouraged the use of the particle *ka*, since the original case marking would be obscured once the noun was generalized as ending in *-i* (or *-y*); notice that the example cited above has a noun ending in *-y* (*poy ka* 'boat', in this instance the *-y* being a part of the etymon and not an accretion), but it is hard to see how that explanation could apply to those dialects which show very little of the *i*-accretion, such as the standard central dialect, nor why it did not apply earlier to the many nouns which basically ended in *-i* or *-y* all along. If we set up a Proto-Korean-Japanese morpheme *\*i* for the nominative/genitive marker, it may be possible to enlarge the original scope of that etymon to include several other morphemes found in the two languages. In Japanese, the verb infinitive *-i*, from which many free nouns are derived, was taken by Martin (1987) as *-Ci* (the missing consonant was perhaps a voiced velar fricative) but the initial may be an internal Japanese hiatus-filler or just an artifact of the analysis; there is also the old Japanese verbal prefix *i-* of unknown semantic force. For Korean we find the postadnominal *i* 'one, person, thing; fact'; the suffix *-i* that derives nouns and adverbs (' *khi* < *kh[u]-i* 'largeness; height', ' *khuy* < *khu-i* 'greatly'); and the deictic ' *i* 'this'.[5]

The genitive marker *s* is obsolete in modern Korean, except as a relic in fossilized compounds, analogous to the Japanese marking of noun compounds by (nasality-and-) voicing that reflects an earlier adnominal marker *n*. In Middle Korean, the two particles *s* and *$^u/_oy$* had identical functions, but attached to different kinds of nouns: the *s* was chosen as the marker for inanimates and exalted (honorific) animates, *$^u/_oy$* for ordinary animates. This may well have been a local and temporary specialization, like the semantically similar distribution of Japanese *no* and *ga* in certain dialects and times. I believe this subsyllabic particle *s* is etymologically identical with the postadnominal *so/to* 'fact', which forms the heart of a number of Middle Korean clause formations (...-*lq s[o] i-la*, ...-*lq t[o] i-la*, ...-*lq so y*, and others). The likely Japanese cognate for this etymon is the obsolete genitive particle *tu*, fairly fossilized already in Old Japanese; this *tu* is often treated as specifically a "locative genitive" (*nifa tu tori* 'the bird in the yard' = 'chicken') but there are examples that point to a wider use, such as *asatuki* 'chives' < *asa tu ki* 'mild onion' with the adjective stem *asa* (-). The non-adnominal forms of the numerals have accreted this morpheme (*hito-tu* < *\*pito tu* 'one') — in at least one instance after a different adnominal marker (*yoro-zu* < *yoro-~du* < *\*yoro n tu* 'ten thousand; many') — as a kind of nominalization of a basically adnominal morpheme, the number, which in seventh-century Japanese often directly preceded a noun without an intervening marker, as did the adjective stem, too.

Japanese *ga* < *\*n ka* probably originated as an emphatic use of the interrogative postadnominal *ka* 'question',[6] attached to the noun by the adnominal marker *n*. The element *n* is sometimes assumed to be a reduced form of the particle *no* (or *ni*), and that, in at least some instances, it may indeed be. But I have a more intriguing idea. We seek the origin of the essive *ni* '[to] be', which I take to be the source of the allative, dative, and other uses of the particle *ni*; we must explain, too, the adnominal use of *no* '... [that] is' and the similar form *na* '... [that] is'. Suppose we assume an essive verb 'be' that has the forms *ni, no, na*. Our *ni* will clearly correspond to the infinitive, but what are the other two? In the case of the superficially similar Old Japanese negative auxiliary verb we find (-)*ni* for the infinitive, as in *sirani* 'knowing not' and (-)*nu* for the attributive/predicative, as in *siranu* '(... that) knows not'. (The predicative later developed as *siran[i] su* > *sira[~] zu* with the auxiliary *su[ru]* 'do'.) The stem of the negative verb appears as the particle *na*, either preposed as an adverb (*na tori so* 'do not take it') or attached as a sentence particle after the predicative form (*toru na* 'take it not'). In the case of the essive verb, we find the infinitive *ni* and the stem *na*, but where we expect the attributive/predicative form *\*nu* we find instead the anomalous attributive /no/. I suggest that this is the attributive expected from the eastern (Azuma) dialect, where the expected predicative form would be *\*nu*; in the central dialect, the attributive and predicative forms merged for this "quadrigrade" conjugation of verb stems except for their accent, and it is to the likely accentual difference that I would ascribe the weakening of the attributive *\*nu* to *n*. The use as a predicative became obsolete before the seventh century, replaced by *n[i a]r-i*, the infinitive of a complex copula consisting of *ni* + auxiliary *ar-*, and the eastern form survived as the attributive /no/ while the western attributive (/predicative) *\*nu* → *n* was limited to compounds.[7]


2.   The accusative particle marks the object of a transitive verb, the path or area of a motion ('walk the line, turn the corner, pass the bank, jump the hurdle'), the point of departure ('leave home', 'depart this world'), the time spent ('sleep seven hours'), and the usual functions found in other languages. In Korean the accusative sometimes substitutes for the allative (cf. English 'attends school' = 'goes to school') or dative ('Gimme' = 'Give it to me'). The forms:

(2.1)    $('^u/_o)l, \cdot l^u/_o l$    —

(2.2)    —    $[w]o ? < *bo^8; wo\ si\text{-}te$

(2.3)    —    $[wo]\ ba < n\ pa$

In the orthography of the 26 songs extant from the old Sinla language, the accusative particle is written with at least three different characters.[9] There are two examples that write the particle with the semanto-phonogram interpreting Sino-Korean $e < $ "$qe$" $< . q(y)o$ 'to; at/in', for which there is a traditional Korean tag translation *nul* (as given in the 1576 character dictionary [Sin-cung] [1]Yuhap) $=$ *nu[l-u]lq*, the imperfect adnominal form of the verb *nul-* 'to increase/advance; to better/best'.[10] Kim Wancin takes this as an attempt to write $l^u/_o l$ in *hyangka* 13: 3 (*NE-\*lul\** 'you') and 17: 10 (*TYE-\*lul\** 'him'). The accusative is usually represented by the character meaning 'Second Stem [of the Twelve Stems]', with the later Sino-Korean reading *ul* ($< $ "$qulq$" $< $ Chinese *qyet*). That appears after consonants (16: 6 *MWOM-ul* 'body', 26: 1 *NIM-ul* 'lord', 22: 6 *MYENG-ul* 'life', 06: 3 *PANG-ul* 'room'; 21: 3 *SWON-ul = swon ol* 'the hands') and at least once after a vowel (20: 4 *PEP-WU-ul* 'a rain of the Law'). But it is also represented by a character meaning 'to bustle; ...', Sino-Korean *hul* $< $ "$hulq$" $< $ Chinese *hyet* (also given the Sino-Korean reading *hil*)[11], which led R. A. Miller (1977) to the immediate conclusion that the "Old Korean" accusative marker was /hel/ (presumably with mid front vowel), for which he would adduce cognateship with a "proto-Altaic" *-g*, based on Turkic *-g* and Mongolian *-(i:)g* and/or with the Tungusic directive-locative *\*ki-lā* and directive-prolative *\*-ki-lī*. Miller (1987) reaffirms his commitment to this notion. There are at most eight examples of the accusative marker written with *hul*, and the noun in seven of these is written with a semantogram for which we must infer the native Korean translation. In three cases, the Korean noun carries a basic final *-h* in later Korean (03: 7 *I STA-hul* 'this ground' $=$ MK *i stah ol*; 07: 1 *MWULWUP-hul* 'knees' $=$ MK *mwulwuph ul* and modern *mwuluph, muleph, mwulwuph-ak, mwulph-ak*) and while 02: 4 *KWOC-hul* 'flower' lacks aspiration in attestations of the fifteenth century (1449 *kwoc ˙ ol* Kok 6), the *-h* is attested in the early seventeenth century (*kwoch ul* 1632 Twusi *cwung-kan* 15: 33) and in modern Korean (*kkoch ul*, with *kk-* from truncation of compounds ... *s kwoch*), so that it may have been present in an unwritten dialect all along. These examples can probably be explained as examples of orthographic conflation (for later examples of which see Martin 1982) or simply as "send-off" cues to indicate that the character is to be taken as its Korean translation rather than given the Chinese reading. (There are similar examples after semantograms that for cues use the phonograms *muy* and *moy* to write ... *m* $^u/_o y$ with the genitive, use *mun* to write ... *m on* with the subdued focus marker, and even use *um-*mul** to write ... *m ul* with the accusative. On these and other orthographic phenomena, see Kim Wancin 1980, one of the more important studies that Miller seems to have overlooked.[12]) More of a problem are the examples of 02: 3 *NA-hul* 'me', 03: 6 *I-hul* 'this', 07: 5 *NWUN-hul* 'eyes', and 16: 07 *TEK-HOY-hul* 'the Sea of Virtue'.[13] (I set aside the example of 03: 5 **han*-hul* 'the people' because of the hypothetical nature of the noun that Kim Wancin proposes as derived from the perfect adnominal *ha-n* '[the] many'; if he is correct, the noun may have picked up a final -*h* under the influence of the initial.) Assuming that these examples are not due to scribal corruption,[14] they may be explained as an attempt to write the variant or allomorph *ol* for which, unlike *ul*, there was no syllable available in the Sino-Korean repertory, and that explanation may well be true of the cases with the aspirate-ending nouns, too. It should be borne in mind that there are accusatives where the *hyangka* texts do not have -*hul* despite a noun that ends in an aspirate in later Korean: 06: 4 *AL-ul* 'egg' = MK *alh ol*, 18: 2 *KIL-ul* 'way' = MK *kilh ul*, 20: 8 *PATH-ul* 'field' = MK *path ol*. There are two other examples of the phonogram *hul* to be found in the *hyangka*: 11: 2 *MEMUS-hul-i-kwo*, which Kim treats as *memus-kulikwo* 'hesitating', and 05: 5 *TWUVUL-hul-un* 'as for the two' (repeated in 05: 6), which Kim treats as *TWUVUl-un*, with the final liquid alone serving as the conflated cue. (He is probably right, but the final aspirate of MK *:twulh* 'two' ? < **twupulh* may invite other notions.)

It may be that the Korean accusative marker will remain isolated, with unknown prehistory and no likely cognates. Before giving up on it, however, I would like to explore parallels between this morpheme and the marker of subdued focus *($^u/_o$)n* 'as for; ...', parallels that are morphophonemic as well as etymological. If we treat the basic shapes as just /n/ and /l/, with epenthetic $^u/_o$ after a consonant and with optional pleonastic formations *n$^u/_o$n* and *l$^u/_o$l* after a vowel, they are the same as the adnominal morphemes -*n* and -*l* that are attached as suffixes to the verb stem to form the perfect and imperfect.

But there is a difference. In Middle Korean, the imperfect adnominal suffix is spelled with a final glottal *-lq*, or a reflex of that in the form of gemination (*-lq ka* = *-l kka* 'whether to [do/be]'); the accusative particle is never spelled that way. Therefore it has been speculated that the modern liquid phoneme may be a merger of two different earlier phonemes /r/ and /l/. Perhaps, however, the *-lq* is an attempt to represent an incorporation of the genitive *s*, for which a bit of other evidence can be adduced (Martin 1982/1983). In the *hyangka*, the imperfect adnominal is written with the phonogram CORPSE: *HO-si-l TI* 'if one deign to do' 3: 4, *HO-l TI* 'if one do' 3: 8, *KU[LI]li-l MOZOM* 'yearning heart' 1: 7, *NYE-l MUL-S-KYEL* 'passing waves' 13: 6, *TAO-l NAL* 'the day I will fulfill [my desire]' 25: 2, *KI[L]l PSU-l PYE[LI]li* 'a star to sweep a path' 7: 10, *CULKI-l* 'to enjoy' 14: 8, .... And CORPSE is also used to write the cue for final *l* in a number of Korean words after a semantogram (such as *NAl twu* 'the day too' 25: 2), so there seems to be no way to avoid the conclusion that in the *hyangka* it is used to represent the liquid and that sound only, despite the misgivings of Miller and others that the phonogram really ought to represent a syllable with a sibilant, as indeed it does in the traditional writing of certain place names and Chinese transcriptions of Korean words. Yu Changkyun and Hashimoto (1973) explained the anomaly as a reflection of the reconstructed initial cluster *\*sl* of archaic Chinese, but the thousand-year discrepancy makes that explanation improbable. A likelier possibility is a scribal abbreviation of a complex character containing the same shape, such as *lwu* < Chinese ' *lyu* 'often', which was used as a phonogram for the Japanese syllable *ru* in the 720 work *Nihon-Shoki*. But even more plausible is the explanation of Kim Wancin (1986) that the character is nothing more than a scribal misunderstanding of a common script form of the character *ul* 'Second Stem'. If that is true, then there is no *hyangka* evidence for a phonemic difference in the accusative marker and the imperfect adnominal, nor for a genitive *s* incorporated into the latter.

The hypothesis I propose would identify the accusative marker *l* with the imperfect adnominal *-l* and the focus marker *n* with the perfect adnominal *-n*.[15] Notice that the focus marker is used to subdue old information that is "known" (= given = done). And the accusative marks the object, the target that is "to be affected" by the verb. It might even be possible to make a case that the two particles are reductions of the adnominal forms of the common auxiliary *ho-* 'do/be/say', namely *ho-n* and *ho-l*, even at the risk of providing grist to the miller of the unaccepted reconstruction \**hel*.[16] The idea that the subdued-focus particle might derive from *ho-n* in the sense of 'said' is not so far-fetched as it might at first appear; notice the modern use of *ila [ha-]n(un)* 'said/saying it to be' → 'as for' and a similar use of the quotative *tte* and *ttara* in Japanese.

3.    The shapes of the Korean particle of subdued focus differ from those of the accusative marker by ending in (or being) a dental nasal /n/ rather than the liquid /l/. The shape after a consonant is $^u/_o n$, conflated with an epenthetic vowel. After a vowel the form is either just *n* or the pleonastic $n^u/_o n$. We assume that the basic shapes of the accusative and the focus are *l* and *n*, respectively, and those forms are found in the earliest Hankul texts, but there are many more examples of the pleonastic $l^u/_o l$ and $n^u/_o n$.[17] For modern Korean, it is convenient to regard forms like *na l* 'me' and *na n* 'as for me' as contractions of *na lul* and *na nun*, but that may not be the best description of their history. Yet, there is evidence for the early existence of the pleonastic forms in the orthography of the *hyangka*, according to Kim Wancin (1980: 14). He cites the use of Sino-Korean *e* < "*qe*" < *.q(y)o* 'to; at/in' as a semanto-phonogram read *nul* = *nu[l-u]lq* 'to increase/advance; to better/best' and used as a way of writing the otherwise untranscribable /lul/, as was mentioned above. He seems to assume that a spelling such as *NE-un* 'as for you' (10 : 2) is intended to represent *ne nun* rather than, as I would take it, *ne n*. Kim Wancin takes many cases of the accusative after a vowel that are written with the regular phono-grams for *ul* (rather than the semanto-phonogram with the traditional reading *nul*) as representing $l^u/_o l$, rather than just *l*, as we would prefer.[18] There is one example of the focus particle written with the phonogram RESENT *hun* ← Chinese *hen·* 'resent' in the character string DAY-CORPSE-RESENT (24 : 5), which is treated as *nal-on* 'as for the day' rather than \**nal-hon* by Kim Wancin (1980: 204) "for the same reason that not all instances of BUSTLE are treated as *hul/hol*".[19] Kim Wancin thinks that vowel harmony can be detected in the *hyangka* choice of phonograms but at the

same time he seems to feel the particles were (at least sometimes) written morphophonemically, as if free words.[20]

The forms for the marker of subdued focus are:

(3.1)    $(\ ^u/_o)n,\ ^{\cdot}n^u/_on$         $(-)$
(3.2)    -n ˙pa 'situation'      ˙wa< fa< *pa 'as for'

The Japanese particle *wa*< *pa must come from the noun *pa'place, situation'; the noun *ba* 'place' results from a truncation of compounds like *[ari]-ba* 'location' < *... n pa* 'place of [being]' with the genitive marker. Compare the use of *... (no) ba-ai* '[in] the situation of ...' to mean 'as for; in the case of; if [it be]'.[21] Corresponding Korean forms with the postadnominal *pa* are obsolescent in the modern colloquial language, but they are well attested in the Hankul texts of earlier centuries.

4.  The focus particle *than* can be regarded as an antonym of Japanese *wa* is *mo* 'too; even; indeed; yet, but', for which the Korean equivalent is the particle *to/twu* < MK ˙*two*,[22] but some of the uses of the Korean particle correspond to the use of a particle *to/do* in earlier Japanese. The opposite of the Japanese (VERB)-*ey ba* 'when/because ...' is (VERB)-*ey do* 'even if ..., though ...'. In the concessive meaning ('even; yet'), we also find morphemes deriving from nouns that mean 'place', Japanese *to[ko]* or *tokoro* and Korean *tey* < ˙*toy* (cf. the 'site').

Japanese has an emphatic sentence particle *zo* 'indeed' and its Ryūkyū reflex *du* underlies a few copular formations (... *du a-* < *zo a[r]-*), but that is thought to go back to a particle *so/zo* that derives from the mesial deictic 'that'. It has been suggested that the particle *koso* 'precisely' (earlier ˙*ko.so*) and perhaps .*kosò*, which imparts a spotlighting focus, derives from *ko* 'this' + *so* 'that'. Yet the Middle Korean particle ˙*kwos* 'precisely, just' corresponds quite nicely in meaning. And there is another mysterious Korean focus particle, *ya/iya* < ˙*i['z]a* and dialect *sa* < *(i/l)* ˙*za*, to be accounted for perhaps in connection with the old Japanese deictic *sa* 'so/that' (and the modern assertive ... *sa!* 'indeed') and the Old Japanese emphatic particle *si*.

It is not easy to track the prehistory of the Japanese particle *mo* 'even; also, indeed; yet, but', from .*mo* or possibly ˙*moò* (see Martin 1987: 170, 347), but I suspect it is a shortening of *o[mo]* '[very]' thing', the initial syllable of which may be cognate with the Korean *mu-* 'wh-' and *amu-/amo-* 'any'. The Miyako version *mai* would seem to argue in different directions, but its unresolved diphthong makes us fairly confident that *mai* is a secondary replacement, which I have proposed to be a contraction of *madi* < *made* 'even; all the way to/till'.

5. There is a profusion of dative and allative particles in both Japanese and Korean. While for particle forms we find narrowed or specialized meanings (dative or allative or locative, personal or impersonal, honorific or non-honorific, static or dynamic), the functions of the basic elements overlap considerably when we take into account earlier usage and dialects. Japanese offers the three forms *ni, e* < *f(y)e* < *\*pe*, and *sa* 'to, in, at, for, …', as well as a number of compound postpositions (like *ate ni* and *ni site*). The most widely used and general is *ni*, which specializes the use of the essive as infinitive of the copula (= noun predicator) into a variety of meanings; the gerund *ni-te* (> *de*) also enjoys a wide range of meanings, including those of circumstance, reason, or cause; means, medium, or instrument; exclusive agent; and general locative.[23] The etymological background of the particle *sa* is unclear (see Martin 1987: 803 – 805). The accentual history of the particle *e*, as well as its vowel, suggests a disyllabic origin *e* < *\*pye* < *\*pi [C]a*, maybe *\*pina* as an early loan from Chinese . *pyen* 'edge, boundary; side, location' (as in Beijing *nèbiar* < *nà (yi) biān* 'there'. In any event, these particles have no direct ties with Korean.

The Korean markers used for dative and allative functions include forms clearly derived from verb forms (*pwokwo* 'looking at', *tele* < *toľ ye* 'leading') or a noun of location, as in *hanthey* < *han tey* < *hon ˙ toy* 'one place' — earlier used as an adverb 'together'. A similar incorporation of a noun meaning 'place' is found in the personal dative forms *eykey* < $\cdot$ $^u$/$_o$*ykey* < $\cdot$ $^u$/$_o$*y-kungey* < $^u$/$_o$*y ku-ng[ek] ey* or $\cdot$ $^u$/$_o$*y-ke ˙ kuy* < $^u$/$_o$*y k[u-nge] ˙ k-uy* (< *ku-[ngek ˙ e]y*) and honorific *kkey* < $\cdot$ *skuy* < *s k[u-ngek] ˙ ey*, all meaning 'to that place of'.[24] The major particle for the dative and allative is *ey* < $\cdot$ $^e$/$_a$*y*, and it is well attested throughout the history of the language. From the evidence of the *hyangka* phonograms we assume that the Old Sinla language had both $^e$/$_a$*y* and a shorter $^e$/$_a$. The Hankul texts of the fifteenth century also often use $^u$/$_o$*y*, indistinguishable from the form of one of the genitive markers, and similar readings have been imputed to some of the *hyangka* examples, but I am not sure those can be supported.[25] The $^e/_a$ form appears before the adnominal (genitive) *s* in *CIP a s PWO la* 'is the jewel of the house' 24 : 7 (a passage so construed by all) and *MOZO[M-u]m a* 'in one's heart' 25 : 9, clearly written with a phonogram read *. [q]a* in Chinese and Sino-Korean. In what Kim Wancin writes as *I ye* (12 : 10) and three others write as *I ya* the initial *y* of `· ya* 'is indeed' cues the reading *i* 'this' for the preceding semantogram and the passage means 'to this'. More of a problem is Kim Wancin's *KYE-ZUL-uy-ye* 'it is in winter' 13: 4 with phonograms *. [ng]uy* 'conclusive particle' and `· ya* 'is indeed'.[26] And I am not sure that *I-uy TYE-uy* 'here and there' (11: 6; phonogram *. [ng]uy* 'conclusive particle') is to be taken as deictic + case-marker. The examples *COYVO[K]-[a]k-huy* 'in the gravel' 4: 6 and *KOS-huy* 'at the side of' carry an initial *h-* in the phonogram meaning 'rare', which Kim Wancin (1980: 69) says is to be disregarded just as is that of the phonogram *hul* used to write the accusative. If we follow what I take is 'Yi Kimun's thinking on the "*hul*" reading, it would be fitting here to reconstruct something like *\*coypokh* 'gravel' and *\*kosh* or *\*kozh* (or, better, *\*ko·soh*) 'edge, side' for these nouns. The longer form $^e/_ay$ is seen in *PWUL-CE[N]-n-ay* 'in front of Buddha' 9: 3. A dissyllabic form *a-hoy* has been proposed for *PWUL-HWOY a-hoy* 'to the assembly of Buddhas' 20: 2.[27] There was a convention among Korean official scribes of the 'Yi dynasty to write the dative-allative postposition with the Chinese-character string *LYANG-TYWUNG* 'good-midst' and to read that "*ahoy*", though we have no evidence that such a pronunciation was used in speech. The string itself was taken from a *hyangka* usage and it has been generally assumed that the scribes were maintaining a phonetic tradition ancestral to the Hankul-attested particle $^e/_ay$. Since most of the clear examples in the *hyangka* do not attest the *-h-*, I suspect that it is an aberrancy; in 20: 2 it could be an echo of the initial of *HWOY* 'assembly'.[28] Miller (1987: 59) toys with a reconstruction of the marker as *\*akai* (> *\*agai* > *ahoy*), which he would associate with a Tungusic *\*kai.* At the same time, he would set up a "locative-directive" *-ak* to account for the example *NALA-ak* (3: 10) with the phonogram 'bad' (Chinese and Sino-Korean *qak*) and modern dialect forms such as *anak* 'inside' and *ttulak* 'in the garden' (Miller's 'in' is gratuitous, the nouns are synonymous variants). But these words are simply conflated (or uncompressed) reflexes of Middle Korean monosyllables ending in another of those overlooked *h*'s: `anh > an / anak,` `ptulh > ttul / ttulak.`[29] And the word for 'nation' is MK *na˙lah*, so that it is appropriate to transcribe the *hyangka* citation as *NAL[A-]ak*. It has been noted that the Japanese place-name *Nara* was written not only in phonograms that clearly indicated the usual pronunciation of the name but also with the character 'joy' carrying the Sino-Japanese reading *raku* (as in *Man'yō-shū* 80 and *Nihon-Shoki* 95), so that a variant *Naraku* may have existed for this place-name, long suspected of being a borrowing from the Korean word. The very peculiar scribal writing of *LYANG-TYWUNG* for the dative-allative particle (however it was pronounced) is a case of an obscure assignment of characters like some of the Japanese "*ate-ji*", such as *RYŪ-SEKI* 'flowing stones' for the adverb *sasuga* 'indeed'. Other cases of the character *LYANG* 'good' may well reflect the liquid initial, however, and one of a more troubling set of examples has led Kim Wancin (1980: 91 – 92) to set up an Old Korean doublet *tolal/tolala* for 'moon', so that "MOON-GOOD" in 12: 9 is taken as the unmarked noun *TOLA[L]-l[a]* = *tolala*, and similarly *TOLA[L]-l[a]-two* = *tolala two* 'the moon too' 12: 6, but in 5: 1 it is taken as *TOLA[L]-la* = *tolal a* 'in the moonlight'.[30] The shorter variant appears in *TO[LAL]-la-li* = *tolal i* 'the moon [as subject]' 4: 2 and 13: 5, and with a semanto-phonogram *al* 'below' in *TOL-*al*-i* = *tolal i* 'the moon [as subject]' 9: 1. There seems to be no other evidence that the word for 'moon' had more than one syllable (1103 *Kyeylim* ʰ*yusa* writes it with a single phonogram), but a compound such as *tol-al* 'under the moon' or **tol-al[h]* 'moon egg [= round object]' can easily be pictured as replacing the simple noun.[31]

Our oldest Korean dative-allative marker, then, appears to be the particle $^e/_a$ and an expanded form with *-y*, which I suspect is an accretion of the copula or the nominative *i*. Perhaps it is unwise to disregard the later scribal particle "*ahoy*" or the troublesome case in 20: 2 cited above. It would be pleasing to have an old Korean locative or allative with a velar-initial element meaning 'place' incorporated, since several Japanese etyma meaning something like 'place' begin with a velar (such as the suffixes *-ka, -ko,* and *-ku* and perhaps the first syllable of *kuni* 'land') but I suspect that if such a velar ever existed in Korean it was before the vowel of the dative, rather than after it, *-[G]a*. And I am reluctant to impute external origins to particular forms until we have tried to account for them internally. The various Ryūkyū dative, allative, and locative particles *nkai, nakai, nai, kai, kee, nai, nee, ...*, are compressions of periphrastic expressions such as *naka ni* 'at/to within', *muka[w]i* < *\*muka-pa-Ci* 'facing', and/or the Old Japanese (-)*gari* = /nkari/ < *\*n ka ari* (< *\*ara-Ci*) 'being place of', rather than directly related to complex forms hypothesized for the languages of the Korean peninsula and further west.


6.   Are there forms in Tungusic, Mongolian, or Turkic that may be cognate with the Korean and Japanese markers treated above? In Tungusic, only four case markers are shared by all the languages, according to Cincius, and two of these are adverbs rather than affixes in Manchu (cf. Benzing 1955: 78). The reconstructions are:

| | |
|---|---|
| Accusative | *\*ba (\*pa)*[32] |
| Dative | *\*dua (\*nu)* |
| Locative | *\*lā, \*du-lā* |
| Directive | *\*tikī, (\*sikī)* |

The instrumental (*\*-ži*) and the genitive (*\*-ŋi*) fall together as *-i* in Manchu (but sometimes *-ni* for the genitive). This resembles the nominative-genitive *i* /$^u$/$_o$y/ of Korean, with possible Japanese cognates, but the initial nasal of the proto-Tungusic marker is unexplained. The accusative *\*ba* (Manchu *be*) loocks promising as a cognate for Japanese *wo* ? < *\*bo* or for the focus particle *wa* < *fa* < *\*pa*, if it was originally different. Manchu *ba* 'place' is strikingly like Japanese *ba* 'place' and the comparison survives even after we take into account the derivation of the Japanese noun from a truncation *... n pa*. In view of Korean *pa* 'place, situation', we are tempted to set up a Japanese-Korean-Tungusic etymon *\*pa* 'place; focus/accusative marker'. But matters are not so simple, for the proto-Tungusic word for 'place' is reconstructed as *\*buga* (Benzing 1955: 80). Is the Tungusic particle *\*ba*, like the Manchu noun *ba* 'place', a compressed form of *\*buga*? Or perhaps the etyma for the accusative and the noun should be kept distinct, the accusative *ba* going with Japanese *wo* (did the vowel assimilate to the labial initial?) and not with *wa* < *\*pa* 'place', recognizing a Korean cognate for the latter but not the former.

In an unpublished paper, J. Ross King has proposed an accusative *ba/*be for both proto-Mongolian and proto-Altaic accusative on the basis of the forms mentioned above together with the elusive Middle Mongolian particle *be* and its variant *ber*, which King suspects may be complex (*be-r*).[33] He also hypothesizes a theme marker *n, which would go well with the Korean subdued-focus particle *n*, and perhaps with the Japanese adnominal *n* or directly with the nominative-genitive *no*, if we defer or reject my suggested derivation of those from an essive stem. In addition, King envisages an engaging scenario whereby a proto-Altaic focus marker *i/yi got specialized as an affix of "definiteness" and from that went on to become the marker of a definite accusative in Mongolian (after *ba/ be lost that function). King does not find Turkic elements to relate to his *ba, but he suspects that the marker *i/yi may be hidden in the "mystery morpheme" hypothesized by Pritsak (1964) to account for the Turkic developments that have been dubbed "lambdacism" and "rhotacism".

7.   It is perhaps misleading to speak of case marking in Japanese and Korean in the way the term is usually applied to suffixes found in the Indo-European languages. The markers are postpositions much like English prepositions, and we see widespread competition, shifting, and semantic specialization among formally disparate morphemes and larger structures, just as the English locative is marked by 'at', 'in', or 'on'; the dative by 'to', 'for', or word order; the agentive by 'by', 'of', or word order; the instrumental by 'by (means of)', 'with (the medium of)', 'through (the use of)', 'in [pencil]', 'on [the computer]', and others. Many of the Japanese and Korean morphemes used for such grammatical functions appear to be cognate with each other. As we try to reach beyond these two languages, our comparisons grow more and more speculative, and this suggests that the time depth for the relationship of Japanese and Korean is less than that for either language with other languages of northern Asia, if such relationships can be shown to exist.

*Notes*

1. The traditional term Middle Korean ("MK") is used to designate early modern Korean of the Hankul texts dating from the middle of the fifteenth century. Most features of modern Korean dialects can be explained as stemming from a

form of the language only slightly older than what we find in the early Hankul texts. Our knowledge of the still earlier language is limited to a few hundred words found in a handful of works written in Chinese during the preceding four hundred years, the transcriptions of Korean-peninsula names found in Chinese works through many centuries, and the 26 *hyangka* discussed below, which are difficult to interpret and subject to much controversy, though they are generally assumed to be written in the language of the Sinla (Shilla) kingdom, which lasted till 935 A. D., and of the early period of its successor, the Kwolye (Kolyŏ) (918 — 1392). The Middle Korean forms are given in a modified version of the Yale romanization: *u* and *o* represent the minimal vowel, the unrounded counterparts of *wu* and *wo*. Modern Korean no longer maintains the unrounded *o* as a distinct phoneme, so that we are free to abbreviate "*wo*" to just "*o*". And *u* is not distinguished from *wu* after labials in modern Korean, so we shorten the transcriptions *mwu* and *pwu* to *mu* and *pu*. The pitch accent of Middle Korean is indicated by dots placed to the left of the syllable, as in the Hankul texts. A high single dot (ˈ) represents high pitch, a double dot or colon (:) indicates a rise that starts low and ends high, and the pitch of unmarked syllables is presumed to be either low or irrelevant.

2. A particle *i* meaning 'in particular (that ...)' has been postulated as an emphatic subject marker for Old Japanese; in the *Man'yō-shū* examples it is usually followed by the focus particles *fa* or *si*. Later it was used only in annotations to help construe texts written in literary Chinese (Kanbun). The adverb *aru-i-wa* 'or; perhaps' is a relic of the postadnominal use of the morpheme. And the morpheme may be present in the verb form ... *ey [-ba/-do]* < *... a-i* (? < *-Ci*). There is little evidence for this particle in later Japanese, but it is reported that *i* is used as a nominative particle in the southern part of Ōita prefecture in Kyūshū: *hito i miyuru* = *hito ga mieru* 'a person appears' (*Hōgen to hyōjun-go* 355). Whitman suggests that some of the nouns ending in the Old Japanese vowels that go back to the diphthongs *Ciy* and *Cey* may display the accretion of this etymon, just as many nouns of north Korean dialects have picked up a final *-i* or *-y*. I would like to propose that the Old Japanese expression *si ga* 'you/that' is from **soy ga* (< **so i n ka*) with a pleonastic accumulation of genitive markers reminiscent of the origin of the modern Korean nominative phrases *nay ka* 'I' < *na i + ka* and *ney ka* 'you' < *ne i + ka*. There is evidence for a second-person pronoun *i* (*ga*) 'you (as subject)' in three Chinese passages of *Koji-ki* and *Nihon-Shoki*, and it is tempting to find in it the missing Japanese cognate for Korean *i/ywo* 'this' but other explanations are possible; perhaps it is merely the Chinese pronoun *i* 'he; this' itself.

3. Korean *:seys* 'three', *:neys* 'four', and *yeˈles* 'several' occur without the *-s* before a noun, and Japanese numerals normally lack the *-tu* before a noun; but Korean *tases* < *taˈsos* 'five' and *yeses* < **yoˈsos* 'six' are usually intact. Matters are further complicated by the occurrence of *-h* rather than *-s* in *ho.nah* 'one' (just *ˈhon* before a noun), *:twulh* ? < **twuˈpulh* 'two' (*:twu* before a noun), *ˈsuˈmulh* 'twenty' (*ˈsuˈmu* before a noun), and *yelh* 'ten'; also, by earlier versions with *-h* and *-k* (*:sek* = *:seh* 'three', *:nek* = *:neh* 'four') or just *-h* (.*yeˈleh* 'several'). I have heard *hanak ssik* 'one each' from a Seoul speaker; if not influenced by the final velar of *ssik*, that seems to indicate *k* rather than *s* for the ancestor of the final *h* of 'one'.

4. Perhaps the postadnominal *no* 'one, fact/thing/person/ ...', which is a kind of resumptive pronoun, has a different source from the particle in its other uses (and from the copula alternant) and could have come from a shortening of [*mo*]*no* 'thing; fact'. But notice that all uses of *ga* and *no* are shared by each in one dialect/time or another (Kōchi uses *ga* as the postadnominal), so that seems unlikely. The probable Korean cognate for Japanese *mono* is the indeterminate *mu*- 'wh-/any-'. I have thought of deriving the adnominal particle *no* from a contraction of *n[-i ar-]o*, the essive infinitive of *ni* + the Azuma adnominal ("attributive") form *-o* of the existential auxiliary *ar*- 'be'. But below we will explore a more interesting hypothesis, also involving the adnominal ending of the old Japanese eastern (Azuma) dialect.

5. The likely cognates for the deictics are askew. The Japanese mesial *so* 'that [near you]' goes with the Korean distal *ce* < ˙*tye* 'that [away from me or you]', the Japanese proximal *ko* 'this [near me]' (and perhaps the deictic verb stem *ko*- 'come [to me]') goes with the Korean *ku* ? < \**ke*. There is no Japanese cognate for Korean proximal *i* 'this', except perhaps in *ima* 'now' ? < *i-ma* 'this interval', unless we so consider the old verbal prefix *i*-; there is no Korean cognate for Japanese *a/ka* 'that [near neither me nor you]', unless we so consider the deictic verb stem *ka*- 'go' (i. e., "to thither"). I will leave open the tantalizing question: whence the Korean deictic verb stem *o*- 'come [to me]'? Also yet to be explained are the Korean forms proximal *yo*, mesial *ko*, and distal *co*. These lively variants are sometimes thought to be quite modern, but the first two are attested in earlier Hankul texts: ˙*ywo* 'this' (1447 Sekpo 11: 19, 1481 Twusi 15: 12), *kwo* 'that' (1517 Sohak 9: 46).

6. The indeterminate *ka* is found in Korean as well as in Japanese. The two languages also have an interrogative postadnominal *ya*; I suspect that the Korean element may derive from an interrogative use of the nominalizing *i* + either the vocative-exclamatory particle /*a*/ or a reduction of [*k*]*a*, and that Japanese *ya*, though quite old, had a similar origin. Ryūkyū dialects attest a Japanese interrogative *i*, as in Shuri *qami* = *qam i* 'does it exist?' and *neeni* = *neen i* 'doesn't it exist?'.

7. I am quite aware that the wider use of *na* in later Japanese to adnominalize adjectival nouns is usually taken (perhaps correctly) to be a shortening, *na[ru]* < *ni aru*, and that the attested Old Japanese use of *na* was limited to a fairly small set of collocations *N na N*, for which the genitive interpretation is generally appropriate. I am also aware of arguments that *na* is a "vowel harmony" alternant of *no*, but I do not find them convincing.

8. Japanese *wo* has sometimes been taken as an expletive, 'lo ...!'. Notice also Korean *pwo*- 'look' ('lo' is short, after all, for 'look!'). An outside possibility is that *wo* may simply be an assimilated version of *wa* < \**pa* despite the problems of chronology *wa* < ? *fa* < \**pa*. For more on this, see below.

9. Songs 1—14 are from 1285 Samkwuk ˡyusa and are attributed to monks and others of the Sin.la period, 15—25 are from 1075 Kyun.ye-cen, and 26 is attributed to the Yeycong period (1105—22). The dates of the texts as we know them are not necessarily so old, and it is unwise to assume a relative chronology for the attestation of the language forms variously claimed to exist in these few poems. In our *hyangka* citations the pure semantograms, including Chinese loanwords, are written in CAPITALS; semanto-phonograms (Korean tag trans-

lations used only for their phonetic values) are delimited by *...*; pure phonograms, with Sino-Korean ("SK") values, are written in lower-case letters. The Chinese ("Ch") phonetic values reflect a rough approximation to some kind of seventh-century Middle Chinese, in the notation of Martin (1987) (*q* = glottal stop; *ng* = velar nasal; preposed low dot = "even" tone; preposed high dot = "rising" tone; postposed high dot = "going" tone). We treat *NE* 'you' in *hyangka* 10: 2 and 13: 3 as a semantogram despite the resemblance of its sound, Ch ˙ *nyo* > SK *nye*, to the Korean translation *ne*; in 16: 10 the semantogram is Ch ˙ *nay* > SK *nay* '(you) there'. The more frequent *na* 'I, me' is consistently written with the semantogram Ch .*ngwo* > SK *[ng]wo* (2: 3, 7: 7, 7: 9, 11: 9, 19: 4, 19: 5, 20: 3, 22: 4, 23: 6, 24: 10, 25: 2).

10. Although this would seem to be evidence against the proposal that the liquid endings of accusative and imperfect adnominal differed phonetically, the evidence is not strong, for the semanto-phonogram could be taken from a slightly different contraction *nul[-ulq]* or from just the verb stem (cf. the semanto-phonogram *twu* from *twu-* 'put away', discussed in note 21). There is something suspect, in any event, about assuming that the imperfect adnominal of *l*-ending stems collapsed the string ... *lulq* (as in modern Korean) since the early Hankul texts show the forms uncontracted; cf. Martin (1982/1983). There are but two passages for which Kim Wancin proposes this "*nul*" as representing the accusative marker, and his construal of the passages may well be wrong.

11. These are the traditional prescriptions; there are no non-Chinese passages that attest this character as part of the Korean language, but it is an entry in the 1447 character dictionary *Tongkwuk cengwun* (1447), with the two readings.

12. Miller failed to consult six of the eight published interpretations of the *hyangka* basing his pronouncements on the oldest two, those of Ogura Shinpei (1929) and ˡYu Cwutong (1942), the latter in part through an English translation inspired more by literary than linguistic interest. The interpretations Miller missed (Ci Hen.yeng 1948, ˡYi Thak 1958, Kim Senki 1967—1975, Se Caykuk 1974, Kim Cwun.yeng 1979, and Kim Wancin's own) are extensively discussed in Kim Wancin (1980), which includes many of the modern Korean translations made by each. Werner Sasse has written a dissertation on *hyangka*, too, but I have not yet had the opportunity to see it. There are probably other studies that have not come to my attention.

13. LKM (1980) implies that he thinks the 80-odd Middle Korean nouns ending in -*h* were but the tip of the iceberg and that there may have been many more earlier, for which our only attestation would be precisely the *hyangka* orthography in question. Presumably that means that Old Korean (meaning the Sinla language, not any old language spoken on the Korean peninsula, an unfortunate extension of the term) would have *nah* 'I/me', *ih* 'this', *nwunh* 'eye'. But other forms of these words occur in the *hyangka* clearly without the -*h* where it would be expected: *NWU[N]-*noy** = *nwun uy* 'of the eye' 1: 5, *NA-*uy** = *na oy* 'my' [genitive] 19: 4 19: 5 24: 10 25: 2, *I-uy : i uy* 'of this' 10: 1 11: 2 11: 6; the vowel quality of phonograms that incorporate the harmonizing Korean vowel may seem discrepant, but that is perhaps because there were no Sino-Korean syllables of the needed type, such as *oy* or *nuy*, so that the phonograms perforce represented an orthographic neutralization of the harmonic vowels. However, perhaps these examples are evidence for a juncture before a genitive *uy* as

contrasted with a nominative *i*; the *hyangka* unfortunately offer no examples of *\*na(?h) i, \*i(?h) i, \*sta(?h) i, \*nwun(?h) i, \*kwoc(?h) i,* or *\*mwulwup(?h) i.* Kim Wancin (1980) seems to assume that the initial "*h*" of the phonogram, if real, is of no etymological relevance. Miller (1987) covers his tracks with respect to the overlooked MK *-h* by explaining it as an analogical extension of the accusative form, which for some reason he seems to think more common, to the other forms of the paradigm; that is, he would have us believe that *mwulwuph* 'knee' got its final *h* by a misanalysis of the morpheme division of *\*mwulwup hel* [sic] as *mwulwuph ol* and extension of that to other members of the paradigm, such as *mwulwuph oy* 'of the knee'.

14. Our earliest extant woodcut edition of *Samkwuk 'yusa* is dated 1512, though the work was written in 1285 and the poems came from earlier sources.

15. The third subsyllabic morpheme of Korean is the nominalizer *-m*, on which a variety of structures are built. That morpheme is likely to be cognate with the Japanese imperfect etymon *\*ma-*, the stem of the auxiliary verb … *mu(ru)*, which underlies the "future" constructions of tentative and hortative. Martin (1968) proposed a cognate relationship between the Korean verbal endings *-m, -n,* and *-l* and proto-Japanese *\*-m, \*-n, \*-r,* verb suffixes reconstructed on the basis of Ryūkyū forms. Tungusic cognates for *\*-r* and *\*-m* may be sought in the Manchu imperfect participle *-r(a)* and the imperfect converb (also a perfect participle?) *-me*.

16. The grist is a Trojan gift, for the *h-* of the Korean auxiliary must come from *\*s-*, as indicated by the likely Japanese cognate *so-*, the original stem of modern *si / su(ru)* 'do', and perhaps by the Korean verb *sikhi-* (first attested in the seventeenth century) < *si˙ki-* (1447 Sek 13: 52) 'cause to do'.

17. Dialect accusative forms *u* and *lu* are secondary developments, probably having to do with the phonetic peculiarities of /l/.

18. Kim Wancin also sees evidence for vowel harmony in the choice of competing phonograms such as *un* = "*qun*" < Ch . *yen* 'secret' versus *en* = "*qen*" < Ch . *yan*/. *hhyan* 'how; (to) this'. That is apparently why he assumes the pleonastic form in *NA non* 'as for me' (phonogram *en*) and *NE nun* 'you' (phonogram *un*). Yet he takes the characters BODY MYRIAD (*man*) SECRET (*un*) as representing *mwoma non*, which would seem to undercut the argument, as it would even if we rejected the hypothesized *mwoma* (> *mwom* 'body') and interpreted the passage as *mwom man on* 'as for just the body'; similar remarks can be made about *CACHWOY-wo-un* interpreted as *cachwoy non* 'as for the traces'. Other passages which show the two phonograms harmonically complementary, such as 3: 1-2-3 and 17: 5-6, are difficult to judge because we do not know whether to assign native or Chinese readings to the character writing the noun that precedes the particle. In fact, the problem of interpreting all of these texts makes statements about Old Korean based upon them highly speculative, to say nothing of claims about Proto-Korean (which must have existed) or "Altaic" (which perhaps did not), as well as assertions that these poems are magnificent literature, which we have no way of judging.

19. The phonogram CORPSE here represents the final liquid of *nal* 'day', *NA[L-u]l on*; see the discussion of the accusative above. The character RESENT is given the traditional reading *hun*, but the Sino-Korean reportory provided no way to write the syllable *hon* except, perforce, the same character. Had the

example not escaped his perusal of the texts, Miller would presumably insist on an interpretation ... *s hen*, with or without discovering "Altaic" congeners. Our notion of what Sino-Korean syllables were available is based on values found in Hankul texts from the middle of the fifteenth century, mostly couched in the prescriptive readings of the character dictionary *Tongkwuk cengwun* (1447), which adhered strictly to the traditions of Chinese phonologists. Within that framework there were no phonograms to write the syllables *nul, *nol, *nel or to write *lul, *lol, *lel. (¹Yi Tonglim 1959: 320 is mistaken in the reading "*lelq*" for *kwelq* 'vacancy', and the character does not even appear in the location he cites, Wel 1: 8.) Characters were available for the sounds *qun, qon,* and *qen*; for *hun* and *hen* but not *hon*; for *hul* and *hel* but not *hol*. Since there was (later and by tradition) a way of writing the syllable *qon*, which appears in Sek 6: 3 in the binom *qon˙-qoy˙* 'favor and love' (modern *un-ay*), we wonder why such a character was not put to use as a phonogram in the *hyangka*, if an effort was indeed made to note vowel harmony. (¹Yi Tonglim 1959: 216 gives variant forms of the character meaning 'secret' as carrying the readings ˙*qon* and *qon˙* but he must be mistaken, for they do not appear in the locations cited, Sek 6: 28 and Wel 10: 38 respectively, nor in *Tongkwuk cengwun*, which gives only the one entry 'favor' for the syllable *qon˙* and reads 'secret' as *qun˙* or ˙*qun*.)

20. And there could be no free word *lul/*lol so perforce it would be written *ul* ("*qulq*") or *hil/hul* (< "*hulq*"), the most innocuous approximation to the non-existent *ol* ("*qolq*"). Perhaps the one instance of "*hun*" for ... *on* (instead of the available "*qon*") was by analogy. We do well to bear in mind that the scribes were probably aware of the Chinese phonological tradition known as *făn-qiè* whereby the sound of a syllable is given by two characters, the first to be read for its onset (the "initial") and the second for the rest of the syllable (the "final" or rime, including the tone).

21. The particle is combined with some of the other particles. The initial labial has a voiced reflex after the accusative, *[w]o ba*, and after certain verb forms with which the focus particle is combined (*-a-ba, -e[y] ba*); the /b/ goes back to the pronunciation [mba] = /npa/, which seems to incorporate the genitive marker *n*.

22. In the *hyangka* this is usually written with the semanto-phonogram PUT AWAY (Ch *tryey˙* > SK *chi*), for which the Korean translation is the verb stem *twu-*. That raises a question about the vowel. Modern Korean *twu* is thought to be a recent raising of the still common pronunciation *two*, the only version found in the Hankul texts before 1586. There are only two passages in the *hyangka* where the particle is written with a phonogram: *PWU[THYE]-thyey two* 'even Buddha [as subject]' 24: 9 with the character meaning 'knife', Ch .*taw* > SK *two* and *THOYK two* 'even a house' 14: 10 with the character for 'capital', Ch .*to* > SK *twu*. We have the unhappy choice of either deciding that the particle must have had variants *two* and *twu* even in early days or concluding that the verb *twu-* raised its vowel from an earlier *two-*, for which no other evidence is to be found. The problem is independent of one's judgment as to the merit of the proposal (by Kim Wancin and others) of a great vowel shift that serves to buttress arguments deriving the horizontal vowel harmony of Korean from an earlier vertical system. Under that interpretation, the pre-Hankul version of *wu* would have been front-rounded and its harmonic counterpart would have been

high: the ancestor of *wu* would be pronounced like some versions of modern *wi* ( < *wuy*) and the ancestor of *[w]o* like modern *wu*.

23. Miller (1987: 279) has the Japanese particle *ni* incorporate a "pre-Jap. *-n.lī*", taken as a "prolative-locative", and fall together with another *ni* ("used for marking the subject of a causative or other secondary verb") that derives from "a nominal stem-final *-n* followed by the original Altaic acc. *-i*", but that seems an improbable scenario.

24. The development of these forms from compounds within Middle Korean is quite clear, and there is no need for Miller (1987: 63−64) to speculate that they indicate a "fairly late (Koryŏ?) borrowing (or, re-borrowing) back into Korean of some Altaic form closely related to the Proto-Tungus suffix *.kai*". The Korean particle *se* (ablative or locative) is from *[i]sye*, the infinitive of *isi-* < *pisi-* 'exist' (modern *iss-* is an irregular development), and *puthe* < *pu'the* '(starting) from' is the infinitive of *puth-* 'adhere'.

25. Kim Wancin has *PA[M]-muy* 'at night' 21: 5 with the phonogram meaning 'not yet', for which we have evidence only of a reading `mi* (as in Sek 13: 59), but perhaps 'not yet' is taken as a graphic abbreviation of some other character, such as 'younger sister' with the reading *moy*`; Kim Wancin was perhaps influenced by the phrase *PAM uy* 6: 4 with the phonogram .*[ng]uy*, but he may be wrong on his construal of that passage and *uy* here is perhaps the genitive. (Of our eight interpreters, only Ogura Shinpei reads *PAM i* for 21: 5, and he reads *PAM ay* for 6: 4.) In the passage *SALOM-moy EP[S]-s[i]-kwon* 19: 6, Kim takes the character for 'rice' as *moy*, but the only reading of the character for which we have evidence is .*mi*. (Of our eight interpreters, only Kim Senki and Kim Cwun.yeng take the passage as *salom i* with the nominative.)

26. I am unsure whether Kim Wancin intends the `ya* character to be taken as a phonogram, with /ye/ a version of /ya/, or as a semanto-phonogram, with *ye* reduced from the copula infinitive *i[y]-e*. If it is the latter, then our transcription should be *I *ye** and *KYEZUL-uy-*ye**. The others are of little help on this, since with one exception they take the passage to mean something quite different. The word for 'winter' was *kye'zolh/kye'zol*, a doublet, in the fifteenth century and 'autumn' was *kozolh/kozol*, also a doublet.

27. Miller (1987) cites another example from ʰYang Cwutong ("...*CWON ohoy*", for which read *CWON uy-huy*; the phonograms are .*[ng]uy* 'conclusive particle' and .*huy* 'rare') but Kim Wancin (1980: 116) makes a good case for a different interpretation of the passage (9: 5, mistakenly cited as "9: 2" by Miller): *MOLO *wos* POLA WUL.WEL-LE* = *molo [G]wos wul[G]welle* 'looking up at the Lofty One Himself', with translational readings for all the characters except the semanto-phonogram 'garment' (as a phonogram read *uy*, SK *quy* < Ch .*qyey*), to represent the lenited form of the particle *kwos* 'precisely', pointing out that the verb 'look up at' is transitive and would take an accusative (here masked by the focus particle), not a dative. Kim Wancin (note 32) rightly cites 1804 Cwuhay Chenca-mun as carrying the passage *molo cwong CWON YA*, roughly 'the character, read *cwong* and glossed as height, means venerated' (26 v), but for *cwon* 'venerated' itself the gloss (14 v) is *nophul* 'lofty'.

28. I have two thoughts on the intervocalic -*h*- implied by the phonograms in *ahoy*. First, perhaps *ahoy* consists of the simple particle *ᵉ/ₐ* followed by a reduced form of *ho.ya*, the infinitive of the auxiliary *ho-* 'do; be', with a unique -*y*- of

258     *Samuel E. Martin*

unexplained origin. (For an analogy, look at the Japanese ... *ni site* and ... *ku site*.) Second, the scribes may have tried to cope with the same problem facing later spellers: since their *-h-* between voiced sounds readily drops, Koreans often omit an etymologically appropriate *-h-* and also, like a good Cockney, sometimes supply an haitch for which there is no morphophonemic or etymological motivation. The non-initial syllables of Korean words have been subject to lenition and compression throughout the history of the language; their vowel color has been neutralized in harmony with the preceding vowel and/or reduced to the minimal vowel quality of *u/o* (vowels that are rare in word-initial position), and even dropped altogether.

29. On words of this type, see Kim Tongso (1982). Miller took the notion of a suffix *-ak* 'within' from [1]Yang Cwutong, who would thus account for the use of the character for 'bad' (Ch and SK *qak*) in the first phrase of the troublesome line 20: 2, *PEP-KYEY ak OY s PWUL-HWOY ahoy*, taken as meaning 'to the assembly of Buddhas of within the realms of the Law (*dharmadhātu*)', but it seems strange for such a suffix to be attached to a Chinese binom, and I am surprised that Miller did not simply take *akoy* as forming a doublet with *ahoy*, thus avoiding a pleonastic genitive (*[...-ak] oy s*) in favor of a genitivized locative (... *akoy s*). I am not happy with the interpretations of this passage and would reserve judgment on them as evidence for linguistic forms.

30. There is no connection with the Beijing word *yuèliang* 'moon', with the adjective *liàng* 'bright' suffixed to the noun, which must be a late coinage in northern China, for in a similar formation Cantonese uses the equivalent of *guāng* 'shine'.

31. In a scolding of the tradition of "scholarship in the Old Korean texts", Miller (1987: 315) claims the phonogram *LYANG* 'good' has been "uniformly taken as" ... *ay* on the basis of Hankul *tolay* 'in the moon' in a version of one of the poems in the 1493 Ak-hak kweypem. The long passage found there (224−225 of the 1973 reproduction published in set 2 of *Hankwuk kocen chongse*) is a retelling of the story of Che-yong (as found in the Chinese text of *Samkwuk [1]yusa*) in the colloquial language of the day, for which the expression *tolay* was appropriate, but that passage has certainly not kept the philological interpreters from treating the relevant line of the poem itself in other ways, as witness both Kim Wancin and Se Caykok.

32. The parenthesized forms appear in certain restricted environments and can be ignored for our purposes.

33. On the Mongolian particle, see Street (1981) and the sources cited there.

*References*

An Pyenghuy
1968        "Cwungsey kwuk.e uy sok.kyek emi '-s' ey tay-ha.ye", [1]*Yi Swung-nyeng paksa songswu kinyem [1]nonmun-chong* 337−345.
Benzing, Johannes
1955        *Die tungusischen Sprachen: Versuch einer vergleichenden Grammatik* (Wiesbaden: Steiner).
Chōsen sōtoku-fu
1937        *Rito shūsei = Litwu cipseng* (Keijō [= Seoul]).

Ci Hen.yeng
1948        *Hyangka ¹Ye-yo sinsek.*
Cincius, V. I.
1975 – 1977  *Sravnitel'nyy slovar' tunguso-man'čžurskix jazykov* 1 – 2 (Leningrad: Nauka).
Co Yuncey
1963        *Hankwuk munhak sa* (Tongkwuk munhwa-sa).
Hamada Atsushi
1970        "Shukaku-joshi *ka* seiritsu no katei", *Chōsen-shiryō ni yoru Nihon-go kenkyū* 255 – 286 (Iwanami).
Hatsutarō, Ōishi – Uemura Yukio, eds.
1975        Hōgen to hyōjun-go (Chikuma-shobō).
Hong Kimun
1957        *Litwu yenkwu* (Phyengyang: KDR Academy of Sciences).
Hong Yunphyo
1953        "Cwuqkyek emi 'ka' ey tay-ha.ye", *Kwuk.e-hak* 3.
Kim Cwun.yeng
1979        *Hyangka munhak.*
Kim Hyengkyu
1954        "Cwuqkyek tho 'ka' ey tay-han soko", *Choy Hyenpay sensayng hwankap ¹nonmun-cip* 93 – 107.
Kim Hyengkyu
1964        " 'Ka' cwuqkyek tho ey tay-han kochal", (*Kim:*) *Kwuk.e-sa yenkwu³* 199 – 211.
Kim Panghan
1957        "Kwuk.e cwuqkyek cep.mi-sa 'i' ko", *Seoul University Theses* 5: 67 – 108.
1965        "Kwuk.e cwuqkyek emi 'i' ko caylon", *Hakswul-wen ¹nonmun-cip* 5: 32 – 61, [English summary 61].
Kim Senki
1967 – 1975  "Hyangka uy saylowun phul.i", *Hyentay munhak* 145 – 250.
Kim Sungkon
1971        "Tho-ssi 'oy/uy' uy palqtal ul salphim", *Hankul Hak.hoy 50-tol kinyem ¹nonmun cip* 185 – 200.
Kim Tongso
1982        "H-mal.um myengsa uy uywen" [Co Kyusel kyoswu hwakap kinyem] *Kwuk.e-hak ¹non.chong* 285 – 299 (Taykwu: Hyelsel chwulphan-sa).
Kim Wancin
1980        *Hyangka haytok-pep yenkwu* (Sewul Tay-hak.kyo).
1986        "Decipherment of hyangga and textual criticism" Korean Linguistics 4: 21 – 32.
LKM = Lee, Ki-Moon = ¹Yi Kimun
1972        "A study on Korean rebus of Chinese characters", *Tonga munhwa* 11: 231 – 269.
1980        "Arutai shogo to Kankoku-go", *Kyōto-daigaku Kokusai gengo-ka-gaku kenkyū-jo shohō* 1.3: 104 – 112.

1984            "Kotay samkwuk-e yenkwu wa saykim uy muncey" [paper presented at the Third International Conference on Korean Linguistics, Bochum].

LSN = Lee Sung Nyong = ᴵYi Swungnyeng
1955            "Sinla sitay uy phyokiq-pep ey kwan-han siko", *Seoul University Theses* 2: 62–166.
1958            "Cwuqkyek "ka" uy palqtal kwa ku haysek", *Kwuk.e-kwuk.mun-hak* 19: 53–57.

Martin, Samuel E.
1968            "Grammatical evidence relating Korean to Japanese", *8th Congress of Anthropological and Ethnological Sciences* B-9: 405–407.
1975            *A reference grammar of Japanese* (New Haven, Conn.: Yale University Press).
1982            "Features, markedness, and order in Korean phonology", *Linguistics in the Morning Calm* 601–618 (Seoul: Hanshin).
1982/1983      "On the consonant distinctions of earlier Korean", *Hankul* 175: 59–172 (1982); corrected and revised, New Haven (1983).
1987            *The Japanese language through time* (New Haven, Conn.: Yale University Press).
1990            "On dating changes in the phonetic rules of earlier Korean", in: *Festschrift für Bruno Lewin* (Bochum).

Miller, Roy A.
1976            "The Altaic accusatives in the light of Old & Middle Korean', *MSFOu* 158: 157–169.
1979 a          "Old Korean and Altaic", *Ural-Altaische Jahrbücher* 51: 1–54.
1979 b          "Old Japanese and the Koguryŏ fragments: a re-survey", in G. Bedell (ed.), *Explorations in Linguistics*, 348–368.
1987            "Preliminary notes toward a history of case in Korean", *Kwuk.e-hak kwa Althaie-hak [Pak Un.yong paksa hoykap kinyem ᴵnonchong]* (Ha.yang, N. Kyengsang: Hyoseng ⁿYeca Tay-hak.kyo).

Nam Kwangwu
1957            "Cwuqkyek cosa 'ka' ey tay-ha.ye", *Cwungang Tay-hak.kyo munliqkwa tayhak munkyeng* 4: 11–7; reproduced in (Nam:) *Kwuk.e-hak ᴵnonmun-cip* 371–378 (1960, 4th ed. 1974) – see also 310–311.

Ogura Shinpei
1929            *Kyōka oyobi ritō no kenkyū. Keijō teikoku-daigaku hōbungaku-bu kiyō* 1 (Seoul).

Pak Pyengchay
1965            "Kotay kwuk.e uy kyek-hyeng", *Korea University Commemorative Theses Humanities* 119–181.

Pritsak Omeljan
1964            "Der 'Rhotazismus' und 'Lambdazismus' ", *Ural-Altaische Jahrbücher* 35: 337–349.

Sasse, Werner
1982            "[CORPSE] as a phonogram in early Korean writing", *Linguistics in the Morning Calm* 709–719 (Seoul: Hanshin).
1984            "On deciphering hyangga" [paper presented at the Third International Conference on Korean Linguistics, Bochum].

Se Caykuk
1974          *Sinla hyangka uy ehwi yenkwu.*
Se Cengmok
1982          "15-seyki kwuk.e tongmyeng-sa naypho-mun uy cwue uy kak ey tay-ha.ye", *Cintan-hakpo* 53.4: 171 — 194.
Se Thaylyong
1980          "Tongmyeng-sa wa hwuchi-sa '-un, -ul' uy kipon uymi", *Cintan-hakpo* 50: 97 — 120.
Street, John C.
1981          "The particle *ber* in the Secret History", *Ural-Altaische Jahrbücher* N. F. 1: 141 — 168.
[1]Yang Cwutong
1942          *Cosen koka yenkwu* [revised edition: 1965].
[1]Yi Kimun: see LKM
[1]Yi Sungwuk
1981          "Putongsa uy hesa-hwa — cwuqkyek celmi-sa 'ka' uy palqtal ey tay-ha.ye", *Cintan-hakpo* 51: 183 — 202.
[1]Yi Swungnyeng: see LSN
[1]Yi Thak
1958          "Hyangka sin haytok", *Kwuk.e-hak* [1]*nonko.*
[1]Yi Tonglim
1959          *[Cwuhay] Sekpo sangcel* (Seoul: Tongkwuk tay-hak, kyo).
Yu Changkyun — Hashimoto Mantarō
1973          "Hyangka phyoki yongca uy sangkwoseng-cek chukmyen", *Sinla-Kaya munhwa* 5: 1 — 29.
Yu Changsik = Yu Changkyun
1956          "Hyangka ey nathanun [CORPSE] uy munqpep-cek kinung kwa umqka", *Kwuk.e-kwukmun-hak* 15: 36 — 61.

# A survey of Omotic grammemes

*M. Lionel Bender*

## 1. Lexicon

In an earlier series of three papers (Bender 1986 a, in press a, b), I developed the case for Omotic as being composed of nine groups: 01 North Ometo, 02 South Ometo, 03 Chara, 04 Gimira, 05 Yemsa, 06 Gonga or Kefoid, 07 Dizoid, 08 Mao, 09 Aroid. See map 1 for locations of groups. The first split in Omotic lexically is between Aroid (which can thus also be called South Omotic) and all the rest (North Omotic). North and South Ometo clearly belong together and Chara is next, making a "Macro-Ometo" consisting of 01, 02, 03. Gimira is always next, although not as clearly as Chara was at the previous step. The rest is not so clear. Results differ somewhat according to how much lexicon is compared. Either Yemsa and Gonga are coordinate or (using maximal lexicon available) Gonga is closer to Gimira-Macro-Ometo. Dizoid follows, then Mao, although the two are about equally distant if one uses maximal lexicon (see Bender in press b). One could represent the situation for the first 100 items as in figure 1, which is probably more accurate, given the problems of data gaps and loans in less-basic lexicon.

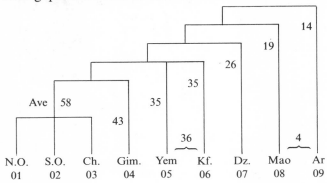

*Figure 1.* Comparison of lexical items

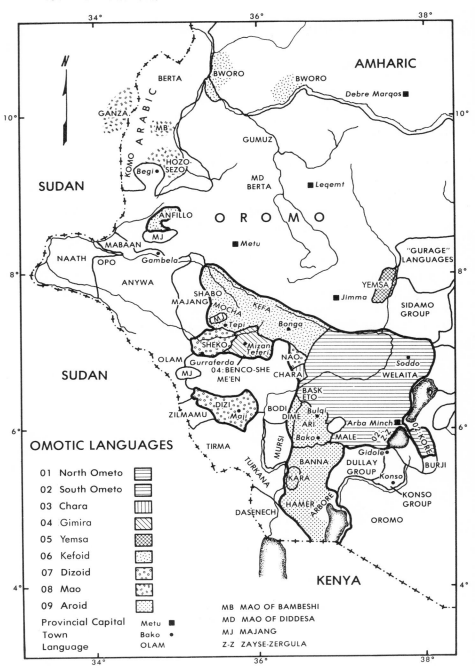

*Map 1.* Omotic languages

## 2. Morphology

What does morphology tell us? Does it support the main outlines of the above and perhaps lend weight to one of the alternatives, or does it give other cross-cutting isotones? At this point I am grateful that I consulted the level-headed discussion by Hodge (1975). "Chronomorphs", long-lasting lexical and morphological items, are what we seek, even if the structures they occur in have changed. The lexical items used in the calculations of section 1 above included about 15 grammatical items in the first 200 and a few more in the total of 532 — ideally these should perhaps have been excluded, since they will be repeated among the morphological items.

For morphology, there are 120 items, divided into seven major broadly defined categories as follows:

> I Pronouns (27)
> II Demonstratives (25)
> III Interrogatives (11)
> IV Nouns (13)
> V Tense-Mode-Aspect (17)
> VI Copulas (11)
> VII Derivations (16)

Table 1 lays out the exponents of these categories in Proto-languages of Afrasian, Cushitic, Omotic, and Nilo-Saharan. The main sources are as follows:

> *Afrasian: Diakonoff 1965; Hetzron 1980
> *Cushitic: Hetzron 1980; Ehret 1985 manuscript
> *Omotic and *Nilo-Saharan: my own reconstructions.

I also looked at Egyptian, Berber, Proto-Semitic, Beja, and Proto-Chad, but I will not report on these here. In the following sections I refer to table 1 and discuss the situation in Omotic in more detail (see note 1).

## 3. Independent Pronouns

### 3.1 First and second singular

The most perplexing problem in Omotic pronouns is how Omotic got first singular *ta*/second singular *ne* in place of the typical Afrasian *ani/a(n)ti*. Conti Rossini (1925: 630) says *ta* was originally a possessive and that *ta/ne* preserves "Nilotic" *a/e* (see *Nilo-Saharan in table 1: the *a/i* pattern, often found as *a/i/e*, is pervasive). But he gives no evidence for *ta* being an original first-person possessive, and we shall see (I hope) that the bulk of the evidence disfavors a Nilo-Saharan membership of Omotic languages. Note that *ta/ne* transparently characterizes only groups 01−06 and that 07−09 have other formatives.

Another tempting possibility, which I resisted as long as I could, is to consider a switch from Afrasian first singular *n*/second singular *t* to Omotic *t/n* (see note 2). Recalling that Hetzron (1980: 14−15) argues convincingly for Cushitic nominative *-i*, accusative or absolute *-a*, we can then guess at a Cushitic-Omotic shared second person *anti/anta*. One could then account for the various forms quite reasonably as follows:

*Cushitic-Omotic

first singular *ani/ana*, second singular *anti/anta*
Omotic first singular:

| | | |
|---|---|---|
| 01−06 | Cushitic-Omotic | second singular absolute *anta* → *ta* |
| 07, 08 | Cushitic-Omotic | *anta* → *nata* (Sheko), *na* (Hozo) |
| 08 | Cushitic-Omotic | *anti* → *ti, di* (Ganza), *tiya* (Bambeshi) |
| 09 | Cushitic-Omotic | *anti* → *at-* (Dime) |
| | | *anti* → *inta* (Hamer), *ita* (Ari) |

Innovations: 07 Dizi first singular *(y)ínù* generalization of first plural *(y)ínú*; 08 Sezo *haa-ŋga*.

Omotic second singular:

| | |
|---|---|
| 01−06 | Cushitic-Omotic first singular *ani* → *ne* (why *-e*?) |
| 07 | Cushitic-Omotic *ani* → *ne* (Nao), *niya* (Sheko, feminine) |
| | (perhaps *niya* → *ne,* and *niya* is *ni* + *a*, but source of *-a*?) |
| 07 | Cushitic-Omotic absolute *ana* → *na* (Nao) |
| 08 | → *nä* (Ganza) |
| 09 | → *ana* (Ari) |

*Table 1.* Grammemes in proto-languages

1.1 Pronouns

| Independent | *Afrasian | | *Cushitic | *Omotic | *Nilo-Saharan |
|---|---|---|---|---|---|
| | Prefix | Suffix | | | |
| 101 1 sg | ank, ink | ku, ni | ʔani, ana | acc. anta / nom. anti | akʷa (> ai, wa) |
| 102 2 m. s. | ntk | kua, kai | ku, ko } ʔ(n)t, | acc. ana / nom. ani | ini |
| 103 2 f. s. | ntt | ke, ki | ki, ke } (a)ti | (is)i | } from DEMS |
| 104 3 m. s. | h, su | su | | (is)a | } N, T, K, S |
| 105 3 f. s. | s; ti | t | | | |
| 106 1 pl. | nkn | n, mu | (h)ann- (?) | nu | } pls. based |
| | | | -nn-, nu | | } on sgs. |
| 107 2 m. pl. | sg. + m, n | | } k-n-V | } ant-u-n | } 1 a/2 i pattern in |
| 108 2 f. pl. | | | | } > Int (In) or It- | } both sg. and pl. |
| 109 3 m. pl. | | | | } (is)u (?) | |
| 110 3 f. pl. | | | | | |
| *Affixes* | | | | | |
| 111 1 sg. | Ø, ʔ- | | V-   -Ø | -n ta   -a | Incl./Excl. |
| 112 2 m. s. | t- | | tV-  -t  ˊ | } -t ne  } -i-n; isi; | in 1 pl.: |
| 113 2 f. s. | t- | | yV-  -Ø | -isa   -n | trace of ŋ/w, o? |
| 114 3 m. s. | Ø, y- | | tV-  -t | | |
| 115 3 f. s. | t- | | nV-  -n | -nu   -i | |
| 116 1 pl. | n- | | -tʔ? | | |
| 117 2 m. pl. | } t- ... -n | | } tV- ... -n | } -int   -u-n | |
| 118 2 f. pl. | | | } -tV-n | | |

Table 1. Continued

| | *Afrasian | *Cushitic | *Omotic | *Nilo-Saharan |
|---|---|---|---|---|
| 119 3 m. pl. | Ø, y- ... -n | -u? / yV- ... -n / -V-n | -ints / -n | trace: m. R |
| 120 3 f. pl. | | | | f. B n. N |
| **Gender** | | | | |
| 121 masc. | $k^{(w)}$ | u | ko → o → a | a    i |
| 122 fem. | t | i; t | ti → i | i    a |
| **Number** | | | | |
| 123 sg. | — | — | — | — |
| 124 pl. | -m, -n; -u(?) | -n | -(n)t; o, u | K; N? |
| **Case** | | | | sg. N/pl. K; d, t, n |
| 125 nom. | — | i | -ni (?) | — |
| 126 acc. | trace: n(?) | a | -na (?) | K; N? |
| 127 gen. | -i | -i; m. k/f. t | Ø | sg. N/pl. K; d, t, n |

1.2 Demonstratives

| | *Afrasian | *Cushitic | *Omotic | *Nilo-Saharan |
|---|---|---|---|---|
| 201 this, m. | Greenberg 1960: basic: m. n, f. t, pl. n | kuni | hage | ne   I near |
| 202 f. | | tini | han- (?) | |
| 203 pl. | Diakonoff 1965: based on d or n | | | |
| 204 that, m. | | | (h)i; en/se(K) | te  far |
| 205 f. | | | | A, U |
| 206 pl. | | | | |
| 207–209 yonder | | | | A, U |
| 210–212 relative | | | | |
| 213–215 referential | | | | Secondary in 201–206; K, R, T; -V → -VV |
| 216 def., det. m. | art. -m(a) ~ na, ni | ka | | |

*Table 1.* Continued

|  | *Afrasian | *Cushitic | *Omotic | *Nilo-Saharan |
|---|---|---|---|---|
| 217 f. |  |  |  |  |
| 218 pl. |  |  |  |  |
| 219 here |  | ti | ⎱ same as 201; | I  A and 'polar' |
| 220 there |  |  | ⎰ 204 plus | U  I forms |
| 221 over there |  |  | -s, -k, -d, -n |  |
| 222 sg. |  |  |  | A |
| 223 pl |  |  |  | I |
| 224 "to" |  |  |  | A  I and 'polar' |
| 225 "away" |  |  |  | I, U  U forms |

1.3 Interrogatives

|  | *Afrasian | *Cushitic | *Omotic | *Nilo-Saharan |
|---|---|---|---|---|
| 301 what? | ma (n, t)- | maa (?) | ⎱ am | ⎱ widespread |
| 302 who? | mi (n, t)- | ayll (?) | ⎰ | ⎰ n(d)V, n- |
| 303 where? | na |  | ⎱ ay (k)on(e) |  |
| 304 when? |  | maa + DATIVE | ⎰ compounds |  |
| 305 why? |  | mee? (?) | ⎱ with LOC |  |
| 306 how? |  |  | ⎰ cmpd. with DAT |  |
| 307 how many, much? |  |  |  | often = 301–302 |
| 308 which? |  | i- (?) | -(i)ya, -ay | -(y)a; b, m, wa |
| 309 marker |  |  |  |  |
| 310 sg. |  |  |  | K; N |
| 311 pl. |  |  |  |  |

*Table 1.* Continued

| | *Afrasian | *Cushitic | *Omotic | *Nilo-Saharan |
|---|---|---|---|---|
| **1.4 Nouns** | | | | |
| 401 nom. | abs. ∅; -a | -i | -(n)i  (?) | |
| 402 gen. | -ii second: n, d (?) | n; -i with | i; t; k; -n; -s(?) | Second.: m, b; a; pl. k, r, l |
| 403 loc. | state: -u motion: -s | m. k-/f. t- d/l ~ l/d | | trace: k(?) |
| 404 acc. | def. acc. -t obj. suf. -n; -a | abs. a | -n;    -a(?) | |
| 405 dat. | -s | dat./bene. s, h, k, g | | |
| 406 abl. | | | -s | |
| 407 masc. | kʷ-, ku-; u̯ | -ku acc. -ka | o, a } cf. prns. | Ed   Second.: b, p, m; h |
| 408 fem. | t- | -ti acc. -ti; ta (innov. as sufs. only) | i, e | b, p, m |
| 409 other | | | | |
| 410 sg. | | | | N; A; T |
| 411 singulative | indiv.: -ān, -ām -á; á(n); -V → -VV; ablaut | -c(c). | trace: -c(c) (?) | trace: -c(c) |
| 412 pl. | | | t; -nts (cf. prns.) | K; E; T |
| 413 dual | direct: -ấ obliq.: -aị̯ | | | |

*Table 1.* Continued

### 1.5 Tense-mode-aspect-system

| | *Afrasian | *Cushitic | *Omotic | *Nilo-Saharan |
|---|---|---|---|---|
| 501 prf./pst. | form: *ya-prus-suf.* | -*i, ay, ey, ye;* *n* or labial; -*a* in 2, 3 pl. pst. | *i* $\}$ *d, t-i, e* | *K* |
| 502 impf./prs. | form: *ya-paras-suf.* | (*a*)*a; ya* | *a* $]$ | *nn;* |
| 503 future | | | | *l* |
| 504–507: progressive, habitual, narrative, conditional | | | | |
| 508 juss. sg. | based on old past $\}$ | internal -*a*- and -*u, o* $\}$ | labial, *o, u* / *a; i, e* / (*i*)*te* $\}$ | not collected yet $\}$ trace: *K, N* |
|      pl. | *i* | *i* | | |
| 510 impv. sg. | *a* (?) | *a* (?) | | |
| 511      pl. | none orig.; later *u, a* / from nom. forms $\}$ | | | |
| 512 subjunct. | | | | |
| 513 converb | | | | |
| 514 neg. tns. | *n, m, r, l, ka, b, -wa* | | retain *B, K, N, R;* innov. *S, T* $\}$ | Second: *š, bV, KV, mV* / *n, A, T* / *nT, ŋ* $\}$ |
| 515 neg. impv. | *m, la, baa* | | | |
| 516 neg. non-vb. | *n, b, la* | | | |
| 517 neg. vbs. | | old vb. in *b* (?) | | |

*Table 1.* Continued

| | *Afrasian | *Cushitic | *Omotic | *Nilo-Saharan |
|---|---|---|---|---|
| **1.6 Copulas** | | | | |
| 601 exist | | | | Ti; ka, ko |
| 602 ident. | hai, hui (?) | ʔ-x; ha- (?) | de, ti | (y)E; |
| 603 attrib. | | | | (y)a |
| 604 place | | | usu. = 601 | ti; ka, ko |
| 605 possess. | uri, li (?) | | usu. = 601 + obj. | Second: L, KE |
| 606 "become" | | | | |
| 607 other | | | | |
| 608 and | | | n(e); na | Second: KA, |
| 609 or | | | | KE, n(T)a, o, bV |
| 610 sg. | | | | trace: n/k |
| 611 pl. | | | | |
| **1.7 Derivations** | | | | |
| 701 rel. | -ii, -ai, -awa | | t(s); š | K |
| 702 adj. | ma(i)- | | Second.: ai, | Second: |
| 703 abst. | ma(i)-, -(n)ti, -(n)ta | -umma, mma(?) | ii, m, n(T), K | n, m, b |
| 704 agt. | | -ana | kl | T, L |
| 705 vb. n. | | | | |
| 706 infin. | | | | |
| 707 other | part., place, instr., action: ma(i)- | | | |
| 708 caus. | s-ı < "make"; duplic. | s, š, h | s, š | Second.: T, K, L, N, S |
| 709 pas. | t- | -am (?) | | Second.: T, E, R, S, N, M, K |
| 710 intrans. | | | | |
| 711 recip./refl. | m-; n- | | (V)t | |
| 712 dative | | | Second.: n | "to": I Second.: T |
| 713 plural | iter: duplic. freq.: duplic. | | | Second.: K, T, U, R |
| 714 intens. | | | | |
| 715 incept. | | | | |

Innovations:

07 Dizi *(y)étù*, Sheko masculine and Nao feminine *yɛta*,

08 Hozo *hii*, Sezo *hin*, Bambeshi *hiya*, Ganza accusative *ye*

09 Hamer *(y)a*, Dimé masculine *yá(ai)*, feminine (rare) *ayto*

All from a) back-formed second plural (quod vide) or b) Nilotic: most of North Nilotic and part of Central Nilotic has *yi(n)*.

But how did the switch in persons happen? One possibility is as follows. All current Omotic languages are SOV, of the "rigid" type described by Heine (1976: 44). But there is good reason to suspect that Cushitic was once of type VO (see Hetzron 1980: 94—96), and Semitic was probably VSO. Thus, if Omotic also comes from an earlier VSO syntax, then in the change to SOV, some languages (01—06) may have reinterpreted first person and second as a result of restructuring of the verb complex:

|  | *d̶es-tane* |  |  |
|---|---|---|---|
| VSO order: | *(ani-)d̶es-ta* | *ani* | *(ata)* |
| 'see-I-you' | (Subject)-Verb-Object | Subject | (Object) |
|  | Verb Complex |  |  |
|  | V | S | O |

|  | *d̶es-a-neta* |  |  |
|---|---|---|---|
| → SOV order | *(ani)* | *(ata)* | *d̶es-ani-ata* |
| 'I-you-see' | (Subject) | (Object) | Verb-Subject-Object |
|  |  |  | Verb Complex |
|  | S | O | V |

(Assuming old nominative/accusative 'I' *ani/ana*, old nominative/accusative 'you' *ati/ata*.) If at one point *d̶es-tane* is reinterpreted as a new SOV-order verb complex, then *ta* will be taken as (first person) subject and *ne* as (second person) object.

## 3.2 Other persons

The other pronouns are not so perplexing, although there are many problems of detail. The following is a brief summary, including first and second singular. Since shared innovations of an arbitrary nature

*Table 2.* Isomorphs in Omotic

| | 01 | 02 | 03 | 04 | 05 | 06 | 07 | 08 | 09 |
|---|---|---|---|---|---|---|---|---|---|
| 1. 1 sg. prn. from *inta* | × | × | × | × | × | × | | | × |
| 2. 1 sg. prn. *ta* | × | × | × | × | × | × | | | |
| 3. 2 pl. prn. without first *-n-* | | | | | × | × | × | × | |
| 4. 3 sg. or pl. prn. with *b* | | | | | × | × | | | |
| 5. 3 sg. prn. with *r* | | | | | × | × | | | |
| 6. Demon. with fem. *n* | × | × | | × | | | × | | |
| 7. Rel. vb. suf. *m, w* | | | | | × | × | | | |
| 8. 'who?' *(k)one* | × | × | × | × | × | × | | | |
| 9. 'who?' *ode* | × | × | | | | | | | |
| 10. 'how?' *akka* | | | × | × | × | | | | |
| 11. 'how?' *as* | | | | | | | × | | × |
| 12. 'how many?' *appun* | × | × | | | × | | | | |
| 13. 'how many?' *ambitsa* | | | × | | | × | | | |
| 14. Interrog. marker with *d* | × | × | | | | | × | | |
| 15. Dative/instrumental *r* | × | × | × | | | | | | |
| 16. Ablative *pa, fe* | × | × | | | | | | | |
| 17. Locative *k* | × | × | | | | | | | × |
| 18. Perfect *S* | × | × | × | × | | | | | × |
| 19. Perfect *n* | × | × | | × | | | | × | × |
| 20. Perfect *k* | | | | | | × | × | | × |
| 21. Impf./Fut. Aux. *ana* | × | × | × | | | | | | |
| 22. Impf./Fut. Aux. *bV* | | | × | | | × | | × | × |
| 23. Impf. with *o, u* | | | × | | × | | | | |
| 24. Prs./Fut. with *nk* | | | | | | | × | | × |
| 25. Prog./Cont. with *m* | | | | | | × | | | × |
| 26. Negative *ana* | | | × | | × | × | | | |
| 27. Negative *hin* | | × | | | | × | | | |
| 28. Copula *fa-* | | | | | × | × | | | |
| 29. Copula 'be, sit' *be* | | | × | | | × | | | |
| 30. 'become' *gid* | × | × | | | | | | | |
| 31. 'be in a place, sit' *kot* | | | × | | | × | | | |
| 32. Noun formative *-bo* | × | | | | × | × | | | |
| 33. Noun formative *(di)f* | | | | | × | × | | | |

are the safest criteria for sub-classification of languages, I will attempt to highlight these: they are identified by superscripts and collected in table 2.

First singular/second singular.   Since the *t/n* reversal seems to have occurred in all branches (obvious in 01−06, least clear in Dizoid, see especially Ganza in Mao, clear in Ari), it can serve as a strong isomorph for Omotic as a whole, but not for subgrouping. However, the precise form *ta/ne* is universal in 01−06 and *inta, ita* occurs only in 09. It is thus reasonable to consider the following isomorphs: *anta → *inta¹ (in 01 − 06, 09), *inta → *ta (in 01 − 06)². (Beginning here, raised numerals refer to table 2).

First plural. All groups except Aroid have reflexes of *nu, although there are several odd forms (see 07 Nao, Shako; 08 Sezo and Bambeshi) either related to *nu or apparently "wild cards". Aroid plural pronouns could be borrowed from Nilotic (and are one reason for a suggested Nilotic membership of Aroid). Indeed North Nilotic has plural forms in w/y/k, as do Aroid languages, though otherwise the forms are not very similar; more striking are Teso second plural yɛsɪ, third plural kɛsɪ (see Hamer ye(si), ko(si), Lotuxo second plural ɪtaɪ; (see Ari yeta, Dimé yɛtɔ). It is hard to deny this likely Nilotic influence on Aroid, but the exact provenience is unclear: the nearest Nilotes today to Aroids are neighboring Nyangatom (part of the Turkana), whose second plural/third plural are èesi/kèci (similar to Teso).

Second plural. All but Aroid can easily be derived from *(a)ntun with retention of the first -n- (01 − 04) or loss (05 − 08)³ and various idiosyncratic reshapings (even 08 Hozo dɔ-; note Sezo first plural daa-, dɔl-, another instance of polarity?). Various Afrasian plural elements are found: -na, -o ~ -u, -ši (latter in Agew as -ji?) but in no clear pattern.

Third singular and plural. As expected, a variety of forms occur, most probably deriving from demonstrative elements. The only likely isomorphs are -b- in 05, 06 singular and plural⁴ and -r- in 05, 06 singular.⁵

# 4. Verb affixes

There are two basic patterns involved in affixes: n/t or t/n (based on pronouns) and i, e/a or a/i, e (in the first and second persons). As Fleming has pointed out (1976: 313 ff.), n/t is in line with other Afrasian forms and is probably the older pattern, but as I tried to justify above, it seems that the Omotic switch to t/n in independents affected all branches. Third person is also included, since several patterns appear with it also. (The following are extracted from table 3.)

| | | |
|---|---|---|
| singular | *I/A/I* | (i.e., first singular *i, e* / second singular *a* / third singular *i, e*): 01, 02 |
| | *A/I/-* | 03, 04, 06, 08 (this pattern is also found strongly in Nilo-Saharan). |
| plural | *U/I/U* | 01, 02, 03 partial, 04 partial, 06, 08 (in form *u/o/i?*). |
| singular | *t/n/s* | 02, 03, 04, 08 partial |
| | *n/t/s* | 05 partial, 07 |
| plural | *n/t/s* | 02, 07, 08 partial? (*n/d/-* ∼ *d/n/-*) |
| | *n/nt/(t)s* | 03, 04 (variant of above?) |
| singular | *t/n/n* | 02, 06 partial, 08 partial, 09 singular and plural |
| plural | *n/t/t* | 05, 06 |

The distribution of *A/I* and *I/A* patterns in the singular (in all groups but 05, 07, 09) suggests it is ancient and that in the three exceptional groups it has been independently levelled. The same can be said for the plural pattern *U/I/U* (the levelling is different in each case and thus does not constitute an isomorph). If *n/t/-* is the older pattern, then it is retained by 05 and 07 in the singular and by all but 01, 09 in the plural. North Ometo (01) has *t/t/n* in the plural and no consonants in the singular, while Aroid (09) is the only group having innovated *t/n/-* in both singular and plural. Since the independents show signs of the innovated *t/n/-* in all groups, we cannot use it for subgrouping here either, and the occurrence of various third-person forms may reflect retention of different Afrasian demonstrative elements, so it will not serve either. Although the peculiar *n/nt/(t)s* forms in 03 and 04 are intriguing, they may be retentions of older forms which gave rise to *n, t, s,* or combinations in modern languages (see table 1: 117 – 118, 119 – 120).

## 5. Gender

Velar and coronal elements seem to be associated with masculine and feminine genders respectively in Afrasian: in fact, *$k^w$/ti* seems to be a reasonable reconstruction of the markers incorporating both consonants and vowels. Hetzron (1980: 18 – 21) sets up an isomorph

*Table 3.* Selected verb affixes in Omotic

| | 01 | 02 | 03 | 04 | 05 | 06 | 07 | 08 | 09 |
|---|---|---|---|---|---|---|---|---|---|
| sg. | | | indeps. used: | | | | | | |
| 1. | -ay ~ e, i | e    t | ta | tan- | i, en | e    a | no | nan-  ha-  (a)ti-  it(e) | -t |
| 2. | -a | a    n | ne | nen- | i, ete | i    i    n | to | hi-  hiin-  a(y)-  aye | -n |
| 3. | -e, | e    š, z, ni | iz-i | m. yis-  f. wus- | i, ee, m. or com. | e    a    n | zo | (y)a-  haan-  iša  a | -n |
| | masc. or common | | | | | | | | |
| pl. | | | indeps. used: | | | | | | |
| 1. | etu, -o | | nu, no | nin-, nun- | -n | o    n | -no | nu-  dol- | -t |
| 2. | ita | tit | hintendi | int- | (o)ti | it, ut, no    t | i-to | do-  nam- | -n |
| 3. | osuna, osona | s    u | itsendi | -s- | i; eti | -no    t, n | -šo | in-    išk- | -n |

of *-ku/-ti* exclusively as suffixes in Cushitic and states that *-i* is a Cushitic innovation (and that \*Afrasian was \**ku/t*). Hetzron states that *k/t* is not found in Omotic. However, 01 Basketo 'that' has masculine *sekants*, feminine *yetánts*; 'this' has masculine *sɛkə́nna*, feminine *yétanná*. Otherwise what we find is:

a/i:    01, 02 (also in demonstratives), 04 (nouns), 05 (*a/e* in nouns), 06, 07 (*a/e* also with demonstratives in Dizi), 08

i/a:    01, 03

a/o:    01 (*-a/iyo* in nouns), 06 (*a/u* in nouns)
o/a:    02, 09 (also *u/a*)

o/i:    06 (as *o/e*, also in nouns as *o/i, o/e*)
i/o:    01, 02 (as *e/o*), 04 (as *yi/wu, u/e* in 'that'), 09

e/i:    02 (also *e/i ~ i/e* with demonstratives)

ø/a:    01, 05 (as *ø/-wa*), 07
ø/t:    07 (Nao?), 09 (Dimé)

Also, *ø-e, o, -iya* in nouns (01, Gofa), *ø, ʌ, a / -e, -in* in nouns (07, Dizi), *(t)a/(to)no* in nouns (09, Hamer), *-ob/-ɩnd* with adjectives (09, Dimé), *k, g/n* in demonstratives in 01, 02, 04, 07 (in the latter two feminine nouns only); *k/t* in 01 as noted above; *s/y* in 01; *s* or *s/ m, n* in 04, 07; tone changes in 06; no gender in demonstratives in 08, 09.

If the proto-form was \**kʷ/ti*, then only Basketo (of the many Ometo languages checked) preserves both consonants, while a new *n* has come in for the feminine in demonstratives in 01, 02, 04, 07.[6] The direct reflex *o/i* (or its "polar form" *i/o*) occurs in 01, 02, 04, 06, 09. The preservation of feminine *t* is seen in 07 and 09. South Ometo (02) stands alone in shifting to *e/i* or *i/e*. The fairly natural shift from *o/i* to *a/i* (or *i/a*) is seen in all but 09. The less natural shift to *a/o* or *o/a* is seen in 01, 02, 06, 09. If *ø/a, wa* belongs to the *i/a* or *o/a* sets, it would not affect the *i/a* set but would expand the *o/a* set to 01, 02, 05, 06, 07, 09. The switch of feminine *t→ n* is considered a shared innovation shedding light on subgrouping. For further details, see Bender in press b.

## 6. Number

As noted earlier, several Afrasian pronoun plurals are found in Omotic. No distinctive singular is found. Vocalic *o* or *u* is found in 01, 02, 06, 08, 09. Combinations such as *nd, nt, ns, tt* are found in 01 – 06 and can be considered retentions, though *t* is not noted in table 1 for Afrasian or Cushitic plurals (but recall that Diakonoff 1965: 103 considers *-nt* as occurring in Afrasian second and third persons and *-t* in all pronouns). Some individual group innovations are 03: *-kn*, 07: tone, 08: *-le*. Both Kefoid (06) and Aroid (09) have plurals reminiscent of Awngi *-ji* (and also some Central Sudanic *j, s, z*); Kefa *-ši*, Hamer *-si*, Dimé *-se* (but recall that the last two may be from Nilotic). Noun plurals will be taken up in section 10.

## 7. Case

Macro-Ometo (01 – 03) have nominative *-ni* / accusative *-na*, while 01, 02, 07 have nominative *-i ~ y*. This seems to be a retention of Cushitic *-i/-a*. Hetzron (1980: 15) mentions the presence of *n* in the Oromo nominative as unexplained: perhaps it is the same *n* showing up in Macro-Ometo in both nominative and accusative. In fact, *n* in the accusative is found elsewhere in Afrasian (e. g., Amharic definite accusative *-n*), and in pronouns *-n* is also found in the accusative in 05, 06, 07, 09 (as *-(d)am* in 09 Hamer). Other idiosyncratic nominatives and accusatives are found in tables 1.1 and 1.4.

The genitive with pronouns is most often unmarked. But the following occur with a pronoun or noun:

*s*:  02 (with noun, = Dative), 06 (with noun, as *-ci*, *-sō*), 08 (with noun, *š*), 09 (with noun, *-sa*).

*n*:  05 (pronoun and noun), 06 (with noun, *-ni*), 08 (with noun, *-n, -ŋ*), 09 (pronoun and noun, *-n, -nɛ*, *-no*).

*k*:  01 (pronoun, *ko*), 04 (*aga*, noun), 05 (noun, rare *ka*), 06 (pronoun and noun, masculine *ka* / feminine *ki*), 07 (noun inalienable *-kn*), 09 (pronoun and noun, masculine *ko-o*, feminine *ka-a* with pronoun).

*d, t*:  06 (*edi, eete*, noun), 08 (noun), 09 (noun or pronoun, *ta*).

Afrasian *-i* is retained as such only in 02 and 06 with nouns, although it may show up also with consonantal support. It could well be that the *k* and *d, t* markers are remnants of the Afrasian masculine/feminine respectively, but this is not obvious (e. g., *n* feminine shows up in 01, 02, 04, 07, but genitive *-ni* does not occur in any of these). Note also that the Nilo-Saharan genitive is often singular *N* (= *n, ŋ*, etc.) / plural *K* (= *k, g*, etc.) and secondarily *d, t, M* (= *m, b, w*, etc.). I cannot see any of the above case markers as shared innovations: all seem to be retentions of gender or genitive markers in Afrasian.

## 8. Demonstrative elements

The pattern *a* "near"/*i, e* "far" is nearly universal in Omotic (only in Aroid does the "polar" *i/a* seem to occur and the situation in Kefoid is unclear). The "near" form is basically *ha-* in 01 — 06 (often extended to *haga*), and *ka-* or *ga-* in 07, 08, 09. In some cases where the "near" form is *ha-* 'here' (213 of table 1.2), *ha-* is extended by *-ga, -ka, -ki, -c* (in 01, 02, 06). This suggests the interaction of a deictic *ha-* and a locative *-ga* (in fact, 01, 02, 09 have locatives with nouns of the form *-ka, -ga*). But we cannot make much of this division since both are probable retentions.

The "far" form is divided between something like *(h)in-, en-* (in 01, 02, 04 feminine) and something like *s(ek), seʔ* (in 01, 02, 03, 05, 07, 08). Both must be considered now as retentions. An extension of the "here" or "there" forms by *-s* or *-š-* in 01, 07 — 09 suggests another locative (but the *s-* locative with a noun is found only for 06). Interesting is the occurrence of *soyga* ('that') in 02, *soy* ('this') in 04, and *sokas* 'that' in 07, as well as *soy* or *šoy* in Nilo-Saharan C (Maba), Surma (of East Sudanic), and two branches of Central Sudanic (always as 'that'). Coincidence?

Gender in demonstratives has already been covered in section 5. None of the other categories of table 1.2 is very revealing (surely, partly for lack of data), except 210 — 212 (relative) and 216 — 218 (determiner/definite). Ometo (North and South) share relative *-ida*, which has been compared to the *-ɗa* of Oromo. Ometo and Mao have *s, z, š*; this could be from the "far" demonstrative. Yemsa (05) and 09 (Ari) have *-na*, whereas Yemsa (05) and Gonga (06, Kefa) have a verb suffix of the form *-wa* or *-ba* and *-mm-o* (reminiscent of Amharic relative *-mm-*) respectively.[7] As for the determiner/ definite, Yemsa, Kefoid, and perhaps Aroid have *-s, -z* while 02, 04, 07, and 09 have *-tV*, usually *-ta*. It is difficult to tell whether these are also related to demonstrative elements. The distributions of all elements (if they are really the same) are widespread in one or another function, except for *b, m, w*, which is therefore counted as an isomorph for 05, 06, relative.

# 9. Interrogatives

Omotic preserves Cushitic and Afrasian *maa* 'what?' in the form *am* (in 02, 03, 05, 06) and also Cushitic *\*ay* 'what?' as either 'who' or 'what?' in 01, 02, 03, 04, 06, 09. A new *(h)ar, al* appears in 02, 03, 04 and perhaps 07 (as *yɪr*). I hesitate to regard the latter as a shared innovation, since the *r, l* forms appear alongside *ay* in 02, 03, 04 and may perhaps be derived from it (more usual is the process *r, l → y*). For table 1 302 'who?' we see innovated[8] *on(e)* in 01 − 05 and *kone* in 06. Several idiosyncratic forms are found in table 1.3 (e. g., 01, 02 *ode*[9], 07 *ig-te*, 08 *kinda*).

Compounds involving 'what?' and 'who' are found in other interrogatives. For 303 'where?', nothing much turns up; for 304 'when?', 01 − 03 and 09 have forms in *-de, -di, -do, -te*. This may be another example of the locative, in this case, *-t* (see section 8 above) and I will reluctantly not count it as a shared innovation. Similarly, 305 'why?' is often a compound involving a dative case marker, as in Cushitic.

The interrogative 'how?' shows three potentially strong iso-morphs: *akka*[9] in 03, 05, 06; *ais, as(i), aziz-*[10] in 07, 09; *wat, wet, wid, wos*[11] in 01, 02, 04, 09 (the last-named questionable: 'which?' *ɪsnu widə* Ray). 'How many, much?' shows *appun, affun*[12], etc. in 01, 02, 05 and *ambitsa, ambissina, ambicco* in 03, 06[13] (but *am-* is probably 'what?' and *abic-* is 'how?' in Kefa).

The sentence-interrogative marker *-i, -e* (as in Cushitic) is found in 01, 03, 05, while *-a(a), -ay, -iya* (similar to Nilo-Saharan) is found in 01 − 03, 08, 09. It is not clear if they are independent of each other, and not much can be made of the possible coincidence with Nilo-Saharan. A *-d-* element[14] is seen in 01 (*-d-* or *-anda*), 02 (*adi*), and 07 (*-da*), perhaps related to Berber *-idd*, but for now, a shared innovation.

All the suggested innovations of this section must remain suspect until their distribution in Afrasian can be further studied.


# 10. Nouns

Case in nouns has already been partially discussed (nominative, accusative and genitive in section 7 above). Omotic has retained the *-s* dative of Afrasian (in 01 − 03, 06 − 09, perhaps in 04 as *-esn*). Otherwise, dative[15] occurs as *-ro, -ri, -ra* in 02, 03 (and 01 has instrumental *-ra*). These could all be retentions of what shows up as locative *d ∼ l* in Cushitic, but in Omotic we see no alternation, so could count *r* as a Macro-Ometo isomorph. Note locative *r, l* in Nilo-Saharan. Dative *-n* occurs in 04, 05, 09, locative *n* in 01, 02, 08, ablative *-n* in 06, instrumental *-n* in 02 and 06. I hesitate to see any isomorphs here. Ometo (01, 02) has a unique ablative *apa, fe,* etc.[16] Finally, *k* appears as a locative[17] in 01 (motion), 02, and 09. (09 also has dative *-kɛn*, perhaps *kɛ-n*?)

Gender has been treated above in (5). As for number, nouns in Omotic usually end in vowels in singular *-a, -e, -o* in 01, 02; usually *-a* in 03 (*-e, -i* rare, *-o* very rare); *-a, -o, -u* in 05 (*-i* very rare, *-e* in loans); *-e* in 08; *-a, i-* in 09. Also, *-na, -ra, -ta, (t)sa,* and *-Ce* in 02; *-(t)a* (masculine), *(to)no* (feminine) in 09. For further details, see Bender (in press c). A rare *-c(c)o-* singulative is found in 06 Kefa — perhaps from Sidamo languages. (Also reminiscent of Surma singulars *-ic* in Nilo-Saharan − further distribution needs to be examined.)

Plural in *-t* is found in 01, 02, 04 (as *-nd*); 05 (*kin: -ota*); 07 (masculine plural adjective *-da*); 08 (as *-toka* or *-tuwi*, 'head'); and 09 (global plural *(to)no*). Is this an isomorph or a miscellaneous assemblage? Groups 01, 02, 06, 08 have plurals in *-V(n)(t)s:* 01 (*-nts*); 02 (*-atse*, archaic for *kin*); 06 (*-Vtsi*); 08 (*-anse, inze*), reminiscent of third person pronouns. This must be considered a retention.

# 11. Tense-mode-aspect system (TMA)

This is perhaps second only to pronouns as a crucial system in Afrasian classification work. It will require a much more thorough investigation.

Zaborski (1986) argued for an isomorph which, in his view, rejoins Omotic to Cushitic as "West Cushitic." This is the presence of characteristic vowels in verb conjugations, *i* perfect, *a* imperfect, *o* jussive. Alemayehu Haile looked into this proposed isomorph further in his Master's thesis at Addis Abeba University in 1980—81, and I reported on it in Bender (1986 b). A summary and updating follows:

|     |          | Perfect   | Imperfect        | Jussive            |
|-----|----------|-----------|------------------|--------------------|
| 01: | Gofa     | *a, i*    | *s*              | *o, u*             |
|     | Kullo    | *d*       | *di, de*         | ?                  |
|     | Basketo  | *d, s*    | *ana* (Auxiliary)| ?                  |
|     | Malé     | *eni*     | *ane* (Auxiliary)| *o-*               |
| 02  | Zaysé    | *ide*     | *te*             | ?                  |
|     | Koré     | *o, u*    | *a*              | *i, e*             |
| 03  | Chara    | *i,e-š*   | *o, u-š*         | ?                  |
| 04  | Bensho   | *e, u*    | *u?*             | *ham-?*            |
| 05  | Yemsa    | *i*       | *a*              | *f*                |
| 06  | Bworo    | *e*       | *e*              | *o*                |
|     | Kefa     | *e*       | *V*              | first plural *o*   |
| 07  | Dizi     | *(k)i*    | *(d)e, i*        | *e, a*             |
| 08  | Hozo     |           | *e*              | ?                  |
|     | Sezo     |           | duplication      | ?                  |
|     | Bambeshi | *ø*       | *b*              | ?                  |
| 09  | Ari      | *t*       | *d ~ φ*          | *+er*, converb *o* |
|     | Hamer    | *a*       | *e*              | *a, e* purposive *o*|
|     | Dimé     | *e*       | *t*              | ?                  |

Full support is found only in Malé (01). Two-thirds support is found in Gofa (01), Yemsa (05), Bworo (06), and also Kefa in the first plural jussive but not in other jussive forms. If one accepts "polarization" (perfect *a*, imperfect *e*,) then Hamer (09) gives full support. Bensho needs further checking, but one could perhaps consider the labial jussive in Bensho (04) and Yemsa (05) as supportive.

If *i/a/o* is a "Cushomotic" isomorph (i. e., common to Cushitic and Omotic, not necessarily requiring that Omotic be restored as "West Cushitic"), then perfect *i* is best-retained (instances in every group but 08). Both 01 and 02 have *d* in the perfect; however, it also shows up in the imperfect, while Dizi and Ari have it in the imperfect only. 06, 08, and 09 also have *t* or *t'* in the perfect. There is reason to believe that at least some of these may be incorporated auxiliaries (recall from my lexical study that Omotic *\*t'* occurs as *d* in Macro-Ometo and Aroid; 1986 a: 25). More plausible as an isomorph[18] is *s, š,* found in 01, 02 as Auxiliary, 03 (in both perfect and imperfect — maybe really indicative), and 09. Also plausible[19] is *ene* in 01, 02 (emphatic *n*), 04 (as *en(d)*), 08 (*an*), and 09 (*n*). A *k* element[20] appears in 06 (*(e)ger*), 07 (*ki*), and 09 (*x*).

In the imperfect and future an auxiliary[21] *ana, ane* ('be') occurs in Macro-Ometo. Another auxiliary *b* occurs in 03 (*ba*) and 06 (*be-*). I assume that *b* in 08 (and in 09 perfect) are other instances of this.[22] Vowel *o, u* occurs only in 03 and 05 (along with *a* in the latter) in the imperfect.[23] Notable also are Dizi (07) present *(n)k* and Ari (09) contingent *denk.*[24] Progressive/continuous marking by *m* is found in 06 Kefa (*emmi*) and 09 Hamer (*-Im*).[25] It is not clear whether the Kefa form is related to relative *-mm-* (see section 8 above).

Imperative singular *-(w)a*/plural *-(i)t(e)* is widespread, especially plural (in all but 08; singular *-(w)a* is found in 01—03, 08, 09). In 08, Bambeshi has plural *-(u)wa* while Hozo has *-(m)*; given *-uwate* in 01 Malé and *-wayte* in 02 Koré, one wonders if the *-te* has dropped in Mao. Or should we relate 01 Basketo pl. *-Vfte* to the above and perhaps Dizi hortative *we(e)...a*? Another possibility is that 03 plural *-na*, 06 Bworo *-ar, -er,* and Hozo *-(m)* are related (Bworo *r* for *n* and Aroid *m* for *n* have been noted — more investigation is needed). Imperative singular *-i, e* is even more widespread than *-a* (*-i, e* found in 01, 02, 05, 06, 08, 09); both will here be considered as retained.

# 12. Negatives

Afrasian had a variety of negative markers (see table 1.4: 514 – 517). Of these, *B, K, N* and *R ~ L* are strongly retained in Omotic:

*B*:     01, 02 (as *ba, wa*), 05 (*af*), 08 (*bay, wa*)

*K*:     in all but 05; specifically as *kay, koy* in 03, 04, 06 (*k'aj, k'az* 'leave'), 07, 08 (*ke*), 09 (*k'ay, kay, koy*).

*N*:     in all but 04, 07; as *ana* in 03 (*na*), 05, 06 (*an, ano*)[26]; as *hin*[27] in 02, 06.

*R, L*:   04 (*arg*), 06 (*al*).

New forms in *S* and *T* have emerged. In 01 – 02, *base, wase, basso, wasso* suggest -*s* suffix to the common negative verb *ba*- (found also in Cushitic, e. g., Sidamoid, and in Nilo-Saharan). In 05 (*vza*), 06 (*as*), 07 (-*is*) occur. *T* forms are more widespread: as *te* or *ta* in 01, 05, 06, 09 and in various other forms in 02 (*ut', ot*) and 06 (*to*-). I consider both *S* and *T* as innovated at Omotic or higher level.

# 13. Copulas

Broadly construed, this includes here verbs of existence, location, 'have', 'become', 'and', 'or', etc. There seems to be an Omotic 'exist' verb of form *de(?)* or *da* in 01, 02, 03, 09 or *(i)ti, te* in 07 and 08. (Recall the comment in section 11 above about the distribution of *d ~ t'* in Omotic.) Interestingly, *ti* is also the form of a probable Nilo-Saharan copula, found strongly in 7 of 12 families. (Note that *de* means 'stand' in 01 Basketo.) Nasal forms are found in 01 (*en, ni*), 06 (*ne*), 09 (*ne*); also *na* (cf. the use of auxiliary 'be' *ana*; see section 11 above) in 01, 06. *K* forms are found in 01, 02 (*ukk*-), 07 (*k*-), 08 (*k'ɛ* 'live'). *S* forms are in 01 (interrogative *za*), 02 (*es*), 05 (*so, zo*), 08 (*š, sə*). A possible isomorph[28] is *far* in Yemsa (05) and Bworo (06, as *fa?*), but note *fa-i* in Beja, so perhaps a retention; another[29] is *be* 'be, sit' in 03 and 06.

There is no pervasive 'become' morph: 01 and 03 have *gid*[30]. Gofa (01) has *pe* 'pass the day' and Bensho has *pet* 'become', but this may be far-fetched. Being in a place is usually expressed by a verb such as *kot* 'sit' (03 and 06)[31]; the distribution needs to be further checked (e. g., does 02 *uts* 'sit' go with this?). Possession is usually expressed by 'exist to me', etc.

Given the drawing on various perhaps widespread lexical items such as 'sit, stand, reside', I cannot be very confident about the four iso-morphs suggested above and will not propose *N, K,* or *S* forms.

Finally, widespread *-n(e), -na* (in all but 04, 07, 09) makes this a likely protoform for 'and' (also found elsewhere in Afrasian, e. g., Amharic, in Niger-Kordofanian, e. g., Swahili, and Nilo-Saharan). *T* forms are found in 01 and 07 (in converb suffix); *K* is found in 01, 07, and 09; *-o* in 06 and 09 — all three are also found in Nilo-Saharan. I think limited choice and chance are responsible here. The alternative 'or' connective shows an Amharic loan of the form *wǝy* in 01, 07 (*we*)?, and 09 (*woi*).

# 14. Derivations

Here are included major nouns and verbs derived from other forms. In the case of nouns, relative, adjective, and abstract can be treated together. Agent, verbal noun, participle, and infinitive show more independence, although the lines are not sharply drawn, of course. Forms reminiscent of Afrasian (see table 1.7: 701 − 703) occur as fol-lows:

| | |
|---|---|
| *-i, e*: | 02 (infinitive), 04 (participle), 06 (infinitive), 08 (ver-bal noun), 09 (relative, verbal noun) |
| *-a(i), iya*: | 01 (adjective, agent), 04 (participle), 06 (infinitive), 07 (participle), 09 (relative, agent) |
| *-awa*: | 01 (agent) |
| *ma(i)-* or *-m-*: | 01 (adjective), 02 (meaning?), 08 (abstract), 09 (ab-stract, infinitive) |
| *-(n)ti, -(n)ta*: | 01 (relative), 05 (adjective), 06 |

In addition, note the following:

| | |
|---|---|
| *ki, ke*: | 03 (verbal noun), 04 (participle), 07 (infinitive), 09 (infinitive) |
| other *k, g*: | 01 (relative, verbal noun), 02 (verbal noun, "say"), 06 (agent, verbal noun), 07 (infinitive), 08 (abstract) |
| *(n)d*: | 01 (verbal noun), 02 (verbal noun), 04 (participle), 07 (verbal noun, infinitive, participle), 08 (abstract?), 09 (verbal noun) |

| | |
|---|---|
| *ts*: | 01 (abstract), 02 (relative), 03 (verbal noun), 04 (participle), 06 (adjective) |
| *s, š*: | 01 (agent), 02 (relative), 04 (adjective, participle), 05 (adjective), 06 (abstract, agent, emphatic), 07 (adjective, agent, participle), 08 (verbal noun, infinitive) |
| *n*: | 01 (verbal noun, infinitive), 04 (infinitive, participle), 06 (adjective, participle) |
| *-bo*:[32] | 01 (result *-ba*?), 05 (adjective), 06 (abstract) |
| *-baab*: | 07 ("owner"), 09 (agent) |
| *-o*: | 01 (abstract), 06 (verbal noun, infinitive), 09 (relative) |

Of the above, *(n)d* (in 01, 02, 04, 07, 08?, 09) seems to be strong for the verbal noun and is counted as such in table 1.7. Perhaps *n* of 01, 04, 06 should be adjoined to it. Perhaps, also, *ts* and *s* should be joined, putting the two together in every group except Aroid (09) (see table 1.7). Interesting (and counted here as an isomorph) is *-bo*, questionable in 01, but less so in 05, 06. I do not find *-o* convincing though, given that it is a single phone. Finally, *-baab* (reminiscent of Amharic *bal-*, "owner") is likely to be a loan from Dizi to Ari or vice-versa, even though the two are not geographically adjacent.

Verb derivations are simpler. Afrasian causative *s, š* shows up in all groups. Variants *ts* (in 06) and *c* (in 02, 04, 06) are not unprecedented elsewhere. More interesting are *t* in 09, *nt* and *nts'* in 01. Note that Nilo-Saharan has several causatives: *T* is the most widespread (in 7 of 12 families), and *S* is found in five families. As for passive/intransitive/reflexive/reciprocal, Afrasian *t* is found in all groups except 08 (data is weak) usually as *(V)t*. Other forms are minor, but note *-(V)nt* or *-ns* in 01, 02. Finally, a derivative in *f* is found in 06 and in 05 (*dif*, 'sit').[33]

# 15. Conclusions

What light does the preceding survey throw on problems of Omotic classification? In particular, I think it points to definite answers in four areas.

## 15.1 Is Omotic Afrasian?

Referring to table 2, one can see that Omotic shows numerous points on which derivability from Afrasian is straightforward. These are (number of features in parentheses):

> independent pronouns — all singular (recalling the "polarization" of one singular and two singular and one plural) (4);
> pronoun affixes — first singular and second singular "polarized", all plural (5);
> pronoun plural in *n* (1);
> masculine and feminine gender (2);
> demonstrative plural *n* (1);
> interrogative — 'what?' (1);
> noun cases — genitive, dative, accusative (3);
> imperative singular *-i* (1);
> negatives in *B, K, N, R* (4);
> noun formatives in *-ai, -ii, m, -nt* (4);
> causative in *S* and passive (etc.) in *t* or *n* (3).

The total is about 29 genetic features. Of course this is a debatable figure, given serious data gaps and problems of incomparability, etc. But let us see how it compares with some others.

## 15.2 What is the relationship of Omotic and Cushitic?

Here, a distinction must be made between what Omotic and Cushitic share with Afrasian as against what they share uniquely.
First, jointly shared with Afrasian:

> the same pronoun features as in 15.1, but *Cushitic third singular unknown (11);
> interrogative '-what?' (1);
> same noun cases as in 15.1 (3);
> imperative singular in *i-* (1);
> negative verb *b* (1);
> noun formative in *m* (1).

Second, unique to "Cushomotic":

> pronoun nominative and accusative (2);
> interrogative *ay* and 'why?' (2);
> noun case — nominative (1);
> trace of *-cc-* singulative (1);
> perfect/imperfect as *i/a* (2);
> jussive in *o, u* (1).

The total of shared Afrasian features is 18; the total of Cushomotic unique features is 9. Because of gaps, especially in Proto-Cushitic documentation, the result is not directly comparable to that of 15.1 (crucially lacking are pronoun third plural, demonstrative plural, 'here, there', negatives, place and possession copulas, 'and', noun formatives). Still, three-fifths of the Omotic-Afrasian features are also Omotic-Cushitic, while Omotic-Cushitic picks up nine more (half of the previous total). Impressionistically, I would say the picture is one of Cushitic and Omotic as independent, but not dissimilar, members of Afrasian. A more definitive answer could be provided if one took the same kind of look at Egyptian, Berber, Beja, and Chadic in Afrasian so that a comparative basis could be provided.

## 15.3 Could Omotic be Nilo-Saharan?

Now that we have a feeling for the degree of relatedness of Omotic to Cushitic and Afrasian, we are in a position to look elsewhere. In particular, based on my own on-going reconstructions of Nilo-Saharan, we see:

> Independent and affixed pronouns — the *ta/ne* pattern can be (and has been) compared with Nilo-Saharan *a/i*. Further, second singular *ne* can certainly be compared to Nilo-Saharan *\*ini*. But this is a case of deceptive "look-alikes", I think. Afrasian (and Omotic) pronouns are based throughout on *n* and *t*, while Nilo-Saharan has *-kʷ-* in first singular and Nilo-Saharan plurals are varied, but generally based on singulars. Furthermore, if I am right, Omotic *ne* comes from the Afrasian first

person, not second. Dizoid and Aroid may have Nilotic loans in pronouns, as we have seen.

Noun case — Nilo-Saharan has a secondary accusative *N*, but *K* is primary; interrogative marker *-(i)ya, ay*;

genitive *n-* primary in Nilo-Saharan, secondary in Omotic (and maybe really a gender marker);

singulative in *-cc-*: Surma singular (and other groups) *-ic* one of many in Nilo-Saharan;

plural in *t* — secondary in Nilo-Saharan;

perfect/imperfect — Nilo-Saharan has a basic *K/n* pattern, but secondarily *T* and vowels are involved;

negative — Nilo-Saharan basically has *m*, but *B, K, N* also occur;

copula — *ti* in both families;

connective *ne, na* — primary in Omotic, one of several in Nilo-Saharan;

noun formative — agent *ki* in Omotic; *K* a primary noun formative in Nilo-Saharan;

causative — *S* primary in Omotic, secondary in Nilo-Saharan.

I hope the reader will agree with me that none of the above is very convincing for an Omotic relationship to Nilo-Saharan: usually it involves a single consonant which is one of several in Nilo-Saharan. The copula *ti* and interrogative *ay* are the best cases, but I am inclined to say "chance convergence" — both are surely popular choices in world languages.

## 15.4 Subgrouping of Omotic

Finally, the question posed at the beginning (what will morphology contribute to the lexical classification scheme?) needs to be addressed. In table 4 the occurrences of the shared innovations identified as numbers 1 − 33 in the text are summarized.

Some observations:
North and South Ometo, as expected, form a clear group (01 − 02: Ometo).

*Table 4.* Frequency of cross-group occurrences

|    | 01 | 02 | 03 | 04 | 05 | 06 | 07 | 08 |
|----|----|----|----|----|----|----|----|----|
| 02 | 11 |    |    |    |    |    |    |    |
| 03 | 9  | 6  |    |    |    |    |    |    |
| 04 | 5  | 5  | 3  |    |    |    |    |    |
| 05 | 5  | 4  | 6  | 3  |    |    |    |    |
| 06 | 4  | 4  | 9  | 3  | 11 |    |    |    |
| 07 | 2  | 2  | 0  | 1  | 1  | 3  |    |    |
| 08 | 1  | 1  | 1  | 1  | 1  | 2  | 1  |    |
| 09 | 4  | 4  | 3  | 2  | 1  | 4  | 3  | 1  |

Chara (03), Yemsa (05), and Gonga (06) form a group overlapping with Ometo.

Dizoid (07), Mao (08), and Aroid (09) do not form a group. But contrary to the lexical results, Aroid is closer to 01 – 06 than Dizoid or Mao are.

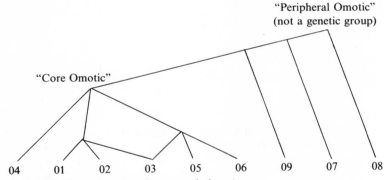

*Figure 2.* Suggested structure based on morphology

There is a problem in the overlap of 03 (Chara) with 01 – 02 (Ometo) on one side and 05 – 06 (Yemsa-Gonga) on the other. The three-way split involving 04 (Gimira), 01 – 02 (Ometo), and 03, 05, 06 (Chara-Yemsa-Gonga) is uncomfortable. The differences are so small that the exact relations of the "peripheral Omotic" groups is shaky. At this point, an examination of the entire picture is needed: geography and history (e. g., Gonga and Mao connections), lexicon (e. g., Nilotic influence on Aroid), and grammar (filling data gaps, better survey of the literature, more analysis and study).

## Notes

1. The table of grammemes in individual Omotic languages is too extensive to be included here. A copy may be obtained from the author.
2. The phenomenon of interchange of exponents of this sort has often been referred to as "polarity", though there are differences of opinion regarding its exact nature and the appropriate application of the term. For example, Semitists may prefer to limit it to the occurrence of masculine plurals for feminine nouns and vice-versa, while others (see Hock 1986, index references) suggest other uses. I have noted frequent occurrences in Nilo-Saharan, e. g., singular *i-*/plural *-a* or singular *-a*/ plural *-i*, near *-o*/far *-a* or near *-a*/far *-o*. Santandrea (1976) was unhappy that *g...r* ~ *g...l* served as both "right" and "left" in Central Sudanic. I suspect that polarization is not a unitary phenomenon and am planning a paper on the subject.

## References

The older, descriptive literature is covered very well in the bibliographies provided by Tucker—Bryan (1956), Fleming (1976), and other Omotic articles in Bender (1976). Presumably, updated bibliographies will be available in Bechhaus-Gerst—Serzisko (in press) and Hayward (in press). (All of these are listed under B below.)

### A. Major language sources old and new

*Aroid*

Ari: Bender, Dennis Tully, modest notes; Harold Fleming, notes.
Hamer-Kara-Bana: Jean Lydall, extensive notes; Fleming, notes.
Dimé: Fleming, extensive lexicon.
 Slight materials in:
 Cerulli, Enrico, 1942: "Il linguaggio degli Amar Cocchè [Hamer] e quello degli arbore nella zona del Lago Stefania", *Rassegna di Studi Etiopici* 2.3: 260—272.
 Conti Rossini, Carlo, 1927: "Sui linguaggi parlati a nord dei laghi Rodolfo e Stefania", *Festschrift Meinhof*, 247—255 [Kara, Hamer, and others].
 Da Trento, Gabriele, 1941: "Vocaboli in lingue [Ari, Hamer] dell'Etiopia meridionale", *Rassegna di Studi Etiopici* 1.2: 203—207.
 There are said to be extensive Cerulli manuscript notes.

*Dizoid*

Dizi (Maji): Edward Allen, Bender, Fleming, Joseph Keefer, Mary Breeze, notes.
Sheko: Bender, Fleming, notes.
Nao: Fleming, notes.
 Breeze, Mary, in press: "A comparison of the phonological features of Gimira and Dizi", in: Bechhaus-Gerst and Serzisko (eds.).
 Chiomio, Giovanni, 1941: "I Magi (Masi) nell'Etiopia del sud-ovest", *Rassegna di Studi Etiopici* 1: 271—304.

Conti Rossini, Carlo, 1925: "Sui linguaggi dei Naa e dei Ghimirra", *Rendiconti della Reale Accademia dei Lincei* 2: 621—636.

1937: "Il popolo dei Magi nell'Etiopia meridionale e il suo linguaggio", *Atti III Congresso Studi Coloniale* (Firenze), 108—116.

Lydall, Jean, 1976: "17. Hamer", in: Bender (editor) [see under B. General below], 393—438.

Montandon, George, 1913: *Au pays Ghimirra* (Neuchâtel: Attinger).

Toselli, Fr. Giovanni, 1939: *Elementi di lingua Magi* (Torino: Istituto Missioni Consolata).

## Mao

Hozo-Sezo: Bender and Atieb Ahmed Dafallah, modest notes.
Mao of Bambeshi/Diddesa: Bender and Atieb lexicon.
Ganza: Wendy James, few words.

Bender, M. L., 1985: "Gumuz, Koman, Mao, and Omotic", *Studies in African Linguistics Supplement* 9: 19—21.

in press a: "The limits of Omotic", in: R. Hayward (ed.) [see under B General references].

Bryan, Margaret, 1945: "A linguistic no-man's land", *Africa* 15.4: 188—205 [mentions slight material on Ganza].

Grottanelli, Vinigi, 1940: *I Mao* 1 (Roma: Reale Accademia d'Italia) [Hozo-Sezo, other Mao].

1946: "Materiali della lingua Coma", *Rassegna di Studi Etiopici* 5: 122—155 [includes Mao].

## Kefoid

Here the sources of Kefa are fairly extensive. Only major sources will be listed. A thorough bibliography as of 1976 is found in:

Fleming, Harold C., 1976: "15. Kefa (Gonga) languages", in: Bender (ed.), 351—376, 430.
Kefa and Mocha: Fleming and Herbert Lewis, notes on several varieties.

Cerulli, Enrico, 1951: *Studi Etiopici IV: La lingua Caffina* (Roma: Istituto per l'Oriente).

Leslau, Wolf, 1958: "Mocha, a tone language of the Kafa group in southwestern Ethiopia", *Africa* 28: 135—147.

Reinisch, Leo, 1888: *Die Kafa-Sprache in Nordost-Afrika* (Sitzungsberichte der phil.-hist. Classe der kaiserlichen Akademie der Wissenschaften 116.3).

1959: *A dictionary of Moca (Southwestern Ethiopia)* (Berkeley, etc.: University of California, Press).
Anfillo (nearly extinct): Bender, Fleming, few notes, Grottanelli 1940 (see under "Mao" above).
Bworo (Shinasha): Bender, Fleming, few notes; Franz Rottland, lexicon.

Grottanelli, Vinigi, 1941: "Gli Scinascia del Nilo Azzurro ed alcuni lessico poco noti della loro lingua", *Rassegna di Studi Etiopici* 1.3: 234—270.

Plazikowsky-Brauner, Herma, 1950: "Schizzo morfologico dello sinasa", *Rassegna di Studi Etiopici* 9: 65—83.

*Yemsa (Janjero)*

Yemsa: Klaus and Charlotte Wedekind, notes.
   Cerulli, Enrico, 1938: *Il linguaggio dei Giangero ed alcune lingue Sidama dell'Omo (Basketo, Ciara, Zaisse)* (Studi Etiopici III) (Roma: Istituto per l'Oriente).

*Gimira*

Benco-She: Mary Breeze, Klaus Wedekind, Fleming, notes.
Nao: Fleming, notes.
   Conti Rossini, Carlo, 1925 (see under Dizoid above [Nao]).
   Breeze, Mary, forthcoming (see under Dizoid above).
   Montandon, George, 1913 (see under Dizoid above [Benco]).

*Chara*

Chara: Fleming, notes.
   Cerulli, Enrico, 1938 (see under Yemsa above).

*Ometo*

   There are many varieties and a corresponding relative wealth of sources. Some major ones follow.
Malo-Zala, Oyda, Gidicho, Gatsamba: Fleming, notes.
Basketo: Fleming, extensive lexicon.
Male: Donald Donham, Herbert Lewis, Bender, notes.
   Allen, Edward J., 1976: "14. Kullo", in: Bender (ed.) [see under B General references], 324–350.
   Cerulli, Enrico, 1929: "Note su alcune popolazione Sidama dell'Abbisinia meridionale: I: I Sidamo orientali", *Revista degli Studi Orientale* 10: 597–692 [Welaita, Gofa, Zala, Kore].
   1938: (see under Yemsa above [Basketo, Chara, Zayse-Zergula]).
   Chiomio, Giovanni, 1938: *Brevi appunti di lingue Uollamo (Africa Orientale Italiana): Grammatica e dizionario* (Torino: Istituto Missione Consolata).
   Conti Rossini, Carlo, 1936: "Contributi per la conoscenza della lingua Haruro [Gidicho] (Isole del Lago Margherita)", *Rendiconti Reale Accademia dei Lincei* 16.2: 621–679.
   da Luchon, P., 1938: *Grammatica della lingua Uollamo* (Roma).
   da Trento, Gabriele, 1941: (see under Aroid above [Welaita, Male]).
   Hayward, Richard, 1982: "Notes on the Koyra language", *Afrika und Übersee* 65.2: 211–268.
   Moreno, Mario Martino, 1938: *Introduzione alle lingua Ometo* (Milano: Mondadori) [Gofa].

**D. General references**

Bechhaus-Gerst, Marianne – Franz Serzisko (eds.)
   in press    *Proceedings of the First Symposium on Cushitic and Omotic Languages* (Hamburg: Buske).

Bell, Alan
    1978         "Language samples", in: J. H. Greenberg (ed.), *Universals of human language 1: Theory and method* (Stanford: Stanford University Press), 123−156.

Bender, M. Lionel
    1981         "Some Nilo-Saharan isoglosses", in: Thilo Schadeberg−M. Lionel Bender (eds.), *Nilo-Saharan* (Dordrecht: Foris), 253−267.
    1986 a     "First steps toward Proto-Omotic", in: David Odden (ed.), *Proceedings of the 15th African Linguistics Conference* (Dordrecht: Foris), 21−45.
    1986 b     "A possible Cushomotic isomorph", *Afrikanistische Arbeitspapiere* 6: 149−155.
    in press a  "The limits of Omotic", in: Richard Hayward (ed.), *Omotic language studies.*
    in press b  "Proto-Omotic phonology and lexicon", in: Bechhaus-Gerst−Serzisko (eds.).
    in press c  "Gender in Omotic", *Journal of Afroasiatic Linguistics* 3.

Bender, M. Lionel (ed.)
    1976         *The non-Semitic languages of Ethiopia* (East Lansing, Mich.: African Studies Center, Michigan State University).

Bynon, James (ed.)
    1984         *Current progress in Afro-Asiatic linguistics* (Amsterdam: Benjamins) [reviewed by M. Lionel Bender in *Journal of African Languages and Linguistics* 7: 173−175, 1985].

Bynon, James−Theodora Bynon (eds.)
    1975         *Hamito-Semitica* (Janua Linguarum Series Practica 200) (The Hague: Mouton).

Dalby, David
    1966         "Levels of relationship in the comparative study of African languages", *African Language Studies* 7: 171−179.
    1970         "Reflections on the classification of African languages...", *African Language Studies* 11: 147−171.

Diakonoff, Igor M.
    1965         *Semito-Hamitic Languages* (Moskva: Nauka).
    1984         [Letter to the conference regarding recent work in the USSR on the comparative historical vocabulary of Afrasian], in: Bynon (ed.), 1−10.

Ehret, Christopher
    1985         [manuscript on Cushitic Proto-lexicon].

Fleming, Harold C.
    1969         "The classification of West Cushitic within Hamito-Semitic", in: Daniel McCall et al. (eds.), *Eastern African history* (New York: Praeger), 3−27.
    1974         "Omotic as an Afroasiatic family", *Studies in African linguistics, Supplement* 5: 81−94.
    1976         "Omotic overview", in: Bender (ed.), 298−323.
    in press    "Reconstruction of Proto-South Omotic", in: Bechhaus-Gerst−Serzisko (ed.).

296    M. Lionel Bender

Fodor, Istvan
1966 *The problems in the classification of the African languages* (Budapest: Center for Afro-Asian Research of the Hungarian Academy of Sciences).

Fronzaroli, Pelio (ed.)
1978 *Atti del Secondo Congresso Internazionale di Linguistica Camito-Semitica* (Firenze: Istituto di Linguistica e di Lingue Orientali, Universita di Firenze).

Goodman, Morris
1970 "Some questions on the classification of African languages", *International Journal of American Linguistics* 36.2: 117–122.

Greenberg, Joseph H.
1955 *Studies in African linguistic classification* (Branford, Conn.: Compass).
1960 "An Afro-Asiatic pattern of gender and number agreement", *Journal of the American Oriental Society* 80: 317–321.
1963 (reprinted 1970) *The languages of Africa* (Bloomington, Ind.: Indiana University; The Hague: Mouton).

Gregersen, Edgar A.
1972 "Kongo-Saharan", *Journal of African Languages* 11.2: 69–89.

Hayward, Richard (ed.)
in press *Omotic language studies.*

Heine, Bernd
1976 *A typology of African languages* (Berlin: Reimer).

Hetzron, Robert
1980 "The limits of Cushitic", *Sprache und Geschichte in Afrika* 2: 7–126.

Hock, Hans H.
1986 *Principles of historical linguistics* (Berlin–New York: Mouton de Gruyter).

Hodge, Carleton T.
1975 "The linguistic cycle", in: Bynon–Bynon (eds.), 171–191.

Meinhof, Karl
1912 *Die Sprachen der Hamiten* (Hamburg: Kolonialinstitut).

Rottland, Franz
1982 *Die südnilotischen Sprachen* (Kölner Beiträge zur Afrikanistik 7) (Berlin: Reimer).

Ruhlen, Merritt
1987 *A guide to the world's languages* 1: *Genetic classification* (Stanford: Stanford University Press).

Santandrea, Stefano
1976 *The Kresh group* (Napoli: Istituto Universitario Orientale).

Tucker, Archibald N.
1967 "Fringe Cushitic", *Bulletin of the School of Oriental and African Studies* 30: 655–680.

Tucker, Archibald N.–Margaret A. Bryan
1956 *The non-Bantu languages of northeastern Africa* (Oxford: Oxford University Press).

1966           *Linguistic analyses: The non-Bantu languages of northeastern Africa*
               (Oxford: Oxford University Press).
Zaborski, Andrzej
1986           "Can Omotic be reclassified as West Cushitic?", in: Gideon Golden-
               berg (ed.), *Ethiopian Studies* (Proceedings of the Sixth International
               Conference, Tel Aviv 1980) (Rotterdam: Balkema), 525–530.

# The regularity of sound change: A Semitistic perspective

*Stephen J. Lieberman*

We all know how important the recognition of the unities of the Indo-European family was to the beginnings of the modern study of languages and particularly to the development of historical linguistics as it is usually practiced. It seems promising to try to expand the perspective on method provided by that linguistic phylum, and to ask whether all human languages are comparable webs made of the same type of material which necessarily always develop in the same way. It also seems particularly fitting that the Afro-Asiatic phylum, which includes both Semitic and Egyptian among its branches, should have something to contribute to such questions, given the thousands of years for which some of these languages have been studied.

The most recent survey of comparative Semitic, Moscati (1964), is no less dated these days than the earlier attempts at such synthesis by Brockelmann (1908 – 1913) or Wright (1890). This is true, in part, because that synthesis pays but little heed to the rest of the phylum. It is also the case, however, because, as we shall see, if we are to represent even the Semitic family accurately, it is essential that we go back to the data, rather than rely on assumed reconstructions. This is a result of the large body of recent work which is now putting the study of even the classical Semitic languages on a sound, inductive, manuscript-based footing, rather than relying on the forms presented by the grammarians. Despite the length of time during which Semitic has been studied, then, we are still quite far from having the comprehensive descriptions on which an outsider needs must rely.

In some ways, such work currently being done by Semitists is comparable to the data gathering and description of students of the Berber, Chadic, Cushitic, and Omotic branches of the phylum. There is serious linguistic study of the manuscript sources for various branches of the Semitic family, particularly Akkadian, Arabic, Aramaic, and Hebrew. Such investigations are now slowly advancing both grammatical and lexical studies of these classical Semitic languages beyond the period when what passed for a grammar or lexicon was simply a translation into a Western language of the views expressed by native, "medieval", grammarians and lexicographers, sometimes spruced up with modern terminology and restated. Unfortunately, from the momentary point of view of the historical linguist, some of these developments are connected with the nationalistic thrusts of modern politics, and much of the best work being done on early Hebrew, for instance, is published in Israeli Hebrew, which many students of the classical languages are not adept at reading. Here, the individual interested in comparison of the whole phylum runs into serious communication problems, as evidenced by the appearance of a number of articles written in Hausa listed in the most recent *Chadic Newsletter*[1]. There are, alas, few (or no) individuals who can read Hausa, modern Arabic and Hebrew, and Akkadian cuneiform with enough facility to keep up with the literature, even if there were no limits to the time devoted to the task. While newly-written Akkadian texts are of scant interest, there is a constant flow of newly-excavated and published tablets. Even after all of the texts which have direct linguistic importance for the historical reconstruction of the earliest stages of Arabic have been investigated, and all of the hitherto undescribed Chadic languages which are spoken by diminishing numbers of speakers have been recorded, we will still have no lack of work excavating, publishing, and interpreting the remains of Akkadian.

We would like to raise some questions concerning the regularity of sound change,[2] in the hope of addressing questions which may be of relevance to the wider field of historical linguistics, and will illustrate our views primarily from Semitic. It is generally accepted among linguists that languages have a certain uniformity in their development. This regularity is but a particular manifestation of the assumption by natural sciences that nature is uniform (cf. Chen 1977: 198). One must note, however, that while the perceived regularity of sound systems and their development is probably the greatest claim of linguistics to be more precise ("scientific") than other social sciences or the humanities, such claims of regularity should, perhaps, in fact be viewed as something to be demonstrated, rather than as a given.

The essential nature of languages as semeiotic systems, conveying information, makes them human artifacts, rather than part of "nature". It is this essence, as a means of communication, which seems to result in both the presumed universality of sound change and the apparent exceptions to the rules.

In fact, however, linguists regularly assume that languages do not develop completely regularly. Let us consider, for a moment, the widespread use of vocabulary lists based on Morris Swadesh's studies. He drew up lists of "noncultural" vocabulary (Swadesh 1971: 281). Such lists were intended to avoid those parts of the vocabulary which are thought to be most affected by cultural change: technological developments, contact with outsiders, and the like. The compiling of such lists and their use implies that the rates of replacement of words from the various semantic spheres of a language are not uniform. On the other hand, it was an assumption of the original purpose of his list-making, namely glottochronological lexicostatistics, that sound change occurred at a constant rate.

It seems that the assumption of nonuniformity underlying Swadesh's list is widespread among linguists, and that most would agree that the speed of vocabulary replacement and the speed of sound change are not interrelated, whether one considers either of these easily measurable or constant, or not. This means that while one aspect of language, the phonemes used to express a word, follows one set of rules, the other aspect, its vocabulary, follows another. It might follow that the phonological systems of languages were part of nature while their systems of vocabulary were part of culture. Such a view of languages as Janus-faced seems problematic. While the sound matter with which speech is expressed is surely governed by physical reality, all linguists know that phonological systems are cultural, not natural, artifacts. Otherwise, all attempts to describe phonological systems would be unnecessary, and we could rely on the sound spectrograph to write the first parts of our grammars.

Put in Peirceian terms, the sound-systems of languages are "symbolic", that is, signs governed by convention.[3] As such, they are cultural, not natural, and governed by history, not nature, in their development, whatever the constraints that the physical world puts on them. History, as we all know, is rather less amenable to the ascription of rigid laws than nature.

Before turning to an example of the problems one encounters when absolutely regular sound change is assumed, it may be good to point out some of our presuppositions.

It matters but little whether we choose to study a whole phylum, a family, a single language, a sociolect or an idiolect. If there is regularity in sound change, it will be evident at all of these levels, and if there is not, then it must be accounted for, no matter what the magnitude of the linguistic entity studied. If we investigate forms from two closely-related idiolects, it will, no doubt, be easier to guess at the intermediary steps which link them: the differences between them will be smaller and clearer. Nonetheless, no conceptual difference should result. If there is regular development, it will be evident whatever the distances between the language samples we are working with. Irregularity, as well, should manifest itself without regard for the extent of the gaps between the speech forms from which we draw our examples, but with greater gaps we will probably feel freer to assume the presence of unattested intermediary stages.

Likewise, the correct determination of genetic groupings and subgroupings does not affect the discernment of sound correspondences, though a proper classification will clearly make the preparation and presentation of our observations more efficient. It is, then, not necessary for us to have classified the Afro-Asiatic phylum correctly before we make meaningful statements about the histories of particular words and morphemes. The retention of archaic forms and the introduction of innovations do not necessarily always follow the simple historical patterns implied by a classification.

Johannes Schmidt's substitution of *Wellentheorie* for the *Stammbaum* does not provide a simple solution to the underlying problems here, for there are many eddys and subsurface streams in the ocean of human language. Individuals can move about even more easily than groups, and one person may have happened to acquire the form of a particular word from someone not in the mainstream.

As an example, we will look at some of the sound correspondences of a couple of the names for the cardinal numbers in Semitic and in Afro-Asiatic. The word "number" is used to refer strictly to speech forms, while "numeral" is reserved for writing-systems. These words are thought to change slowly, and their presumed conservative character should make them illustrative of the usual sound correspondences. For reference, some of the Semitic sound correspondences from Moscati (1964) are given in table 1. The order of the columns has been slightly rearranged; the changed order does not reflect any new classificatory scheme.

*Table 1.* Some of the Semitic sound correspondences (after Moscati 1964: 43—44)

| Proto-Semitic | Akkadian | Ethiopic | Arabic | Hebrew | Syriac | Ugaritic | Epigraphic South Arabian |
|---|---|---|---|---|---|---|---|
| ʾ | ʾ | ʾ | ʾ | ʾ | ʾ | ʾ | ʾ |
| ḥ | ʾ | ḥ | ḥ | ḥ | ḥ | ḥ | ḥ |
| d | d | d | d | d | d | d | d |
| c | ʾ | c | c | c | c | c | c |
| θ | š | s | θ | š | t | θ | θ |
| n | n | n | n | n | n | n | n |

In table 2, some additional sound correspondences are given. These are not shown in tabular form in Moscati (1964), but the facts are, by and large, recorded in his summarizing volume, and represent the scholarly consensus. The information given for Hebrew is for the Babylonian vocalization, not the usual Tiberian one, which is the one recorded in Moscati's volume. In the Tiberian system, which is the only one ever taught, there are further developments, but we will not concentrate on the vowels.

*Table 2.* Some additional sound correspondences

| Proto-Semitic | Akkadian | Ethiopic | Arabic | Hebrew | Syriac | Ugaritic | Epigraphic South Arabian |
|---|---|---|---|---|---|---|---|
| (in initial position) | | | | | | | |
| w | w (>ʾ ca. 1600 B.C.E) | w | w | y | y | y | w |
| a | a > e | a | a | a | a > ə | a | ? |
| i | i > e | i | i | i | i > ə | i | ? |

(Developments shown occur only in certain sound environments.)

The sound changes which affect the phonemes shown in table 2 are quite small. If we want to summarize them succinctly, we can do so in a sentence or two, or in a chart such as that given in table 3, which shows only the differences from Proto-Semitic.

*Table 3.* Summary of some Semitic sound correspondences

| Proto-Semitic | Akkadian | Ethiopic | Arabic | Hebrew | Syriac | Ugaritic | Epigraphic South Arabian |
|---|---|---|---|---|---|---|---|
| ʾ | | | | | | | |
| ḥ | ʾ | | | | | | |
| d | | | | | | | |
| c | ʾ | | | | | | |
| θ | š | | s | š | t | | |
| n | | | | | | | |

(in initial position)

| | | | | | | | |
|---|---|---|---|---|---|---|---|
| w | > ʾ | | | y | y | y | |
| a | > e | | | | > ə | | |
| i | > e | | | | > ə | | |

(Developments shown occur only in certain sound environments.)

Swadesh (1971) included the numeral 'one' and 'two' in his list, but a glance at the list given in table 4 will show that in Semitic we start our problems at the beginning, with 'one'. For this form, Akkadian has a morpheme which is not related to the form in the other languages. In order to clarify it, the listing extends to 'eleven', since we find cognates in some of the West-Semitic forms of that word.[4]

We should note that the listing in table 4 contains certain allowable shortcuts in order to present the stems more clearly. Concerning the form of the Akkadian word for 'one', it has been necessary to revise the form which is to be found in the standard grammars and dictionaries. They give an /i/ vowel which is not proved by the attested spellings, even if the known orthographies do permit the usual interpretation. Since the cuneiform syllable graphemes employed are not used in a way which distinguishes between these, and there is no additional evidence which shows which phoneme is involved, we are left knowing that the first vowel was a front vowel, but not certain which. The known spellings of the first syllable are shown in table 5. Based on the obvious etymological connection with Hebrew ʿaštê (cf. 'eleven'), the /e/ vowel most likely developed as follows: *ʿašt... > *ʿešt... > ʾešt... The Akkadian change of /a/ to /e/ in the environment of /*ʿ/ is well-known.

*Table 4.* Cardinal numbers in the Classical Semitic languages

| | Akkadian (absolute state all but 6 m) | Ethiopic⁵ | Arabic | Hebrew (B = Babylonian T = Tiberian else both or B not attested) | Syriac | Ugaritic | Sabaic |
|---|---|---|---|---|---|---|---|
| 1m | ʾeštiʾān < *ᶜašti+ān > ʾeštên | ʾaḥadu {ʾaḥadû} | ʾaḥadu ~ wāḥidu | ʾaḥaḏ ~ ʾaḥāḏ (B) ~ ʾeḥaḏ (T) ~ ḥāḏ (B) ~ ḥaḏ (T) | ḥaḏ | aḥd | ʾḥd |
| 2m | šina⁶ | kalʾē {kəloʾ} | ʾiθnā(ni) ~ θnyn ~ tnyn | šnê | tərēn | tn | tny |
| 3f | šalāš | šalās ~ šalas {šāllás} ~ šélse ~ | θalāθu | šālōš ~ šālôš | təlāt | tlt | s²lt > tlt |
| 4f | ʾarbaʾ > ʾerbe | ʾarbāᶜ{ə} ~ rəbᶜ {rēbʾə} | ʾarbaᶜu | ʾarbaᶜ ~ ʾarbāᶜ (B) | ʾarbaᶜ | arbᶜ | ʾrbᶜ |
| 5f | ḫamiš | ḫams{ə} ~ ḫāms {ḥámsə} | ḫamsu | ḥāmēš ~ ḥāmaš (B) | ḥameš | ḫmš | ḫms¹ |
| 6f⁷ | šedeštum | sessu ~ sədəs {~ sédsə} | sittu | šēš | šet | tt | s¹dt > s¹t |

| Akkadian (absolute state all but 6m) | Ethiopic[5] | Arabic | Hebrew (B = Babylonian T = Tiberian else both or B not attested) | Syriac | Ugaritic | Sabaic |
|---|---|---|---|---|---|---|
| ordinal | | sādis | | | t̲dt̲ | |
| 7f  sebe | sabᶜu ~sabᶜ{ə} | sabᶜu | šābaᶜ (B) ~šabᶜā (B) ~šēbaᶜ (T; spelled šēbᶜa) | šəbaᶜ | šbᶜ | s¹bᶜ |
| ordinal  sebʔu | | | | | | |
| 8f  samāne | samānī ~samen {sémnə} | tamānī > tamān | šəmōnāh (B) šəmōnah (B) šəmōneh (T) | təmānē | tmn | tmny > tmn |
| construct state | | tamānī | | | | |
| 9f  tiše | tesᶜu ~tasᶜu {e ʔə, tásʔə} | tisᶜu | tēᶜ/ēšaᶜ | tešaᶜ | **tšᶜ | ts¹ᶜ |
| 10f  ʔešer | ᶜašru ~ᶜəšr {ᶜasrú, ᶜəsrə} | ᶜašru | ᶜaśar (B) ~ᶜaśār (B: pausal) ~ᶜeśer (T) | ᶜesar | ᶜšr | ᶜs²r |
| 11m  ʔešten  -ešret | ᶜašru wa-ʔaḥatti {ʔassārtú wā-ʔaḥadū} | ʔaḥada ʔḥd(ᶜḏ) -ᶜaša | ʔaštê ~ʔaḥad -ᶜaśāra | ḥədᶜəsar | ᶜšt -ᶜšr(h) | ʔḥd -ᶜs²r |

\* = reconstructed forms

\*\* =

{…} = traditional pronunciation according to Argaw (1984)

*Table 5.* Spellings of the first syllable of 'one' in Akkadian

---

Old Akkadian
        *iš-* to be interpreted as (glottal stop followed by) /e/ *or* /i/ + /s/ *or*
        /š/ (*or* /z/ *or* /ṣ/)
  (ca. 2300–2000 B. C. E.)

later, also

Old-Babylonian
  (ca. 2000–1600 B. C. E.)
  Mari:
        *UŠ-* (Dossin 1951: 10 10′), to be interpreted as (glottal stop followed
        by) /e/ *or* /i/ + /s/ *or* /š/ (*or* /z/ *or* /ṣ/)

Middle Babylonian and Middle Assyrian and later
  (i. e., after ca. 1600 B. C. E.)
        *il-t...*
  (already in Old-Babylonian, sibilant followed /t/ > /lt/)

Neo-Assyrian
  (ca. 1000–600 B. C. E.)
        *eš-* (in 'eleven' in "Enuma Eliš" III 36 [Lambert–Parker 1966: 16]
          and as borrowed into Sumerian in "Ea" II 237 [Landsberger 1979:
          257]
        *is-se (is = es)*
        *i-se*
        (in NA /lt/ > /ss/)

---

A Babylonian spelling with *i-* would show /i/ rather than /e/, but (neo-)Assyrian /ʾi/ is sometimes spelled *e-* and etymological /ʾe/ as *i-* (cf. Deller 1959: § 25).

We may note that in order to determine what the forms of most Akkadian words were, we depend in part on comparisons of just the type which are in question in the present paper. The general shape of the syllables represented by a cuneiform syllable grapheme may be determined by comparing their usage with forms which Semitists conventionally reconstruct for the language. Fortunately, a study of the pattern of usage of the graphemes can advance us beyond the circularity inherent in basing our Akkadian forms on Semitistic hypotheses and then basing later Proto-Semitic reconstructions on the forms posited. Such systematic graphemic study has been carried out for the classical, Old-Babylonian, "dialect" of Akkadian, where regional differences in spelling practice sometimes allow one to gain the firm footing of distinct spelling patterns which can then put so much of a dent on the circle of reasoning that it is unlikely to roll off into never-never land. With the help of such detailed study, presumed phonemic patterns and structuring can be determined based purely on the surviving evidence, rather than on catenations of linguistic reconstructions (cf. Lieberman 1977: 96—117).

The form of the word we are to reconstruct for Hebrew 'one' may be taken as a sample of what is required when we try to reconstruct the earliest attested state of that language. As everyone knows, Hebrew is commonly written with a system of graphemes ("letters") which leave many of the vowels undistinguished. Long after it had ceased to be spoken, various systems of pointing were introduced in order to rectify this situation. One system, the Tiberian,[8] gained absolute ascendancy over its rivals, the Babylonian and Palestinian. Only within the last one hundred and fifty years or so have manuscripts and fragments of manuscripts with these obsolete systems become widely known and available, and it is only fairly recently that there has been any comprehensive linguistic study of these materials.[9] There is no printed text of all of the Bible which records the preserved pointings of either of these supralinear systems, just as we still lack a text which presents the variations in pointing of the Tiberian tradition. Current dictionaries of "Biblical" Hebrew simply ignore such information (Murtonen 1986 is an attempt at improving the situation). The most commonly used grammars of Hebrew do not even record the non-Tiberian spellings, though at least a couple of the reference grammars give one some inkling that Palestinian and Babylonian systems existed. The forms of the word for 'one' in the Hebrew of the Bible are presented in table 6.

*Table 6.* 'One' in Hebrew

|  | Tiberian | Babylonian (does not distinguish /e/ from /a/) |
|---|---|---|
| (Absolute) |  |  |
|  | 'aḥad̲ 6 x | 'aḥad̲ |
|  | 'eḥād̲ passim (pausal used in place of contextual) | •'aḥād̲ |
|  | ḥad̲ | ḥād̲ |

What is of particular interest for the question of sound change is not the Akkadian non-cognate, but the form with initial /w/ in Arabic, and its relatives. Wright's Arabic grammar gives *'aḥadu* and *wāḥidu* as simple variants (Wright 1896–1898, I: 253). The word with /w/ is, of course, simply the participle of an unaugmented verb stem which begins with that phoneme. The listing of words meaning 'one' is, then, not sufficient to explore this Semitic vocable, since there are clear cognates with initial /w/ or /y/ elsewhere in classical Semitic. Some of these are given in table 7.

*Table 7.* Comparative evidence for *waḥad*

---

Old-Babylonian Akkadian (also attested in Old Akkadian in personal names)
    *u̯êdum* (also cf. derivatives)
    'individual'
Ugaritic
    *yḥd* (Herdner 1963: 63) ["Epic of Krt"] 96 (// *aḫd* (Herdner 1963: 65) ["Epic of Krt"] 184)
    'loner'
El-Amarna ("Canaanite" ca. 1400 B. C. E.)
    *u̯a-hu-du-un-ni* (glossing *a-na-ku-ma*) (Thureau-Dangin 1922: 108–124)
    (*u̯a* = *i̯a*8; < /...dōnī/ < /...dānī/)
    ('I') alone
                cf. *'êdēnu*(/û) 'aloneness' passim in these letters
Hebrew
    \**yēḥad* (cf. 3fs *tēḥad* Genesis 49:6, etc.)
    'he will become one'
Old Aramaic
    *hwḥd* (Zkr stele)
    'bring together' (Causative 3 masc. sg. suff.)
Syriac
    *yawḥēd*
    'set alone'
Ethiopic
    *weḥda*
    'he was few/small'

---

The development of initial /w/ to /y/ in Northwest Semitic and Ugaritic is well-known, but there is no regular correspondence with /'/. Standard accounts take the Hebrew form which begins with /ḥ/ to be the result of Aramaic influence (the phrase is a semantic doublet, and left out in the Septuagint translation of the passage in Ezekiel). The Arabic form for 'eleven' without either glottal stop or /w/ is apparently the only form attested in the papyri of the first three centuries after the Hejira, that is, no Arabic manuscript before the tenth century C. E. has a /w/ or /'/ in this form (Hopkins 1984: 116). Some dictionaries refer to the two forms as being of relevance one for another, but this is usually merely a suggestion to "compare" the second form, and some sound change from /'/ to /w/ or /y/ or vice versa is not necessarily implied.[10]

The alternative assumption, that what is involved here is some base /ḥad/ which was augmented with both /'/ and /w/ or /y/ outside of Aramaic, but was preserved in its pristine state only in Aramaic is most unlikely, even if one might, possibly, want to posit such a base for Proto-Afro-Asiatic. Like Hebrew and Arabic, Punic also has an aleph-less biconsonantal form, but all such forms seem most likely to be the result of Aramaic influence.[11]

The form for 'two' shows the regular correspondences, except for Ethiopic, where one can find a cognate outside of the cardinal (*sanuy* means 'second day/night [of the week/month]'). Syriac also shows a couple of peculiarities as compared with Proto-Semitic, but both of them result from regular, well-known Aramaic developments. The forms with a second /n/ are duals. The Ethiopic word for the number 'two' has several Semitic cognates outside of the number system, but they need not detain us.

It is well known that if we turn to the other Afro-Asiatic families searching for cognate numbers, by looking at their cardinal numbers, the relationships are not always clear.[12] It seems likely that the presence of cognate Semitic verbs in unaugmented, base stem, the *qal* or *Grundstamm* form, might well account for the lack of correspondences. I have listed a few of these Semitic verbs in table 8. The numerals may well be derived from verbs.

Simple, unadorned, derivation from the verbal system will not, however, account for the interchange between /'/ and /w/ which we seem to find in the Arabic words for 'one', and the apparent relationship between the cardinal number 'one' and the verbs which begin with /w/ or /y/ in the other languages.

This example, then, may be used to consider whether sound change is completely regular. If we follow the usual viewpoint and grant the assertion that all exceptions are to be explained away by subsidiary sound laws or by borrowing, we may set out to find such complications, but it seems unlikely that any will be discovered. A third cause of exceptions to apparent sound laws, namely analogical influence, has been used to account *(inter alia)* for the inconsistent

*Table 8.* A sampling of the related meanings of cognate unaugmented verbal stems in Semitic.

| | |
|---|---|
| 2 | 'change (oneself) (*i*)' (Akkadian, Hebrew), 'fold/bend (*i*)' (Arabic) |
| 3 | 'do three times (*i* ~ *u* > *a/u*)' (Akkadian), 'take a third part of something (*u*)' (Arabic) |
| 4 | 'do fourth (*u*)' (Akkadian),[13] 'drink every fourth day (camels), gallop (horse) (*a*)' (Arabic) |
| 5 | 'do five times, divide into five (*u*)' (Akkadian) 'take the fifth part of somebody's goods (*u*); be fifth, complete the number five, twist five-stranded rope (*i*)' (Arabic) |
| 6 | 'be the sixth (*i*), take the sixth part from somebody (*u*)' (Arabic) |
| 7 | 'take an oath' (Hebrew: pass. part; nif.; hif.),[14] 'be seventh, revile somebody, frighten somebody (*a*)' (Arabic) |
| 8 | 'take the eighth part of somebody's goods (*u*); become the eighth (*i*)' (Arabic) |
| 9 | 'be ninth, take the ninth part, make something nine (*a, u*)' (Arabic) |
| 10 | 'muster (*a/u*)' (Akk.: *ašāru*),[15] 'tithe (*u*)' (Hebrew,[16] Arabic), 'make up the number ten, be the tenth (*i*)' (Arabic) |

Vowels in ( ) indicate *Ablaut* classes.

correspondences between the sibilants of the Semitic numbers. No doubt, some such set of explanations must be invoked there, but it seems unlikely that such analogical factors can be brought to account for the apparent irregularity of the number 'one'. Neither borrowing, phonological rules, nor analogy can provide an explanation, except on an *ad hoc* basis. Like thousands of other examples, this may well lead us to reconsider the validity of the claim that sound change is completely regular.

We believe that the claim is not valid. While granting that most sound change follows rules, else they would not be rules, we cannot accept the contention that sound change is exceptionless, and that any variance from the "laws" is to be explained by making those laws more complex or assuming that there has been some borrowing or analogical influence. The claim that sound change is exceptionless must be viewed as a hypothesis which requires verification. Any acceptance of the absolute regularity of sound-change laws would require that we allow for the possibility of "falsifying" the hypothesis, as Karl Popper would have insisted. Linguists have not, however, to my knowledge, considered the question on some inductive basis, and it is hard to see how any test of the regularity hypothesis could be made that would satisfy its advocates. They always insist on the possibility of other, undiscovered, factors modifying the basic rules, and concede the necessarily incomplete nature of our knowledge of all of the details.

When we admit that hitherto undiscovered complications in the rules or borrowing or analogy or some combination of such factors may be needed to account for exceptions to our supposed rules, we are conceding that we have not arrived at some final, comprehensive statement of sound laws. We are thus affirming our faith in the regularity of the universe, or, rather, the phonological part of languages, rather than making any testable, scientific assertion.[17]

It seems that we can, in fact, counter such an a priori assertion only on a reasoned (i. e., non-empirical) basis. We must, then, go beyond the claims of absolute regularity to a consideration of why there should be any regularity at all. Regularity is necessary to languages because it is more efficient to communicate with a system, rather than with some collection of tokens, each of which represents a different particular entity in the physical world. The use of a "system" requires that an easily available key to its understanding be present. Regularity facilitates the availability of such a key, even if it is not an absolute *conditio sine qua non*. Without some system, the plethora of things we might want to refer to in speech would have to be matched with an equally large collection of different words. It is only by recognizing and imposing regularities on the physical universe that it becomes manipulatable by us. Nonetheless, we all know that such regularities are not absolute or completely uniform.

The (synchronic) use of a language to communicate imposes both upper and lower limits on both its regularities and its irregularities. Using one word for each thing or action would give us a most precise means of expression, but it would require such a large number of tokens or symbols that it would be completely unwieldy in its application. Such a structureless concatenation of forms would not differ greatly from ostentation, and would require a tremendous memory merely to store the lexicon. At the other extreme, the simplest "system" of all would be to have but a single speech form which meant everything, or rather, anything the speaker wanted, but this would obviously also be useless. It would put us in the position of Humpty Dumpty in *Through the Looking-Glass* who insists that, "When *I* use a word, it means just what I choose it to mean — neither more nor less". Alice, you will recall, answers that, "The question is whether you *can* make words mean so many different things," and he responds that, "The question is which is to be master — that's all," (Carroll 1982: 136).

The structure that we find in languages mediates between the two extremes of a single word for each object in the universe and one word for all of them. It means that we are not absolute "masters" of our own speech, but must conform to social conventions in order to communicate. Alice implies this when she next asks Humpty Dumpty what one of his words means. In a like fashion, the regularity of sound change is imposed by the sociocultural conventions used by speakers, and their need to communicate.

Roman Jakobson used to speak of synchronic diachrony, of the fact that the actual linguistic repertoire of an individual speaker of a language was not a simple absolutely uniform whole. It seems that such an approach is essential when we try to assess the regularity of sound change. The historically uniform samplings of a language which we find in classical texts have been predigested for us by native grammarians, even when those "grammarians" are the writers themselves. Likewise, poetry or recitation in "high style" is a construct imposed on diverse linguistic realities by speakers. The actual, everyday utterances, and certainly the linguistic repertoires of speakers, are more complex and less uniform than one might like.

The regularity of sound change is governed by the needs of communication which impose, or allow, both upper and lower limits on it. If sound change is too irregular, that is, if change takes place completely unpredictably, then communication must cease, since the listener won't know the new repertory of symbols. If sound change is absolutely regular, then we lose some of the richness of nuance which is added to speech by its being more complex than simple ostentation.

Were sound change overly irregular, we would be put in the position of Alice, having to start learning the language over again, and being forced to ask "what that means". In order to continue speaking the same language or some clear derivative of it, there must be a small range of possible phonemes from which a sound derives. I must be able to map the phone-type used by interlocutor against one or a couple of my own phonemes, or I will not be able to understand. So long as there is a fairly simple correspondence between the speech we hear and that we are used to, we will be able to fill in the gaps by using the linguistic and situational context. We will learn the correspondences quickly, and understand a person, even if we think he or she speaks oddly.

If sound change is too regular, and all of the usual changes are inevitably made for every form, the possibility, for example, of retaining some unchanged earlier forms with their emotional and/ or referential overtones would be lost. Retention of such forms is a variety of dialect mixing, in which some linguistic form which does not follow the rules is retained because of its special value. This process results, we know, in biforms, in which a single linguistic token has two descendants which differ in some way or other. Dialect mixing can be made by combining forms from the multiple linguistic repertoires of a single speaker. Since the use of more than one historical stage of a language is within our capabilities, we can switch between the usually distinct sub-codes which are part of our total linguistic repertoire. However, since the distinction between and the differentiation of some sets of sub-codes are not necessarily part of the linguistic sphere, it seems wrong to consider such inconsistencies to be simply additional instances of "borrowing".

We can illustrate these two potential tendencies from the number 'one' in the various Semitic languages. Without either /ʾ/ or /y/ (~ /w/) in the name of the number, Aramaic has completely neutralized any possible distinction between the two (presumed) stems. Hebrew distinguishes between verbal stems with /ʾ/ as a first radical and those with /y/ as a first radical. In the piʿel, the form with /ʾ/ means 'unite' (Ben Yehuda 1948–1959. I: 141), and that with /y/ 'join, designate, specialize, leave alone, proclaim "one"' (Ben-Yehuda 1948–1959. IV: 2010–2011), at least in post-Biblical Hebrew. Hebrew makes this distinction, it should be noted, despite the fact that only the form with /ʾ/ is used for the cardinal number. Arabic, as a third possibility, uses both forms with /ʾ/ and /w/ for the cardinal number, but does not seem to distinguish them semantically. The different frequencies of their use in some syntactic positions (Wright 1896–1898. II: 236a) are, however, apparently distinguished stylistically, but in Christian Palestinian Arabic before 1000, the differences "have become blurred" (Blau 1966: 375, § 255). In the papyri of the first three centuries after the Hejira, with the decads (where there is no syntactic or stylistic variation in the "classical" language) there seems to be a clear preference for the form with /ʾ/, though /ʾwāḥid/ occurs at least once, in '71' (Hopkins 1984: 118).

Usage in these three languages seems to illustrate, then, some of the possible effects of sound change: no distinction of form or meaning, as in Aramaic; distinction in form and meaning, as in Hebrew; and distinction in form and usage, but perhaps not in meaning, as in Arabic.

With completely constant form, resulting apparently from wholly regular sound change, as for Aramaic, the language comes to have but a single form. Without universal application of sound shift, we come to have biforms, which can be distinguished semantically, as seems to be the case for Hebrew, or syntactically and stylistically, as seems true in Arabic.

For the symbols (i.e., words, etc.) of a language to remain constant, their shapes must change uniformly. As with substitution ciphers, correspondences must be unvarying to allow simple decipherment and understanding. However, the presence of context means that imprecision in such change can be allowed, and this permits the survival of both a form and its relative. When these two become part of a single system, then they commonly come to be differentiated in one way or another. This necessarily means, of course, change of one kind or another in the language. With incompletely uniform sound change (whatever the cause), then, other ramifications necessarily result.

In brief, then, it seems to us that on a theoretical level we cannot assume that sound change operates completely regularly. On a factual level, we all know that we can cite numerous exceptions to presumed mechanically-operating sound laws.

What practical conclusions should one draw from such a view? How are we to proceed? It seems that the assumption that there are uniformly operating sound laws is useful, if not heuristically indispensible. Even if it seems wrong-headed to expect the social phenomena we see exemplified by languages to conform absolutely with exceptionless laws, only the search for such regularity can lead to further understanding of them, and to adumbration of the approximations of rule-governed behavior which do seem possible.

To return to the numeral 'one', and its variation between initial /ʾ/ and initial /w/ or /y/, we have here no simple sound change (outside of Akkadian, where words beginning with /w/ regularly — but not universally — develop into words beginning with /ʾ/ at some point around the year 1600 B. C. E. (cf. Lieberman 1977: 8, note 21 b). What is involved is, most likely, a hitherto unrecognized derivational pattern where /ʾa/ is prefixed to a stem which begins with a consonant cluster. That such a pattern is used in forming cardinal numbers in Semitic has long been obvious from the numeral /ʾarbaᶜ/ 'four' which has /ʾa/ plus a stem in all of the classical Semitic languages (cf. table 4). When one compares the ordinal used for 'fourth' (cf. table 9), it seems to become clear that the /ʾa/ is an afformative[18] and reflects a broader Afro-Asiatic nominal pattern.

*Table 9.* The ordinal 'fourth' in Classical Semitic (according to Argaw 1984)

| Akkadian | Ethiopic | Arabic | Hebrew | Syriac | Ugaritic | Sabaic[19] |
|---|---|---|---|---|---|---|
| rebûm | rābəᶜ {rabə́ɔə} | rābiᶜu | rəḇi/îᶜî | rəḇīāyā | rbᶜ | rbᶜ |
| < rabûm (1 × in Middle-Assyrian) | | | | | | |

Carleton Hodge has been working on this Afro-Asiatic aleph nominal pattern,[20] and it seems that we have an instance of it in the word for the Semitic cardinal 'one' outside of Akkadian. We would propose that this word, that is, the form beginning with /ʾ/, is a derivative of /*wḥd/ by prefixing /(ʾ)a/. The reconstructed form /ʾawḥad/ would then have had its first syllable reduced, in due course, to /ʾa/. Hebrew then formed a secondary verb from the cardinal, one which began with a glottal stop, and was differentiated semantically from the original stem which was /*yḥd/ there.

I would stop here, but am afraid that I might be accused of having been pitched four balls and, despite the walk, not getting off of first base. Let us, then, move briefly to second place in conclusion, that is to the number 'two'. We might well see the same cardinal-forming prefix known for 'four', which we have posited for 'one' behind that numeral. Without having time to review all of the complex details here (in 1878 Phillippi took 78 pages to study the numeral), 'two' would likewise seem to have remnants of the same prefix and of the same pattern. The fact that the first two radicals of the Arabic /ʾiθnāni/ have no vowel between them, and that this is true for Hebrew as well (cf. now Hoberman, 1989), suggests that we have at hand the same nominal pattern despite the absence of any prothetic aleph. The retention of this pattern might even, ultimately, account for the anomaly of the feminine form of Hebrew 'two', /štayîm/, which violates the rules of Hebrew phonology. Those rules are said not to allow either an initial consonant cluster or an unspirantized /t/ with preceding vowel, which keeps us from interpreting the shwa under the šin as a shwa mobile, that is, as phonetic shwa. It must be understood as representing "no vowel" or "zero" in linguistic parlance. The loss of a full aleph in these forms might, perhaps, result from the suffixing of the dual to the Arabic and Hebrew citation forms of this word.

We have ended with a morphological explanation for a phenomenon which was used to argue a phonological point. The dangers inherent in making any claim that sound change need not be wholly regular as a basis for allowing irregularity into our historical accounts of languages too quickly are evident from the example. It is not only phonological regularities which may be lost if we stop our search for order too soon in our investigations, but morphology as well. The common assumption of "exceptionless" regularity, then, seems to be the only reasonable working hypothesis with which we can approach the study of sound change, even if is not justifiable in the final analysis, and we should always expect a residue of exceptions in practice.

Our morphological explanation of the problem underlines once again a peculiarity that we seem to encounter over and over in the reconstruction of Afro-Asiatic. The most readily apparent connections between the families in the phylum seem to be found not in the lexicon, but in morphology.

## Notes

1. *Chadic Newsletter* 16/17, published in April 1987 by the Chadic Working Group of the (German) West African Linguistic Society, and edited by H. Jungraithmayr.
2. We use this term in a narrow sense, to refer to a diachronic change between the (surface) phonemes with which a word is realized. We consider a change "phonological" only when there is some alteration in the number or patterning of the phonemes of the language.

   In his latest statement on "the principles of genetic linguistic classification", Joseph Greenberg (1987: 17–18, 30–31) cites, and refers to, some materials concerning scholars' accepting the absence of absolutely exceptionless sound laws. Wilbur (1977) reprints some of the literature on the question, with an insightful introduction.

3. For an accessible introduction to the relevant thought of C. S. Peirce, see Hardwick (1977).
4. There is also a cognate in the Aramaic texts from Elephantine, and, as A. Faber noted in her conference presentation, beyond Semitic, in the Berber family. In Epigraphic South Arabian, the presumed Minaean cognate is epigraphically quite uncertain (cf. Höffner 1943: 130 n. 1), while the Qatabanian is rather less problematic.
5. We have included the secondary forms of the Ethiopic numbers in our listing below (cf. Dillman 1899: 325).
6. For the spelling *ši-in-ni* in an Old-Babylonian letter, cf. Frankena (1978: 115).
7. Eilers (1986: 35) ignores the South Arabian evidence in his attempt to reconstruct 'six' on a biradical basis.
8. For an overview of Hebrew graphemics, particularly the Tiberian system, cf. Lieberman (in press).
9. Yeivin (1985) is an excellent study of the Babylonian system.
10. Cf., for instance Levy—Goldschmidt (1924. 2: 232 b), Ben-Yehuda—Tur-Sinai (1948—1959. 4: 2010 n. 2), Hava (1964: 4 b), or Koehler—Baumgartner (1967: 29, 1974: 387).
11. In addition, there are also Punic forms without /ḥ/, and one without /ʿ/ or /ḥ/, cf. Fuentes Estañol (1980: 63), who labels these "graphic errors".
12. A partial bibliography on the topic may substitute, here, for an attempt to reconstruct the number systems for the various families. For Egyptian, one should consult Gunn (1916); for Berber: Vycichl (1952), Zavadovskij (1975); for Cushitic: Zaborski (1987; with bibliography); Mukarovsky (1987) treats Chadic, Cushitic, and Omotic, while contributions to the study of the Semitic numerals not mentioned elsewhere in the present paper include: Al-sāmarrāʾī (1960), Brugnatelli (1982; with further extensive bibliography), Brugnatelli (1984), Cantineau (1943), and Powell (1979).
13. This verb is attested in Greengus (1986: 23, no. 24, l. 15).
14. That is, probably, 'say something definitively'.
15. It seems that this, rather than the expected *ʾešēru*, is used to avoid homonomy with Akkadian *ʾešēru* 'be straight'.
16. Attested in II Samuel vii 15 and 17.
17. It may well be correct to consider the claim of the Junggrammatiker that sound change was exceptionless to be tautological, as H. M. Hoenigswald argued in the paper he delivered to the Indo-European section of the Stanford Conference. Leskien (1876: xxviii cited in Wilbur 1977: XXV—XXVI) put it succinctly: "Lässt man aber die beliebigen zufälligen, unter einander in keinen Zusammenhang zu bringenden Abweichungen zu, so erklärt man in Grunde dazu, dass das Objekt der Untersuchung, die Sprache, der wissenschaftlichen Erkenntniss nicht zugänglich ist." Such a claim that only the regular part of language is amenable to "scientific" study is, however, vacuous (like all tautologies). So long as there is no specification of some externally-determined means to develop criteria for delineating the rule-governed part of language (or any other object of scientific study), such a meaning for the concept "exceptionless sound change" is probably

best left unaccounted for. If the student of some object of scientific study is allowed to pick and choose that part of his topic which is governed by the type of regularity for which he clamors, there remains but little means to control fantastic theories. Thus, adumbrating a scientific law for the order in which leaves detach themselves from deciduous trees on their way to the ground, and claiming that only the "regular" instances of that process (namely just that part for which one can give a satisfactory account) are amenable to "scientific" study, may well mean that most of the falling leaves will be unaccounted for. At any rate, Leskien's understanding of the designation "scientific," depends on an overly narrow definition of the concept, as was common in the last century, but no longer thought adequate.

An example from the area of decipherment may clarify our view. Given a body of (hitherto) undeciphered texts (B), one may propose an interpretation which holds for only some of them (I). (The likelihood of the acceptance of the hypothesis will be greater if the numbers of texts in both of these groups are integers (i), i.e. if one excludes only *whole* documents from the corpus.) If, furthermore, one can find some additional characteristic or characteristics which distinguish the successfully interpreted texts (I) from the uninterpreted texts (U), whether in the external form of the documents or in the circumstances of their discovery, this division of the corpus will be seen as justifying the partial distinction. That is, if there is some reason, other than the proposed decipherment, to eliminate the uninterpretable texts from consideration and justify the equation $B^{(i)}-U^{(i)} = I^{(i)}$.

A statement of linguistic law may be compared with the successful deciphering of the whole body of texts. If one simply asserts that the hypothesis holds only for (I) (where $I < B$), and does not justify the exclusion of the materials unaccounted for (i.e., show why I and U differ), it will not gain authority. Making the hypothesis more complex will not aid in the query, since it merely increases the size of (I) (unless (I) grows so large that $U = \emptyset$). Excluding materials from (I) by claiming they are foreign is circular, and remains so until some non-linguistic grounds are preferred.

There commonly remain texts which are difficult to interpret in any corpus, and instances of changes in sounds which do not conform to some proposed rule. As long as we know that we are treating of a single language, as we commonly do, it may be hard to find non-tautological grounds to exclude exceptions. Neither discarding the largely operable rule nor ignoring the problems can be anything other than arbitrary. (Our failure to understand passages in texts, or even whole texts, on the other hand, may commonly, and correctly, be ascribed to the fact that we do not know the circumstances which surrounded their production, i.e., their contexts.)

18. One is rather startled to read the opinion expressed in an article in the volume edited by Rochberg-Halton (1987: 405) that the cardinal 'four' is a quadriradical, and derivatives based on a "verkürzte, dreiradikalige" root.

19. Beeston (1984: 34) gives *'rb^c* which is a simple error for the form given below, cf. the dictionaries and his earlier description.

20. Hodge (1985; in press a, b). We would like to thank Professor Hodge for his generosity in sharing pre-publication forms of this work. He does not consider the preformatives which have different vowels or glottal stop rather than *hamzat al-waṣl* (euphonic glottal stop) distinct.

# References

Al-sāmarrā'ī, Ibrahim A.
1960       "The numerals in Arabic", *Sumer* 16: 25—27 [in Arabic].

Argaw, Makonnen
1984       *Matériaux pour l'étude de la prononciation traditionelle du Guèze* (Mémoire, 44) (Paris: Editions Recherche sur les Civilisations).

Beeston, Alfred F. L.
1984       *Sabaic grammar* (Journal of Semitic Series, Monograph 6) (Manchester: University of Manchester).

Ben Yehuda, Eliezer — Naftali H. Tur-Sinai (eds.)
1948—1959  *A complete dictionary of Ancient and Modern Hebrew* (Jerusalem/New York: Ben Yehuda/Yoseloff).

Blau, Joshua
1966       *A grammar of Christian Arabic, based mainly on South Palestinian texts from the first millennium* (Corpus Scriptorum Christianorum Orientalium, vols. 267—269, subsidia, tomes 27—29) (Louvain: CorpusSCO).

Bodine, Walter (ed.)
in press   *Linguistics and Biblical Hebrew.*

Brockelmann, Carl
1908—1913  *Grundriß der vergleichenden Grammatik der semitischen Sprachen* 1—2 (Berlin: Reuther & Reichard) [reprint (Hildesheim: Olms) 1961, 1982].

Brugnatelli, Vermondo
1982       *Questioni di morfologia e sintassi dei numerali cardinali semitici* (Pubblicazioni della facoltà dell'Università di Milano, XCIII. Sezione a cura dell'Istituto di Glottologia 7) (Firenze: La Nuova Italia).
1984       "Some remarks on Semitic numerals and the Ebla texts", in: Fronzaroli (ed.), 85—99.

Cantineau, Jean
1943       "Le nom de nombre 'six' dans les langues sémitiques", *Bulletin des études arabes* 3: 72—73.

Carroll, Lewis
1982       *The complete illustrated works of Lewis Carroll* (New York: Avenel) [originally published in 1871].

Chen, Matthew Y.
1972       "The time dimension: Contribution toward a theory of sound change", *Foundations of Language* 8. 457—498 [reprinted in: Wang 1977: 197—247].

Deller, Karlheinz
1959       *Lautlehre des Neuassyrischen* [unpublished dissertation, University of Vienna].

Dillmann, August
1899       *Grammatik der äthiopischen Sprache*² (Leipzig: Tauchnitz) [reprint Graz: Akademische Druck- und Verlagsanstalt, 1959].

Dossin, Georges
1951        *Archives royales de Mari* IV: *Lettres* (Musée du Louvre, Département des antiquités orientales, Textes cunéiformes, vol. XXV) (Paris: Geuthner).

Eilers, Wilhelm
1986        "Einige akkadische Etymologien", in: Meid — Trenkwalder (eds.), 31 — 44.

Frankena, Rintje
1978        *Kommentar zu den altbabylonischen Briefen aus Lagaba und anderen Orten* (Studia ad tabulas cuneiformes a F. M. Th. de Liagre Böhl collectas pertinentia IV) (Leiden: Nederlands Instituut voor het nabije Oosten).

Fronzaroli, Pelio (ed.)
1984        *Studies on the language of Ebla* (Quaderni di Semitistica 13) (Firenze: Università di Firenze).

Fuentes Estañol, María-José
1980        *Vocabulario fenicio* (Biblioteca Fenicia 1) (Barcelona: Diamante).

Greenberg, Joseph H.
1987        *Language in the Americas* (Stanford: Stanford University Press).

Greengus, Samuel
1986        *Studies in Ishchali documents* (Bibliotheca Mesopotamica 19) (Malibu: Undena).

Gunn, Battiscombe
1916        Review of K. Sethe, *Von Zahlen und Zahlworten bei den alten Ägyptern, Journal of Egyptian Archaeology* 3: 279 — 286.

Hardwick, Charles S. (ed.)
1977        *Semiotic and significs: The correspondence between Charles S. Peirce and Victoria Lady Welby* (Bloomington and London: Indiana University Press).

Hava, Joseph G.
1964        *Al-Faraid Arabic-English dictionary* (Beirut: Catholic Press).

Herdner, André
1963        *Corpus des tablettes en cunéiformes alphabétiques découvertes à Ras Shamra-Ugarit de 1929 à 1939* (Mission de Ras Shamra X) (Paris: Imprimerie nationale).

Hoberman, Robert
1989        "Initial consonant clusters in Hebrew and Aramaic" *Journal of Near Eastern Studies*, 48: 25 — 29.

Hodge, Carleton T.
1985        Review of W. R. Garr, *Dialect geography of Syria-Palestine, Anthropological Linguistics* 27. 3: 319 — 326.
in press a  "Prothetic alif and canonical form in Egyptian" [to appear in the Stockwell Festschrift].
in press b  "A relative matter", *LACUS* 1985.

Höffner, Maria
1943        *Altsüdarabische Grammatik* (Porta Linguarum Orientalium XXIV) (Leipzig: Harrassowitz).

Hopkins, Simon
1984        *Studies in the grammar of Early Arabic based upon papyri datable to before 300 A.H./912 A.D.* (London Oriental Series 37) (Oxford: Oxford University Press).

Jungraithmayr, Hermann — Wolfgang W. Müller (eds.)
1987        *Proceedings of the fourth international Hamito-Semitic congress, Marburg 20 — 22 September, 1983* (Amsterdam Studies in the Theory and History of Linguistic Science, Series IV, vol. 44) (Amsterdam: Benjamins).

Koehler, Ludwig — Walter Baumgartner et al.
1967        *Hebräisches und aramäisches Lexikon zum Alten Testament* 1³ (Leiden: Brill).
1974        *Hebräisches und aramäisches Lexikon zum Alten Testament* 2³ (Leiden: Brill).

Lambert, Wilfred G. — Simon B. Parker
1966        *Enuma Eliš: The Babylonian epic of creation: The cuneiform text* (Oxford: Clarendon Press).

[Landsberger, Benno] — Miguel Civil et al. (eds.)
1979        *Ea A : 'nâqu', Aa A = 'nâqu' with their forerunners and related texts* (Materials for the Sumerian Lexicon XIV) (Roma: Pontificium Institutum Biblicum).

Leskien, August
1876        *Die Declination im Slawisch-Litauischen und Germanischen* (Leipzig: Weidmann).

Levy, Jacob — Lazarus Goldschmidt (eds.)
1924        *Wörterbuch über die Talmudim und Midrashim. Nebst Beiträgen von H. L. Fleischer,* in 4 vols. (Berlin: Harz).

Lieberman, Stephen J.
1977        *The Sumerian loanwords in Old-Babylonian Akkadian* (Harvard Semitic Series 22) (Missoula: Harvard Semitic Museum/Scholars Press).
in press     "Towards a graphemics of the Tiberian Bible", in: Bodine (in press).

Meid, Wolfgang — Helga Trenkwalder
1986        *Im Bannkreis des alten Orients* (Innsbrucker Beiträge zur Kulturwissenschaft 24) (Innsbruck: Institut für Sprachwissenschaft der Universität Innsbruck).

Moscati, Sabatino (ed.)
1964        *An introduction to the comparative grammar of the Semitic languages* (Wiesbaden: Harrassowitz).

Mukarovsky, Hermann G.
1987        "Grundzahlwörter im Tschadischen, Kuschitischen und Omotischen", in: Jungraithmayr — Müller (eds.), 25 — 46.

Murtonen, A.
1986        *Hebrew in its West Semitic setting: A comparative survey of non-Masoretic Hebrew dialects and traditions* 1: *A comparative lexicon,* A: *Proper names* (Studies in Semitic Languages and Linguistics 13) (Leiden: Brill).

Philippi, Friedrich W. M.
1878    "Das Zahlwort zwei im Semitischen", *Zeitschrift der deutschen mor-genländischen Gesellschaft* 32: 21—98.
Powell, Marvin
1979    "Notes on Akkadian numbers and number syntax", *Journal of Semitic Studies* 24: 13—18.
Rochberg-Halton, Francesca (ed.)
1987    *Language, literature, and history: Philological and historical studies presented to Erica Reiner* (American Oriental Series 67) (New Haven: American Oriental Society).
Swadesh, Morris
1971    *The origin and diversification of language* (Chicago: Aldine) [ed.: Joel Sherzer].
Thureau-Dangin, François
1922    "Nouvelles lettres d'El-Amarna", *Revue d'Assyriologie et d'archéologie orientale* 19: 91—108.
Vycichl, Werner
1952    "Das berberische Ziffernsystem von Ghadames und sein Ursprung", *Rivista di Studi Orientali* 27: 81—83.
Wang, William S.-Y. (ed.)
1977    *The lexicon in phonological change* (The Hague: Mouton).
Wilbur, Terence H. (ed.)
1977    *The Lautgesetz controversy: A documentation (1885—86)* (Amsterdam Studies in the Theory and History of Linguistic Science I, Amsterdam Classics in Linguistics 9) (Amsterdam: Benjamins).
Wright, William
1890    *Lectures on the comparative grammar of the Semitic languages* (Cambridge: Cambridge University Press/New York: Macmillan) [reprint: Amsterdam: Philo, 1966 and 1981].
Wright, William — William Robertson Smith — Michael Jan de Goeje (eds.)
1896—1898    *A grammar of the Arabic language*[3] (Cambridge: University Press).
Yeivin, Israel
1985    *The Hebrew language tradition as reflected in the Babylonian vocalization* (Academy of the Hebrew Language, Texts and Studies XII) (Jerusalem: The Academy) [in Hebrew].
Zaborski, Andrzej
1987    "Basic numerals in Cushitic", in: Jungraithmayr—Müller (eds.), 317—347.
Zavadovskij, Jurij N.
1975    "Problema berberskix čislitel'nyx v svete sravnitel'nogo semito-xamitskogo jazykoznanija" [The problem of the Berber numerals in the light of Semito-Hamitic comparative linguistics], *Drevnij Vostok* (Moskva, 1: 43 ff.).

# Subject index

# Language index

This index contains the names of individual languages (e. g. Latin), genetic groups and subgroups (e. g. Austronesian and Melanesian), areal groups (e. g. African), and proto-languages (e. g. Proto-Dravidian).

# Author index

# Hans Henrich Hock
# Principles of Historical Linguistics

Second Edition. Revised and updated 1991 (first edition 1986).
22,8 x 14,8 cm. XIV, 706 pages. With 18 illustrations.
Paperback. DM 68,–
ISBN 3-11-012962-0

It is the widespread use of **Principles of Historical Linguistics** in university linguistics courses that has prompted this revised and updated edition.

This book provides in up-to-date form an understanding of the principles of historical linguistics and the related fields of comparative linguistics and linguistic reconstruction. In addition, it provides a very broad exemplification for the principles of historical linguistics.

In this second edition, the bibliography has been significantly expanded and updated. Revisions and changes cover both matters of content and presentation as well as the correction of misprints that are not self-correcting and factual errors that were contained in the first edition. Some of the corrections have been made in the text itself, others in the Notes section.

# mouton de gruyter

Berlin · New York